WITHDRAWN

15-45

TO PROVE A VILLAIN: *The Case of King Richard III*

TO PROVE A VILLAIN

VILLAIN

THE CASE OF KING RICHARD III

TAYLOR LITTLETON

and

ROBERT R. REA

AUBURN UNIVERSITY

The Macmillan Company

PRINTING   67891011   YEAR   3456789

Library of Congress catalog card number: 64—16051

THE MACMILLAN COMPANY
866 THIRD AVENUE, NEW YORK, NEW YORK 10022
Collier—Macmillan Canada, Ltd., Toronto, Ontario

Printed in the United States of America

For our "schoolboys":

PAM, DOWE, GEORGE, *and* FRANKLIN

ACKNOWLEDGMENTS

We are indebted to the estate of Elizabeth Mackintosh for the use of her novel *Daughter of Time* and to The Macmillan Company and Professor Oscar James Campbell for the text and notes of Shakespeare's *The Tragedy of King Richard the Third*. We particularly wish to thank the editors of *History Today* and Professor Alec R. Myers of the University of Liverpool for their generous permission to reprint "The Character of Richard III." For permission to reprint "A Note on *Richard III:* The Bishop of Ely's Strawberries," we wish to thank Professor J. Dover Wilson, the Modern Humanities Research Association, and the General Editor of the *Modern Language Review*, in which the article first appeared. "Richard III, A Doubtful Verdict Reviewed," by Sir Clements R. Markham, is reprinted by courtesy of *The English Historical Review* and Messrs. Bleaymire and Shepherd, on behalf of the Executors of the late Fredrick Rice Markham. University Microfilms, Inc., furnished the original texts upon which our edited versions of a number of works are based.

TABLE OF CONTENTS

INTRODUCTION

As every schoolboy knows, villainy hath charms that never fade, and as Shakespeare taught, King Richard the Third, humpbacked Dickon o' Gloucester, was the greatest villain of them all. If further proof were needed, two great Lord Chancellors said so—one was a saint and the other was a scientist. Victorian maids wept copious tears at the thought of the poor innocent little princes murdered in their bed, and generations shuddered with delight at the royal actor's bloody cry, "Off with his head!" Ultimately, of course,

> For want of a nail, the shoe was lost,
> For want of a shoe, the horse was lost,
> For want of a horse, the rider was lost.

And, with a sigh of relief at the triumph of virtue, personified in the God-sent Henry Tudor, the book of history closes on Richard's evil deeds.

History? There may be more of history in a modern detective story than in all of Shakespeare! At least it is a different history, and one that will intrigue as much as the history purloined by the Bard from an imaginative copyist who got it from the usurper's propagandist. Richard's missing horse might have told a truer tale!

Whatever the truth may be, it is the unsolved mystery of Richard's character that has caught and held men's minds for well-nigh five hundred years. He may be the monster that More, Shakespeare, and the old historians portray; if so, we glory in his total wickedness, and modern critics may find in him the concentrated venom of a whole people's iniquity that must be divinely exorcised. In him the troubles of a nation reach their peak, and in his fall they pass. We have him to thank for the lesson and the propitiation. Yet if he should be the victim of lies and treachery surpassing that of which he is accused (and remember that "Dickon thy master is bought and sold"), another lesson may be learned.

THE HISTORICAL BACKGROUND

The reign of Richard III is the culmination of a turbulent phase of England's history extending from the late fourteenth century to the end of the fifteenth century. In the declining years of Edward III (1327–1377), English success in the war against France turned sour, and as the old king sank into senility, his sons took up a struggle for power which ended at Bosworth Field. Edward's grandson and successor, Richard II (1377–1399), was unable to maintain himself against baronial machinations and fell before a revolt which placed Henry of Lancaster on the throne. Richard did not long survive his deposition. The new Lancastrian, Henry IV (1399–1413), beat the baronial factions into submission; his son Henry V (1413–1422) led his countrymen to victory at Agincourt and won tenuous control of northern France before his untimely death. Henry VI (1422–1461) inherited the crown as an infant; dependent on his uncles during his minority, the feeble Henry never controlled his realm of England and soon lost his lands in France. Military defeat and national humiliation, governmental inefficiency and bankruptcy, and the unpopularity of Henry's long-fruitless marriage to the French princess Margaret of Anjou led to open conflict between the supporters of the king and those of Richard, Duke of York, who claimed the crown in his own right. In 1455 began the civil war known as the Wars of the Roses—the red rose of Lancaster and the white rose of York. Richard of York was killed early in the strife, but his eldest son, Edward, supported by Richard Neville, Earl of Warwick ("the Kingmaker"), overcame all opposition and secured the crown in 1461 as Edward IV.

The triumphant Yorkists were shortly at odds with one another. Warwick, antagonized by the marriage of Edward IV and Elizabeth Woodville (1464) at the very moment when he was negotiating for a royal marriage in

France, turned against the king. With the aid of France, Margaret of Anjou (whose son, the Prince of Wales, was betrothed to Warwick's daughter Anne), and Edward's brother George, Duke of Clarence (who was also Warwick's son-in-law), the Kingmaker deposed the Yorkist king in 1470 and restored Henry VI. Edward and his loyal brother, Richard of Gloucester, escaped to Burgundy. Returning to England in 1471, they persuaded Clarence to betray Warwick, and in a brief, brilliant campaign the Yorkists defeated Warwick at Barnet and Margaret at Tewkesbury. The Lancastrian Prince of Wales was killed in the latter engagement, and as soon as Edward and Richard secured the Tower of London, they announced that poor Henry VI had died "of pure displeasure and melancholy."

From 1471 to 1483, Edward IV governed England with a firm hand. He was popular notwithstanding his many amours, and save for the jealous rivalry between the older nobility and Queen Elizabeth's Woodville relatives, the nation seemed well settled. "False, fleeting, perjured Clarence" met a not altogether undeserved end in 1478, attainted of high treason. All was upset, however, by Edward's unexpected death in 1483, while he was yet in the prime of life.

Once more England faced the dangers of a royal minority. Edward V was only twelve years old, and the nobles would inevitably fight for control of his government; no promises to a dead king could bind them. The Woodvilles formed a party—the Queen Mother, Elizabeth; her brother, Earl Rivers; and her son, the Marquis Dorset. Richard of Gloucester opposed them. Great barons like Buckingham, Hastings, and Stanley had to find their way between these rival forces or perish. And across the Channel in France, young Henry Tudor was patiently awaiting the outcome of events.

Such was the stage on which the actors moved—or could be made to move, by monkish chronicler, historian, dramatist, or novelist. As will be seen, from first to last, each formed the plot to suit his purposes, each turned to the Muse of History to help him "prove a villain."

Thus there are many Richards, and this fact brings us to one final point. The student will find implicit in this book not merely a series of readings about a complex medieval figure, but also a moral problem of distinct significance. In our attempts to frame judgments of men and ideas we are constantly faced, perhaps more today than ever before, with the sinister fog of propaganda, a fog that must either blur our vision or dissipate before our efforts to get at the truth. The reputation of King Richard III is shrouded in just such a mist, and if the student seriously engages himself with the problem of proving or disproving Richard a villain, he must also grapple with the larger question: What is the truth and how does one recognize it? The answer to this question is not easily attained, and the student may not be able to say with finality that truth is what emerges from the conflict. But he will undoubtedly find satisfaction in having participated in the struggle.

The Text

Although the material in this book may, in fact, be used in any order and for several purposes, the authors have thought it best to introduce the subject in its best-known form: Shakespeare's Richard, the classic portrait. There follows, in roughly chronological order, a selection of sources in which the Tudor myth is firmly stated and then challenged. The text concludes with Josephine Tey's intriguing statement of the case for Richard in that most modern form, the detective novel. This arrangement should demonstrate the development of ideas and lend itself to comparative analysis. We have taken such liberties with spelling, punctuation, and word usage in the primary sources as seemed best calculated to make them palatable to American university students without entirely sacrificing their antique flavor. For the satisfaction of scholarly curiosities we refer student and teacher to the bibliography.

TO PROVE A VILLAIN: *The Case of King Richard III*

WILLIAM SHAKESPEARE

From The Third Part of King Henry the Sixth[1]

RICHARD. Why, love forswore me in my
    mother's womb:
And, for I should not deal in her soft laws,
She did corrupt frail nature with some bribe,
To shrink mine arm up like a wither'd shrub;
To make an envious mountain on my back,
Where sits deformity to mock my body;
To shape my legs of an unequal size;
To disproportion me in every part,
Like to a chaos, or an unlick'd bear-whelp
That carries no impression like the dam.
And am I then a man to be belov'd?
O monstrous fault! to harbour such a thought.
Then, since this earth affords no joy to me
But to command, to check, to o'erbear such
As are of better person than myself,
I'll make my heaven to dream upon the crown;
And, whiles I live, to account this world but
    hell,
Until my mis-shap'd trunk that bears this head
Be round impaled with a glorious crown.
And yet I know not how to get the crown,
For many lives stand between me and home:
And I, like one lost in a thorny wood,

That rents the thorns and is rent with the
    thorns,
Seeking a way and straying from the way;
Not knowing how to find the open air,
But toiling desperately to find it out,
Torment myself to catch the English crown:
And from that torment I will free myself,
Or hew my way out with a bloody axe.
Why, I can smile and murder whiles I smile,
And cry, "Content," to that which grieves my
    heart,
And wet my cheeks with artificial tears,
And frame my face to all occasions.
I'll drown more sailors than the mermaid shall;
I'll slay more gazers than the basilisk;
I'll play the orator as well as Nestor,
Deceive more slily than Ulysses could,
And, like a Sinon, take another Troy.
I can add colors to the chameleon,
Change shapes with Proteus for advantages,
And set the murd'rous Machiavel to school.
Can I do this, and cannot get a crown?
Tut! were it further off, I'll pluck it down.

[1] Act III, Scene ii, 153–195.

The Tragedy of King Richard the Third

DRAMATIS PERSONÆ

KING EDWARD *the Fourth.*

EDWARD, *Prince of Wales, after-* } *sons to the*
  wards KING EDWARD V., } *King.*
RICHARD, *Duke of York,* }

GEORGE, *Duke of Clarence,* } *brothers to*
RICHARD, *Duke of Gloucester,* } *the King.*
  afterwards KING RICHARD III., }

A young son of Clarence.

HENRY, *Earl of Richmond, afterwards* KING
  HENRY VII.

CARDINAL BOURCHIER, *Archbishop of Canter-*
  bury.

THOMAS ROTHERHAM, *Archbishop of York.*

JOHN MORTON, *Bishop of Ely.*

DUKE OF BUCKINGHAM.

DUKE OF NORFOLK.

EARL OF SURREY, *his son.*

EARL RIVERS, *brother to Elizabeth.*

MARQUIS OF DORSET *and* LORD GREY, *sons to*
  Elizabeth.

EARL OF OXFORD.

LORD HASTINGS.

LORD STANLEY, *called also* EARL OF DERBY.

LORD LOVEL.

SIR THOMAS VAUGHAN.

SIR RICHARD RATCLIFF.

SIR WILLIAM CATESBY.

SIR JAMES TYRREL.

SIR JAMES BLOUNT.

SIR WALTER HERBERT.

SIR ROBERT BRAKENBURY, *Lieutenant of the*
  Tower.

CHRISTOPHER URSWICK, *a priest. Another Priest.*

TRESSEL *and* BERKELEY, *gentlemen attending on*
  the Lady Anne.

LORD MAYOR *of London.* SHERIFF of Wiltshire.

ELIZABETH, *queen to King Edward IV.*

MARGARET, *widow of King Henry VI.*

DUCHESS OF YORK, *mother to King Edward IV.*

LADY ANNE, *widow of Edward Prince of*
  Wales, son to King Henry VI.; afterwards
  married to Richard.

A young daughter of Clarence (MARGARET
  PLANTAGENET).

GHOSTS *of those murdered by Richard III.,*
  LORDS *and other* ATTENDANTS; *a* PURSUIVANT,
  SCRIVENER, CITIZENS, MURDERERS, MESSENGERS,
  SOLDIERS, *&c.*

SCENE: *England.*

ACT I

SCENE I. *London. A street.*

[*Enter* RICHARD, DUKE OF GLOUCESTER, *solus.*]

GLOU. Now is the winter of our discontent
Made glorious summer by this sun of York;
And all the clouds that lour'd upon our house
In the deep bosom of the ocean buried.
Now are our brows bound with victorious
  wreaths;   5
Our bruised arms hung up for monuments;
Our stern alarums changed to merry meetings,
Our dreadful marches to delightful measures.
Grim-visaged war hath smooth'd his wrinkled
  front;
And now, instead of mounting barbéd
  steeds   10

Act I, Scene i: 2. sun, pun on "son." Because these suns had appeared to King Edward at the Battle of Morti-mer's Cross, Edward took the sun as his badge. 6. monuments, trophies. 8. measures, dances. 10. barbed, covered with armor.

1

To fright the souls of fearful adversaries,
He capers nimbly in a lady's chamber
To the lascivious pleasing of a lute.
But I, that am not shaped for sportive tricks,
Nor made to court an amorous looking-glass;
I, that am rudely stamp'd, and want love's
    majesty   16
To strut before a wanton ambling nymph;
I, that am curtail'd of this fair proportion,
Cheated of feature by dissembling nature,
Deform'd, unfinish'd, sent before my time 20
Into this breathing world, scarce half made
    up,
And that so lamely and unfashionable
That dogs bark at me as I halt by them;
Why, I, in this weak piping time of peace,
Have no delight to pass away the time,   25
Unless to spy my shadow in the sun
And descant on mine own deformity:
And therefore, since I cannot prove a lover,
To entertain these fair well-spoken days,
I am determinéd to prove a villain   30
And hate the idle pleasures of these days.
Plots have I laid, inductions dangerous,
By drunken prophecies, libels and dreams,
To set my brother Clarence and the king
In deadly hate the one against the other: 35
And if King Edward be as true and just
As I am subtle, false and treacherous,
This day should Clarence closely be mew'd
    up,
About a prophecy, which says that G
Of Edward's heirs the murderer shall be. 40
Dive, thoughts, down to my soul: here Clar-
    ence comes.

[*Enter* CLARENCE, *guarded, and*
BRAKENBURY.]

Brother, good day: what means this arméd
    guard
That waits upon your grace?
    CLAR.   His majesty,
Tendering my person's safety, hath appointed
This conduct to convey me to the Tower. 45
    GLOU. Upon what cause?
    CLAR.   Because my name is George.
    GLOU. Alack, my lord, that fault is none of
    yours;

He should, for that, commit your godfathers:
O, belike his majesty hath some intent
That you shall be new-christen'd in the
    Tower.   50
But what's the matter, Clarence? may I know?
    CLAR. Yea, Richard, when I know; for I
    protest
As yet I do not: but, as I can learn,
He hearkens after prophecies and dreams;
And from the cross-row plucks the letter
    G,   55
And says a wizard told him that by G
His issue disinherited should be;
And, for my name of George begins with G,
It follows in his thought that I am he.
These, as I learn, and such like toys as
    these   60
Have moved his highness to commit me now.
    GLOU. Why, this it is, when men are ruled
    by women:
'Tis not the king that sends you to the Tower;
My Lady Grey his wife, Clarence, 'tis she
That tempers him to this extremity.   65
Was it not she and that good man of wor-
    ship,
Anthony Woodville, her brother there,
That made him send Lord Hastings to the
    Tower,
From whence this present day he is deliver'd?
We are not safe, Clarence; we are not safe. 70
    CLAR. By heaven, I think there's no man is
    secure
But the queen's kindred and night-walking
    heralds
That trudge betwixt the king and Mistress
    Shore.
Heard ye not what an humble suppliant
Lord Hastings was to her for his delivery? 75
    GLOU. Humbly complaining to her deity
Got my lord chamberlain his liberty.
I'll tell you what; I think it is our way,
If we will keep in favour with the king,
To be her men and wear her livery: 80
The jealous o'erworn widow and herself,
Since that our brother dubb'd them gentle-
    women,
Are mighty gossips in this monarchy.

---

14. sportive, amorous. 17. ambling, walking affectedly.
19. feature, normal form; dissembling, cheating. 22. unfashionable, deformed. 23. halt, limp. 24. piping, unmar-
tial music of pipes. 27. descant, play variations on.
32. inductions, beginnings 38. mew'd up, shut up like a
hawk while it is moulting. 54. hearkens after, inquiries
about. 55. cross-row, alphabet. 60. toys, trifles. 65. tempers . . . extremity, makes him capable of following this
extreme course. 73. Mistress Shore, the King's mistress,
wife of a London tradesman. 77. lord chamberlain, i.e.,
Hastings. 81. widow, i.e., the Queen. 83. gossips, cronies.

BRAK. I beseech your graces both to pardon me;

His majesty hath straitly given in charge 85
That no man shall have private conference,
Of what degree soever, with his brother.

GLOU. Even so; an't please your worship, Brakenbury,
You may partake of any thing we say:
We speak no treason, man: we say the king 90
Is wise and virtuous, and his noble queen
Well struck in years, fair, and not jealous;
We say that Shore's wife hath a pretty foot,
A cherry lip, a bonny eye, a passing pleasing tongue;
And that the queen's kindred are made gentlefolks: 95
How say you, sir? can you deny all this?

BRAK. With this, my lord, myself have naught to do.

GLOU. Naught to do with Mistress Shore! I tell thee, fellow,
He that doth naught with her, excepting one,
Were best he do it secretly, alone. 100

BRAK. What one, my lord?

GLOU. Her husband, knave: wouldst thou betray me?

BRAK. I beseech your grace to pardon me, and withal
Forbear your conference with the noble duke.

CLAR. We know thy charge, Brakenbury, and will obey. 105

GLOU. We are the queen's abjects, and must obey.
Brother, farewell: I will unto the king;
And whatsoever you will employ me in,
Were it to call King Edward's widow sister,
I will perform it to enfranchise you. 110
Meantime, this deep disgrace in brotherhood
Touches me deeper than you can imagine.

CLAR. I know it pleaseth neither of us well.

GLOU. Well, your imprisonment shall not be long;
I will deliver you, or else lie for you: 115
Meantime, have patience.

CLAR.   I must perforce. Farewell.

[Exeunt CLARENCE, BRAKENBURY, and GUARD.

GLOU. Go, tread the path that thou shalt ne'er return,
Simple, plain Clarence! I do love thee so,
That I will shortly send thy soul to heaven,

If heaven will take the present at our hands.
But who comes here? the new-deliver'd Hastings?   121

[Enter LORD HASTINGS.]

HAST. Good time of day unto my gracious lord!

GLOU. As much unto my good lord chamberlain!
Well are you welcome to the open air.
How hath your lordship brook'd imprisonment?   125

HAST. With patience, noble lord, as prisoners must:
But I shall live, my lord, to give them thanks
That were the cause of my imprisonment.

GLOU. No doubt, no doubt; and so shall Clarence too;
For they that were your enemies are his, 130
And have prevail'd as much on him as you.

HAST. More pity that the eagle should be mew'd,
While kites and buzzards prey at liberty.

GLOU. What news abroad?

HAST. No news so bad abroad as this at home;   135
The king is sickly, weak and melancholy,
And his physicians fear him mightily.

GLOU. Now, by Saint Paul, this news is bad indeed.
O, he hath kept an evil diet long,
And overmuch consumed his royal person. 140
'Tis very grievous to be thought upon.
What, is he in his bed?

HAST. He is.

GLOU. Go you before, and I will follow you.

[Exit HASTINGS.

He cannot live, I hope; and must not die 145
Till George be pack'd with post-horse up to heaven.
I'll in, to urge his hatred more to Clarence,
With lies well steel'd with weighty arguments;
And, if I fail not in my deep intent,
Clarence hath not another day to live: 150
Which done, God take King Edward to his mercy,
And leave the world for me to bustle in!
For then I'll marry Warwick's youngest daughter.

106. abjects, slaves. 109. King Edward's widow, i.e., the widow he has made Queen. 115. lie, pun on (1) tell lies, (2) lie in prison. 125. brook'd, endured. 132. mewed, caged. 137. fear him, are anxious about him. 146. with post-horse, at full speed. 153. Warwick's . . . daughter, i.e., Lady Anne, widow of Edward, Prince of Wales and daughter-in-law of Henry VI.

What though I kill'd her husband and her
    father?
The readiest way to make the wench
    amends   155
Is to become her husband and her father:
The which will I; not all so much for love
As for another secret close intent,
By marrying her which I must reach unto.
But yet I run before my horse to market: 160
Clarence still breathes; Edward still lives and
    reigns:
When they are gone, then must I count my
    gains.   [*Exit.*

SCENE II. *The same. Another street.*

[*Enter the corpse of* KING HENRY *the Sixth,*
GENTLEMEN *with halberds to guard it;* LADY
ANNE *being the mourner.*]

ANNE. Set down, set down your honourable
    load,
If honour may be shrouded in a hearse,
Whilst I awhile obsequiously lament
The untimely fall of virtuous Lancaster.
Poor key-cold figure of a holy king!   5
Pale ashes of the house of Lancaster!
Thou bloodless remnant of that royal blood!
Be it lawful that I invocate thy ghost,
To hear the lamentations of poor Anne,
Wife to thy Edward, to thy slaughter'd
    son,   10
Stabb'd by the selfsame hand that made these
    wounds!
Lo, in these windows that let forth thy life,
I pour the helpless balm of my poor eyes.
Cursed be the hand that made these fatal
    holes!
Cursed be the heart that had the heart to
    do it!   15
Cursed the blood that let this blood from
    hence!
More direful hap betide that hated wretch,
That makes us wretched by the death of thee,
Than I can wish to adders, spiders, toads,
Or any creeping venom'd thing that lives! 20
If ever he have child, abortive be it,
Prodigious, and untimely brought to light,

Whose ugly and unnatural aspect
May fright the hopeful mother at the view;
And that be heir to his unhappiness!   25
If ever he have wife, let her be made
As miserable by the death of him
As I am made by my poor lord and thee!
Come, now towards Chertsey with your holy
    load,
Taken from Paul's to be interréd there;   30
And still, as you are weary of the weight,
Rest you, whiles I lament King Henry's corse.

[*Enter* GLOUCESTER.]

    GLOU. Stay, you that bear the corse, and
        set it down.
    ANNE. What black magician conjures up
        this fiend,
To stop devoted charitable deeds?   35
    GLOU. Villains, set down the corse; or, by
        Saint Paul,
I'll make a corse of him that disobeys.
    GENT. My lord, stand back, and let the
        coffin pass.
    GLOU. Unmanner'd dog! stand thou, when
        I command:
Advance thy halberd higher than my
    breast,   40
Or, by Saint Paul, I'll strike thee to my foot,
And spurn upon thee, beggar, for thy bold-
    ness.
    ANNE. What, do you tremble? are you all
        afraid?
Alas, I blame you not; for you are mortal,
And mortal eyes cannot endure the devil. 45
Avaunt, thou dreadful minister of hell!
Thou hadst but power over his mortal body,
His soul thou canst not have; therefore, be
    gone.
    GLOU. Sweet saint, for charity, be not so
        curst.
    ANNE. Foul devil, for God's sake, hence,
        and trouble us not;   50
For thou hast made the happy earth thy
    hell,
Fill'd it with cursing cries and deep exclaims.
If thou delight to view thy heinous deeds,
Behold this pattern of thy butcheries.
O, gentlemen, see, see! dead Henry's wounds

Scene ii: 3. obsequiously, in a way appropriate for a
funeral. 4. Lancaster, i.e., Henry VI. 13. helpless, useless. 17. hap betide, fortune befall. 22. prodigious, monstrous. 25. that, i.e., the unnatural child; unhappiness,
evil nature. 30. Paul's, St. Paul's Church in London.

31. still, meanwhile. 34. black magician, one in league
with the devil. 35. devoted, pious. 42. spurn upon, kick.
46. Avaunt, begone; minister, servant. 49. curst, shrewish.
54. pattern, example.

Open their congeal'd mouths and bleed
    afresh!   56
Blush, blush, thou lump of foul deformity;
For 'tis thy presence that exhales this blood
From cold and empty veins, where no blood
    dwells;
Thy deed, inhuman and unnatural,   60
Provokes this deluge most unnatural.
O God, which this blood madest, revenge his
    death!
O earth, which this blood drink'st, revenge
    his death!
Either heaven with lightning strike the mur-
    derer dead,
Or earth, gape open wide and eat him
    quick,   65
As thou dost swallow up this good king's
    blood,
Which his hell-govern'd arm hath butcheréd!
    GLOU. Lady, you know no rules of charity,
Which renders good for bad, blessings for
    curses.
    ANNE. Villain, thou know'st no law of God
    nor man: 70
No beast so fierce but knows some touch of
    pity.
    GLOU. But I know none, and therefore am
    no beast.
    ANNE. O wonderful, when devils tell the
    truth!
    GLOU. More wonderful, when angels are so
    angry.
Vouchsafe, divine perfection of a woman, 75
Of these supposéd evils, to give me leave,
By circumstance, but to acquit myself.
    ANNE. Vouchsafe, defused infection of a
    man,
For these known evils, but to give me leave,
By circumstance, to curse thy cursed self. 80
    GLOU. Fairer than tongue can name thee, let
    me have
Some patient leisure to excuse myself.
    ANNE. Fouler than heart can think thee, thou
    canst make
No excuse current, but to hang thyself.
    GLOU. By such despair, I should accuse my-
    self.   85
    ANNE. And, by despairing, shouldst thou
    stand excused;

For doing worthy vengeance on thyself,
Which didst unworthy slaughter upon others.
    GLOU. Say that I slew them not?
    ANNE.   Why, then they are not dead:
But dead they are, and, devilish slave, by
    thee.   90
    GLOU. I did not kill your husband.
    ANNE.   Why, then he is alive.
    GLOU. Nay, he is dead; and slain by Edward's
    hand.
    ANNE. In thy foul throat thou liest: Queen
    Margaret saw
Thy murderous falchion smoking in his
    blood;
The which thou once didst bend against her
    breast,   95
But that thy brothers beat aside the point.
    GLOU. I was provokéd by her slanderous
    tongue,
Which laid their guilt upon my guiltless
    shoulders.
    ANNE. Thou wast provokéd by thy bloody
    mind,
Which never dreamt on aught but butcher-
    ies: 100
Didst thou not kill this king?
    GLOU.   I grant ye.
    ANNE. Dost grant me, hedgehog? then, God
    grant me too
Thou mayst be damnéd for that wicked deed!
O, he was gentle, mild, and virtuous!
    GLOU. The fitter for the King of heaven,
    that hath him.   105
    ANNE. He is in heaven, where thou shalt
    never come.
    GLOU. Let him thank me, that holp to send
    him thither;
For he was fitter for that place than earth.
    ANNE. And thou unfit for any place but
    hell.
    GLOU. Yes, one place else, if you will hear
    me name it.   110
    ANNE. Some dungeon.
    GLOU.   Your bed-chamber.
    ANNE. Ill rest betide the chamber where
    thou liest!
    GLOU. So will it, madam, till I lie with you.
    ANNE. I hope so.
    GLOU.   I know so. But, gentle Lady
    Anne,

---

56. **bleed afresh**, alludes to the superstitious belief that a corpse bled in the presence of its murderer. 65. **quick**, alive. 77. **circumstance**, relating the facts. 78. **defused**, shapeless. 82. **patient**, calm. 84. **current**, good (as of money), hence that will pass muster. 94. **falchion**, sword. 101. **grant ye**, acknowledge it. 102. **hedgehog**, reference to Richard's heraldic device—a boar.

To leave this keen encounter of our wits, 115
And fall somewhat into a slower method,
Is not the causer of the timeless deaths
Of these Plantagenets, Henry and Edward,
As blameful as the executioner?

ANNE. Thou art the cause, and most accursed effect.   120

GLOU. Your beauty was the cause of that
effect;
Your beauty, which did haunt me in my
sleep
To undertake the death of all the world,
So I might live one hour in your sweet bosom.

ANNE. If I thought that, I tell thee, homicide,   125
These nails should rend that beauty from my
cheeks.

GLOU. These eyes could never endure sweet
beauty's wreck;
You should not blemish it, if I stood by:
As all the world is cheered by the sun,
So I by that; it is my day, my life.   130

ANNE. Black night o'ershade thy day, and
death thy life!

GLOU. Curse not thyself, fair creature; thou
art both.

ANNE. I would I were, to be revenged on
thee.

GLOU. It is a quarrel most unnatural,
To be revenged on him that loveth you.   135

ANNE. It is a quarrel just and reasonable,
To be revenged on him that slew my husband.

GLOU. He that bereft thee, lady, of thy husband,
Did it to help thee to a better husband.

ANNE. His better doth not breathe upon the
earth.   140

GLOU. He lives that loves thee better than
he could.

ANNE. Name him.

GLOU.   Plantagenet.

ANNE.   Why, that was he.

GLOU. The selfsame name, but one of better
nature.

ANNE. Where is he?

GLOU.   Here. [*She spitteth at him.*]
Why dost thou spit at me?   145

ANNE. Would it were mortal poison, for
thy sake!

GLOU. Never came poison from so sweet a
place.

ANNE. Never hung poison on a fouler toad.
Out of my sight! thou dost infect my eyes.

GLOU. Thine eyes, sweet lady, have infected
mine.   150

ANNE. Would they were basilisks, to strike
thee dead!

GLOU. I would they were, that I might die
at once;
For now they kill me with a living death.
Those eyes of thine from mine have drawn
salt tears,
Shamed their aspect with store of childish
drops: 155
These eyes, which never shed remorseful tear,
No, when my father York and Edward wept,
To hear the piteous moan that Rutland made
When black-faced Clifford shook his sword
at him;
Nor when thy warlike father, like a child, 160
Told the sad story of my father's death,
And twenty times made pause to sob and
weep,
That all the standers-by had wet their cheeks,
Like trees bedash'd with rain: in that sad
time
My manly eyes did scorn an humble tear;   165
And what these sorrows could not thence
exhale,
Thy beauty hath, and made them blind with
weeping.
I never sued to friend nor enemy;
My tongue could never learn sweet smooth-
ing words;
But, now thy beauty is proposed my fee,   170
My proud heart sues and prompts my tongue
to speak. [*She looks scornfully at him.*
Teach not thy lips such scorn, for they were
made
For kissing, lady, not for such contempt.
If thy revengeful heart cannot forgive,
Lo, here I lend thee this sharp-pointed
sword;   175
Which if thou please to hide in this true
bosom,
And let the soul forth that adoreth thee,
I lay it naked to the deadly stroke,

117. timeless, untimely. 120. effect, agent. 151. basilisks,
mythical serpents, the offspring of a rooster's egg hatched
by a toad or snake, who killed by their glance. 158. Rutland, Richard's brother slain by Lord Clifford. 163. That

so that. 169. smoothing, flattering. 170. Is . . . fee.
is my proposed reward.

And humbly beg the death upon my knee.
  [*He lays his breast open: she offers at it
                                    with his sword.*
Nay, do not pause; for I did kill King Henry,
But 'twas thy beauty that provokèd me.   181
Nay, now dispatch; 'twas I that stabb'd young
    Edward,
But 'twas thy heavenly face that set me on.
              [*Here she lets fall the sword.*
Take up the sword again, or take up me.
  ANNE. Arise, dissembler: though I wish thy
    death,   185
I will not be the executioner.
  GLOU. Then bid me kill myself, and I will
    do it.
  ANNE. I have already.
  GLOU.   Tush, that was in thy rage:
Speak it again, and, even with the word,
That hand, which, for thy love, did kill thy
    love,   190
Shall, for thy love, kill a far truer love;
To both their deaths thou shalt be accessary.
  ANNE. I would I knew thy heart.
  GLOU. 'Tis figured in my tongue.
  ANNE. I fear me both are false.   195
  GLOU. Then never man was true.
  ANNE. Well, well, put up your sword.
  GLOU. Say, then, my peace is made.
  ANNE. That shall you know hereafter.
  GLOU. But shall I live in hope?   200
  ANNE. All men, I hope, live so.
  GLOU. Vouchsafe to wear this ring.
  ANNE. To take is not to give.
  GLOU. Look, how this ring encompasseth
    thy finger,
Even so thy breast encloseth my poor
    heart;   205
Wear both of them, for both of them are
    thine.
And if thy poor devoted suppliant may
But beg one favour at thy gracious hand,
Thou dost confirm his happiness for ever.
  ANNE. What is it?   210
  GLOU. That it would please thee leave these
    sad designs
To him that hath more cause to be a
    mourner,
And presently repair to Crosby Place;
Where, after I have solemnly interr'd

At Chertsey monastery this noble king,   215
And wet his grave with my repentant tears,
I will with all expedient duty see you:
For divers unknown reasons, I beseech you,
Grant me this boon.
  ANNE. With all my heart; and much it joys
    me too,   220
To see you are become so penitent.
Tressel and Berkeley, go along with me.
  GLOU. Bid me farewell.
  ANNE.   'Tis more than you deserve;
But since you teach me how to flatter you,
Imagine I have said farewell already.   225
    [*Exeunt* LADY ANNE, TRESSEL, *and* BERKELEY.
  GLOU. Sirs, take up the corse.
  GENT.   Towards Chertsey, noble lord?
  GLOU. No, to White-Friars; there attend my
    coming.   [*Exeunt all but* GLOUCESTER.
Was ever woman in this humour woo'd?
Was ever woman in this humour won?
I'll have her; but I will not keep her long. 230
What! I, that kill'd her husband and his father,
To take her in her heart's extremest hate,
With curses in her mouth, tears in her eyes,
The bleeding witness of her hatred by;
Having God, her conscience, and these bars
    against me,   235
And I nothing to back my suit at all,
But the plain devil and dissembling looks,
And yet to win her, all the world to nothing!
Ha!
Hath she forgot already that brave prince,
Edward, her lord, whom I, some three months
    since,   241
Stabb'd in my angry mood at Tewksbury?
A sweeter and a lovelier gentleman,
Framed in the prodigality of nature,
Young, valiant, wise, and, no doubt, right
    royal,   245
The spacious world cannot again afford:
And will she yet debase her eyes on me,
That cropp'd the golden prime of this sweet
    prince,
And made her widow to a woful bed?
On me, whose all not equals Edward's
    moiety?   250
On me, that halt and am unshapen thus?
My dukedom to a beggarly denier,

---

194. figured, portrayed. 202. Vouchsafe, consent. 213.
Crosby Place, Richard's residence. 215. Chertsey, a
town in Surrey. 217. with . . . duty, as expeditiously as
my respect (for you) requires. 218. unknown, secret.
227. White-Friars, a Carmelite priory in London; attend,
await. 228. humour, our mood. 244. in the prodigality of
nature, i.e., when nature was most generous. 250. moiety,
half. 252. denier, small copper coin.

I do mistake my person all this while:
Upon my life, she finds, although I cannot,
Myself to be a marvellous proper man.   255
I'll be at charges for a looking-glass,
And entertain some score or two of tailors,
To study fashions to adorn my body:
Since I am crept in favour with myself,
I will maintain it with some little cost.   260
But first I'll turn yon fellow in his grave;
And then return lamenting to my love.
Shine out, fair sun, till I have bought a glass,
That I may see my shadow as I pass.   [*Exit*.

SCENE III. *The palace.*

[*Enter* QUEEN ELIZABETH, LORD RIVERS, *and*
LORD GREY.]

RIV. Have patience, madam: there's no doubt
his majesty
Will soon recover his accustom'd health.
GREY. In that you brook it ill, it makes him
worse:
Therefore, for God's sake, entertain good
comfort,
And cheer his grace with quick and merry
words.   5
Q. ELIZ. If he were dead, what would be-
tide of me?
RIV. No other harm but loss of such a lord.
Q. ELIZ. The loss of such a lord includes all
harm.
GREY. The heavens have bless'd you with a
goodly son,
To be your comforter when he is gone.   10
Q. ELIZ. Oh, he is young, and his minority
Is put unto the trust of Richard Gloucester,
A man that loves not me, nor none of you.
RIV. Is it concluded he shall be protector?
Q. ELIZ. It is determined, not concluded
yet   15
But so it must be, if the king miscarry.

[*Enter* BUCKINGHAM *and* DERBY.]

GREY. Here come the lords of Buckingham
and Derby.
BUCK. Good time of day unto your royal
grace.

DER. God make your majesty joyful as you
have been!
Q. ELIZ. The Countess Richmond, good my
Lord of Derby,   20
To your good prayers will scarcely say amen.
Yet, Derby, notwithstanding she's your wife,
And loves not me, be you, good lord, assured
I hate not you for her proud arrogance.
DER. I do beseech you, either not believe   25
The envious slanders of her false accusers;
Or, if she be accused in true report,
Bear with her weakness, which, I think, pro-
ceeds
From wayward sickness, and no grounded
malice.
RIV. Saw you the king to-day, my Lord of
Derby?   30
DER. But now the Duke of Buckingham and
I
Are come from visiting his majesty.
Q. ELIZ. What likelihood of his amendment,
lords?
BUCK. Madam, good hope; his grace speaks
cheerfully.
Q. ELIZ. God grant him health! Did you
confer with him?   35
BUCK. Madam, we did: he desires to make
atonement
Betwixt the Duke of Gloucester and your
brothers,
And betwixt them and my lord chamberlain;
And sent to warn them to his royal presence.
Q. ELIZ. Would all were well! but that will
never be: 40
I fear our happiness is at the highest.

[*Enter* GLOUCESTER, HASTINGS, *and* DORSET.]

GLOU. They do me wrong, and I will not
endure it:
Who are they that complain unto the king,
That I, forsooth, am stern and love them not?
By holy Paul, they love his grace but
lightly   45
That fill his ears with such dissentious
rumours.
Because I cannot flatter and speak fair,
Smile in men's faces, smooth, deceive and cog,
Duck with French nods and apish courtesy,
I must be held a rancorous enemy.   50

---

255. proper, handsome. 256. be at charges for, buy.
261. turn . . . in, tip into. Scene iii: 3. brook, bear.
6. betide of, happen to. 15. determined, not concluded,
decided on, not yet ratified. 16. miscarry, die. 20. Countess
Richmond, Margaret Beaufort. Her first husband was the

Earl of Richmond, by whom she became mother of Henry
VII. Lord of Derby, Margaret's third husband. 36. atonement, reconcilement. 39. warn, summon. 46. dissentious,
trouble making. 48. smooth, flatter; cog, cheat.

Cannot a plain man live and think no harm,
But thus his simple truth must be abused
By silken, sly, insinuating Jacks?

RIV. To whom in all this presence speaks
your grace?

GLOU. To thee, that hast nor honesty nor
grace.   55

When have I injured thee? when done thee
wrong?

Or thee? or thee? or any of your faction?

A plague upon you all! His royal person,—

Whom God preserve better than you would
wish!—

Cannot be quiet scarce a breathing-while,   60

But you must trouble him with lewd complaints.

Q. ELIZ. Brother of Gloucester, you mistake
the matter.

The king, of his own royal disposition,

And not provoked by any suitor else;

Aiming, belike, at your interior hatred,   65

Which in your outward actions shows itself

Against my kindred, brothers, and myself,

Makes him to send; that thereby he may
gather

The ground of your ill-will, and so remove it.

GLOU. I cannot tell: the world is grown so
bad,   70

That wrens make prey where eagles dare not
perch:

Since every Jack became a gentleman,

There's many a gentle person made a Jack.

Q. ELIZ. Come, come, we know your mean-
ing, brother Gloucester;   74

You envy my advancement and my friends':

God grant we never may have need of you!

GLOU. Meantime, God grants that we have
need of you:

Our brother is imprison'd by your means,

Myself disgraced, and the nobility

Held in contempt; whilst many fair promotions   80

Are daily given to ennoble those

That scarce, some two days since, were worth
a noble.

Q. ELIZ. By Him that raised me to this careful height

From that contented hap which I enjoy'd,

I never did incense his majesty   85

Against the Duke of Clarence, but have been

An earnest advocate to plead for him.

My lord, you do me shameful injury,

Falsely to draw me in these vile suspects.

GLOU. You may deny that you were not the
cause   90

Of my Lord Hastings' late imprisonment.

RIV. She may, my lord, for—

GLOU. She may, Lord Rivers! why, who
knows not so?

She may do more, sir, than denying that:

She may help you to many fair prefer-
ments;   95

And then deny her aiding hand therein,

And lay those honours on your high deserts.

What may she not? She may, yea, marry, may
she,—

RIV. What, marry, may she?

GLOU. What, marry, may she! marry with a
king,   100

A bachelor, a handsome stripling too:

I wis your grandam had a worser match.

Q. ELIZ. My Lord of Gloucester, I have too
long borne

Your blunt upbraidings and your bitter scoffs:

By heaven, I will acquaint his majesty   105

With those gross taunts I often have endured.

I had rather be a country servant-maid

Than a great queen, with this condition,

To be thus taunted, scorn'd, and baited at:

[*Enter* QUEEN MARGARET, *behind.*]

Small joy have I in being England's queen.

Q. MAR. And lessen'd be that small, God,
I beseech thee!   111

Thy honour, state and seat is due to me.

GLOU. What! threat you me with telling of
the king?

Tell him, and spare not: look, what I have
said

I will avouch in presence of the king: 115

I dare adventure to be sent to the Tower.

'Tis time to speak; my pains are quite forgot.

Q. MAR. Out, devil! I remember them too
well:

Thou slewest my husband Henry in the
Tower,

And Edward, my poor son, at Tewksbury.

GLOU. Ere you were queen, yea, or your
husband king,   121

53. Jacks, upstarts. 61. lewd, vile. 63. disposition, inclination. 65. interior, inner. 76. have need of you, be in
trouble because of you. 82. noble, coin worth 13s, 4d.
83. careful, full of care. 84. hap, fortune. 89. suspects,
suspicions. 98. marry, by the Virgin Mary. 109. baited
at, harassed. 115. avouch, openly affirm. 116. adventure
to be, risk being.

I was a pack-horse in his great affairs;
A weeder-out of his proud adversaries,
A liberal rewarder of his friends:
To royalise his blood I spilt mine own.   125
  Q. MAR. Yea, and much better blood than
    his or thine.
  GLOU. In all which time you and your hus-
    band Grey
Were factious for the house of Lancaster;
And, Rivers, so were you. Was not your
  husband
In Margaret's battle at Saint Alban's slain?
Let me put in your minds, if you forget,   131
What you have been ere now, and what you
  are;
Withal, what I have been, and what I am.
  Q. MAR. A murderous villain, and so still
    thou art.
  GLOU. Poor Clarence did forsake his father,
    Warwick;   135
Yea, and forswore himself,—which Jesu par-
  don!—
  Q. MAR. Which God revenge!
  GLOU. To fight on Edward's party for the
    crown;
And for his meed, poor lord, he is mew'd up.
I would to God my heart were flint, like
  Edward's;   140
Or Edward's soft and pitiful, like mine:
I am too childish-foolish for this world.
  Q. MAR. Hie thee to hell for shame, and leave
    the world,
Thou cacodemon! there thy kingdom is.
  RIV. My Lord of Gloucester, in those busy
    days   145
Which here you urge to prove us enemies,
We follow'd then our lord, our lawful king:
So should we you, if you should be our king.
  GLOU. If I should be! I had rather be a
    pedlar:
Far be it from my heart, the thought of it!   150
  Q. ELIZ. As little joy, my lord, as you sup-
    pose
You should enjoy, were you this country's
  king,
As little joy may you suppose in me,
That I enjoy, being the queen thereof.
  Q. MAR. A little joy enjoys the queen
    thereof;   155

For I am she, and altogether joyless.
I can no longer hold me patient. [*Advancing.*
Hear me, you wrangling pirates, that fall out
In sharing that which you have pill'd from
  me!
Which of you trembles not that looks on me?
If not, that, I being queen, you bow like
  subjects,   161
Yet that, by you deposed, you quake like
  rebels?
O gentle villain, do not turn away!
  GLOU. Foul wrinkled witch, what makest
    thou in my sight?
  Q. MAR. But repetition of what thou hast
    marr'd;   165
That will I make before I let thee go.
  GLOU. Wert thou not banished on pain of
    death?
  Q. MAR. I was; but I do find more pain in
    banishment
Than death can yield me here by my abode.
A husband and a son thou owest to me;   170
And thou a kingdom; all of you allegiance:
The sorrow that I have, by right is yours,
And all the pleasures you usurp are mine.
  GLOU. The curse my noble father laid on
    thee,
When thou didst crown his warlike brows
  with paper   175
And with thy scorns drew'st rivers from his
  eyes,
And then, to dry them, gavest the duke a clout
Steep'd in the faultless blood of pretty Rut-
  land,—
His curses, then from bitterness of soul
Denounced against thee, are all fall'n upon
  thee;   180
And God, not we, hath plagued thy bloody
  deed.
  Q. ELIZ. So just is God, to right the inno-
    cent.
  HAST. O, 'twas the foulest deed to slay that
    babe,
And the most merciless that e'er was heard
  of!
  RIV. Tyrants themselves wept when it was
    reported.   185

---

130. **battle,** i.e., battle fought at St. Albans in 1461.
133. **withal,** besides. 139. **meed,** reward; **mew'd,** cooped
up. 144. **cacodemon,** evil spirit. 159. **pill'd,** robbed.
162. **yet . . . deposed,** yet because you have deposed me,
your true queen. 165. **But . . . marr'd,** I only rehearse
your crimes. 167. **banished,** Margaret was really dead
before the historical time of this scene. 170. **thou,** Richard.
171. **thou,** Queen Elizabeth. 175. **When,** at the battle of
Wakefield (1460). 177. **clout,** cloth, handkerchief. 183.
that babe, young Rutland.

DOR. No man but prophesied revenge for it.

BUCK. Northumberland, then present, wept to see it.

Q. MAR. What! were you snarling all before I came,

Ready to catch each other by the throat,

And turn you all your hatred now on me? 190

Did York's dread curse prevail so much with heaven

That Henry's death, my lovely Edward's death,

Their kingdom's loss, my woful banishment,

Could all but answer for that peevish brat?

Can curses pierce the clouds and enter heaven?   195

Why, then, give way, dull clouds, to my quick curses!

If not by war, by surfeit die your king,

As ours by murder, to make him a king!

Edward thy son, which now is Prince of Wales,

For Edward my son, which was Prince of Wales,   200

Die in his youth by like untimely violence!

Thyself a queen, for me that was a queen,

Outlive thy glory, like my wretched self!

Long mayst thou live to wail thy children's loss;

And see another, as I see thee now,   205

Deck'd in thy rights, as thou art stall'd in mine!

Long die thy happy days before thy death;

And, after many lengthen'd hours of grief,

Die neither mother, wife, nor England's queen!

Rivers and Dorset, you were standers by, 210

And so wast thou, Lord Hastings, when my son

Was stabb'd with bloody daggers: God, I pray him,

That none of you may live your natural age,

But by some unlook'd accident cut off!

GLOU. Have done thy charm, thou hateful wither'd hag!   215

Q. MAR. And leave out thee? stay, dog, for thou shalt hear me.

If heaven have any grievous plague in store

Exceeding those that I can wish upon thee,

O, let them keep it till thy sins be ripe,

And then hurl down their indignation   220

On thee, the troubler of the poor world's peace!

The worm of conscience still begnaw thy soul!

Thy friends suspect for traitors while thou livest,

And take deep traitors for thy dearest friends!

No sleep close up that deadly eye of thine, 225

Unless it be whilst some tormenting dream

Affrights thee with a hell of ugly devils!

Thou elvish-mark'd, abortive, rooting hog!

Thou that wast seal'd in thy nativity

The slave of nature and the son of hell!   230

Thou slander of thy mother's heavy womb!

Thou loathed issue of thy father's loins!

Thou rag of honour! thou detested—

GLOU. Margaret.

Q. MAR.   Richard!

GLOU.   Ha!

Q. MAR.   I call thee not.

GLOU. I cry thee mercy then, for I had thought   235

That thou hadst call'd me all these bitter names.

Q. MAR. Why, so I did; but look'd for no reply.

O, let me make the period to my curse!

GLOU. 'Tis done by me, and ends in 'Margaret.'

Q. ELIZ. Thus have you breathed your curse against yourself.   240

Q. MAR. Poor painted queen, vain flourish of my fortune!

Why strew'st thou sugar on that bottled spider,

Whose deadly web ensnareth thee about?

Fool, fool! thou whet'st a knife to kill thyself.

The time will come when thou shalt wish for me   245

To help thee curse that poisonous bunch-back'd toad.

HAST. False-boding woman, end thy frantic curse,

Lest to thy harm thou move our patience.

Q. MAR. Foul shame upon you! you have all moved mine.

187. Northumberland, the Third Earl was on the Lancastrian side. 196. quick, lively. 206. stall'd, installed. 228.
Elvish-mark'd, marked at his birth by elves and so
deformed. 230. slave of nature, by nature contemptible.
234. Ha! i.e., did you call me? 235. Cry thee mercy, beg
your pardon. 238. period, conclusion. 241. Poor . . .
fortune, poor artificial picture of a Queen! A mere showy
portrait of what I once was. 242. bottled, shaped like a
bottle.

RIV. Were you well served, you would be taught your duty.   250

Q. MAR. To serve me well, you all should do me duty,

Teach me to be your queen, and you my subjects:

O, serve me well, and teach yourselves that duty!

DOR. Dispute not with her; she is lunatic.

Q. MAR. Peace, master marquess, you are malapert: 255

Your fire-new stamp of honour is scarce current.

O, that your young nobility could judge

What 'twere to lose it, and be miserable!

They that stand high have many blasts to shake them;

And if they fall, they dash themselves to pieces.   260

GLOU. Good counsel, marry: learn it, learn it, marquess.

DOR. It toucheth you, my lord, as much as me.

GLOU. Yea, and much more: but I was born so high,

Our aery buildeth in the cedar's top,

And dallies with the wind and scorns the sun.   265

Q. MAR. And turns the sun to shade; alas! alas!

Witness my son, now in the shade of death;

Whose bright out-shining beams thy cloudy wrath

Hath in eternal darkness folded up.

Your aery buildeth in our aery's nest.   270

O God, that seest it, do not suffer it;

As it was won with blood, lost be it so!

BUCK. Have done! for shame, if not for charity.

Q. MAR. Urge neither charity nor shame to me:

Uncharitably with me have you dealt,   275

And shamefully by you my hopes are butcher'd.

My charity is outrage, life my shame;

And in that shame still live my sorrow's rage!

BUCK. Have done, have done.

Q. MAR. O princely Buckingham, I'll kiss thy hand,   280

In sign of league and amity with thee:

Now fair befall thee and thy noble house!

Thy garments are not spotted with our blood,

Nor thou within the compass of my curse.

BUCK. Nor no one here; for curses never pass   285

The lips of those that breathe them in the air.

Q. MAR. I'll not believe but they ascend the sky,

And there awake God's gentle-sleeping peace.

O Buckingham, take heed of yonder dog!

Look, when he fawns, he bites; and when he bites,   290

His venom tooth will rankle to the death:

Have not to do with him, beware of him;

Sin, death, and hell have set their marks on him,

And all their minsters attend on him.

GLOU. What doth she say, my Lord of Buckingham?   295

BUCK. Nothing that I respect, my gracious lord.

Q. MAR. What, dost thou scorn me for my gentle counsel?

And soothe the devil that I warn thee from?

O, but remember this another day,

When he shall split thy very heart with sorrow,   300

And say poor Margaret was a prophetess!

Live each of you the subjects to his hate,

And he to yours, and all of you to God's!

                                                          [Exit.

HAST. My hair doth stand on end to hear her curses.

RIV. And so doth mine: I muse why she's at liberty.   305

GLOU. I cannot blame her: by God's holy mother,

She hath had too much wrong; and I repent

My part thereof that I have done to her.

Q. ELIZ. I never did her any, to my knowledge.

GLOU. But you have all the vantage of her wrong.   310

I was too hot to do somebody good,

That is too cold in thinking of it now.

Marry, as for Clarence, he is well repaid;

He is frank'd up to fatting for his pains:

God pardon them that are the cause of it!   315

RIV. A virtuous and a Christian-like conclusion,

---

255. malapert, impudent. 256. fire-new, fresh from the mint. 264. aery, eagle's brood. 277. My . . . outrage, the only charity I receive is outrage. 291. rankle, make fester.

298. soothe, humor. 305. muse why, wonder that. 314. frank'd up, shut up in a sty.

To pray for them that have done scathe to us.

GLOU. So do I ever: [*Aside*] being well advised.

For had I cursed now, I had cursed myself.

[*Enter* CATESBY.]

CATES. Madam, his majesty doth call for you;   320
And for your grace; and you, my noble lords.

Q. ELIZ. Catesby, we come. Lords, will you go with us?

RIV. Madam, we will attend your grace.
                    [*Exeunt all but* GLOUCESTER.

GLOU. I do the wrong, and first begin to brawl.

The secret mischiefs that I set abroach   325
I lay unto the grievous charge of others.

Clarence, whom I, indeed, have laid in darkness,

I do beweep to many simple gulls;

Namely, to Hastings, Derby, Buckingham;

And say it is the queen and her allies   330
That stir the king against the duke my brother.

Now, they believe it; and withal whet me

To be revenged on Rivers, Vaughan, Grey:

But then I sigh; and, with a piece of scripture,

Tell them that God bids us do good for evil:

And thus I clothe my naked villany   336
With old odd ends stolen out of holy writ;

And seem a saint, when most I play the devil.

[*Enter two* MURDERERS.]

But, soft! here come my executioners.

How now, my hardy, stout resolvéd mates!

Are you now going to dispatch this deed? 341

FIRST MURD. We are, my lord; and come to have the warrant,

That we may be admitted where he is.

GLOU. Well thought upon; I have it here about me.   [*Gives the warrant.*

When you have done, repair to Crosby Place.   345

But, sirs, be sudden in the execution,

Withal obdurate, do not hear him plead;

For Clarence is well-spoken, and perhaps

May move your hearts to pity, if you mark him.

FIRST MURD. Tush!   350
Fear not, my lord, we will not stand to prate;

Talkers are no good doers: be assured

We come to use our hands and not our tongues.

GLOU. Your eyes drop millstones, when fools' eyes drop tears:

I like you, lads; about your business straight;   355
Go, go, dispatch.

FIRST MURD. We will, my noble lord.
                    [*Exeunt.*

SCENE IV. *London. The Tower.*

[*Enter* CLARENCE *and* BRAKENBURY.]

BRAK. Why looks your grace so heavily today?

CLAR. O, I have pass'd a miserable night,

So full of ugly sights, of ghastly dreams,

That, as I am a Christian faithful man,

I would not spend another such a night,   5

Though 'twere to buy a world of happy days,

So full of dismal terror was the time!

BRAK. What was your dream? I long to hear you tell it.

CLAR. Methoughts that I had broken from the Tower,

And was embark'd to cross to Burgundy;   10

And, in my company, my brother Gloucester;

Who from my cabin tempted me to walk

Upon the hatches: thence we look'd toward England,

And cited up a thousand fearful times,

During the wars of York and Lancaster   15

That had befall'n us. As we paced along

Upon the giddy footing of the hatches,

Methought that Gloucester stumbled; and, in falling,

Struck me, that thought to stay him, overboard,

Into the tumbling billows of the main.   20

Lord, Lord! methought, what pain it was to drown!

What dreadful noise of waters in mine ears!

What ugly sights of death within mine eyes!

Methought I saw a thousand fearful wrecks;

Ten thousand men that fishes gnaw'd upon;

Wedges of gold, great anchors, heaps of pearl,   26

---

317. scathe, harm. 325. set abroach, set going. 326. I . . . other, I attribute to others by accusing them of the crimes.

Scene iv: 10. Burgundy, the Netherlands, where Clarence had lived as a boy. 14. cited up, called to mind.

Inestimable stones, unvalued jewels,
All scatter'd in the bottom of the sea:
Some lay in dead men's skulls; and, in those holes
Where eyes did once inhabit, there were crept,   30
As 'twere in scorn of eyes, reflecting gems,
Which woo'd the slimy bottom of the deep,
And mock'd the dead bones that lay scatter'd by.
   BRAK. Had you such leisure in the time of death
To gaze upon the secrets of the deep?   35
   CLAR. Methought I had; and often did I strive
To yield the ghost: but still the envious flood
Kept in my soul, and would not let it forth
To seek the empty, vast and wandering air;
But smother'd it within my panting bulk,   40
Which almost burst to belch it in the sea.
   BRAK. Awaked you not with this sore agony?
   CLAR. O, no, my dream was lengthen'd after life;
O, then began the tempest to my soul,
Who pass'd, methought, the melancholy flood,   45
With that grim ferryman which poets write of,
Unto the kingdom of perpetual night.
The first that there did greet my stranger soul,
Was my great father-in-law, renowned Warwick;
Who cried aloud, "What scourge for perjury   50
Can this dark monarchy afford false Clarence?"
And so he vanish'd: then came wandering by
A shadow like an angel, with bright hair
Dabbled in blood; and he squeak'd out aloud,
"Clarence is come; false, fleeting, perjured Clarence,   55
That stabb'd me in the field by Tewksbury;
Seize on him, Furies, take him to your torments!"
With that, methoughts, a legion of foul fiends
Environ'd me about, and howled in mine ears
Such hideous cries, that with the very noise
I trembling waked, and for a season after   61
Could not believe but that I was in hell,

Such terrible impression made the dream.
   BRAK. No marvel, my lord, though it affrighted you;
I promise you, I am afraid to hear you tell it.   65
   CLAR. O Brakenbury, I have done those things,
Which now bear evidence against my soul,
For Edward's sake; and see how he requites me!
O God! if my deep prayers cannot appease thee,
But thou wilt be avenged on my misdeeds,   70
Yet execute thy wrath in me alone,
O, spare my guiltless wife and my poor children!
I pray thee, gentle keeper, stay by me;
My soul is heavy, and I fain would sleep.
   BRAK. I will, my lord: God give your grace good rest!   [CLARENCE *sleeps.*]   75
Sorrow breaks seasons and reposing hours,
Makes the night morning, and the noon-tide night.
Princes have but their titles for their glories,
An outward honour for an inward toil;
And, for unfelt imagination,   80
They often feel a world of restless cares:
So that, betwixt their titles and low names,
There's nothing differs but the outward fame.

[*Enter the two* MURDERERS.]

   FIRST MURD. Ho! who's here?
   BRAK. In God's name what are you, and how came you hither?   85
   FIRST MURD. I would speak with Clarence, and I came hither on my legs.
   BRAK. Yea, are you so brief?
   SEC. MURD. O sir, it is better to be brief than tedious. Show him our commission; talk no more.   [BRAKENBURY *reads it.*   91
   BRAK. I am, in this, commanded to deliver
The noble Duke of Clarence to your hands:
I will not reason what is meant hereby,
Because I will be guiltless of the meaning.   95
Here are the keys, there sits the duke asleep.
I'll to the king; and signify to him
That thus I have resign'd my charge to you.
   FIRST MURD. Do so, it is a point of wisdom: fare you well.   [*Exit* BRAKENBURY.   100

27. unvalued, invaluable. 37. envious, malicious. 45. melancholy flood, i.e., the river Styx. 46. ferryman, Charon, who ferried the souls of the dead across the Styx. | 53. shadow, Prince Edward, son of Henry VI. 55. fleeting, fickle, disloyal. 80. for unfelt imagination, for the sake of unreal splendor. 90. commission, written instructions.

SEC. MURD. What, shall we stab him, as he sleeps?

FIRST MURD. No; then he will say 'twas done cowardly, when he wakes.

SEC. MURD. When he wakes! why, fool, he shall never wake till the judgement-day.   106

FIRST MURD. Why, then he will say we stabbed him sleeping.

SEC. MURD. The urging of that word "judgement" hath bred a kind of remorse in me.   110

FIRST MURD. What, art thou afraid?

SEC. MURD. Not to kill him, having a warrant for it; but to be damned for killing him, from which no warrant can defend us.

FIRST MURD. I thought thou hadst been resolute.   116

SEC. MURD. So I am, to let him live.

FIRST MURD. Back to the Duke of Gloucester, tell him so.

SEC. MURD. I pray thee, stay a while: I hope my holy humour will change; 'twas wont to hold me but while one would tell twenty. 122

FIRST MURD. How dost thou feel thyself now?

SEC. MURD. 'Faith, some certain dregs of conscience are yet within me.

FIRST MURD. Remember our reward, when the deed is done.

SEC. MURD. 'Zounds, he dies: I had forgot the reward.

FIRST MURD. Where is thy conscience now?

SEC. MURD. In the Duke of Gloucester's purse.   131

FIRST MURD. So when he opens his purse to give us our reward, thy conscience flies out.

SEC. MURD. Let it go; there's few or none will entertain it.   135

FIRST MURD. How if it come to thee again?

SEC. MURD. I'll not meddle with it: it is a dangerous thing: it makes a man a coward: a man cannot steal, but it accuseth him; he cannot swear, but it checks him; he cannot lie with his neighbour's wife, but it detects him: 'tis a blushing shamefast spirit that mutinies in a man's bosom; it fills one full of obstacles: it made me once restore a purse of gold that I

found; it beggars any man that keeps it: it is turned out of all towns and cities for a dangerous thing; and every man that means to live well endeavours to trust to himself and to live without it.   148

FIRST MURD. 'Zounds, it is even now at my elbow, persuading me not to kill the duke.

SEC. MURD. Take the devil in thy mind, and believe him not: he would insinuate with thee but to make thee sigh.   153

FIRST MURD. Tut, I am strong-framed, he cannot prevail with me, I warrant thee.

SEC. MURD. Spoke like a tall fellow that respects his reputation. Come, shall we to this gear?   158

FIRST MURD. Take him over the costard with the hilts of thy sword, and then we will chop him in the malmsey-butt in the next room. 161

SEC. MURD. O excellent device! make a sop of him.

FIRST MURD. Hark! he stirs: shall I strike?

SEC. MURD. No, first let's reason with him.

CLAR. Where art thou, keeper? give me a cup of wine.   166

SEC. MURD. You shall have wine enough, my lord, anon.

CLAR. In God's name, what art thou?

SEC. MURD. A man, as you are.

CLAR. But not, as I am, royal.   170

SEC. MURD. Nor you, as we are, loyal.

CLAR. Thy voice is thunder, but thy looks are humble.

SEC. MURD. My voice is now the king's, my looks mine own.

CLAR. How darkly and how deadly dost thou speak!   175

Your eyes do menace me: why look you pale?
Who sent you hither? Wherefore do you come?

BOTH. To, to, to—

CLAR. To murder me?

BOTH. Ay, ay.

CLAR. You scarcely have the hearts to tell me so,   180

And therefore cannot have the hearts to do it.
Wherein, my friends, have I offended you?

FIRST MURD. Offended us you have not, but the king.

CLAR. I shall be reconciled to him again.

120. humour, mood. 121. tell, count. 135. entertain, listen to. 141. shamefast, bashful. 151. take the devil, subdue your conscience (which is a devil). 152. insinuate, worm himself into favor. 156. tall, brave. 159. costard, head.

literally a kind of apple. 160-1. chop . . . malmsey-butt, pop him into a keg of malmsey wine. 162. sop, bread dipped into wine. 175. darkly, mysteriously.

SEC. MURD. Never, my lord; therefore prepare to die.   185

CLAR. Are you call'd forth from out a world of men
To slay the innocent? What is my offence?
Where are the evidence that do accuse me?
What lawful quest have given their verdict up   189
Unto the frowning judge? or who pronounced
The bitter sentence of poor Clarence' death?
Before I be convict by course of law,
To threaten me with death is most unlawful.
I charge you, as you hope to have redemption
By Christ's dear blood shed for our grievous sins,   195
That you depart and lay no hands on me:
The deed you undertake is damnable.

FIRST MURD. What we will do, we do upon command.

SEC. MURD. And he that hath commanded is the king.

CLAR. Erroneous vassal! the great King of kings   200
Hath in the tables of his law commanded
That thou shalt do no murder: and wilt thou, then,
Spurn at his edict and fulfil a man's?
Take heed; for he holds vengeance in his hands,
To hurl upon their heads that break his law. 205

SEC. MURD. And that same vengeance doth he hurl on thee,
For false forswearing and for murder too:
Thou didst receive the holy sacrament,
To fight in quarrel of the house of Lancaster.

FIRST MURD. And, like a traitor to the name of God,   210
Didst break that vow; and with thy treacherous blade
Unrip'dst the bowels of thy sovereign's son.

SEC. MURD. Whom thou wert sworn to cherish and defend.

FIRST MURD. How canst thou urge God's dreadful law to us,
When thou hast broke it in so dear degree? 215

CLAR. Alas! for whose sake did I that ill deed?
For Edward, for my brother, for his sake:
Why, sirs,
He sends ye not to murder me for this;

For in this sin he is as deep as I.   220
If God will be revenged for this deed,
O, know you yet, he doth it publicly:
Take not the quarrel from his powerful arm;
He needs no indirect nor lawless course
To cut off those that have offended him. 225

FIRST MURD. Who made thee, then, a bloody minister,
When gallant-springing brave Plantagenet,
That princely novice, was struck dead by thee?

CLAR. My brother's love, the devil, and my rage.

FIRST MURD. Thy brother's love, our duty, and thy fault,   230
Provoke us hither now to slaughter thee.

CLAR. Oh, if you love my brother, hate not me;
I am his brother, and I love him well.
If you be hired for meed, go back again,
And I will send you to my brother Gloucester,
Who shall reward you better for my life   236
Than Edward will for tidings of my death.

SEC. MURD. You are deceived, your brother Gloucester hates you.

CLAR. O, no, he loves me, and he holds me dear:
Go you to him from me.

BOTH.   Aye, so we will. 240

CLAR. Tell him, when that our princely father York
Bless'd his three sons with his victorious arm,
And charged us from his soul to love each other,
He little thought of this divided friendship:
Bid Gloucester think of this, and he will weep.

FIRST MURD. Ay, millstones; as he lesson'd us to weep,   246

CLAR. O, do not slander him, for he is kind.

FIRST MURD. Right,
As snow in harvest. Thou deceivest thyself:
'Tis he that sent us hither now to slaughter thee.   250

CLAR. It cannot be; for when I parted with him,
He hugg'd me in his arms, and swore, with sobs,
That he would labour my delivery.

SEC. MURD. Why, so he doth, now he delivers thee

189. quest, jury. 192. convict, convicted. 200. Erroneous, misled. 207. forswearing, perjury. 215. dear, great, grievous. 227. gallant-springing, youthful blossoming. 228. novice, youth. 234. meed, reward. 249. snow in harvest,

cf. Proverbs XXVI.1, "As snow in summer, and as rain in harvest, so honor is not seemly for a fool." 253. labour my delivery, work for my deliverance.

From this world's thraldom to the joys of
    heaven.   255
  FIRST MURD. Make peace with God, for you
    must die, my lord.
  CLAR. Hast thou that holy feeling in thy soul,
To counsel me to make my peace with God,
And art thou yet to thy own soul so blind,
That thou wilt war with God by murdering
    me?   260
Ah, sirs, consider, he that set you on
To do this deed will hate you for the deed.
  SEC. MURD. What shall we do?
  CLAR.   Relent, and save your souls.
  FIRST MURD. Relent! 'tis cowardly and wo-
    manish.
  CLAR. Not to relent is beastly, savage, devil-
    ish.   265
Which of you, if you were a prince's son,
Being pent from liberty, as I am now,
If two such murderers as yourselves came to
    you,
Would not entreat for life?
My friend, I spy some pity in thy looks; 270
O, if thine eye be not a flatterer,
Come thou on my side, and entreat for me,
As you would beg, were you in my distress:
A begging prince what beggar pities not?
  SEC. MURD. Look behind you, my lord.
  FIRST MURD. Take that, and that: if all this
    will not do,   [Stabs him.
I'll drown you in the malmsey-butt within.
                        [Exit, with the body.
  SEC. MURD. A bloody deed, and desperately
    dispatch'd!
How fain, like Pilate, would I wash my hands
Of this most grievous guilty murder done! 280

[Re-enter FIRST MURDERER.]

  FIRST MURD. How now! what mean'st thou,
    that thou help'st me not?
By heavens, the duke shall know how slack
    thou art!·
  SEC. MURD. I would he knew that I had saved
    his brother!
Take thou the fee, and tell him what I say;
For I repent me that the duke is slain. [Exit.
  FIRST MURD. So do not I: go, coward as thou
    art.   286
Now must I hide his body in some hole,

Until the duke take order for his burial:
And when I have my meed, I must away;
For this will out, and here I must not stay. 290
                                       [Exit.

ACT II

SCENE I. *London. The palace.*

[*Flourish. Enter* KING EDWARD *sick,* QUEEN
ELIZABETH, DORSET, RIVERS, HASTINGS, BUCK-
INGHAM, GREY, *and others.*]

  K. EDW. Why, so: now have I done a good
    day's work:
You peers, continue this united league:
I every day expect an embassage
From my Redeemer to redeem me hence;
And now in peace my soul shall part to
    heaven,   5
Since I have set my friends at peace on earth.
Rivers and Hastings, take each other's hand;
Dissemble not your hatred, swear your love.
  RIV. By heaven, my heart is purged from
    grudging hate;
And with my hand I seal my true heart's
    love.   10
  HAST. So thrive I, as I truly swear the like!
  K. EDW. Take heed you dally not before
    your king;
Lest he that is the supreme King of kings
Confound your hidden falsehood, and award
Either of you to be the other's end.   15
  HAST. So prosper I, as I swear perfect love!
  RIV. And I, as I love Hastings with my heart!
  K. EDW. Madam, yourself are not exempt in
    this,
Nor your son Dorset, Buckingham, nor you;
You have been factious one against the other.
Wife, love Lord Hastings, let him kiss your
    hand;   21
And what you do, do it unfeignedly.
  Q. ELIZ. Here, Hastings; I will never more
    remember
Our former hatred, so thrive I and mine!
  K. EDW. Dorset, embrace him; Hastings, love
    Lord Marquess.   25

267. pent, shut off. 288. take order. make arrangement.
290. out, be revealed. Act. II, Scene i: 8. Dissemble . . .
love, Do not merely hide your hatred, openly express your
love. 12. dally, trifle. 15. Either, each; end, death.
20. factious, at enmity.

DOR. This interchange of love, I here protest,
Upon my part shall be unviolable.
HAST. And so swear I, my lord.
                                        [*They embrace.*
K. EDW. Now, princely Buckingham, seal
    thou this league
With thy embracements to my wife's allies, 30
And make me happy in your unity.
    BUCK. Whenever Buckingham doth turn his
        hate
On you or yours [*to the* QUEEN], but with all
    duteous love
Doth cherish you and yours, God punish me
With hate in those where I expect most love!
When I have most need to employ a friend,
And most assuréd that he is a friend,   37
Deep, hollow, treacherous, and full of guile,
Be he unto me! this do I beg of God,
When I am cold in zeal to you or yours.   40
                                        [*They embrace.*
K. EDW. A pleasing cordial, princely Buck-
    ingham,
Is this thy vow unto my sickly heart.
There wanteth now our brother Gloucester
    here,
To make the perfect period of this peace.
    BUCK. And, in good time, here comes the
        noble duke.   45

[*Enter* GLOUCESTER.]

GLOU. Good morrow to my sovereign king
    and queen;
And, princely peers, a happy time of day!
    K. EDW. Happy, indeed, as we have spent
        the day.
Brother, we have done deeds of charity;
Made peace of enmity, fair love of hate,   50
Between these swelling wrong-incenséd peers.
    GLOU. A blesséd labour, my most sovereign
        liege:
Amongst this princely heap, if any here,
By false intelligence, or wrong surmise,
Hold me a foe;   55
If I unwittingly, or in my rage,
Have aught committed that is hardly borne
By any in this presence, I desire
To reconcile me to his friendly peace:
'Tis death to me to be at enmity;   60
I hate it, and desire all good men's love.
First, madam, I entreat true peace of you,

Which I will purchase with my duteous serv-
    ice;
Of you, my noble cousin Buckingham,   64
If ever any grudge were lodged between us;
Of you, Lord Rivers, and Lord Grey, of you;
That all without desert have frown'd on me;
Dukes, earls, lords, gentlemen; indeed, of all.
I do not know that Englishman alive
With whom my soul is any jot at odds   70
More than the infant that is born to-night:
I thank my God for my humility.
    Q. ELIZ. A holy day shall this be kept here-
        after:
I would to God all strifes were well com-
    pounded.
My sovereign liege, I do beseech your Maj-
    esty   75
To take our brother Clarence to your grace.
    GLOU. Why, madam, have I offer'd love for
        this,
To be so flouted in this royal presence?
Who knows not that the noble duke is dead?
                                        [*They all start.*
You do him injury to scorn his corse.   80
    RIV. Who knows not he is dead! who knows
        he is?
    Q. ELIZ. All-seeing heaven, what a world is
        this!
    BUCK. Look I so pale, Lord Dorset, as the
        rest?
    DOR. Ay, my good lord; and no one in this
        presence
But his red colour hath forsook his cheeks. 85
    K. EDW. Is Clarence dead? the order was
        reversed.
    GLOU. But he, poor soul, by your first order
        died,
And that a wingéd Mercury did bear;
Some tardy cripple bore the countermand,
That came too lag to see him buriéd.   90
God grant that some, less noble and less loyal,
Nearer in bloody thoughts, but not in blood,
Deserve not worse than wretched Clarence
    did,
And yet go current from suspicion!

[*Enter* DERBY.]

    DER. A boon, my sovereign, for my service
        done!   95

---

41. cordial, stimulant. 44. period, conclusion. 51. swelling, i.e., with anger. 53. heap, gathering. 54. intelligence, report. 57. hardly borne, resented. 67. without desert, i.e., on my part. 70. any . . . odds, the least bit in discord. 74. compounded, made up. 90. lag, late. 94. current, free.

K. EDW. I pray thee, peace: my soul is full
of sorrow.

DER. I will not rise, unless your highness
grant.

K. EDW. Then speak at once what is it thou
demand'st.

DER. The forfeit, sovereign, of my servant's
life;

Who slew to-day a riotous gentleman   100
Lately attendant on the Duke of Norfolk.

K. EDW. Have I a tongue to doom my
brother's death,

And shall the same give pardon to a slave?

My brother slew no man; his fault was
thought,

And yet his punishment was cruel death. 105

Who sued to me for him? who, in my rage,

Kneel'd at my feet, and bade me be advised?

Who spake of brotherhood? who spake of
love?

Who told me how the poor soul did forsake

The mighty Warwick, and did fight for me?

Who told me, in the field by Tewksbury, 111

When Oxford had me down, he rescued me,

And said, "Dear brother, live, and be a king"?

Who told me, when we both lay in the field

Frozen almost to death, how he did lap me 115

Even in his own garments, and gave himself,

All thin and naked, to the numb cold night?

All this from my remembrance brutish wrath

Sinfully pluck'd, and not a man of you

Had so much grace to put it in my mind. 120

But when your carters or your waiting-vassals

Have done a drunken slaughter, and defaced

The precious image of our dear Redeemer,

You straight are on your knees for pardon,
pardon;

And I, unjustly too, must grant it you: 125

But for my brother not a man would speak,

Nor I, ungracious, speak unto myself

For him, poor soul. The proudest of you all

Have been beholding to him in his life;

Yet none of you would once plead for his life.

O God, I fear thy justice will take hold 131

On me, and you, and mine, and yours for this!

Come, Hastings, help me to my closet. Oh,
poor Clarence!

[*Exeunt some with* KING *and* QUEEN.

99. forfeit, forgiving the forfeit. 107. advised, careful,
deliberate. 127. ungracious, without mercy. 129. beholding, indebted. 133. closet, private room. 137. still, continually. Scene ii: 8. cousins, relatives. 18. Incapable,

GLOU. This is the fruit of rashness! Mark'd
you not

How that the guilty kindred of the queen 135

Look'd pale when they did hear of Clarence'
death?

O, they did urge it still unto the king!

God will revenge it. But come, let us in,

To comfort Edward with our company.

BUCK. We wait upon your grace.   140

[*Exeunt.*

SCENE II. *The palace.*

[*Enter the* DUCHESS OF YORK, *with the two
children of* CLARENCE.]

BOY. Tell me, good grandam, is our father
dead?

DUCH. No, boy.

BOY. Why do you wring your hands, and
beat your breast,

And cry "O Clarence, my unhappy son!"

GIRL. Why do you look on us, and shake
your head,   5

And call us wretches, orphans, castaways,

If that our noble father be alive?

DUCH. My pretty cousins, you mistake me
much;

I do lament the sickness of the king,

As loath to lose him, not your father's death; 10

It were lost sorrow to wail one that's lost.

BOY. Then, grandam, you conclude that he
is dead.

The king my uncle is to blame for this:

God will revenge it; whom I will importune

With daily prayers all to that effect.   15

GIRL. And so will I.

DUCH. Peace, children, peace! the king doth
love you well:

Incapable and shallow innocents,

You cannot guess who caused your father's
death.

BOY. Grandam, we can; for my good uncle
Gloucester   20

Told me, the king, provokéd by the queen,

Devised impeachments to imprison him:

And when my uncle told me so, he wept,

And hugg'd me in his arm, and kindly kiss'd
my cheek;

Bade me rely on him as on my father,   25

And he would love me dearly as his child.

i.e., of understanding; shallow, simple-minded. 22. impeachments, accusations.

DUCH. Oh, that deceit should steal such gen-
tle shapes,
And with a virtuous vizard hide foul guile!
He is my son; yea, and therein my shame;
Yet from my dugs he drew not this deceit. 30
BOY. Think you my uncle did dissemble,
grandam?
DUCH. Ay, boy.
BOY. I cannot think it. Hark! what noise is
this?

[*Enter* QUEEN ELIZABETH, *with her hair about
her ears;* RIVERS *and* DORSET *after her.*]

Q. ELIZ. Oh, who shall hinder me to wail and
weep,
To chide my fortune, and torment myself?   35
I'll join with black despair against my soul,
And to myself become an enemy.
DUCH. What means this scene of rude im-
patience?
Q. ELIZ. To make an act of tragic violence:
Edward, my lord, your son, our king, is dead.
Why grow the branches now the root is
wither'd?   41
Why wither not the leaves the sap being gone?
If you will live, lament; if die, be brief,
That our swift-wingéd souls may catch the
king's;
Or, like obedient subjects, follow him   45
To his new kingdom of perpetual rest.
DUCH. Ah, so much interest have I in thy
sorrow
As I had title in thy noble husband!
I have bewept a worthy husband's death,
And lived by looking on his images: 50
But now two mirrors of his princely sem-
blance
Are crack'd in pieces by malignant death,
And I for comfort have but one false glass,
Which grieves me when I see my shame in
him.
Thou art a widow; yet thou art a mother,   55
And hast the comfort of thy children left thee:
But death hath snatch'd my husband from mine
arms,
And pluck'd two crutches from my feeble
limbs,
Edward and Clarence. O, what cause have I,
Thine being but a moiety of my grief,   60

To overgo thy plaints and drown thy cries!
BOY. Good aunt, you wept not for our
father's death;
How can we aid you with our kindred tears?
GIRL. Our fatherless distress was left un-
moan'd;
Your widow-dolour likewise be unwept!   65
Q. ELIZ. Give me no help in lamentation;
I am not barren to bring forth complaints:
All springs reduce their currents to mine eyes,
That I, being govern'd by the watery moon,
May send forth plenteous tears to drown the
world!   70
Oh for my husband, for my dear lord Ed-
ward!
CHIL. Oh for our father, for our dear lord
Clarence!
DUCH. Alas for both, both mine, Edward and
Clarence!
Q. ELIZ. What stay had I but Edward? and
he's gone.
CHIL. What stay had we but Clarence? and
he's gone.   75
DUCH. What stays had I but they? and they
are gone.
Q. ELIZ. Was never widow had so dear a loss!
CHIL. Were never orphans had so dear a loss!
DUCH. Was never mother had so dear a loss!
Alas, I am the mother of these moans!   80
Their woes are parcell'd, mine are general.
She for an Edward weeps, and so do I;
I for a Clarence weep, so doth not she:
These babes for Clarence weep, and so do I;
I for an Edward weep, so do not they: 85
Alas, you three, on me, threefold distress'd,
Pour all your tears! I am your sorrow's nurse,
And I will pamper it with lamentations.
DOR. Comfort, dear mother; God is much
displeased
That you take with unthankfulness his doing:
In common worldly things, 'tis call'd ungrate-
ful,   91
With dull unwillingness to repay a debt
Which with a bounteous hand was kindly lent;
Much more to be thus opposite with heaven,
For it requires the royal debt it lent you. 95
RIV. Madam, bethink you, like a careful
mother,
Of the young prince your son: send straight
for him;

28. vizard, mask. 39. To . . . violence, as the end of an
act in a violent tragedy. 40. Edward, King Edward IV.
50. images, i.e., children. 51. semblance, likeness. 53.
false glass, i.e., Richard. 60. moiety, snare. 67. barren,

unable. 68. reduce, bring back. 74. stay, support. 94.
opposite with, in opposition to. 95. requires . . . you, asks
the return of the King's life regarded as a loan from God.

Let him be crown'd; in him your comfort lives:

Drown desperate sorrow in dead Edward's grave,

And plant your joys in living Edward's throne.   100

[*Enter* GLOUCESTER, BUCKINGHAM, DERBY, HAST-INGS, *and* RATCLIFF.]

GLOU. Madam, have comfort: all of us have cause

To wail the dimming of our shining star;

But none can cure their harms by wailing them.

Madam, my mother, I do cry you mercy;

I did not see your grace: humbly on my knee

I crave your blessing.   106

DUCH. God bless thee; and put meekness in thy mind,

Love, charity, obedience, and true duty!

GLOU. [*Aside*] Amen; and make me die a good old man!

That is the butt-end of a mother's blessing:

I marvel why her grace did leave it out.   111

BUCK. You cloudy princes and heart-sorrow-ing peers,

That bear this mutual heavy load of moan,

Now cheer each other in each other's love:

Though we have spent our harvest of this king,   115

We are to reap the harvest of his son.

The broken rancour of your high-swoln hearts,

But lately splinter'd, knit, and join'd together,

Must gently be preserved, cherish'd, and kept:

Meseemeth good, that, with some little train,

Forthwith from Ludlow the young prince be fetch'd   121

Hither to London, to be crown'd our king.

RIV. Why with some little train, my Lord of Buckingham?

BUCK. Marry, my lord, lest, by a multitude,

The new-heal'd wound of malice should break out;   125

Which would be so much the more danger-ous,

By how much the estate is green and yet un-govern'd:

Where every horse bears his commanding rein,

And may direct his course as please himself,

As well the fear of harm, as harm apparent, 130

In my opinion, ought to be prevented.

GLOU. I hope the king made peace with all of us;

And the compact is firm and true in me.

RIV. And so in me; and so, I think, in all:

Yet, since it is but green, it should be put   135

To no apparent likelihood of breach,

Which haply by much company might be urged:

Therefore I say with noble Buckingham,

That it is meet so few should fetch the prince.

HAST. And so say I.   140

GLOU. Then be it so; and go we to determine

Who they shall be that straight shall post to Ludlow.

Madam, and you, my mother, will you go

To give your censures in this weighty busi-ness?

Q. ELIZ.⎫
DUCH. ⎬ With all our hearts.   145

[*Exeunt all but* BUCKINGHAM *and* GLOUCESTER.

BUCK. My lord, whoever journeys to the prince,

For God's sake, let not us two be behind;

For, by the way, I'll sort occasion,

As index to the story we late talk'd of,

To part the queen's proud kindred from the king.   150

GLOU. My other self, my counsel's consistory,

My oracle, my prophet! My dear cousin,

I, like a child, will go by thy direction.

Towards Ludlow then, for we'll not stay be-hind.   [*Exeunt.*

SCENE III. *London. A street.*

[*Enter two* CITIZENS, *meeting.*]

FIRST CIT. Neighbour, well met: whither away so fast?

SEC. CIT. I promise you, I scarcely know my-self:

Hear you the news abroad?

FIRST CIT.   Ay, that the king is dead.

---

112. cloudy, clouded with sorrow. 117. The . . . hearts, the figure is that of a boil coming to a head and break-ing. 118. splinter'd, put into splints. 120. little train, few followers. 121. Ludlow, a royal castle in Shropshire. 127. estate is green, government is newly established.

130-1. We should forestall suspected as well as obvious danger. 137. urged, encouraged. 142. post, hasten. 144. censures in, judgment on. 148. sort, find. 149. index, preface. 150. king, i.e., the new boy king. 151. consistory, council chamber, i.e., the highest court.

SEC. CIT. Bad news, by 'r lady; seldom comes
the better:
I fear, I fear 'twill prove a troublous world. 5

[*Enter another* CITIZEN.]

THIRD CIT. Neighbours, God speed!
FIRST CIT.   Give you good morrow, sir.
THIRD CIT. Doth this news hold of good King
Edward's death?
SEC. CIT. Ay, sir, it is too true; God help the
while!
THIRD CIT. Then, masters, look to see a trou-
blous world.
FIRST CIT. No, no; by God's good grace his
son shall reign.   10
THIRD CIT. Woe to that land that's govern'd
by a child!
SEC. CIT. In him there is a hope of govern-
ment,
That in his nonage council under him,
And in his full and ripen'd years himself,
No doubt, shall then and till then govern well.
FIRST CIT. So stood the state when Henry the
Sixth   16
Was crown'd in Paris but at nine months old.
THIRD CIT. Stood the state so? No, no, good
friends, God wot;
For then this land was famously enrich'd
With politic grave counsel; then the king   20
Had virtuous uncles to protect his grace.
FIRST CIT. Why, so hath this, both by the
father and mother.
THIRD CIT. Better it were they all came by the
father,
Or by the father there were none at all;
For emulation now, who shall be nearest,   25
Will touch us all too near, if God prevent not.
O, full of danger is the Duke of Gloucester!
And the queen's sons and brothers haught and
proud:
And were they to be ruled, and not to rule,
This sickly land might solace as before.   30
FIRST CIT. Come, come, we fear the worst;
all shall be well.
THIRD CIT. When clouds appear, wise men
put on their cloaks;
When great leaves fall, the winter is at hand;
When the sun sets, who doth not look for
night?
Untimely storms make men expect a dearth. 35

All may be well; but, if God sort it so,
'Tis more than we deserve, or I expect.
SEC. CIT. Truly, the souls of men are full of
dread:
Ye cannot reason almost with a man
That looks not heavily and full of fear.   40
THIRD CIT. Before the times of change, still
is it so:
By a divine instinct men's minds mistrust
Ensuing dangers; as, by proof, we see
The waters swell before a boisterous storm.
But leave it all to God. Whither away?   45
SEC. CIT. Marry, we were sent for to the
justices.
THIRD CIT. And so was I: I'll bear you com-
pany.

[*Exeunt.*

SCENE IV. *London. The palace.*

[*Enter the* ARCHBISHOP OF YORK, *the young*
DUKE OF YORK, QUEEN ELIZABETH, *and the*
DUCHESS OF YORK.]

ARCH. Last night, I hear, they lay at North-
ampton;
At Stony-Stratford will they be to-night:
To-morrow, or next day, they will be here.
DUCH. I long with all my heart to see the
prince:
I hope he is much grown since last I saw him. 5
Q. ELIZ. But I hear, no; they say my son of
York
Hath almost overta'en him in his growth.
YORK. Ay, mother; but I would not have it
so.
DUCH. Why, my young cousin, it is good to
grow.
YORK. Grandam, one night, as we did sit at
supper,   10
My uncle Rivers talk'd how I did grow
More than my brother: "Ay," quoth my uncle
Gloucester,
"Small herbs have grace, great weeds do grow
apace:"
And since, methinks, I would not grow so
fast,
Because sweet flowers are slow and weeds
make haste.   15
DUCH. Good faith, good faith, the saying did
not hold

In him that did object the same to thee:
He was the wretched'st thing when he was
 young,
So long a-growing and so leisurely,
That, if this rule were true, he should be
 gracious.   20
 ARCH. Why, madam, so, no doubt, he is.
 DUCH. I hope he is; but yet let mothers doubt.
 YORK. Now, by my troth, if I had been re-
 member'd,
I could have given my uncle's grace a flout,
To touch his growth nearer than he touch'd
 mine.   25
 DUCH. How, my pretty York? I pray thee,
 let me hear it.
 YORK. Marry, they say my uncle grew so fast
That he could gnaw a crust at two hours old:
'Twas full two years ere I could get a tooth.
Grandam, this would have been a biting jest.
 DUCH. I pray thee, pretty York, who told
 thee this?   31
 YORK. Grandam, his nurse.
 DUCH. His nurse! why, she was dead ere thou
 wert born.
 YORK. If 'twere not she, I cannot tell who
 told me.
 Q. ELIZ. A parlous boy: go to, you are too
 shrewd.   35
 ARCH. Good madam, be not angry with the
 child.
 Q. ELIZ. Pitchers have ears.

[*Enter a* MESSENGER.]

 ARCH. Here comes a messenger. What news?
 MESS. Such news, my lord, as grieves me to
 unfold.
 Q. ELIZ. How fares the prince?
 MESS.   Well, madam, and in health. 40
 DUCH. What is thy news, then?
 MESS. Lord Rivers and Lord Grey are sent
 to Pomfret,
With them Sir Thomas Vaughan, prisoners.
 DUCH. Who hath committed them?
 MESS.   The mighty dukes
Gloucester and Buckingham.
 Q. ELIZ.   For what offence? 45
 MESS. The sum of all I can, I have disclosed;
Why or for what these nobles were committed

Is all unknown to me, my gracious lady.
 Q. ELIZ. Ay me, I see the downfall of our
 house!
The tiger now hath seized the gentle hind; 50
Insulting tyranny begins to jet
Upon the innocent and aweless throne:
Welcome, destruction, death, and massacre!
I see, as in a map, the end of all.
 DUCH. Accurséd and unquiet wrangling
 days,   55
How many of you have mine eyes beheld!
My husband lost his life to get the crown;
And often up and down my sons were toss'd,
For me to joy and weep their gain and loss:
And being seated, and domestic broils   60
Clean over-blown, themselves, the conquerors,
Make war upon themselves; blood against
 blood,
Self against self: O, preposterous
And frantic outrage, end thy damnéd spleen;
Or let me die, to look on death no more! 65
 Q. ELIZ. Come, come, my boy; we will to
 sanctuary.
Madam, farewell.
 DUCH.   I'll go along with you.
 Q. ELIZ. You have no cause.
 ARCH.   My gracious lady, go;
And thither bear your treasure and your
 goods.
For my part, I'll resign unto your grace 70
The seal I keep: and so betide to me
As well I tender you and all of yours!
Come, I'll conduct you to the sanctuary.
                                [*Exeunt.*

ACT III

SCENE I. *London. A street.*

[*The trumpets sound. Enter the young* PRINCE,
the DUKES OF GLOUCESTER *and* BUCKINGHAM,
CARDINAL BOURCHIER, CATESBY, *and others.*]

 BUCK. Welcome, sweet prince, to London,
 to your chamber.

Scene iv: 17. did . . . thee, i.e., suggested that the saying
applied to you; object, apply. 23. remember'd, reminded.
24. grace, good-will; flout, gibe. 25. touch . . . nearer,
to hit his method of growing more clearly. 35. parlous,
bold, precocious; shrewd, bitter. 46. can, know. 50. hind,
doe. 51-2. jet upon, treat with insolence. 54. map, picture.

61. clean over-blown, entirely finished. 64. spleen, anger.
66. sanctuary, a church was an inviolable place of refuge
from pursuers. 71-2. and so . . . yours, may I be fortunate in proportion as I serve you and yours. Act III,
Scene i: 1. chamber, i.e., London, often called "the King's
chamber."

GLOU. Welcome, dear cousin, my thoughts'
    sovereign:
The weary way hath made you melancholy.
    PRINCE. No, uncle; but our crosses on the
    way
Have made it tedious, wearisome, and heavy: 5
I want more uncles here to welcome me.
    GLOU. Sweet prince, the untainted virtue of
    your years
Hath not yet dived into the world's deceit:
Nor more can you distinguish of a man
Than of his outward show; which, God he
    knows,   10
Seldom or never jumpeth with the heart.
Those uncles which you want were dangerous;
Your grace attended to their sugar'd words,
But look'd not on the poison of their hearts:
God keep you from them, and from such false
    friends!   15
    PRINCE. God keep me from false friends! but
    they were none.
    GLOU. My lord, the mayor of London comes
    to greet you.

[*Enter the* LORD MAYOR, *and his train.*]

    MAY. God bless your grace with health and
    happy days!
    PRINCE. I thank you, good my lord; and
    thank you all.   19
I thought my mother, and my brother York,
Would long ere this have met us on the way:
Fie, what a slug is Hastings, that he comes not
To tell us whether they will come or no!

[*Enter* LORD HASTINGS.]

    BUCK. And, in good time, here comes the
    sweating lord.
    PRINCE. Welcome, my lord: what, will our
    mother come?   25
    HAST. On what occasion, God he knows,
    not I,
The queen your mother, and your brother
    York,
Have taken sanctuary: the tender prince
Would fain have come with me to meet your
    grace,
But by his mother was perforce withheld. 30
    BUCK. Fie, what an indirect and peevish
    course

Is this of hers! Lord Cardinal, will your grace
Persuade the queen to send the Duke of York
Unto his princely brother presently?
If she deny, Lord Hastings, go with him,   35
And from her jealous arms pluck him perforce.
    CARD. My Lord of Buckingham, if my weak
    oratory
Can from his mother win the Duke of York,
Anon expect him here; but if she be obdurate
To mild entreaties, God in heaven forbid   40
We should infringe the holy privilege
Of blessèd santuary! not for all this land
Would I be guilty of so deep a sin.
    BUCK. You are too senseless-obstinate, my
    lord,
Too ceremonious and traditional: 45
Weigh it but with the grossness of this age,
You break not sanctuary in seizing him.
The benefit thereof if always granted
To those whose dealings have deserved the
    place,
And those who have the wit to claim the
    place:
This prince hath neither claim'd it nor de-
    served it;   51
And therefore, in mine opinion, cannot have
    it:
Then, taking him from thence that is not
    there,
You break no privilege nor charter there.
Oft have I heard of sanctuary men;   55
But sanctuary children ne'er till now.
    CARD. My lord, you shall o'er-rule my mind
    for once.
Come on, Lord Hastings, will you go with me?
    HAST. I go, my lord.
    PRINCE. Good lords, make all the speedy
    haste you may.   60

[*Exeunt* CARDINAL *and* HASTINGS.

Say, uncle Gloucester, if our brother come,
Where shall we sojourn till our coronation?
    GLOU. Where it seems best unto your royal
    self.
If I may counsel you, some day or two
Your highness shall repose at the Tower: 65
Then where you please, and shall be thought
    most fit

---

4. crosses, misfortunes, i.e., the arrest of his uncle. 11.
jumpeth, agrees with. 22. slug, snail. 26. On what
occasion, for what reason. 28. sanctuary, i.e., in Westminster. 31. indirect and peevish, lawless and childish.

34. presently, at once. 39. anon, soon. 44. senseless, unrea-
sonably. 45. ceremonious, observant of forms. 46. grossness, moral laxity. 47. you . . . him, it is no breach of
sanctuary to arrest him. 65. Tower, was then a palace
as well as a prison.

For your best health and recreation.

PRINCE. I do not like the Tower, of any place.

Did Julius Cæsar build that place, my lord?

BUCK. He did, my gracious lord, begin that place; 70

Which, since, succeeding ages have re-edified.

PRINCE. Is it upon record, or else reported

Successively from age to age, he built it?

BUCK. Upon record, my gracious lord.

PRINCE. But say, my lord, it were not regis-ter'd, 75

Methinks the truth should live from age to age,

As 'twere retail'd to all posterity,

Even to the general all-ending day.

GLOU. [Aside] So wise so young, they say, do never live long.

PRINCE. What say you, uncle? 80

GLOU. I say, without characters, fame lives long,

[Aside] Thus, like the formal vice, Iniquity,

I moralize two meanings in one word.

PRINCE. That Julius Cæsar was a famous man;

With what his valour did enrich his wit, 85

His wit set down to make his valour live:

Death makes no conquest of this conqueror;

For now he lives in fame, though not in life.

I'll tell you what, my cousin Buckingham,—

BUCK. What, my gracious lord? 90

PRINCE. An if I live until I be a man,

I'll win our ancient right in France again,

Or die a soldier, as I lived a king.

GLOU. [Aside] Short summers lightly have a forward spring.

[Enter young YORK, HASTINGS, and the CARDINAL.]

BUCK. Now, in good time, here comes the Duke of York. 95

PRINCE. Richard of York! how fares our lov-ing brother?

YORK. Well, my dread lord; so must I call you now.

PRINCE. Ay, brother, to our grief, as it is yours:

Too late he died that might have kept that title,

Which by his death hast lost much majesty.

GLOU. How fares our cousin, noble Lord of York? 101

YORK. I thank you, gentle uncle. O, my lord,

You said that idle weeds are fast in growth:

The prince my brother hath outgrown me far.

GLOU. He hath, my lord.

YORK. And therefore is he idle? 105

GLOU. O, my fair cousin, I must not say so.

YORK. Then he is more beholding to you than I.

GLOU. He may command me as my sover-eign;

But you have power in me as in a kinsman.

YORK. I pray you, uncle, give me this dagger. 110

GLOU. My dagger, little cousin? with all my heart.

PRINCE. A beggar, brother?

YORK. Of my kind uncle, that I know will give;

And being but a toy, which is no grief to give.

GLOU. A greater gift than that I'll give my cousin. 115

YORK. A greater gift! O, that's the sword to it.

GLOU. Ay, gentle cousin, were it light enough.

YORK. O, then, I see, you will part but with light gifts;

In weightier things you'll say a beggar nay.

GLOU. It is too heavy for your grace to wear. 120

YORK. I weigh it lightly, were it heavier.

GLOU. What, would you have my weapon, little lord?

YORK. I would, that I might thank you as you call me.

GLOU. How?

YORK. Little. 125

PRINCE. My Lord of York will still be cross in talk:

Uncle, your grace knows how to bear with him.

YORK. You mean, to bear me, not to bear with me:

Uncle, my brother mocks both you and me;

Because that I am little, like an ape, 130

He thinks that you should bear me on your shoulders.

68. of any place, of all places. 71. re-edified, rebuilt. 81. characters, (1) letters, (2) moral qualities. 82. vice, a stock character half clown, half villain, in the morality plays. 83. moralize, comment upon. 94. lightly, ordi-narily. 99. late, lately. 105. idle, useless. 114. toy, trifle. 118. light, of little value. 119. say . . . nay, say "no" to

one who begs. 121. I weigh it lightly, I should consider it a matter of no importance. 126. cross, impudent. 130-1. Because . . . shoulders, a common attraction at fairs was a tame bear carrying a monkey on his back.

BUCK. With what a sharp-provided wit he reasons!
To mitigate the scorn he gives his uncle,
He prettily and aptly taunts himself:
So cunning and so young is wonderful.   135
  GLOU. My lord, will't please you pass along?
Myself and my good cousin Buckingham
Will to your mother, to entreat of her
To meet you at the Tower and welcome you.
  YORK. What, will you go unto the Tower, my lord?   140
  PRINCE. My lord protector needs will have it so.
  YORK. I shall not sleep in quiet at the Tower.
  GLOU. Why, what should you fear?
  YORK. Marry, my uncle Clarence' angry ghost:
My grandam told me he was murder'd there.
  PRINCE. I fear no uncles dead.   146
  GLOU. Nor none that live, I hope.
  PRINCE. An if they live, I hope I need not fear.
But come, my lord; and with a heavy heart,
Thinking on them, go I unto the Tower.   150

[*A Sennet. Exeunt all but* GLOUCESTER, BUCKINGHAM *and* CATESBY.

  BUCK. Think you, my lord, this little prating York
Was not incensed by his subtle mother
To taunt and scorn you thus opprobriously?
  GLOU. No doubt, no doubt: O, 'tis a parlous boy;
Bold, quick, ingenious, forward, capable: 155
He is all the mother's, from the top to toe.
  BUCK. Well, let them rest. Come hither, Catesby.
Thou art sworn as deeply to effect what we intend
As closely to conceal what we impart:
Thou know'st our reasons urged upon the way;   160
What think'st thou? is it not an easy matter
To make William Lord Hastings of our mind,
For the instalment of this noble duke
In the seat royal of this famous isle?

  CATE. He for his father's sake so loves the prince,   165
That he will not be won to aught against him.
  BUCK. What think'st thou, then, of Stanley? what will he?
  CATE. He will do all in all as Hastings doth.
  BUCK. Well, then, no more but this: go, gentle Catesby,
And, as it were far off, sound thou Lord Hastings,   170
How he doth stand affected to our purpose;
And summon him to-morrow to the Tower,
To sit about the coronation.
If thou dost find him tractable to us,
Encourage him, and show him all our reasons:
If he be leaden, icy-cold, unwilling,   176
Be thou so too; and so break off your talk,
And give us notice of his inclination:
For we to-morrow hold divided councils,
Wherein thyself shalt highly be employ'd.   180
  GLOU. Commend me to Lord William: tell him, Catesby,
His ancient knot of dangerous adversaries
To-morrow are let blood at Pomfret-castle;
And bid my friend, for joy of this good news,
Give Mistress Shore one gentle kiss the more.
  BUCK. Good Catesby, go, effect this business soundly.   186
  CATE. My good lords both, with all the heed I may.
  GLOU. Shall we hear from you, Catesby, ere we sleep?
  CATE. You shall, my lord.
  GLOU. At Crosby Place, there shall you find us both.   [*Exit* CATESBY.   190
  BUCK. Now, my lord, what shall we do, if we perceive
Lord Hastings will not yield to our complots?
  GLOU. Chop off his head, man; somewhat we will do:
And, look, when I am king, claim thou of me
The earldom of Hereford, and the moveables
Whereof the king my brother stood possess'd.
  BUCK. I'll claim that promise at your grace's hands.   197
  GLOU. And look to have it yielded with all willingness.

---

132. sharp-provided furnished with keenness. 141. needs will, i.e., requires me to go. 147. Nor . . . hope, i.e., fear of the uncles just arrested. 152. incensed, set on. 154. parlous, mischievous. 160. upon the way, i.e., on the journey to London. 163. instalment, enthroning. 170. far off, indirectly, discreetly. 173. sit, i.e., in council. 179.

divided councils, i.e., for Richard to seize the crown, for Hastings and his party to arrange for the coronation. 183. are let blood, i.e., will be executed. 185. Mistress Shore, after the death of Edward IV she became Hastings' mistress. 186. effect, carry out. 192. complots, conspiracies. 195. moveables, goods.

Come, let us sup betimes, that afterwards
We may digest our complots in some form. 200
[*Exeunt.*

SCENE II. *Before* LORD HASTINGS' *house.*

[*Enter a* MESSENGER.]

MESS. What, ho! my lord!
HAST. [*Within*] Who knocks at the door?
MESS. A messenger from the Lord Stanley.

[*Enter* LORD HASTINGS.]

HAST. What is 't o'clock?
MESS. Upon the stroke of four. 5
HAST. Cannot thy master sleep these tedious
    nights?
MESS. So it should seem by that I have to say.
First, he commends him to your noble lord-
    ship.
HAST. And then?
MESS. And then he sends you word 10
He dreamt to-night the boar had razed his
    helm:
Besides, he says there are two councils held;
And that may be determined at the one
Which may make you and him to rue at the
    other.
Therefore he sends to know your lordship's
    pleasure, 15
If presently you will take horse with him,
And with all speed post with him toward the
    north,
To shun the danger that his soul divines.
HAST. Go, fellow, go, return unto thy lord;
Bid him not fear the separated councils: 20
His honour and myself are at the one,
And at the other is my servant Catesby;
Where nothing can proceed that toucheth us
Whereof I shall not have intelligence.
Tell him his fears are shallow, wanting in-
    stance: 25
And for his dreams, I wonder he is so fond
To trust the mockery of unquiet slumbers:
To fly the boar before the boar pursues,
Were to incense the boar to follow us
And make pursuit where he did mean no
    chase. 30
Go, bid thy master rise and come to me;

And we will both together to the Tower,
Where, he shall see, the boar will use us
    kindly.
MESS. My gracious lord, I'll tell him what
    you say. [*Exit.*

[*Enter* CATESBY.]

CATE. Many good morrows to my noble
    lord! 35
HAST. Good morrow, Catesby; you are early
    stirring:
What news, what news, in this our tottering
    state?
CATE. It is a reeling world, indeed, my lord.
And I believe 'twill never stand upright
Till Richard wear the garland of the realm. 40
HAST. How! wear the garland! dost thou
    mean the crown?
CATE. Ay, my good lord.
HAST. I'll have this crown of mine cut from
    my shoulders
Ere I will see the crown so foul misplaced.
But canst thou guess that he doth aim at it?
CATE. Ay, on my life; and hopes to find you
    forward 46
Upon his party for the gain thereof:
And thereupon he sends you this good news,
That this same very day your enemies,
The kindred of the queen, must die at Pom-
    fret. 50
HAST. Indeed, I am no mourner for that
    news,
Because they have been still mine enemies:
But, that I'll give my voice on Richard's side,
To bar my master's heirs in true descent,
God knows I will not do it, to the death. 55
CATE. God keep your lordship in that gra-
    cious mind!
HAST. But I shall laugh at this a twelve-
    month hence,
That they who brought me in my master's
    hate,
I live to look upon their tragedy.
I tell thee, Catesby,— 60
CATE. What, my lord?
HAST. Ere a fortnight make me elder,
I'll send some packing that yet think not on it.
CATE. 'Tis a vile thing to die, my gracious
    lord,

---

200. digest, arrange. Scene ii: 11. boar, i.e., Richard;
razed, cut off. 14. rue at, grieve for. 25. instance, proof.
33. kindly, (1) gently, (2) according to his nature. The
second meaning is an example of dramatic irony.

46-7. forward . . . Upon his party, zealous, on his side.
52. still, always. 55. to the death, i.e., even though my
refusal cost me my life. 56. gracious, holy.

When men are unprepared and look not for
it.   65
  HAST. O monstrous, monstrous! and so falls
    it out
With Rivers, Vaughan, Grey: and so 'twill do
With some men else, who think themselves as
    safe
As thou and I; who, as thou know'st, are dear
To princely Richard and to Buckingham.   70
  CATE. The princes both make high account
    of you;
  [Aside] For they account his head upon the
    bridge.
  HAST. I know they do; and I have well de-
    served it.

[Enter LORD STANLEY.]

Come on, come on; where is your boar-spear,
    man?
Fear you the boar, and go so unprovided?   75
  STAN. My lord, good morrow; good morrow,
    Catesby:
You may jest on, but, by the holy rood,
I do not like these several councils, I.
  HAST. My lord,
I hold my life as dear as you do yours;   80
And never in my life, I do protest,
Was it more precious to me than 'tis now:
Think you, but that I know our state secure,
I would be so triumphant as I am?
  STAN. The lords at Pomfret, when they rode
    from London,   85
Were jocund, and supposed their state was
    sure,
And they indeed had no cause to mistrust;
But yet, you see, how soon the day o'ercast.
This sudden stab of rancour I misdoubt:
Pray God, I say, I prove a needless coward!   90
What, shall we toward the Tower? the day is
    spent.
  HAST. Come, come, have with you. Wot you
    what, my lord?
To-day the lords you talk of are beheaded.
  STAN. They, for their truth, might better
    wear their heads
Than some that have accused them wear their
    hats.   95
But come, my lord, let us away.

[Enter a PURSUIVANT.]

  HAST. Go on before; I'll talk with this good
    fellow.   [Exeunt STANLEY and CATESBY.
How now, sirrah! how goes the world with
    thee?
  PURS. The better that your lordship please
    to ask.
  HAST. I tell thee, man, 'tis better with me
    now   100
Than when I met thee last where now we
    meet:
Then was I going prisoner to the Tower,
By the suggestion of the queen's allies;
But now, I tell thee—keep it to thyself—
This day those enemies are put to death,   105
And I in better state than e'er I was.
  PURS. God hold it, to your honour's good
    content!
  HAST. Gramercy, fellow: there, drink that
    for me.   [Throws him his purse.
  PURS. God save your lordship!   [Exit.

[Enter a PRIEST.]

  PRIEST. Well met, my lord; I am glad to see
    your honour.   110
  HAST. I thank thee, good Sir John, with all
    my heart.
I am in your debt for your last exercise;
Come the next Sabbath, and I will content
    you.   [He whispers in his ear.

[Enter BUCKINGHAM.]

  BUCK. What, talking with a priest, lord
    chamberlain?
Your friends at Pomfret, they do need the
    priest;   115
Your honour hath no shriving work in hand.
  HAST. Good faith, and when I met this holy
    man,
Those men you talk of came into my mind.
What, go you toward the Tower?
  BUCK. I do, my lord; but long I shall not
    stay: 120
I shall return before your lordship thence.
  HAST. 'Tis like enough, for I stay dinner
    there.
  BUCK. [Aside] And supper too, although
    thou know'st it not.

75. unprovided, unprepared. 77. rood, cross. 89. misdoubt, mistrust. 92. have with you, come on. 95. wear their hats, keep their offices. s.d. Pursuivant, a herald's attendant. 98. sirrah, form of address used to social inferiors. 103. suggestion, instigation. 107. God hold it, may God preserve it. 111. Sir, form of address to priests. 112. exercise, sermon. 116. shriving work, confession and absolution.

66. falls it out, it happens. 71. make . . . you, have a high opinion of you. 72. the bridge, that is, London Bridge, on which the heads of traitors were impaled.

Come, will you go?

HAST. I'll wait upon your lordship.   125

[Exeunt.

SCENE III. *Pomfret Castle.*

[*Enter* SIR RICHARD RATCLIFF, *with halberds, carrying* RIVERS, GREY, *and* VAUGHAN *to death.*]

RAT. Come, bring forth the prisoners.

RIV. Sir Richard Ratcliff, let me tell thee this:

To-day shalt thou behold a subject die

For truth, for duty, and for loyalty.

GREY. God keep the prince from all the pack of you!   5

A knot you are of damnèd blood-suckers.

VAUG. You live that shall cry woe for this hereafter.

RAT. Dispatch; the limit of your lives is out.

RIV. O Pomfret, Pomfret! O thou bloody prison,

Fatal and ominous to noble peers!   10

Within the guilty closure of thy walls

Richard the second here was hack'd to death;

And, for more slander to thy dismal seat,

We give thee up our guiltless blood to drink.

GREY. Now Margaret's curse is fall'n upon our heads,   15

For standing by when Richard stabb'd her son.

RIV. Then cursed she Hastings, then cursed she Buckingham,

Then cursed she Richard. O, remember, God,

To hear her prayers for them, as now for us!

And for my sister and her princely sons,   20

Be satisfied, dear God, with our true blood,

Which, as thou know'st, unjustly must be spilt.

RAT. Make haste; the hour of death is expiate.

RIV. Come, Grey, come, Vaughan, let us all embrace:

And take our leave, until we meet in heaven.

[Exeunt.   25

SCENE IV. *The Tower of London.*

[*Enter* BUCKINGHAM, DERBY, HASTINGS, *the* BISHOP OF ELY, RATCLIFF, LOVEL, *with others, and take their seats at a table.*]

HAST. My lords, at once: the cause why we are met

Is, to determine of the coronation.

In God's name, speak: when is the royal day?

BUCK. Are all things fitting for that royal time?

DER. It is, and wants but nomination.   5

ELY. To-morrow, then, I judge a happy day.

BUCK. Who knows the lord protector's mind herein?

Who is most inward with the noble duke?

ELY. Your grace, we think, should soonest know his mind.

BUCK. Who, I, my lord! we know each other's faces,   10

But for our hearts, he knows no more of mine,

Than I of yours;

Nor I no more of his, than you of mine.

Lord Hastings, you and he are near in love.

HAST. I thank his grace, I know he loves me well;   15

But, for his purpose in the coronation,

I have not sounded him, nor he deliver'd

His gracious pleasure any way therein:

But you, my noble lords, may name the time;

And in the duke's behalf I'll give my voice,   20

Which, I presume, he'll take in gentle part.

[*Enter* GLOUCESTER.]

ELY. Now in good time, here comes the duke himself.

GLOU. My noble lords and cousins all, good morrow.

I have been long a sleeper; but, I hope,

My absence doth neglect no great designs,   25

Which by my presence might have been concluded.

BUCK. Had not you come upon your cue, my lord,

William Lord Hastings had pronounced your part,—

I mean, your voice,—for crowning of the king.

GLOU. Than my Lord Hastings no man might be bolder;   30

His lordship knows me well, and loves me well.

HAST. I thank your grace.

GLOU.   My lord of Ely!

ELY.   My lord?

Scene iii: s.d. halberds, bearers of halberds, battle axes fixed to long poles. 8. Dispatch, make ready for going; limit, allotted time. 23. expiate, arrived in all its fulness.

Scene iv: 2. determine of, decide upon. 5. nomination, designation (of the day). 8. inward, intimate. 20. voice, vote. 21. take . . . part, kindly approve.

GLOU. When I was last in Holborn,
I saw good strawberries in your garden there:
I do beseech you send for some of them.   35
ELY. Marry, and will, my lord, with all my
heart.   [*Exit.*
GLOU. Cousin of Buckingham, a word with
you.   [*Drawing him aside.*]
Catesby hath sounded Hastings in our busi-
ness,
And finds the testy gentleman so hot,
As he will lose his head ere give consent   40
His master's son, as worshipful he terms it,
Shall lose the royalty of England's throne.
BUCK. Withdraw you hence, my lord, I'll
follow you.

[*Exit* GLOUCESTER, BUCKINGHAM *following.*

DER. We have not yet set down this day of
triumph.
To-morrow, in mine opinion, is too sudden; 45
For I myself am not so well provided
As else I would be, were the day prolong'd.

[*Re-enter* BISHOP OF ELY.]

ELY. Where is my lord protector? I have
sent for these strawberries.
HAST. His grace looks cheerfully and smooth
to-day;   50
There's some conceit or other likes him well,
When he doth bid good morrow with such a
spirit.
I think there's never a man in Christendom
That can less hide his love or hate than he;
For by his face straight shall you know his
heart.   55
DER. What of his heart perceive you in his
face
By any likelihood he show'd to-day?
HAST. Marry, that with no man here he is
offended;
For, were he, he had shown it in his looks.
DER. I pray God he be not, I say.   60

[*Re-enter* GLOUCESTER *and* BUCKINGHAM.]

GLOU. I pray you all, tell me what they
deserve
That do conspire my death with devilish plots
Of damnèd witchcraft, and that have prevail'd

Upon my body with their hellish charms?
HAST. The tender love I bear your grace,
my lord,   65
Makes me most forward in this noble presence
To doom the offenders, whatsoever they be:
I say, my lord, they have deserved death.
GLOU. Then be your eyes the witness of this
ill:
See how I am bewitch'd; behold mine arm   70
Is, like a blasted sapling, wither'd up:
And this is Edward's wife, that monstrous
witch,
Consorted with that harlot strumpet Shore,
That by their witchcraft thus have marked
me.
HAST. If they have done this thing, my gra-
cious lord,—   75
GLOU. If! thou protector of this damned
strumpet,
Tellest thou me of 'ifs'? Thou art a traitor:
Off with his head! Now, by Saint Paul I swear,
I will not dine until I see the same.
Lovel and Ratcliff, look that it be done: 80
The rest, that love me, rise and follow me.
[*Exeunt all but* HASTINGS, RATCLIFF, *and* LOVEL.
HAST. Woe, woe for England! not a whit
for me;
For I, too fond, might have prevented this.
Stanley did dream the boar did raze his helm;
But I disdain'd it, and did scorn to fly: 85
Three times to-day my foot-cloth horse did
stumble,
And startled, when he look'd upon the Tower,
As loath to bear me to the slaughter-house.
O, now I want the priest that spake to me:
I now repent I told the pursuivant,   90
As 'twere triumphing at mine enemies,
How they at Pomfret bloodily were butch-
er'd,
And I myself secure in grace and favour.
O Margaret, Margaret, now thy heavy curse
Is lighted on poor Hastings' wretched head! 95
RAT. Dispatch, my lord; the duke would be
at dinner:
Make a short shrift; he longs to see your head.
HAST. O momentary grace of mortal men,
Which we more hunt for than the grace of
God!

---

33. Holborn, a district of London, where the Bishop of
Ely's palace was situated. 47. prolong'd, postponed. 50.
smooth, untroubled. 51. conceit, idea; likes, pleases.

69. ill, misfortune. 82. Woe . . . me, that is, pity England
but not me at all. 83. fond, foolish. 86. foot-cloth, cloth
hanging to the ground on each side of a fully caparisoned
horse; stumble, a sign of bad luck. 97. shrift, confession
and absolution.

Who builds his hopes in air of your good
    looks,   100
Lives like a drunken sailor on a mast,
Ready, with every nod, to tumble down
Into the fatal bowels of the deep.
    LOV. Come, come, dispatch; 'tis bootless to
    exclaim.
    HAST. O bloody Richard! miserable Eng-
    land!   105
I prophesy the fearfull'st time to thee
That ever wretched age hath look'd upon.
Come, lead me to the block; bear him my
    head:
They smile at me that shortly shall be dead.
                        [Exeunt.

SCENE V. *The Tower-walls.*

[*Enter* GLOUCESTER *and* BUCKINGHAM, *in rotten
armour, marvellous ill-favoured.*]

    GLOU. Come, cousin, canst thou quake, and
    change thy colour,
Murder thy breath in middle of a word,
And then begin again, and stop again,
As if thou wert distraught and mad with
    terror?
    BUCK. Tut, I can counterfeit the deep
    tragedian;   5
Speak and look back, and pry on every side,
Tremble and start at wagging of a straw,
Intending deep suspicion: ghastly looks
Are at my service, like enforced smiles;
And both are ready in their offices,   10
At any time, to grace my stratagems.
But what, is Catesby gone?
    GLOU. He is; and, see, he brings the mayor
    along.

[*Enter the* MAYOR *and* CATESBY.]

    BUCK. Lord mayor,—
    GLOU. Look to the drawbridge there!   15
    BUCK. Hark! a drum.
    GLOU. Catesby, o'erlook the walls.
    BUCK. Lord mayor, the reason we have
    sent—.
    GLOU. Look back, defend thee, here are
    enemies.

    BUCK. God and our innocency defend and
    guard us!   20
    GLOU. Be patient, they are friends, Ratcliff
    and Lovel.

[*Enter* LOVEL *and* RATCLIFF, *with* HASTINGS'
head.]

    LOV. Here is the head of that ignoble traitor,
The dangerous and unsuspected Hastings.
    GLOU. So dear I loved the man, that I must
    weep.
I took him for the plainest harmless crea-
    ture   25
That breathed upon this earth a Christian;
Made him my book, wherein my soul re-
    corded
The history of all her secret thoughts:
So smooth he daub'd his vice with show of
    virtue,
That, his apparent open guilt omitted,   30
I mean, his conversation with Shore's wife,
He lived from all attainder of suspect.
    BUCK. Well, well, he was the covert'st
    shelter'd traitor
That ever lived.
Would you imagine, or almost believe,   35
Were't not that, by great preservation,
We live to tell it you, the subtle traitor
This day had plotted, in the council-house
To murder me and my good Lord of Glouces-
    ter?
    MAY. What, had he so?   40
    GLOU. What, think you we are Turks or
    infidels?
Or that we would, against the form of law,
Proceed thus rashly to the villain's death,
But that the extreme peril of the case,
The peace of England and our persons'
    safety,   45
Enforced us to this execution?
    MAY. Now, fair befall you! he deserved his
    death;
And you my good lords, both have well pro-
    ceeded,
To warn false traitors from the like attempts.
I never look'd for better at his hands,   50
After he once fell in with Mistress Shore.
    GLOU. Yet had not we determined he should
    die,
Until your lordship came to see his death;

---

100. in air, i.e., without foundation. 104. bootless, useless. Scene v. s.d. rotten, rusty; ill favored, ugly. 6. pry,
look intently. 8. intending, pretending. 10. offices, employment. 32. Attainder of suspect, taint of suspicion.

35. almost, even. 36. preservation, divine protection.
47. fair . . . you, good luck to you.

Which now the loving haste of these our
    friends,
Something against our meanings, have pre-
    vented;   55
Because, my lord, I would have had you heard
The traitor speak, and timorously confess
The manner and the purpose of his treasons;
That you might well have signifi'd the same
Unto the citizens, who haply may   60
Misconstrue us in him and wail his death.
    MAY. But, my good lord, your grace's words
    shall serve
As well as I had seen and heard him speak;
And do not doubt, right noble princes both,
That I'll acquaint our duteous citizens   65
With all your just proceedings in this case.
    GLOU. And to that end we wish'd your lord-
    ship here,
To avoid the censures of the carping world.
    BUCK. But since you come too late of our
    intent,
Yet witness what you hear we did intend.   70
And so, my good Lord Mayor, we bid fare-
    well.   [*The* LORD MAYOR *goes out.*
    GLOU. Go, after, after, cousin Buckingham.
The mayor towards Guildhall hies him in all
    post.
There, at your meetest vantage of the time,
Infer the bastardy of Edward's children   75
Tell them how Edward put to death a citizen,
Only for saying he would make his son
Heir to the crown; meaning indeed his house,
Which, by the sign thereof, was termed so.
Moreover, urge his hateful luxury,   80
And bestial appetite in change of lust;
Which stretch'd unto their servants, daugh-
    ters, wives,
Even where his raging eye or savage heart,
Without control, lusted to make a prey.
Nay, for a need, thus far come near my
    person: 85
Tell them, when that my mother went with
    child
Of that insatiate Edward, noble York
My princely father then had wars in France;
And, by just computation of the time,

Found that the issue was not his begot;   90
Which well appeared in his lineaments,
Being nothing like the noble duke my father:
But touch this sparingly, as 'twere far off;
Because you know, my lord, my mother lives.
    BUCK. Fear not, my lord, I'll play the
    orator   95
As if the golden fee for which I plead
Were for myself: and so, my lord, adieu.
    GLOU. If you thrive well, bring them to
    Baynard's Castle;
Where you shall find me well accompanied
With reverend fathers and well-learned
    bishops.   100
    BUCK. I go; and towards three or four
    o'clock
Look for the news that the Guildhall affords.
                                      [*Exit.*
    GLOU. Go, Lovel, with all speed to Doctor
    Shaw;
[*To Cate.*] Go thou to Friar Penker; bid them
    both
Meet me within this hour at Baynard's Castle.
                     [*Exeunt all but* GLOUCESTER.]
Now will I in, to take some privy order,   106
To draw the brats of Clarence out of sight;
And to give notice, that no manner of person
At any time have recourse unto the princes.
                                      [*Exit.*

SCENE VI. *The same. A street*

[*Enter a* SCRIVENER, *with a paper in his hand.*]

    SCRIV. This is the indictment of the good
    Lord Hastings;
Which in a set hand fairly is engross'd,
That it may be this day read o'er in Paul's.
And mark how well the sequel hangs to-
    gether:
Eleven hours I spent to write it over,   5
For yesternight by Catesby was it brought
    me;
The precedent was full as long a-doing:
And yet within these five hours lived Lord
    Hastings,

---

55. something . . . prevented, somewhat contrary to our intention have forestalled. 61. misconstrue . . . him, misjudge our action against him. 73. post, haste. 74. meet'st advantage, earliest opportunity. 75. Infer, allege. 78. the crown, the citizen's house was named from the sign of his shop—a crown. 80. luxury, lust. 81. in change of lust, in changing the objects of his lust. 83. raging, lascivious. 84. lusted, desired. 85. for a need, in case of necessity.

96. golden fee, i.e., the crown. 98. Baynard's Castle, on the Thames, near the Blackfriars', once owned by Richard's father. 103-4. Doctor Shaw . . . Friar Penker, popular preachers favorable to Richard's claims (Scene vi: III) s.d. Scrivener, notary public. 2. which . . . engrossed, of which a fair copy in legal form has been made. 4. the sequel, what happened. 5. write it over, make a copy. 7. precedent, written copy, i.e., the one Catesby brought the scrivener (notary).

Untainted, unexamined, free, at liberty.
Here's a good world the while! Why who's
   so gross,   10
That seeth not this palpable device?
Yet who's so blind, but says he sees it not?
Bad is the world; and all will come to nought,
When such bad dealing must be seen in
   thought.   [Exit.

SCENE VII. *Baynard's Castle.*

[*Enter* GLOUCESTER *and* BUCKINGHAM, *at
several doors.*]

GLOU. How, now, my lord, what say the
   citizens?
BUCK. Now, by the holy mother of our
   Lord,
The citizens are mum and speak not a word.
GLOU. Touch'd you the bastardy of Ed-
   ward's children?
BUCK. I did; with his contract with Lady
   Lucy,   5
And his contract by deputy in France;
The insatiate greediness of his desires,
And his enforcement of the city wives;
His tyranny for trifles; his own bastardy,
As being got, your father then in France,   10
And his resemblance, being not like the duke:
Withal I did infer your lineaments,
Being the right idea of your father,
Both in your form and nobleness of mind:
Laid open all your victories in Scotland,   15
Your discipline in war, wisdom in peace,
Your bounty, virtue, fair humility;
Indeed, left nothing fitting for the purpose
Untouch'd, or slightly handled, in discourse:
And when mine oratory grew to an end,   20
I bid them that did love their country's good
Cry "God save Richard, England's royal king!"
GLOU. Ah! and did they so?
BUCK. No, so God help me, they spake not
   a word;
But, like dumb statuas or breathing stones,   25
Gazed each on other, and look'd deadly pale.
Which when I saw, I reprehended them;
And ask'd the mayor what meant this wilful
   silence:

His answer was, the people were not wont
To be spoke to but by the recorder.   30
Then he was urged to tell my tale again,
"Thus saith the duke, thus hath the duke in-
   ferr'd,"
But nothing spake in warrant from himself.
When he had done, some followers of mine
   own,
At the lower end of the hall, hurl'd up their
   caps,   35
And some ten voices cried "God save King
   Richard!"
And thus I took the vantage of those few,
"Thanks, gentle citizens and friends," quoth I;
"This general applause and loving shout
Argues your wisdoms and your love to Rich-
   ard:"   40
And even here brake off, and came away.
  GLOU. What tongueless blocks were they!
   would they not speak?
BUCK. No, by my troth, my lord.
GLOU. Will not the mayor then and his
   brethren come?
BUCK. The mayor is here at hand: intend
   some fear;   45
Be not you spoke with, but by mighty suit:
And look you get a prayer-book in your hand,
And stand betwixt two churchmen, good my
   lord;
For on that ground I'll build a holy descant:
And be not easily won to our request: 50
Play the maid's part, still answer nay, and
   take it.
  GLOU. I go; and if you plead as well for
   them
As I can say nay to thee for myself,
No doubt we'll bring it to a happy issue.
  BUCK. Go, go, up to the leads; the lord
   mayor knocks.   [*Exit* GLOUCESTER.] 55

[*Enter the* MAYOR *and* CITIZENS.]

Welcome, my lord: I dance attendance here;
I think the duke will not be spoke withal.

[*Enter* CATESBY.]

Here comes his servant: how now, Catesby,
What says he?

---

9. Untainted, unaccused. 10. gross, stupid. 14. seen in
thought, i.e., kept quiet. Scene vii: 5. contract, troth
plight or formal betrothal, which in Elizabethan times was
almost equivalent to a legal marriage. 6. by deputy, Warwick contracted with Louis VI of France the betrothal
of Edward to Lady Bona, his sister-in-law. 13. right idea,
perfect image. 15. Scotland, Richard commanded the English army in its Scottish campaign of 1482. 30. recorder,
custodian of the city's records. 33. in . . . himself, on his
own responsibility. 45. intend, pretend. 46. mighty suit,
urgent petition. 49. descant, a musical variation. i.e., argument. 55. leads, roof. 57. withal, with.

CATE. My lord, he doth entreat your grace
To visit him to-morrow or next day: 60
He is within, with two right reverend fathers,
Divinely bent to meditation;
And in no worldly suit would he be moved,
To draw him from his holy exercise.
  BUCK. Return, good Catesby, to thy lord
    again;   65
Tell him, myself, the mayor and citizens,
In deep designs and matters of great moment,
No less importing than our general good,
Are come to have some conference with his
    grace.
  CATE. I'll tell him what you say, my lord.
      [Exit.
  BUCK. Ah, ha, my lord, this prince is not an
    Edward!   71
He is not lolling on a lewd day-bed,
But on his knees at meditation;
Not dallying with a brace of courtezans,
But meditating with two deep divines;   75
Not sleeping, to engross his idle body,
But praying, to enrich his watchful soul:
Happy were England, would this gracious
    prince
Take on himself the sovereignty thereof:
But, sure, I fear, we shall ne'er win him
    to it.   80
  MAY. Marry, God forbid his grace should
    say us nay!
  BUCK. I fear he will.

    [Re-enter CATESBY.]

How now, Catesby, what says your lord?
  CATE.   My lord,
He wonders to what end you have assembled
Such troops of citizens to speak with him, 85
His grace not being warn'd thereof before:
My lord, he fears you mean no good to him.
  BUCK. Sorry I am my noble cousin should
Suspect me, that I mean no good to him:
By heaven, I come in perfect love to him; 90
And so once more return and tell his grace.
      [Exit CATESBY.]
When holy and devout religious men
Are at their beads, 'tis hard to draw them
    thence,
So sweet is zealous contemplation.

[Enter GLOUCESTER aloft, between two BISHOPS.
    CATESBY returns.]

76. engross, fatten. s.d. aloft, that is, on the gallery
above the stage. 97. stay . . . vanity, prevent his falling

  MAY. See, where he stands between two
    clergymen!   95
  BUCK. Two props of virtue for a Christian
    prince,
To stay him from the fall of vanity:
And, see, a book of prayer in his hand,
True ornaments to know a holy man.
Famous Plantagenet, most gracious prince,
Lend favourable ears to our request;   101
And pardon us the interruption
Of thy devotion and right Christian zeal.
  GLOU. My lord, there needs no such apology:
I rather do beseech you pardon me,   105
Who, earnest in the service of my God,
Neglect the visitation of my friends.
But, leaving this, what is your grace's pleas-
    ure?
  BUCK. Even that, I hope, which pleaseth
    God above,
And all good men of this ungovern'd isle. 110
  GLOU. I do suspect I have done some offence
That seems disgracious in the city's eyes,
And that you come to reprehend my igno-
    rance.
  BUCK. You have, my lord: would it might
    please your grace,
At our entreaties, to amend that fault!   115
  GLOU. Else wherefore breathe I in a Chris-
    tian land?
  BUCK. Then know, it is your fault that you
    resign
The supreme seat, the throne majestical,
The scepter'd office of your ancestors,
Your state of fortune and your due of
    birth,   120
The lineal glory of your royal house,
To the corruption of a blemish'd stock:
Whilst, in the mildness of your sleepy
    thoughts,
Which here we waken to our country's good,
This noble isle doth want her proper
    limbs;   125
Her face defaced with scars of infamy,
Her royal stock graft with ignoble plants,
And almost shoulder'd in the swallowing gulf
Of blind forgetfulness and dark oblivion.
Which to recure, we heartily solicit   130
Your gracious self to take on you the charge
And kingly government of this your land,

into the sin of pride. 112. disgracious, disgraceful.
116. Else, otherwise. 128. shoulder'd, covered up to the
shoulders; gulf, whirlpool. 130. recure, restore.

Not as protector, steward, substitute,
Or lowly factor for another's gain;
But as successively from blood to blood,   135
Your right of birth, your empery, your own.
For this, consorted with the citizens,
Your very worshipful and loving friends,
And by their vehement instigation,
In this just suit come I to move your grace.
   GLOU. I know not whether to depart in
    silence,   141
Or bitterly to speak in your reproof,
Best fitteth my degree or your condition:
If not to answer, you might haply think
Tongue-tied ambition, not replying, yielded
To bear the golden yoke of sovereignty,   146
Which fondly you would here impose on me;
If to reprove you for this suit of yours,
So season'd with your faithful love to me,
Then, on the other side, I check'd my
    friends.   150
Therefore, to speak, and to avoid the first,
And then, in speaking, not to incur the last,
Definitively thus I answer you.
Your love deserves my thanks; but my desert
Unmeritable shuns your high request.   155
First, if all obstacles were cut away,
And that my path were even to the crown,
As my ripe revenue and due by birth;
Yet so much is my poverty of spirit,
So mighty and so many my defects,   160
As I had rather hide me from my greatness,
Being a bark to brook no mighty sea,
Than in my greatness covet to be hid,
And in the vapour of my glory smother'd.
But, God be thanked, there's no need of
    me,   165
And much I need to help you, if need were;
The royal tree hath left us royal fruit,
Which, mellow'd by the stealing hours of
    time,
Will well become the seat of majesty,
And make, no doubt, us happy by his reign.
On him I lay what you would lay on me, 171
The right and fortune of his happy stars;
Which God defend that I should wring from
    him!

   BUCK. My lord, this argues conscience in
    your grace;
But the respects thereof are nice and trivial,
All circumstances well considered.   176
You say that Edward is your brother's son:
So say we too, but not by Edward's wife;
For first he was contract to Lady Lucy—
Your mother lives a witness to that vow— 180
And afterward by substitute betroth'd
To Bona, sister to the King of France.
These both put by, a poor petitioner,
A care-crazed mother of a many children,
A beauty-waning and distressèd widow,   185
Even in the afternoon of her best days,
Made prize and purchase of his lustful eye,
Seduced the pitch and height of all his
    thoughts
To base declension and loathed bigamy:
By her, in his unlawful bed, he got   190
This Edward, whom our manners term the
    prince.
More bitterly could I expostulate,
Save that, for reverence to some alive,
I give a sparing limit to my tongue.
Then, good my lord, take to your royal
    self   195
This proffer'd benefit of dignity;
If not to bless us and the land withal,
Yet to draw forth your noble ancestry
From the corruption of abusing times,
Unto a lineal true-derived course.   200
   MAY. Do, good my lord, your citizens en-
    treat you.
   BUCK. Refuse not, mighty lord, this proffer'd
    love.
   CATE. O, make them joyful, grant their law-
    ful suit!
   GLOU. Alas, why would you heap these cares
    on me?
I am unfit for state and majesty: 205
I do beseech you, take it not amiss;
I cannot nor I will not yield to you.
   BUCK. If you refuse it,—as, in love and zeal,
Loath to depose the child, your brother's
    son;
As well we know your tenderness of heart 210
And gentle, kind, effeminate remorse,
Which we have noted in you to your kin,

134. factor, agent. 136. empery, empire. 137. consorted, joined. 138. worshipful, full of reverence. 143. degree, rank; condition, social position. 150. check'd, rebuked. 155. Unmeritable, undeserving. 157. even, smooth. 158. ripe revenue, inheritance ready to be obtained. 161. greatness, right to the throne. 163. in my greatness, in my royal office. 164. vapour, lustre, brightness. 173. defend, forbid; wring, snatch. 175. respects, reasons (you give); nice, overcareful. 185. widow, Lady Lucy. 187. purchase.

booty. 189. declension, moral deterioration. 192. expostulate, hold forth, i.e., discuss the matter. 193. reverence . . . alive, Edward's mother, the Duchess of York, is the "some alive." 194. sparing limit, i.e., restrain myself from alluding to Edward as the product of a bigamous marriage. 205. state, high places.

And egally indeed to all estates,—
Yet whether you accept our suit or no,
Your brother's son shall never reign our
    king;   215
But we will plant some other in the throne,
To the disgrace and downfall of your house:
And in this resolution here we leave you.—
Come, citizens: 'zounds! I'll entreat no more.
    GLOU. O, do not swear, my lord of Buck-
        ingham.   220
        [*Exit* BUCKINGHAM *with the* CITIZENS.
    CATE. Call them again, my lord, and accept
        their suit.
    ANOTHER. Do, good my lord, lest all the
        land do rue it.
    GLOU. Would you enforce me to a world of
        care?
Well, call them again. I am not made of
    stones,
But penetrable to your kind entreats,   225
Albeit against my conscience and my soul.
        [*Re-enter* BUCKINGHAM *and the rest.*]
Cousin of Buckingham, and you sage, grave
    men,
Since you will buckle fortune on my back,
To bear her burthen, whether I will or no,
I must have patience to endure the load: 230
But if black scandal or foul-faced reproach
Attend the sequel of your imposition,
Your mere enforcement shall acquittance me
From all the impure blots and stains thereof;
For God he knows, and you may partly
    see,   235
How far I am from the desire thereof.
    MAY. God bless your grace! we see it, and
        will say it.
    GLOU. In saying so, you shall but say the
        truth.
    BUCK. Then I salute you with this kingly
        title:
Long live Richard, England's royal king! 240
    MAY. AND CIT. Amen.
    BUCK. To-morrow will it please you to be
        crown'd?
    GLOU. Even when you please, since you will
        have it so.
    BUCK. To-morrow, then, we will attend your
        grace:
And so most joyfully we take our leave. 245

    GLOU. Come, let us to our holy task again.
Farewell, good cousin; farewell, gentle friends.
                                            [*Exeunt.*

ACT IV

SCENE I. *Before the Tower.*

[*Enter, on one side,* QUEEN ELIZABETH, DUCHESS
OF YORK, *and* MARQUESS OF DORSET; *on the
other,* ANNE, DUCHESS OF GLOUCESTER, *leading*
LADY MARGARET PLANTAGENET, CLARENCE'S
young Daughter.]

    DUCH. Who meets us here? my niece
        Plantagenet
Led in the hand of her kind aunt of Glouces-
    ter?
Now, for my life, she's wandering to the
    Tower,
On pure heart's love to greet the tender
    princes.
Daughter, well met.
    ANNE.   God give your graces both 5
A happy and a joyful time of day!
    Q. ELIZ. As much to you, good sister!
        Whither away?
    ANNE. No farther than the Tower; and, as
        I guess,
Upon the like devotion as yourselves,
To gratulate the gentle princes there.   10
    Q. ELIZ. Kind sister, thanks: we'll enter all
        together.

        [*Enter* BRAKENBURY.]

And, in good time, here the lieutenant comes.
Master lieutenant, pray you, by your leave,
How doth the prince, and my young son of
    York?
    BRAK. Right well, dear madam. By your
        patience,   15
I may not suffer you to visit them;
The king hath straitly charged the contrary.
    Q. ELIZ. The king! why, who's that?
    BRAK. I cry you mercy: I mean the lord
        protector.

---

213. egally, equally; all estates, all kinds of people. 232.
your imposition, the duty you have imposed. 233. mere,
unqualified; acquaintance, clear. 244. attend, wait on.

Act IV, Scene i: 1. niece, really her granddaughter
9. like devotion, same devout errand. 10. gratulate, greet.
17. straitly, strictly. 19. cry you mercy, beg your pardon.

Q. ELIZ. The Lord protect him from that
kingly title!   20
Hath he set bounds betwixt their love and
me?
I am their mother; who should keep me from
them?
DUCH. I am their father's mother; I will see
them.
ANNE. Their aunt I am in law, in love their
mother:
Then bring me to their sights; I'll bear thy
blame   25
And take thy office from thee, on my peril.
BRAK. No, madam, no; I may not leave it so;
I am bound by oath, and therefore pardon
me.   [Exit.

[Enter LORD STANLEY.]

STAN. Let me but meet you, ladies, one hour
hence,
And I'll salute your grace of York as mother,
And reverend looker on, of two fair queens. 31
[To Anne] Come, madam, you must straight
to Westminster,
There to be crownèd Richard's royal queen.
Q. ELIZ. O, cut my lace in sunder, that my
pent heart
May have some scope to beat, or else I
swoon   35
With this dead-killing news!
ANNE. Despiteful tidings! O unpleasing
news!
DOR. Be of good cheer: mother, how fares
your grace?
Q. ELIZ. O Dorset, speak not to me, get thee
hence!   39
Death and destruction dog thee at the heels;
Thy mother's name is ominous to children.
If thou wilt outstrip death, go cross the seas,
And live with Richmond, from the reach of
hell:
Go, hie thee, hie thee from this slaughter-
house,
Lest thou increase the number of the dead; 45
And make me die the thrall of Margaret's
curse,
Nor mother, wife, nor England's counted
queen.

STAN. Full of wise care is this your counsel,
madam.
Take all the swift advantage of the hours;
You shall have letters from me to my son 50
To meet you on the way, and welcome you.
Be not ta'en tardy by unwise delay.
DUCH. O ill-dispersing wind of misery!
O my accursèd womb, the bed of death!
A cockatrice hast thou hatch'd to the
world,   55
Whose unavoided eye is murderous.
STAN. Come, madam, come; I in all haste
was sent.
ANNE. And I in all unwillingness will go.
I would to God that the inclusive verge
Of golden metal that must round my brow 60
Were red-hot steel, to sear me to the brain!
Anointed let me be with deadly venom,
And die, ere men can say, God save the
queen!
Q. ELIZ. Go, go, poor soul, I envy not thy
glory;
To feed my humour, wish thyself no harm. 65
ANNE. No! why? When he that is my hus-
band now
Came to me, as I follow'd Henry's corse,
When scarce the blood was well wash'd from
his hands
Which issued from my other angel husband
And that dead saint which then I weeping
follow'd;   70
O, when, I say, I look'd on Richard's face,
This was my wish: "Be thou," quoth I, "ac-
cursed,
For making me, so young, so old a widow!
And, when thou wed'st, let sorrow haunt thy
bed;
And be thy wife—if any be so mad—   75
As miserable by the life of thee
As thou hast made me by my dear lord's
death!"
Lo, ere I can repeat this curse again,
Even in so short a space, my woman's heart
Grossly grew captive to his honey words   80
And proved the subject of my own soul's
curse,

21. bounds, barriers. 31. reverend looker on, one who regards with reverence; two fair queens, Elizabeth and
Anne. 34. pent, shut. According to Elizabethan psychology, grief made the heart swell. 43. Richmond, afterwards Henry VII; from, out of. 47. counted, accepted.
50. son, Stanley was Richmond's stepfather. 52. ta'en
tardy, taken because you are too late. 55. cockatrice, a
fabulous creature thought to come from a rooster's egg,
whose eye was so terrible it killed with a glance. 59.
verge, circle. 65. feed my humour, please me. 69. angel
husband, Edward, son of Henry VI, to whom Anne was
betrothed. He died before the marriage could take place.
73. old, i.e., in grief. 80. grossly, stupidly.

Which ever since hath kept my eyes from
rest;
For never yet one hour in his bed
Have I enjoy'd the golden dew of sleep,
But have been wakèd by his timorous
dreams.   85
Besides, he hates me for my father Warwick;
And will, no doubt, shortly be rid of me.
  Q. ELIZ. Poor heart, adieu! I pity thy com-
  plaining.
  ANNE. No more than from my soul I mourn
  for yours.
  Q. ELIZ. Farewell, thou woful welcomer of
  glory!   90
  ANNE. Adieu, poor soul, that takest thy
  leave of it!
  DUCH. [To Dorset] Go thou to Richmond,
  and good fortune guide thee!
[To Anne] Go thou to Richard, and good
  angels guard thee!
[To Queen Eliz.] Go thou to sanctuary, and
  good thoughts possess thee!
I to my grave, where peace and rest lie with
  me!   95
Eighty odd years of sorrow have I seen,
And each hour's joy wreck'd with a week of
  teen.
  Q. ELIZ. Stay, yet look back with me unto
  the Tower.
Pity, you ancient stones, those tender babes
Whom envy hath immured within your
  walls!   100
Rough cradle for such little pretty ones!
Rude ragged nurse, old sullen playfellow
For tender princes, use my babies well!
So foolish sorrow bids your stones farewell.
                                        [Exeunt.

SCENE II. *London. The palace.*

[*Sennet. Enter* RICHARD, *in pomp, crowned;*
BUCKINGHAM, CATESBY, *a* PAGE, *and others.*]

  K. RICH. Stand all apart. Cousin of Buckingham!
  BUCK. My gracious sovereign?
  K. RICH. Give me thy hand.   [*Here he
  ascendeth his throne.*] Thus high, by thy
  advice

And thy assistance, is King Richard seated:
But shall we wear these honours for a day? 5
Or shall they last, and we rejoice in them?
  BUCK. Still live they and for ever may they
  last!
  K. RICH. O Buckingham, now do I play the
  touch,
To try if thou be current gold indeed:
Young Edward lives: think now what I would
  say.   10
  BUCK. Say on, my loving lord.
  K. RICH. Why, Buckingham, I say, I would
  be king.
  BUCK. Why, so you are, my thrice renownèd
  liege.
  K. RICH. Ha! am I king! 'tis so: but Edward
  lives.
  BUCK. True, noble prince.
  K. RICH.   O bitter consequence,
That Edward still should live! "True, noble
  prince!"   16
Cousin, thou wert not wont to be so dull:
Shall I be plain? I wish the bastards dead;
And I would have it suddenly perform'd.
What sayest thou? speak suddenly; be brief.
  BUCK. Your grace may do your pleasure. 21
  K. RICH. Tut, tut, thou art all ice, thy kind-
  ness freezeth:
Say, have I thy consent that they shall die?
  BUCK. Give me some breath, some little
  pause, my lord,
Before I positively speak herein: 25
I will resolve your grace immediately. [*Exit.*
  CATE. [*Aside to a stander by*] The king is
  angry: see, he bites the lip.
  K. RICH. I will converse with iron-witted
  fools
And unrespective boys; none are for me
That look into me with considerate eyes: 30
High-reaching Buckingham grows circum-
  spect.
Boy!
  PAGE. My lord?
  K. RICH. Know'st thou not any whom cor-
  rupting gold
Would tempt unto a close exploit of death?
  PAGE. My lord, I know a discontented gen-
  tleman,   36

97. teen, woe. 100. envy, malice. Scene ii: 1. s.d. Sennet,
trumpet call. Stand . . . apart, all stand back. 7. still live
they, may they always live. 8. play the touch, make you
serve as a touchstone. 9. current, genuine. 14. Edward,
i.e., Edward V, Henry VI's oldest son. 20. suddenly, at
once. 26. resolve your grace, i.e., give your grace my
decision. 28. iron-witted, unfeeling. 29. unrespective,
heedless. 30. considerate, understanding. 35. close exploit
of death, secret deed of murder.

Whose humble means match not his haughty
   mind:
Gold were as good as twenty orators,
And will, no doubt, tempt him to any thing.
  K. RICH. What is his name?
  PAGE.   His name, my lord, is Tyrrel.
  K. RICH. I partly know the man: go, call
   him hither.   [*Exit* PAGE.
The deep-revolving witty Buckingham   42
No more shall be the neighbour to my
   counsel:
Hath he so long held out with me untired,
And stops he now for breath?

[*Enter* STANLEY.]

      How now! what news with you?
  STAN. My lord, I hear the Marquis Dorset's
  fled
To Richmond, in those parts beyond the sea
Where he abides.   [*Stands apart.*
  K. RICH. Catesby!
  CATE. My lord?   50
  K. RICH. Rumour it abroad
That Anne, my wife, is sick and like to die:
I will take order for her keeping close.
Inquire me out some mean-born gentleman,
Whom I will marry straight to Clarence'
   daughter: 55
The boy is foolish, and I fear not him.
Look, how thou dream'st! I say again, give
  out
That Anne my wife is sick and like to die:
About it; for it stands me much upon,
To stop all hopes whose growth may damage
  me.   [*Exit* CATESBY.] 60
I must be married to my brother's daughter,
Or else my kingdom stands on brittle glass.
Murder her brothers, and then marry her!
Uncertain way of gain! But I am in
So far in blood that sin will pluck on sin: 65
Tear-falling pity dwells not in this eye.

[*Re-enter* PAGE, *with* TYRREL.]

Is thy name Tyrrel?
  TYR. James Tyrrel, and your most obedi-
  ent subject.
  K. RICH. Art thou, indeed?
  TYR. Prove me, my gracious sovereign.

  K. RICH. Darest thou resolve to kill a friend
   of mine?   70
  TYR. Ay, my lord;
But I had rather kill two enemies.
  K. RICH. Why, there thou hast it: two deep
   enemies,
Foes to my rest and my sweet sleep's dis-
   turbers
Are they that I would have thee deal
   upon: 75
Tyrrel, I mean those bastards in the Tower.
  TYR. Let me have open means to come to
  them,
And soon I'll rid you from the fear of them.
  K. RICH. Thou sing'st sweet music. Hark,
   come hither, Tyrrel:
Go, by this token: rise, and lend thine ear: 80
                    [*Whispers.*]
There is no more but so: say it is done,
And I will love thee, and prefer thee too.
  TYR.. 'Tis done, my gracious lord.
  K. RICH. Shall we hear from thee, Tyrrel, ere
   we sleep?
  TYR. Ye shall, my lord.   [*Exit.* 85

[*Re-enter* BUCKINGHAM.]

  BUCK. My lord, I have consider'd in my mind
The late demand that you did sound me in.
  K. RICH. Well, let that pass. Dorset is fled to
   Richmond.
  BUCK. I hear that news, my lord.
  K. RICH. Stanley, he is your wife's son: well,
   look to it.   90
  BUCK. My lord, I claim your gift, my due by
   promise,
For which your honour and your faith is
   pawn'd;
The earldom of Hereford and the moveables
The which you promiséd I should possess.
  K. RICH. Stanley, look to your wife: if she
   convey   95
Letters to Richmond, you shall answer it.
  BUCK. What says your highness to my just
   demand?
  K. RICH. As I remember, Henry the Sixth
Did prophesy that Richmond should be king,
When Richmond was a little peevish boy. 100
A king, perhaps, perhaps,—
  BUCK. My lord!

42. revolving, scheming; witty, clever. 44. held out, kept
up. 53. close, imprisoned. 54. mean-born, low-born. 57.
dream'st, have fallen into a reverie, i.e., you are not
paying attention. 59. stands . . . upon, is of great importance to me. 65. pluck on, draw on, i.e., lead to. 75.
deal upon, go to work on. 82. prefer, promote. 90. he,
i.e., Richmond. 93. moveables, perquisites.

K. RICH. How chance the prophet could not at that time
Have told me, I being by, that I should kill him?
BUCK. My lord, your promise for the earl-
dom,— 105
K. RICH. Richmond! When last I was at Exe-
ter,
The mayor in courtesy show'd me the castle,
And call'd it Rougemont: at which name I started,
Because a bard of Ireland told me once,
I should not live long after I saw Richmond.
BUCK. My lord! 111
K. RICH. Ay, what's o'clock?
BUCK. I am thus bold to put your grace in mind
Of what you promised me.
K. RICH.   Well, but what's o'clock?
BUCK. Upon the stroke of ten.
K. RICH.   Well, let it strike. 115
BUCK. Why let it strike?
K. RICH. Because that, like a Jack, thou keep'st the stroke
Betwixt thy begging and my meditation.
I am not in the giving vein to-day.
BUCK. Why, then resolve me whether you will or no. 120
K. RICH. Tut, tut,
Thou troublest me; I am not in the vein.
        [Exeunt all but BUCKINGHAM.
BUCK. Is it even so? rewards he my true service
With such deep contempt? made I him king for this?
O, let me think on Hastings, and be gone 125
To Brecknock, while my fearful head is on!
        [Exit.

SCENE III. *The same.*

[Enter TYRREL.]

TYR. The tyrannous and bloody deed is done,
The most arch act of piteous massacre
That ever yet this land was guilty of.
Dighton and Forrest, whom I did suborn
To do this ruthless piece of butchery, 5

Although they were flesh'd villains, bloody dogs,
Melting with tenderness and kind compassion
Wept like two children in their deaths' sad stories.
"Lo, thus," quoth Dighton, "lay those tender babes:"
"Thus, thus," quoth Forrest, "girdling one another 10
Within their innocent alabaster arms:
Their lips were four red roses on a stalk,
Which in their summer beauty kiss'd each other.
A book of prayers on their pillow lay;
Which once," quoth Forrest, "almost changed my mind; 15
But O! the devil"—there the villain stopp'd;
Whilst Dighton thus told on: "We smothered
The most replenished sweet work of nature,
That from the prime creation e'er she framed."
Thus both are gone with conscience and remorse; 20
They could not speak; and so I left them both,
To bring this tidings to the bloody king.
And here he comes.

[Enter KING RICHARD.]

        All hail, my sovereign liege!
K. RICH. Kind Tyrrel, am I happy in thy news?
TYR. If to have done the thing you gave in charge 25
Beget your happiness, be happy then,
For it is done, my lord.
K. RICH.   But didst thou see them dead?
TYR. I did, my lord.
K. RICH.   And buried, gentle Tyrrel?
TYR. The chaplain of the Tower hath buried them;
But how or in what place I do not know. 30
K. RICH. Come to me, Tyrrel, soon at after supper,
And thou shalt tell the process of their death.
Meantime, but think how I may do thee good,
And be inheritor of thy desire.
Farewell till soon.   [Exit TYRREL. 35
The son of Clarence have I pent up close;
His daughter meanly have I match'd in marriage;

117. Jack, a figure on old clocks that strikes the hours on a bell. 126. Brecknock, his castle in Wales. Scene iii: 2. arch, wicked. 4. suborn, procure. 6. flesh'd, hunting dogs were trained by feeding them on the game they pur- sued, hence, hardened. 18. replenished, complete. 19. prime, first. 20. gone, overcome. 31. after supper, dessert. 32. process, events. 36. pent up, shut up. 37. meanly, poorly.

The sons of Edward sleep in Abraham's
  bosom,
And Anne my wife hath bid the world good
  night.
Now, for I know the Breton Richmond aims 40
At young Elizabeth, my brother's daughter,
And, by that knot, looks proudly o'er the
  crown,
To her I go, a jolly thriving wooer.

[*Enter* CATESBY.]

CATE. My lord!
K. RICH. Good news or bad, that thou comest
  in so bluntly?   45
CATE. Bad news, my lord: Ely is fled to Rich-
  mond;
And Buckingham, back'd with the hardy
  Welshmen,
Is in the field, and still his power increaseth.
K. RICH. Ely with Richmond troubles me
  more near
Than Buckingham and his rash-levied army.
Come, I have heard that fearful commenting 51
Is leaden servitor to dull delay;
Delay leads impotent and snail-paced beggary:
Then fiery expedition be my wing,
Jove's Mercury, and herald for a king!   55
Come, muster men: my counsel is my shield;
We must be brief when traitors brave the field.
                                   [*Exeunt.*

SCENE IV. *Before the palace.*

[*Enter* QUEEN MARGARET.]

Q. MAR. So, now prosperity begins to mellow
And drop into the rotten mouth of death.
Here in these confines slily have I lurk'd,
To watch the waning of mine adversaries.
A dire induction am I witness to,   5
And will to France, hoping the consequence
Will prove as bitter, black, and tragical.
Withdraw thee, wretched Margaret: who
  comes here?

[*Enter* QUEEN ELIZABETH *and the* DUCHESS OF
  YORK.]

Q. ELIZ. Ah, my young princes! ah, my tender babes!

My unblown flowers, new-appearing sweets!
If yet your gentle souls fly in the air   11
And be not fix'd in doom perpetual,
Hover about me with your airy wings
And hear your mother's lamentation!
  Q. MAR. Hover about her; say, that right for
  right   15
Hath dimm'd your infant morn to aged night.
  DUCH. So many miseries have crazed my
  voice,
That my woe-wearied tongue is mute and
  dumb;
Edward Plantagenet, why art thou dead?
  Q. MAR. Plantagenet doth quit Plantagenet. 20
Edward for Edward pays a dying debt.
  Q. ELIZ. Wilt thou, O God, fly from such
  gentle lambs,
And throw them in the entrails of the wolf?
When didst thou sleep when such a deed was
  done?
  Q. MAR. When holy Harry died, and my
  sweet son.   25
  DUCH. Blind sight, dead life, poor mortal liv-
  ing ghost,
Woe's scene, world's shame, grave's due by
  life usurp'd,
Brief abstract and record of tedious days,
Rest thy unrest on England's lawful earth,
                             [*Sitting down.*]
Unlawfully made drunk with innocents'
  blood!   30
  Q. ELIZ. O, that thou wouldst as well afford
  a grave
As thou canst yield a melancholy seat!
Then would I hide my bones, not rest them
  here.
O, who hath any cause to mourn but I?
                       [*Sitting down by her.*
  Q. MAR. If ancient sorrow be most reverend,
Give mine the benefit of seniory,   36
And let my woes frown on the upper hand.
If sorrow can admit society,
                       [*Sitting down with them.*]
Tell o'er your woes again by viewing mine:
I had an Edward, till a Richard kill'd him; 40
I had a Harry, till a Richard kill'd him:

40. Breton, Richmond was then in Brittany. 42. by that
knot, by virtue of that union. 46. Ely, i.e., John Morton,
Bishop of Ely. 51-2. fearful . . . delay, frightened discussion is the slow servant of delay. 54-5. fiery . . . king,
hot haste be my herald as Mercury was Jove's. 57. brave,

dare take. Scene iv: 5. induction, beginning. 6. consequence, sequel. 10. unblown, unopened. 15. right for
right, just retribution. 17. crazed, cracked. 20. Plantagenet . . . Plantagenet, Edward IV pays for Edward V, son
of Henry VI. 25. Harry, Henry VI. 26. Blind sight, etc.,
she is describing herself. 28. abstract, epitome. 36.
seniory, seniority, hence priority. 39. tell, count. 40.
Edward, her son, once Prince of Wales. 41. Harry,
Henry VI, her husband.

Thou hadst an Edward, till a Richard kill'd
  him;
Thou hadst a Richard, till a Richard kill'd
  him.
  DUCH. I had a Richard too, and thou didst
    kill him;
I had a Rutland too, thou holp'st to kill him. 45
  Q. MAR. Thou hadst a Clarence too, and
    Richard kill'd him.
From forth the kennel of thy womb hath crept
A hell-hound that doth hunt us all to death:
That dog, that had his teeth before his eyes,
To worry lambs and lap their gentle blood, 50
That foul defacer of God's handiwork,
That excellent grand tyrant of the earth,
That reigns in gallèd eyes of weeping souls,
Thy womb let loose, to chase us to our graves.
O upright, just, and true-disposing God, 55
How do I thank thee, that this carnal cur
Preys on the issue of his mother's body,
And makes her pew-fellow with others' moan!
  DUCH. O Harry's wife, triumph not in my
    woes!
God witness with me, I have wept for thine. 60
  Q. MAR. Bear with me; I am hungry for re-
    venge,
And now I cloy me with beholding it.
Thy Edward he is dead, that stabb'd my Ed-
  ward;
Thy other Edward dead, to quit my Edward;
Young York he is but boot, because both
  they 65
Match not the high perfection of my loss:
Thy Clarence he is dead that kill'd my Ed-
  ward;
And the beholders of this tragic play,
The adulterate Hastings, Rivers, Vaughan,
  Grey,
Untimely smother'd in their dusky graves. 70
Richard yet lives, hell's black intelligencer,
Only reserved their factor, to buy souls
And send them thither: but at hand, at hand,
Ensues his piteous and unpitied end:
Earth gapes, hell burns, fiends roar, saints pray,
To have him suddenly convey'd away. 76
Cancel his bond of life, dear God, I pray,

That I may live to say, The dog is dead!
  Q. ELIZ. O, thou didst prophesy the time
    would come 79
That I should wish for thee to help me curse
That bottled spider, that foul bunch-back'd
  toad!
  Q. MAR. I call'd thee then vain flourish of my
    fortune;
I call'd thee then poor shadow, painted queen;
The presentation of but what I was;
The flattering index of a direful pageant; 85
One heaved a-high, to be hurl'd down below;
A mother only mock'd with two sweet babes;
A dream of what thou wert, a breath, a bubble,
A sign of dignity, a garish flag,
To be the aim of every dangerous shot; 90
A queen in jest, only to fill the scene.
Where is thy husband now? where be thy
  brothers?
Where are thy children? wherein dost thou
  joy?
Who sues to thee and cries "God save the
  queen"?
Where be the bending peers that flatter'd
  thee? 95
Where be the thronging troops that follow'd
  thee?
Decline all this, and see what now thou art:
For happy wife, a most distressed widow;
For joyful mother, one that wails the name;
For queen, a very caitiff crown'd with care; 100
For one being sued to, one that humbly sues;
For one that scorn'd at me, now scorn'd of me;
For one being fear'd of all, now fearing one;
For one commanding all, obey'd of none.
Thus hath the course of justice wheel'd about,
And left thee but a very prey to time; 106
Having no more but thought of what thou
  wert,
To torture thee the more, being what thou art.
Thou didst usurp my place, and dost thou not
Usurp the just proportion of my sorrow? 110
Now thy proud neck bears half my burthen'd
  yoke;
From which even here I slip my weary neck,
And leave the burthen of it all on thee.

---

42. Edward, Edward IV. 43. Richard, Duke of York, son
of Edward IV. 44. Richard, her husband, the Duke of
York, father of Richard III, killed at the battle of Wakefield by Margaret's forces. 45. Rutland, son of the foregoing also killed at Wakefield. 49. teeth, a reference to
the tradition that Richard III was born with teeth.
53. galled, red from weeping. 56. carnal, carnivorous.
58. pew-fellow, close associate. 63. Thy Edward, Edward

IV; my Edward, son of Henry VI. 64. other Edward,
Edward V. 65. Young York, the younger of Edward IV's
sons, murdered in the Tower; boot, something thrown in.
69. adulterate, adulterous. 71. intelligencer, messenger.
72. their factor, agent of Hell's fiends. 82. vain flourish,
foolish, showy decoration. 85. index, Table of contents.
89. sign, mere sign. 97. Decline, repeat from beginning to
end. 100. caitiff, wretch. 102. scorn'd at, taunted; scorn'd
of, taunted by. 112. slip, get loose.

Farewell, York's wife, and queen of sad mis-
    chance:
These English woes will make me smile in
    France.   115
  Q. ELIZ. O thou well skill'd in curses, stay
    awhile,
And teach me how to curse mine enemies!
  Q. MAR. Forbear to sleep the nights, and fast
    the days;
Compare dead happiness with living woe;
Think that thy babes were fairer than they
    were,   120
And he that slew them fouler than he is:
Bettering thy loss makes the bad causer worse:
Revolving this will teach thee how to curse.
  Q. ELIZ. My words are dull; O, quicken them
    with thine!
  Q. MAR. Thy woes will make them sharp,
    and pierce like mine.   [Exit.   125
  DUCH. Why should calamity be full of
    words?
  Q. ELIZ. Windy attorneys to their client
    woes,
Airy succeeders of intestate joys,
Poor breathing orators of miseries!
Let them have scope: though what they do
    impart   130
Help not at all, yet do they ease the heart.
  DUCH. If so, then be not tongue-tied: go
    with me,
And in the breath of bitter words let's smother
My damnèd son, which thy two sweet sons
    smother'd.
ı hear his drum: be copious in exclaims.   135

[Enter KING RICHARD, marching, with drums
    and trumpets.]

  K. RICH. Who intercepts my expedition?
  DUCH. O, she that might have intercepted
    thee,
Ry strangling thee in her accursed womb,
From all the slaughters, wretch, that thou hast
    done!
  Q. ELIZ. Hidest thou that forehead with a
    golden crown,   140
Where should be graven, if that right were
    right,

The slaughter of the prince that owed that
    crown,
And the dire death of my two sons and
    brothers?
Tell me, thou villain slave, where are my chil-
    dren?
  DUCH. Thou toad, thou toad, where is thy
    brother Clarence?   145
And little Ned Plantagenet, his son?
  Q. ELIZ. Where is kind Hastings, Rivers,
    Vaughan, Grey?
  K. RICH. A flourish, trumpets! strike alarum,
    drums!
Let not the heavens hear these tell-tale women
Rail on the Lord's anointed: strike, I say! 150
              [Flourish. Alarums.]
Either be patient, and entreat me fair,
Or with the clamorous report of war
Thus will I drown your exclamations.
  DUCH. Art thou my son?
  K. RICH. Ay, I thank God, my father, and
    yourself.   155
  DUCH. Then patiently hear my impatience.
  K. RICH. Madam, I have a touch of your con-
    dition,
Which cannot brook the accent of reproof.
  DUCH. O, let me speak!
  K. RICH.   Do then; but I'll not hear.
  DUCH. I will be mild and gentle in my speech.
  K. RICH. And brief, good mother; for I am
    in haste.   161
  DUCH. Art thou so hasty? I have stay'd for
    thee,
God knows, in anguish, pain and agony.
  K. RICH. And came I not at last to comfort
    you?
  DUCH. No, by the holy rood, thou know'st it
    well,   165
Thou camest on earth to make the earth my
    hell.
A grievous burthen was thy birth to me;
Tetchy and wayward was thy infancy;
Thy school-days frightful, desperate, wild, and
    furious,
Thy prime of manhood, daring, bold, and ven-
    turous,   170
Thy age confirm'd, proud, subtle, bloody,
    treacherous,

---

122. Bettering, exaggerating. 123. revolving, meditating.
127. Windy . . . woes, lawyers who make long-winded
speeches in behalf of their client, woe. 128. intestate,
literally = bequeathing nothing, hence, bankrupt, worthless. 129. breathing . . . miseries, orators uttering miseries. 136. expedition, haste. 141. right were right, justice

prevailed. 142. owed, owned. 149. tell-tale, tattling, chattering. 151. fair, gently. 157. touch . . . condition, a little
bit of your disposition. 168. Tetchy, fretful. 170. prime
of, first of, that is, early. 171. age confirm'd, later manhood.

More mild, but yet more harmful, kind in hatred:
What comfortable hour canst thou name,
That ever graced me in thy company?

    K. RICH. Faith, none, but Humphrey Hour, that call'd your grace   175
To breakfast once forth of my company.
If I be so disgracious in your sight,
Let me march on, and not offend your grace.
Strike up the drum.

    DUCH.   I prithee, hear me speak.

    K. RICH. You speak too bitterly.

    DUCH.   Hear me a word;   180
For I shall never speak to thee again.

    K. RICH. So.

    DUCH. Either thou wilt die, by God's just ordinance,
Ere from this war thou turn a conqueror,
Or I with grief and extreme age shall perish 185
And never look upon thy face again.
Therefore take with thee my most heavy curse;
Which, in the day of battle, tire thee more
Than all the complete armour that thou wear'st!
My prayers on the adverse party fight;   190
And there the little souls of Edward's children
Whisper the spirits of thine enemies
And promise them success and victory.
Bloody thou art, bloody will be thy end; 194
Shame serves thy life and doth thy death attend.   [*Exit.*

    Q. ELIZ. Though far more cause, yet much less spirit to curse
Abides in me; I say amen to all.

    K. RICH. Stay, madam; I must speak a word with you.

    Q. ELIZ. I have no moe sons of the royal blood
For thee to murder: for my daughters, Richard,   200
They shall be praying nuns, not weeping queens;
And therefore level not to hit their lives.

    K. RICH. You have a daughter call'd Elizabeth,
Virtuous and fair, royal and gracious.

    Q. ELIZ. And must she die for this? O, let her live,   205
And I'll corrupt her manners, stain her beauty;
Slander myself as false to Edward's bed;
Throw over her the veil of infamy:
So she may live unscarr'd of bleeding slaughter,
I will confess she was not Edward's daughter.

    K. RICH. Wrong not her birth, she is of royal blood.   211

    Q. ELIZ. To save her life, I'll say she is not so.

    K. RICH. Her life is only safest in her birth.

    Q. ELIZ. And only in that safety died her brothers.

    K. RICH. Lo, at their births good stars were opposite.   215

    Q. ELIZ. No, to their lives bad friends were contrary.

    K. RICH. All unavoided is the doom of destiny.

    Q. ELIZ. True, when avoided grace makes destiny:
My babes were destined to a fairer death,
If grace had bless'd thee with a fairer life. 220

    K. RICH. You speak as if that I had slain my cousins.

    Q. ELIZ. Cousins, indeed; and by their uncle cozen'd
Of comfort, kingdom, kindred, freedom, life.
Whose hand soever lanced their tender hearts,
Thy head, all indirectly, gave direction: 225
No doubt the murderous knife was dull and blunt
Till it was whetted on thy stone-hard heart,
To revel in the entrails of my lambs.
But that still use of grief makes wild grief tame,
My tongue should to thy ears not name my boys   230
Till that my nails were anchor'd in thine eyes;
And I, in such a desperate bay of death,
Like a poor bark, of sails and tackling reft,
Rush all to pieces on thy rocky bosom.

    K. RICH. Madam, so thrive I in my enterprise
And dangerous success of bloody wars,   236
As I intend more good to you and yours
Than ever you or yours were by me wrong'd!

---

175. **Humphrey Hour**, men, hoping in vain to be invited to a meal, used to hang around in Humphrey's, Duke of Gloucester's, walk in St. Paul's. Richard means the happiest time for him was when his mother did not appear for meals. 176. **forth of**, away from. 190. **on,** with.

195. **serves,** accompanies. 199. **moe,** more. 202. **level,** aim. 206. **manners,** morals. 214. **only in,** merely because of. 215. **opposite,** hostile. 217. **unavoided,** unavoidable. 218. **avoided grace,** one devoid of grace or kindness. 222. **cozen'd,** cheated. 229. **still,** continuous. 236. **success,** consequence.

Q. ELIZ. What good is cover'd with the face of heaven,

To be discover'd, that can do me good? 240

K. RICH. The advancement of your children, gentle lady.

Q. ELIZ. Up to some scaffold, there to lose their heads?

K. RICH. No, to the dignity and height of honour,

The high imperial type of this earth's glory.

Q. ELIZ. Flatter my sorrows with report of it;

Tell me what state, what dignity, what honour,

Canst thou demise to any child of mine? 247

K. RICH. Even all I have; yea, and myself and all,

Will I withal endow a child of thine;

So in the Lethe of thy angry soul 250

Thou drown the sad remembrance of those wrongs

Which thou supposest I have done to thee.

Q. ELIZ. Be brief, lest that the process of thy kindness

Last longer telling than thy kindness' date.

K. RICH. Then know, that from my soul I love thy daughter. 255

Q. ELIZ. My daughter's mother thinks it with her soul.

K. RICH. What do you think?

Q. ELIZ. That thou dost love my daughter from thy soul:

So from thy soul's love didst thou love her brothers;

And from my heart's love I do thank thee for it. 260

K. RICH. Be not so hasty to confound my meaning:

I mean, that with my soul I love thy daughter,

And mean to make her queen of England.

Q. ELIZ. Say then, who dost thou mean shall be her king?

K. RICH. Even he that makes her queen: who should be else? 265

Q. ELIZ. What, thou?

K. RICH. I, even I: what think you of it, madam?

Q. ELIZ. How canst thou woo her?

K. RICH.   That I would learn of you,

As one that are best acquainted with her humour.

Q. ELIZ. And wilt thou learn of me?

K. RICH.   Madam, with all my heart. 270

Q. ELIZ. Send to her, by the man that slew her brothers,

A pair of bleeding hearts; thereon engrave

Edward and York; then haply she will weep:

Therefore present to her,—as sometime Margaret 274

Did to thy father, steep'd in Rutland's blood,—

A handkerchief; which, say to her, did drain

The purple sap from her sweet brother's body.

And bid her dry her weeping eyes therewith.

If this inducement force her not to love,

Send her a story of thy noble acts; 280

Tell her thou madest away her uncle Clarence,

Her uncle Rivers; yea, and, for her sake,

Madest quick conveyance with her good aunt Anne.

K. RICH. Come, come, you mock me; this is not the way

To win your daughter.

Q. ELIZ.   There is no other way; 285

Unless thou couldst put on some other shape,

And not be Richard that hath done all this.

K. RICH. Say that I did all this for love of her.

Q. ELIZ. Nay, then indeed she cannot choose but hate thee,

Having bought love with such a bloody spoil.

K. RICH. Look, what is done cannot be now amended: 291

Men shall deal unadvisedly sometimes,

Which after hours give leisure to repent.

If I did take the kingdom from your sons,

To make amends, I'll give it to your daughter. 295

If I have kill'd the issue of your womb,

To quicken your increase, I will beget

Mine issue of your blood upon your daughter:

A grandam's name is little less in love

Than is the doting title of a mother; 300

They are as children but one step below,

Even of your mettle, of your very blood;

Of all one pain, save for a night of groans

Endured of her, for whom you bid like sorrow.

Your children were vexation to your youth,

But mine shall be a comfort to your age. 306

The loss you have is but a son being king,

And by that loss your daughter is made queen.

I cannot make you what amends I would,

her tears. **283.** conveyance, removal. **292.** unadvisedly, without proper consideration. **293.** Which, for which dealing, i.e., inadvised action. **297.** quicken your increase, make your child pregnant. **302.** mettle, disposition. **304.** bid, endured. **307. son being King,** Edward V.

244. imperial type, i.e., the crown; type = badge. **247.** demise, transmit. **250.** Lethe, river of forgetfulness in the classical after-world. **253.** process, story. **259.** from, divorced from. **274.** Therefore, for her weeping, i.e., to dry

Therefore accept such kindness as I can.   310
Dorset your son, that with a fearful soul
Leads discontented steps in foreign soil,
This fair alliance quickly shall call home
To high promotions and great dignity:
The king, that calls your beauteous daughter
    wife,   315
Familiarly shall call thy Dorset brother;
Again shall you be mother to a king,
And all the ruins of distressful times
Repair'd with double riches of content.
What! we have many goodly days to see: 320
The liquid drops of tears that you have shed
Shall come again, transform'd to orient pearl,
Advantaging their loan with interest
Of ten times double gain of happiness.
Go, then, my mother, to thy daughter go; 325
Make bold her bashful years with your ex-
    perience;
Prepare her ears to hear a wooer's tale;
Put in her tender heart the aspiring flame
Of golden sovereignty; acquaint the princess
With the sweet silent hours of marriage joys:
And when this arm of mine hath chastisèd 331
The pretty rebel, dull-brain'd Buckingham,
Bound with triumphant garlands will I come
And lead thy daughter to a conqueror's bed;
To whom I will retail my conquest won, 335
And she shall be sole victress, Cæsar's Cæsar.
    Q. ELIZ. What were I best to say? her father's
    brother
Would be her lord? or shall I say, her uncle?
Or, he that slew her brothers and her uncles?
Under what title shall I woo for thee,   340
That God, the law, my honour and her love,
Can make seem pleasing to her tender years?
    K. RICH. Infer fair England's peace by this
    alliance.
    Q. ELIZ. Which she shall purchase with still
    lasting war.
    K. RICH. Say that the king, which may com-
    mand, entreats.   345
    Q. ELIZ. That at her hands which the king's
    King forbids.
    K. RICH. Say, she shall be a high and mighty
    queen.
    Q. ELIZ. To wail the title, as her mother
    doth.
    K. RICH. Say, I will love her everlastingly.

    Q. ELIZ. But how long shall that title 'ever'
    last?   350
    K. RICH. Sweetly in force unto her fair life's
    end.
    Q. ELIZ. But how long fairly shall her sweet
    life last?
    K. RICH. So long as heaven and nature
    lengthens it.
    Q. ELIZ. So long as hell and Richard likes
    of it.
    K. RICH. Say, I, her sovereign, am her sub-
    ject love.   355
    Q. ELIZ. But she, your subject, loathes such
    sovereignty.
    K. RICH. Be eloquent in my behalf to her.
    Q. ELIZ. An honest tale speeds best being
    plainly told.
    K. RICH. Then in plain terms tell her my
    loving tale.
    Q. ELIZ. Plain and not honest is too harsh
    a style.   360
    K. RICH. Your reasons are too shallow and
    too quick.
    Q. ELIZ. O no, my reasons are too deep and
    dead;
Too deep and dead, poor infants, in their
    grave.
    K. RICH. Harp not on that string, madam;
    that is past.
    Q. ELIZ. Harp on it still shall I till heart-
    strings break.   365
    K. RICH. Now, by my George, my garter,
    and my crown,—
    Q. ELIZ. Profaned, dishonour'd, and the
    third usurp'd.
    K. RICH. I swear—
    Q. ELIZ.   By nothing; for this is no
    oath:
The George, profaned, hath lost his holy
    honour;
The garter, blemish'd, pawn'd his knightly
    virtue;   370
The crown, usurp'd, disgraced his kingly
    glory.
If something thou wilt swear to be believed,
Swear then by something that thou hast not
    wrong'd.
    K. RICH. Now, by the world—
    Q. ELIZ.   'Tis full of thy foul wrongs.

---

312. discontented, sorrowful. 322. orient, shining. 323.
Advantaging, increasing. 328. aspiring flame of, ambitious
desire for. 343. infer, offer a reason for. 348. wail, bewail,
deplore. 354. likes of, is pleased with. 360. harsh, dis-
cordant. 361. quick, hastily given (contrasted with "dead"
in the next line). 366. my George, a pendant showing
St. George slaying the dragon, attached to the insignia
of the order of the Garter.

K. RICH. My father's death—

Q. ELIZ. Thy life hath that dishonour'd. 375

K. RICH. Then, by myself—

Q. ELIZ.   Thyself thyself misusest.

K. RICH. Why then, by God—

Q. ELIZ.   God's wrong is most of all.

If thou hadst fear'd to break an oath by Him,

The unity the king thy brother made   379

Had not been broken, nor my brother slain:

If thou hadst fear'd to break an oath by Him,

The imperial metal, cirling now thy brow,

Had graced the tender temples of my child,

And both the princes had been breathing here,

Which now, two tender playfellows for dust,

Thy broken faith hath made a prey for worms.   386

What canst thou swear by now?

K. RICH.   The time to come.

Q. ELIZ. That thou hast wronged in the time o'erpast;

For I myself have many tears to wash

Hereafter time, for time past wrong'd by thee.   390

The children live, whose parents thou hast slaughter'd,

Ungovern'd youth, to wail it in their age;

The parents live, whose children thou hast butcher'd,

Old wither'd plants, to wail it with their age.

Swear not by time to come; for that thou hast   395

Misused ere used, by time misused o'erpast.

K. RICH. As I intend to prosper and repent,

So thrive I in my dangerous attempt

Of hostile arms! myself myself confound!

Heaven and fortune bar me happy hours! 400

Day, yield me not thy light; nor, night, thy rest!

Be opposite all planets of good luck

To my proceedings, if, with pure heart's love,

Immaculate devotion, holy thoughts,

I tender not thy beauteous princely daughter!

In her consists my happiness and thine; 406

Without her, follows to this land and me,

To thee, herself, and many a Christian soul,

Death, desolation, ruin and decay:

It cannot be avoided but by this;   410

It will not be avoided but by this.

Therefore, good mother,—I must call you so—

Be the attorney of my love to her:

Plead what I will be, not what I have been;

Not my deserts, but what I will deserve: 415

Urge the necessity and state of times,

And be not peevish-fond in great designs.

Q. ELIZ. Shall I be tempted of the devil thus?

K. RICH. Ay, if the devil tempt thee to do good.

Q. ELIZ. Shall I forget myself to be myself?

K. RICH. Ay, if yourself's remembrance wrong yourself.   421

Q. ELIZ. But thou didst kill my children.

K. RICH. But in your daughter's womb I bury them:

Where in that nest of spicery they shall breed

Selves of themselves, to your recomforture.

Q. ELIZ. Shall I go win my daughter to thy will?   426

K. RICH. And be a happy mother by the deed.

Q. ELIZ. I go. Write to me very shortly,

And you shall understand from me her mind.

K. RICH. Bear her my true love's kiss; and so, farewell.   430

            [Exit QUEEN ELIZABETH.]

Relenting fool, and shallow, changing woman!

[Enter RATCLIFF; CATESBY following.]

How now! what news?

RAT. My gracious sovereign, on the western coast

Rideth a puissant navy; to the shore

Throng many doubtful hollow-hearted friends,   435

Unarm'd, and unresolved to beat them back:

'Tis thought that Richmond is their admiral;

And there they hull, expecting but the aid

Of Buckingham to welcome them ashore.

K. RICH. Some light-foot friend post to the Duke of Norfolk: 440

Ratcliff, thyself, or Catesby; where is he?

CATE. Here, my lord.

90. Hereafter, future. 396. o'er past, gone by. 399. myself confound, may I destroy myself. 405. tender not, have not a tender feeling for. 406. consists, dwells. 417. peevish-fond, childishly foolish. 420. myself . . . myself, i.e., what my situation is. 421. wrong yourself, work

to your disadvantage. 424. nest of spicery, the fabled phoenix was consumed by fire in the nest of spicery, whence it arose rejuvenated. 425. recomforture, consolation. 438. hull, float; expecting, awaiting. 440. light-foot, swift-running.

K. RICH. Fly to the duke: [*To* RATCLIFF]
Post thou to Salisbury:
When thou comest thither,— [*To* CATESBY]
Dull, unmindful villain,
Why stand'st thou still, and go'st not to the
duke?   445
CATE. First, mighty sovereign, let me know
your mind,
What from your grace I shall deliver to him.
K. RICH. O, true, good Catesby: bid him
levy straight
The greatest strength and power he can
make,
And meet me presently at Salisbury.   450
CATE. I go.   [*Exit.*
RAT. What is 't your highness' pleasure I
shall do
At Salisbury?
K. RICH. Why, what wouldst thou do there
before I go?
RAT. Your highness told me I should post
before.   455
K. RICH. My mind is changed, sir, my mind
is changed.

[*Enter* LORD STANLEY.]

How now, what news with you?
STAN. None good, my lord, to please you
with the hearing;
Nor none so bad, but it may well be told.
K. RICH. Hoyday, a riddle! neither good
nor bad!   460
Why dost thou run so many mile about,
When thou mayst tell thy tale a nearer way?
Once more, what news?
STAN.   Richmond is on the seas.
K. RICH. There let him sink, and be the seas
on him!
White-liver'd runagate, what doth he there?
STAN. I know not, mighty sovereign, but by
guess.   466
K. RICH. Well, sir, as you guess, as you
guess?
STAN. Stirr'd up by Dorset, Buckingham,
and Ely,
He makes for England, there to claim the
crown.
K. RICH. Is the chair empty? is the sword
unsway'd?   470
Is the king dead? the empire unpossess'd?

What heir of York is there alive but we?
And who is England's king but great York's
heir?
Then, tell me, what doth he upon the sea?
STAN. Unless for that, my liege, I cannot
guess.   475
K. RICH. Unless for that he comes to be
your liege,
You cannot guess wherefore the Welshman
comes.
Thou wilt revolt, and fly to him, I fear.
STAN. No, mighty liege; therefore mistrust
me not.
K. RICH. Where is thy power, then, to beat
him back?   480
Where are thy tenants and thy followers?
Are they not now upon the western shore,
Safe-conducting the rebels from their ships?
STAN. No, my good lord, my friends are in
the north.
K. RICH. Cold friends to Richard: what do
they in the north,   485
When they should serve their sovereign in
the west?
STAN. They have not been commanded,
mighty sovereign:
Please it your majesty to give me leave,
I'll muster up my friends, and meet your
grace
Where and what time your majesty shall
please.   490
K. RICH. Ay, ay, thou wouldst be gone to
join with Richmond:
I will not trust you, sir.
STAN.   Most mighty sovereign,
You have no cause to hold my friendship
doubtful:
I never was nor never will be false.
K. RICH. Well,   495
Go muster men; but, hear you, leave behind
Your son, George Stanley: look your faith be
firm,
Or else his head's assurance is but frail.
STAN. So deal with him as I prove true to
you.   [*Exit*

[*Enter a* MESSENGER.]

MESS. My gracious sovereign, now in Devonshire,   500

443. post, hasten. 450. presently, at once. 460. Hoyday,
an expression of surprise and contempt. 465. White-
liver'd runagate, cowardly renegade. 473. great York,
Richard, Duke of York, father of Edward IV and
Richard III. 475. that, i.e., to seek the crown. 477.
Welshman, Richmond was grandson of the Welshman
Owen Tudor, who married the widow of Henry V. 479.
therefore, for that reason. 488. me leave, i.e., to depart

As I by friends am well advertised,
Sir Edward Courtney, and the haughty prel-
ate
Bishop of Exeter, his brother there,
With many moe confederates, are in arms.

[*Enter another* MESSENGER.]

SEC. MESS. My liege, in Kent the Guild-
fords are in arms;   505
And every hour more competitors
Flock to their aid, and still their power increaseth.

[*Enter another* MESSENGER.]

THIRD MESS. My lord, the army of the Duke
of Buckingham—
K. RICH. Out on you, owls! nothing but
songs of death?   [*He striketh him.*]
Take that, until thou bring me better news.
THIRD MESS. The news I have to tell your
majesty   511
Is, that by sudden floods and fall of waters,
Buckingham's army is dispersed and scatter'd;
And he himself wander'd away alone,
No man knows whither.
K. RICH.   I cry thee mercy: 515
There is my purse to cure that blow of thine.
Hath any well-advisèd friend proclaim'd
Reward to him that brings the traitor in?
THIRD MESS. Such proclamation hath been
made, my liege.

[*Enter another* MESSENGER.]

FOURTH MESS. Sir Thomas Lovel and Lord
Marquis Dorset,   520
'Tis said, my liege, in Yorkshire are in arms.
Yet this good comfort bring I to your grace,
The Breton navy is dispersed by tempest:
Richmond, in Dorsetshire, sent out a boat
Unto the shore, to ask those on the banks 525
If they were his assistants, yea or no;
Who answer'd him, they came from Buck-
ingham
Upon his party: he, mistrusting them,
Hoised sail and made away for Brittany.
K. RICH. March on, march on, since we are
up in arms;   530

If not to fight with foreign enemies,
Yet to beat down these rebels here at home.

[*Re-enter* CATESBY.]

CATE. My liege, the Duke of Buckingham is
taken;
That is the best news: that the Earl of Rich-
mond
Is with a mighty power landed at Milford, 535
Is colder tidings, yet they must be told.
K. RICH. Away towards Salisbury! while we
reason here,
A royal battle might be won and lost:
Some one take order Buckingham be brought
To Salisbury; the rest march on with me. 540
[*Flourish. Exeunt.*

SCENE V. LORD DERBY'S *house.*

[*Enter* DERBY *and* SIR CHRISTOPHER URSWICK.]

DER. Sir Christopher, tell Richmond this
from me:
That in the sty of this most bloody boar
My son George Stanley is frank'd up in hold:
If I revolt, off goes young George's head;
The fear of that withholds my present aid.   5
But, tell me, where is princely Richmond now?
CHRIS. At Pembroke, or at Ha'rford-west, in
Wales.
DER. What men of name resort to him?
CHRIS. Sir Walter Herbert, a renownèd sol-
dier;
Sir Gilbert Talbot, Sir William Stanley;   10
Oxford, redoubted Pembroke, Sir James Blunt,
And Rice ap Thomas, with a valiant crew;
And many moe of noble fame and worth:
And towards London they do bend their
course,
If by the way they be not fought withal.   15
DER. Return unto thy lord; commend me to
him:
Tell him the queen hath heartily consented
He shall espouse Elizabeth her daughter.
These letters will resolve him of my mind.
Farewell.   [*Exeunt.*

501. advertised, informed. 503. his brother, Sir Edward
Courtney was only distantly related to Peter Courtney,
Bishop of Exeter. 506. competitors, confederates. 509.
owls, the hooting of an owl was supposed to portend death.
515. I cry thee mercy, I beg your pardon. 528. Upon
his party, to fight on his side. 529. Hoised, hoisted.
535. power, army; Milford, Milford Haven, on the west
coast of Wales. 538. a royal battle, a battle for a kingdom. Scene v: s.d. Sir Christopher Urswick, a priest,
the confessor to Richmond's (Henry VII's) mother. 3.
frank'd up, penned in a sty. 7. Ha'rford-west, Haverford-
west, near Milford Haven. 8. name, good reputation. 12.
ap, son of.

Act V

Scene i. *Salisbury. An open place.*

[*Enter the* SHERIFF, *and* BUCKINGHAM, *with halberds, led to execution.*]

BUCK. Will not King Richard let me speak with him?

SHER. No, my good lord; therefore be patient.

BUCK. Hastings, and Edward's children, Rivers, Grey,
Holy King Henry, and thy fair son Edward,
Vaughan, and all that have miscarried   5
By underhand corrupted foul injustice,
If that your moody discontented souls
Do through the clouds behold this present hour,
Even for revenge mock my destruction!
This is All-Souls' day, fellows, is it not?   10
   SHER. It is, my lord.
      BUCK. Why, then All-Souls' day is my body's doomsday.
This is the day that, in King Edward's time,
I wish'd might fall on me, when I was found
False to his children or his wife's allies;   15
This is the day wherein I wish'd to fall
By the false faith of him I trusted most;
This, this All-Souls' day to my fearful soul
Is the determined respite of my wrongs:
That high All-Seer that I dallied with   20
Hath turn'd my feignèd prayer on my head
And given in earnest what I begg'd in jest.
Thus doth he force the swords of wicked men
To turn their own points on their masters' bosoms:
Now Margaret's curse is fallen upon my head;
"When he," quoth she, "shall split thy heart with sorrow,   26
Remember Margaret was a prophetess."
Come, sirs, convey me to the block of shame;
Wrong hath but wrong, and blame the due of blame.   [*Exeunt.*

Scene ii. *The camp near Tamworth.*

[*Enter* RICHMOND, OXFORD, BLUNT, HERBERT, *and others, with drum and colours.*]

RICHM. Fellows in arms, and my most loving friends,
Bruised underneath the yoke of tyranny,
Thus far into the bowels of the land
Have we march'd on without impediment;
And here receive we from our father Stanley   5
Lines of fair comfort and encouragement.
The wretched, bloody, and usurping boar,
That spoil'd your summer fields and fruitful vines,
Swills your warm blood like wash, and makes his trough
In your embowell'd bosoms, this foul swine   10
Lies now even in the centre of this isle,
Near to the town of Leicester, as we learn:
From Tamworth thither is but one day's march.
In God's name, cheerly on, courageous friends,
To reap the harvest of perpetual peace   15
By this one bloody trial of sharp war.
   OXF. Every man's conscience is a thousand swords,
To fight against that bloody homicide.
   HERB. I doubt not but his friends will fly to us.
   BLUNT. He hath no friends but who are friends for fear,   20
Which in his greatest need will shrink from him.
   RICHM. All for our vantage. Then, in God's name, march:
True hope is swift, and flies with swallow's wings;
Kings it makes gods, and meaner creatures kings.   [*Exeunt.*

Scene iii. *Bosworth Field.*

[*Enter* KING RICHARD *in arms, with* NORFOLK, *the* EARL OF SURREY, *and others.*]

K. RICH. Here pitch our tents, even here in Bosworth field.
My Lord of Surrey, why look you so sad?
   SUR. My heart is ten times lighter than my looks.

---

19. resolve, inform. Act. V, Scene i: 4 thy, that is, Henry VI.'s. 5. miscarried, perished. 10. All-Soul's day, November 2, the day on which the living are supposed to be able to communicate with the dead. 19. respite, limit; wrongs, wrong-doing. 20. that . . . with, i.e., with whom I trifled. Scene ii: 9. wash, i.e., hog-wash. 10. embowell'd, disembowled. 17. conscience, consciousness of right. 24. meaner, of lower rank.

K. RICH. My Lord of Norfolk,—
NOR.   Here, most gracious liege.
K. RICH. Norfolk, we must have knocks; ha!
  must we not?   5
NOR. We must both give and take, my gra-
  cious lord.
K. RICH. Up with my tent there! here will I
  lie to-night;
But where to-morrow? Well, all's one for
  that.
Who hath descried the number of the foe?
NOR. Six or seven thousand is their utmost
  power.   10
K. RICH. Why, our battalion trebles that ac-
  count:
Besides, the king's name is a tower of strength,
Which they upon the adverse party want.
Up with my tent there! Valiant gentlemen,
Let us survey the vantage of the field;   15
Call for some men of sound direction:
Let's want no discipline, make no delay;
For, lords, to-morrow is a busy day. [Exeunt.

[Enter, on the other side of the field, RICH-
  MOND, SIR WILLIAM BRANDON, OXFORD, and
  others. Some of the SOLDIERS pitch RICH-
  MOND's tent.]

RICHM. The weary sun hath made a golden
  set,
And, by the bright track of his fiery car, 20
Gives signal of a goodly day to-morrow.
Sir William Brandon, you shall bear my stand-
  ard.
Give me some ink and paper in my tent:
I'll draw the form and model of our battle,
Limit each leader to his several charge,   25
And part in just proportion our small strength.
My Lord of Oxford, you, Sir William Bran-
  don,
And you, Sir Walter Herbert, stay with me.
The Earl of Pembroke keeps his regiment:
Good Captain Blunt, bear my good-night to
  him,   30
And by the second hour in the morning
Desire the earl to see me in my tent:
Yet one thing more, good Blunt, before thou
  go'st,
Where is Lord Stanley quarter'd, dost thou
  know?

BLUNT. Unless I have mista'en his colours
  much,   35
Which well I am assured I have not done,
His regiment lies half a mile at least
South from the mighty power of the king.
  RICHM. If without peril it be possible,
Good Captain Blunt, bear my good-night to
  him,   40
And give him from me this most needful
  scroll.
BLUNT. Upon my life, my lord, I'll under-
  take it;
And so, God give you quiet rest to-night!
  RICHM. Good night, good Captain Blunt.
  Come, gentlemen,
Let us consult upon to-morrow's business: 45
In to our tent; the air is raw and cold.
            [They withdraw into the tent.

[Enter, to his tent, KING RICHARD, NORFOLK,
  RATCLIFF, CATESBY, and others.]

K. RICH. What is 't o'clock?
CATE.   It's supper-time, my lord;
It's nine o'clock.
K. RICH.   I will not sup tonight.
Give me some ink and paper.
What, is my beaver easier than it was?   50
And all my armour laid into my tent?
CATE. It is, my liege; and all things are in
  readiness.
K. RICH. Good Norfolk, hie thee to thy
  charge;
Use careful watch, choose trusty sentinels.
NOR. I go, my lord.   55
K. RICH. Stir with the lark to-morrow, gentle
  Norfolk.
NOR. I warrant you, my lord.   [Exit.
K. RICH. Catesby!
CATE. My lord?
K. RICH. Send out a pursuivant at arms
To Stanley's regiment; bid him bring his
  power   60
Before sunrising, lest his son George fall
Into the blind cave of eternal night.
            [Exit CATESBY.]
Fill me a bowl of wine. Give me a watch.
Saddle white Surrey for the field to-morrow.

Scene iii: 8. all's one for that, no matter for that, never
mind. 11. battalion, army. 16. direction, military judgment (executive ability). 25. limit, allot; several charge,
particular command. 29. keeps, stays with. 50. beaver,
face piece of a helmet; easier, made to fit more comfortably. 54. use careful watch, employ attentive guards.
57. I warrant you, i.e., I surely will. 59. pursuivant at
arms, attendant of a herald. 60. power, army. 63. watch,
watch-light, a candle marked in such a way as to keep
time.

Look that my staves be sound, and not too
   heavy.   65
Ratcliff!
  RAT. My lord?
  K. RICH. Saw'st thou the melancholy Lord
    Northumberland?
  RAT. Thomas the Earl of Surrey, and himself,
Much about cock-shut time, from troop to
   troop   70
Went through the army, cheering up the sol-
   diers.
  K. RICH. So, I am satisfied. Give me a bowl
   of wine:
I have not that alacrity of spirit,
Nor cheer of mind, that I was wont to have.
Set it down. Is ink and paper ready?   75
  RAT. It is, my lord.
  K. RICH.   Bid my guard watch; leave
  me.
Ratcliff, about the mid of night come to my
  tent
And help to arm me. Leave me, I say.

[*Exeunt* RATCLIFF *and the other* ATTENDANTS.

[*Enter* DERBY *to* RICHMOND *in his tent,* LORDS
    and others attending.]

  DER. Fortune and victory sit on thy helm!
  RICHM. All comfort that the dark night can
   afford   80
Be to thy person, noble father-in-law!
Tell me, how fares our loving mother?
  DER. I, by attorney, bless thee from thy
   mother,
Who prays continually for Richmond's good:
So much for that. The silent hours steal on, 85
And flaky darkness breaks within the east.
In brief,—for so the season bids us be,—
Prepare thy battle early in the morning,
And put thy fortune to the arbitrement
Of bloody strokes and mortal-staring war. 90
I, as I may—that which I would I cannot,—
With best advantage will deceive the time,
And aid thee in this doubtful shock of arms:
But on thy side I may not be too forward,
Lest, being seen, thy brother, tender George,
Be executed in his father's sight.   96
Farewell: the leisure and the fearful time

Cuts off the ceremonious vows of love
And ample interchange of sweet discourse,
Which so long sunder'd friends should dwell
   upon: 100
God give us leisure for these rites of love!
Once more, adieu: be valiant, and speed well!
  RICHM. Good lords, conduct him to his regi-
  ment:
I'll strive with troubled thoughts, to take a
  nap,
Lest leaden slumber peise me down to-mor-
  row,   105
When I would mount with wings of victory:
Once more, good night, kind lords and gentle-
  men.   [*Exeunt all but* RICHMOND.]
O Thou, whose captain I account myself,
Look on my forces with a gracious eye;
Put in their hands thy bruising irons of wrath,
That they may crush down with a heavy fall
The usurping helmets of our adversaries! 112
Make us thy ministers of chastisement,
That we may praise thee in the victory!
To thee I do commend my watchful soul, 115
Ere I let fall the windows of mine eyes:
Sleeping and waking, O, defend me still!
                           [*Sleeps.*

[*Enter the Ghost of* PRINCE EDWARD, *son to*
    HENRY *the Sixth.*]

  GHOST. [*To* RICHARD] Let me sit heavy on thy
  soul to-morrow!
Think, how thou stab'dst me in my prime of
  youth
At Tewksbury: despair, therefore, and die!
[*To* RICHMOND] Be cheerful, Richmond; for
  the wronged souls   121
Of butcher'd princes fight in thy behalf:
King Henry's issue, Richmond, comforts thee.

[*Enter the Ghost of* HENRY *the Sixth.*]

  GHOST [*To* RICHARD] When I was mortal, my
  anointed body
By thee was punched full of deadly holes: 125
Think on the Tower and me: despair, and die!
Harry the Sixth bids thee despair and die!
[*To* RICHMOND] Virtuous and holy, be thou
  conqueror!

---

65. staves, shafts of lances. 70. cock-shut time, sundown,
when chickens are shut up. 81. father-in-law, stepfather.
83. by attorney, as deputy. 86. And flaky . . . east, the
darkness in the east is broken with streaks of light.
87. seasons, time of day. 88. prepare thy battle, draw up
your troops in battle array. 89. arbitrement, decision,
judgment. 90. mortal-staring, causing death by a glance.
91. that . . . would, i.e., sleep. 92. With best advantage,
to best purpose; deceive the time, i.e., by pretending to
be on Richard's side. 97. leisure, lack of leisure. 105.
poise, weigh. 110. bruising irons, weapons. 119. prime,
early time. 123. issue, son.

Harry, that prophesied thou shouldst be king,
Doth comfort thee in thy sleep: live, and
  flourish!   130

[*Enter the Ghost of* CLARENCE.]

GHOST [*To* RICHARD] Let me sit heavy on thy
  soul to-morrow!
I, that was wash'd to death with fulsome wine,
Poor Clarence, by thy guile betrayed to death!
To-morrow in the battle think on me,
And fall thy edgeless sword: despair, and
  die!—   135
[*To* RICHMOND] Thou offspring of the house
  of Lancaster,
The wrongèd heirs of York do pray for thee:
Good angels guard thy battle! live, and flour-
  ish!

[*Enter the Ghosts of* RIVERS, GREY, *and*
VAUGHAN.]

GHOST OF R. [*To* RICHARD] Let me sit heavy
  on thy soul to-morrow,
Rivers, that died at Pomfret! despair, and die!
GHOST OF G. [*To* RICHARD] Think upon Grey,
  and let thy soul despair!   141
GHOST OF V. [*To* RICHARD] Think upon
  Vaughan, and, with guilty fear,
Let fall thy lance: despair, and die!
ALL. [*To* RICHMOND] Awake, and think our
  wrongs in Richard's bosom
Will conquer him! awake, and win the day!

[*Enter the Ghost of* HASTINGS.]

GHOST. [*To* RICHARD] Bloody and guilty,
  guiltily awake,   146
And in a bloody battle end thy days!
Think on Lord Hastings: despair, and die!
[*To* RICHMOND] Quiet untroubled soul, awake,
  awake!
Arm, fight, and conquer, for fair England's
  sake!   150

[*Enter the Ghosts of the two young* PRINCES.]

GHOSTS. [*To* RICHARD] Dream on thy cousins
  smother'd in the Tower:
Let us be lead within thy bosom, Richard,
And weigh thee down to ruin, shame, and
  death!
Thy nephews' souls bid thee despair and die!

[*To* RICHMOND] Sleep, Richmond, sleep in
  peace, and wake in joy;   155
Good angels guard thee from the boar's annoy!
Live, and beget a happy race of kings!
Edward's unhappy sons do bid thee flourish.

[*Enter the Ghost of* LADY ANNE.]

GHOST. [*To* RICHARD] Richard, thy wife, that
  wretched Anne thy wife,
That never slept a quiet hour with thee,   160
Now fills thy sleep with perturbations:
To-morrow in the battle think on me,
And fall thy edgeless sword: despair, and die!
[*To* RICHMOND] Thou quiet soul, sleep thou a
  quiet sleep;
Dream of success and happy victory!   165
Thy adversary's wife doth pray for thee.

[*Enter the Ghost of* BUCKINGHAM.]

GHOST [*To* RICHARD] The first was I that
  help'd thee to the crown;
The last was I that felt thy tyranny:
O, in the battle think on Buckingham,
And die in terror of thy guiltiness!   170
Dream on, dream on, of bloody deeds and
  death:
Fainting, despair; despairing, yield thy breath!
[*To* RICHMOND] I died for hope ere I could
  lend thee aid:
But cheer thy heart, and be thou not dismay'd:
God and good angels fight on Richmond's
  side;   175
And Richard falls in height of all his pride.
  [*The* GHOSTS *vanish.* KING RICHARD *starts
   out of his dream.*
K. RICH. Give me another horse: bind up my
  wounds.
Have mercy, Jesu!—Soft! I did but dream.
O coward conscience, how dost thou afflict
  me!
The lights burn blue. It is now dead midnight.
Cold fearful drops stand on my trembling
  flesh.   181
What do I fear? myself? there's none else by:
Richard loves Richard; that is, I am I.
Is there a murderer here? No. Yes, I am:
Then fly. What, from myself? Great reason
  why: 185
Lest I revenge. What, myself upon myself?
Alack, I love myself. Wherefore? for any good

---

132. wash'd to death, i.e., drowned in a butt of malmsey
wine; fulsome, nauseating. 135. fall, let fall. 151. cousins,
relatives. 156. bear's annoy, i.e., Richard's attack.

173. for hope, in hope, i.e., futile hope of being able to
help you. 180. lights burn blue, a sign that a ghost
was about.

That I myself have done unto myself?
O, no! alas, I rather hate myself
For hateful deeds committed by myself!   190
I am a villain: yet I lie, I am not.
Fool, of thyself speak well: fool, do not flatter.
My conscience hath a thousand several
    tongues,
And every tongue brings in a several tale,
And every tale condemns me for a villain.   195
Perjury, perjury, in the high'st degree;
Murder, stern murder, in the direst degree;
All several sins, all used in each degree,
Throng to the bar, crying all, Guilty! guilty!
I shall despair. There is no creature loves me;
And if I die, no soul shall pity me: 201
Nay, wherefore should they, since that I my-
    self
Find in myself no pity to myself?
Methought the souls of all that I had murder'd
Came to my tent; and every one did threat
To-morrow's vengeance on the head of Rich-
    ard.   206

[Enter RATCLIFF.]

RAT. My lord!
K. RICH. 'Zounds! who is there?
RAT. Ratcliff, my lord; 'tis I. The early vil-
    lage-cock
Hath twice done salutation to the morn;   210
Your friends are up, and buckle on their ar-
    mour.
K. RICH. O Ratcliff, I have dream'd a fearful
    dream!
What thinkest thou, will our friends prove all
    true?
RAT. No doubt, my lord.
K. RICH.   O Ratcliff, I fear, I fear,—
RAT. Nay, good my lord, be not afraid of
    shadows.   215
K. RICH. By the apostle Paul, shadows to-
    night
Have struck more terror to the soul of Richard
Than can the substance of ten thousand sol-
    diers
Armèd in proof, and led by shallow Rich-
    mond.
It is not yet near day. Come, go with me;   220
Under our tents I'll play the eaves-dropper,
To see if any mean to shrink from me.
                                    [Exeunt.

[Enter the LORDS to RICHMOND, sitting in his
                    tent.]

LORDS. Good morrow, Richmond!
RICHM. Cry mercy, lords and watchful gen-
    tlemen,   224
That you have ta'en a tardy sluggard here.
LORDS. How have you slept, my lord?
RICHM. The sweetest sleep, and fairest-bod-
    ing dreams
That ever enter'd in a drowsy head,
Have I since your departure had, my lords.
Methought their souls, whose bodies Richard
    murder'd,   230
Came to my tent, and cried on victory:
I promise you, my soul is very jocund
In the remembrance of so fair a dream.
How far into the morning is it, lords?
LORDS. Upon the stroke of four.   235
RICHM. Why, then 'tis time to arm and give
    direction.

His Oration to His Soldiers.

More than I have said, loving countrymen,
The leisure and enforcement of the time
Forbids to dwell upon: yet remember this,   239
God and our good cause fight upon our side;
The prayers of holy saints and wronged souls,
Like high-rear'd bulwarks, stand before our
    faces;
Richard except, those whom we fight against
Had rather have us win than him they follow.
For what is he they follow? truly, gentlemen,
A bloody tyrant and a homicide;   246
One raised in blood, and one in blood estab-
    lish'd;
One that made means to come by what he
    hath,
And slaughter'd those that were the means to
    help him;
A base foul stone, made precious by the foil
Of England's chair, where he is falsely set;   251
One that hath ever been God's enemy:
Then, if you fight against God's enemy,
God will in justice ward you as his soldiers;
If you do sweat to put a tyrant down,   255
You sleep in peace, the tyrant being slain;
If you do fight against your country's foes,

---

weapons. **224. Cry mercy,** I beg your pardon. **231. cried
on victory,** shouted "victory." **238. leisure,** lack of leisure;
enforcement, demands, exactions. **250. foil,** a thin piece
of metal placed beneath a jewel to set it off. **251. chair,**
throne. **254. ward,** protect.

193. several, separate. **198. used,** committed. **199. bar,**
i.e.. bar of a court of justice. **218. substance,** actual
bodies. **219. proof,** armor tested and found impervious to

Your country's fat shall pay your pains the
    hire;
If you do fight in safeguard of your wives,
Your wives shall welcome home the con-
    querors;   260
If you do free your children from the sword,
Your children's children quit it in your age.
Then, in the name of God and all these rights,
Advance your standards, draw your willing
    swords.
For me, the ransom of my bold attempt   265
Shall be this cold corpse on the earth's cold
    face;
But if I thrive, the gain of my attempt
The least of you shall share his part thereof.
Sound drums and trumpets boldly and cheer-
    fully;
God and Saint George! Richmond and vic-
    tory!   [*Exeunt.* 270

[*Re-enter* KING RICHARD, RATCLIFF, ATTENDANTS
    and FORCES.]

K. RICH. What said Northumberland as
    touching Richmond?
RAT. That he was never trained up in arms.
K. RICH. He said the truth: and what said
    Surrey then?
RAT. He smiled and said 'The better for our
    purpose.'
K. RICH. He was in the right; and so indeed
    it is.   [*Clock striketh.*] 275
Tell the clock there. Give me a calendar.
Who saw the sun to-day?
RAT.   Not I, my lord.
K. RICH. Then he disdains to shine; for by
    the book
He should have braved the east an hour ago:
A black day will it be to somebody.   280
Ratcliff!
RAT. My lord?
K. RICH. The sun will not be seen to-day;
The sky doth frown and lour upon our army.
I would these dewy tears were from the
    ground.   284
Not shine to-day! Why, what is that to me
More than to Richmond? for the selfsame
    heaven
That frowns on me looks sadly upon him.

[*Enter* NORFOLK.]

NOR. Arm, arm, my lord; the foe vaunts in
    the field.
K. RICH. Come, bustle, bustle; caparison my
    horse.
Call up Lord Stanley, bid him bring his power:
I will lead forth my soldiers to the plain, 291
And thus my battle shall be ordered:
My foreward shall be drawn out all in length,
Consisting equally of horse and foot;
Our archers shall be placed in the midst: 295
John Duke of Norfolk, Thomas Earl of Sur-
    rey,
Shall have the leading of this foot and horse.
They thus directed, we will follow
In the main battle, whose puissance on either
    side
Shall be well winged with our chiefest horse.
This, and Saint George to boot! What think'st
    thou, Norfolk?   301
NOR. A good direction, warlike sovereign.
This found I on my tent this morning.
                    [*He sheweth him a paper.*
K. RICH. [*Reads*] "Jockey of Norfolk, be not
    too bold,
For Dickon thy master is bought and sold."
A thing devised by the enemy.   306
Go, gentlemen, every man unto his charge:
Let not our babbling dreams affright our souls:
Conscience is but a word that cowards use,
Devised at first to keep the strong in awe: 310
Our strong arms be our conscience, swords
    our law.
March on, join bravely, let us to 't pell-mell;
If not to heaven, then hand in hand to hell.

His Oration to His Army.

What shall I say more than I have inferr'd?
Remember whom you are to cope withal; 315
A sort of vagabonds, rascals, and runaways,
A scum of Bretons, and base lackey peasants,
Whom their o'er-cloyed country vomits forth
To desperate ventures and assured destruction.
You sleeping safe, they bring to you unrest;
You having lands, and blest with beauteous
    wives,   321
They would restrain the one, distain the other.

258. fat, wealth. 262. quit, repay. 265. ransom, price of
failure. 276. tell, count the strokes. 278. book, calendar.
279. braved, made splendid. 288. vaunts, exults. 289.
caparison, put on the battle equipment. 293. foreward,
vanguard. 299. main battle, main body of troops. 300.
winged, flanked. 301. to boot, to give us aid besides.
304. Jockey, Jack. This couplet appears in the Chronicles.
305. Dickon, i.e., Richard; bought and sold, betrayed
through bribery. 308. babbling, senseless. 312. join, meet
the enemy. 314. inferr'd, stated. 317. lackey, servile,
obsequious. 318. o'er-cloyed, nauseated from over-eating.
322. distain, stain, defile.

And who doth lead them but a paltry fellow,
Long kept in Bretagne at our mother's cost?
A milk-sop, one that never in his life   325
Felt so much cold as over shoes in snow?
Let's whip these stragglers o'er the seas again;
Lash hence these overweening rags of France,
These famish'd beggars, weary of their lives;
Who, but for dreaming on this fond exploit,
For want of means, poor rats, had hang'd
    themselves: 331
If we be conquer'd, let men conquer us,
And not these bastard Bretons; whom our
    fathers
Have in their own land beaten, bobb'd, and
    thump'd,
And in record, left them the heirs of shame.
Shall these enjoy our lands? lie with our
    wives?   336
Ravish our daughters? [Drums afar off.]
    Hark! I hear their drum.
Fight, gentlemen of England! fight, bold
    yeomen!
Draw, archers, draw your arrows to the head!
Spur your proud horses hard, and ride in
    blood;   340
Amaze the welkin with your broken staves!

[Enter a MESSENGER.]

What says Lord Stanley? will he bring his
    power?
MESS. My lord, he doth deny to come.
K. RICH. Off with his son George's head!
NOR. My lord, the enemy is past the
    marsh: 345
After the battle let George Stanley die.
K. RICH. A thousand hearts are great within
    my bosom:
Advance our standards, set upon our foes;
Our ancient word of courage, fair Saint
    George,
Inspire us with the spleen of fiery dragons!
Upon them! Victory sits on our helms.   351
    [Exeunt.

SCENE IV. *Another part of the field.*

[*Alarum: excursions. Enter* NORFOLK *and
    forces fighting; to him* CATESBY.]

CATE. Rescue, my Lord of Norfolk, rescue,
    rescue!

The king enacts more wonders than a man,
Daring an opposite to every danger:
His horse is slain, and all on foot he fights,
Seeking for Richmond in the throat of
    death.   5
Rescue, fair lord, or else the day is lost!

[*Alarums. Enter* KING RICHARD.]

K. RICH. A horse! a horse! my kingdom for a
    horse!
CATE. Withdraw, my lord; I'll help you to
    a horse.
K. RICH. Slave, I have set my life upon a
    cast,
And I will stand the hazard of the die: 10
I think there be six Richmonds in the field;
Five have I slain to-day instead of him.
A horse! a horse! my kingdom for a horse!
    [*Exeunt.*

SCENE V. *Another part of the field.*

[*Alarum. Enter* RICHARD *and* RICHMOND; *they
    fight.* RICHARD *is slain. Retreat and flourish.
    Re-enter* RICHMOND, DERBY *bearing the
    crown, with divers other* LORDS.]

RICHM. God and your arms be praised, vic-
    torious friends;
The day is ours, the bloody dog is dead.
DER. Courageous Richmond, well hast thou
    acquit thee.
Lo, here, this long-usurped royalty
From the dead temples of this bloody wretch 5
Have I pluck'd off, to grace thy brows withal:
Wear it, enjoy it, and make much of it.
RICHM. Great God of heaven, say Amen to
    all!
But, tell me, is young George Stanley living?
DER. He is, my lord, and safe in Leicester
    town;   10
Whither, if it please you, we may now with-
    draw us.
RICHM. What men of name are slain on
    either side?
DER. John Duke of Norfolk, Walter Lord
    Ferrers,

324. mother's, Richmond's mother was not Richard's. The mistake occurs also in the Chronicles. Richmond was "kept" by his brother-in-law, Charles of Burgundy.

334. bobb'd, thrashed. 341. Amaze . . . staves, frighten the sky with the sound of breaking lances. 343. deny, refuse. 350. spleen, anger. Scene iv: s.d. excursions, sounds of battle. 3. Daring . . . danger, boldly meeting every danger of battle. 10. I . . . die, I will take the luck that the turn of the die brings. Scene v: 3. well . . . thee, you have given a good account of yourself. 12. name, high rank.

Sir Robert Brakenbury, and Sir William
    Brandon.

RICHM. Inter their bodies as becomes their
    births: 15
Proclaim a pardon to the soldiers fled
That in submission will return to us:
And then, as we have ta'en the sacrament,
We will unite the white rose and the red:
Smile heaven upon this fair conjunction,   20
That long have frown'd upon their enmity!
What traitor hears me, and says not amen?
England hath long been mad, and scarr'd
    herself;
The brother blindly shed the brother's blood,
The father rashly slaughter'd his own son, 25
The son, compell'd, been butcher to the sire:
All this divided York and Lancaster,

18. as . . . sacrament, as have sworn upon the sacrament
to do. 35. Abate the edge, blunt the swords. 36. reduce,
bring back. 38. increase, coming prosperity.

Divided in their dire division,
O, now, let Richmond and Elizabeth,
The true succeeders of each royal house, 30
By God's fair ordinance conjoin together!
And let their heirs, God, if thy will be so,
Enrich the time to come with smooth-faced
    peace,
With smiling plenty and fair prosperous days!
Abate the edge of traitors, gracious Lord, 35
That would reduce these bloody days again,
And make poor England weep in streams of
    blood!
Let them not live to taste this land's increase
That would with treason wound this fair
    land's peace!
Now civil wounds are stopp'd, peace lives
    again: 40
That she may long live here, God say amen!
                                  [*Exeunt.*

From The History of King Richard III[1]

George, Duke of Clarence, was a goodly noble prince, and at all points fortunate, if either his own ambition had not set him against his brother, or the envy of his enemies his brother against him. For were it by the queen and the lords of her blood which highly maligned the king's kindred (as women commonly not of malice but of nature hate them whom their husbands love) or were it a proud appetite of the duke himself intending to be king, at the leastwise heinous treason was there laid to his charge, and finally, were he faulty were he faultless, attainted was he by parliament and judged to the death, and thereupon hastily drowned in a butt of Malmsey, whose death King Edward (albeit he commanded it) when he wist it was done, piteously bewailed and sorrowfully repented.

Richard the third son, of whom we now entreat, was in wit and courage equal with either of them, in body and prowess far under them both, little of stature, ill featured of limbs, crook backed, his left shoulder much higher than his right, hard favored of visage . . . he was malicious, wrathful, envious and, from before his birth, ever froward. It is for truth reported, that the duchess his mother had so much ado in her travail, that she could not be delivered of him uncut: and that he came into the world with the feet forward . . . and (as the fame runneth) also not untoothed, whether men of hatred report above the truth, or else that nature changed her course in his beginning, which in the course of his life many things unnaturally committed. None evil captain was he in the war, as to which his disposition was more meetly than for peace. Sundry victories had he, and sometime overthrows, but never in default, as for his own person, either of hardiness or politic order; free was he called of dispense, and somewhat above his power liberal; with large

gifts he got him unsteadfast friendship, for which he was fain to pillage and spoil in other places, and get him steadfast hatred. He was close and secret, a deep dissumulator, lowly of countenance, arrogant of heart, outwardly companionable where he inwardly hated, not letting to kiss whom he thought to kill; dispiteous and cruel, not for evil will always, but often for ambition, and either for the surety or increase of his estate. Friend and foe was much what indifferent, where his advantage grew; he spared no man's death whose life withstood his purpose. He slew with his own hands King Henry the Sixth, being prisoner in the Tower, as men constantly say, and that without commandment or knowledge of the king [Edward IV], who would undoubtedly, if he had intended that thing, have appointed that butcherly office to some other than his own born brother. Some wise men also ween that his drift, covertly conveyed, lacked not in helping forth his brother Clarence to his death: which he resisted openly, howbeit somewhat (as men deemed) more faintly than he that was heartily minded to his welfare. And they that thus deem, think that he long time in King Edward's life forethought to be king in case that the king his brother (whose life he looked that evil diet should shorten) should happen to decease (as indeed he did) while his children were young. And they deem, that for this intent he was glad of his brother's death the Duke of Clarence, whose life must needs have hindered him so intending, whether the same Duke of Clarence had kept him true to his nephew the young king, or enterprised to be king himself. But of all this point there is no certainty, and whoso divineth upon conjectures may as well shoot too far as too short. . . .

But now to return to the course of this history, were it that the Duke of Gloucester had of old foreminded this conclusion, or was now at first thereunto moved and put in hope by the occasion of the tender age of the

[1] In *The Works of Sir Thomas More* (London, 1557).

young princes his nephews (as opportunity and likelihood of speed putteth a man in courage of that he never intended), certain it is that he contrived their destruction, with the usurpation of the regal dignity upon himself. And for as much as he well wist and helped to maintain a long continued grudge and heart-burning between the queen's kindred and the king's blood, either party envying the other's authority, he now thought that their division should be (as it was indeed) a furtherly beginning to the pursuit of his intent, and a sure ground for the foundation of all his building if he might first, under the pretext of revenging of old displeasure, abuse the anger and ignorance of the one party, to the destruction of the other: and then win to his purpose as many as he could: and those that could not be won, might be lost ere they looked therefore. For of one thing he was certain, that if his intent were perceived, he should soon have made peace between both parties with his own blood.

King Edward in his life, albeit that this dissension between his friends somewhat irked him, yet in his good health he somewhat the less regarded it, because he thought whatsoever business should fall between them, himself should always be able to rule both the parties. But in his last sickness, when he perceived his natural strength so sore enfeebled that he despaired all recovery, then . . . well foreseeing that many harms might grow by their debate, while the youth of his children should lack discretion of themselves and good counsel of their friends, of which either party should counsel for their own commodity and rather by pleasant advice to win themselves favor, than by profitable advertisement to do the children good, he called some of them before him that were at variance, and in especial the Lord Marquis Dorset, the queen's son by her first husband, and Richard Lord Hastings, a nobleman, then lord chamberlain, against whom the queen specially grudged, for the great favor the king bore him, and also for that she thought him secretly familiar with the king in wanton company. Her kindred also bore him sore, as well for that the king had made him captain of Calais (which office Lord Rivers, brother to the queen, claimed of the king's former promise) as for diverse other great gifts which he received, that they looked for. When these lords with diverse other of both the parties were come in presence, the king lifting up himself and underset with pil-

lows, as it is reported on this wise said unto them.

"My lords, my dear kinsmen and allies, in what plight I lie you see, and I feel. By which the less while I look to live with you, the more deeply am I moved to care in what case I leave you, for such as I leave you, such be my children like to find you. Which if they should (that God forbid) find you at variance, might hap to fall themselves at war ere their discretion would serve to set you at peace. You see their youth, of which I reckon the only surety to rest in your concord. For it sufficeth not that all you love them, if each of you hate the other. If they were men, your faithfulness happily would suffice. But childhood must be maintained by men's authority, and slipper youth underpropped with elder counsel, which neither they can have, but you give it, nor you give it, if you agree not. For where each labors to break that the other makes and, for hatred of each of other's person, impugns each other's counsel, there must it needs be long ere any good conclusion go forward. . . .

"But if you among yourselves in a child's reign fall at debate, many a good man shall perish and haply he too, and you too, ere this land find peace again. Wherefore in these last words that ever I look to speak with you, I exhort you and require you all, for the love that you have ever borne to me, for the love that I have ever borne to you, for the love that our Lord beareth to us all, from this time forward, all griefs forgotten, each of you love the other. Which I verily trust you will, if you anything earthly regard, either God or your king, affinity or kindred, this realm, your own country, or your own surety."

And there withal the king no longer enduring to sit up, laid him down on his right side, his face toward them: and none was there present that could refrain from weeping. But the lords comforting him with as good words as they could, and answering for the time as they thought to stand with his pleasure, there in his presence (as by their words appeared) each forgave other, and joined their hands together, when (as it after appeared by their deeds) their hearts were far asunder.

As soon as the king was departed, the noble prince his son drew toward London, which at the time of his decease, kept his household at Ludlow in Wales. Which country being far off from the law and recourse to justice, was begun to be far out of good will and waxed wild, robbers and reivers walking at liberty uncorrected. And for this reason the prince was in the life of his father sent thither, to the end that the authority of his presence should refrain evil disposed persons from the boldness of their former outrages. To the governance and ordering of this young prince . . . was there appointed Sir Anthony Woodville, Lord Rivers and brother unto the queen, a right honorable man, as valiant of hand as politic in counsel. Adjoined were there unto him other of the same party, and in effect every one as he was nearest of kin unto the queen, so was planted next about the prince. That drift by the queen was not unwisely devised, whereby her blood might of youth be rooted in the prince's favor, the Duke of Gloucester turned unto their destruction, and upon that ground set the foundation of all his unhappy building. For whomsoever he perceived either at variance with them, or bearing himself their favor, he broke unto them, some by mouth, some by writing and secret messengers, that it neither was reason nor in anywise to be suffered, that the young king, their master and kinsman, should be in the hands and custody of his mother's kindred, sequestered in manner from their company and attendance. . . .

With these words and writings and such other, the Duke of Gloucester soon set afire them that were of themselves easy to kindle, and in especial two, Edward, Duke of Buckingham, and Richard Lord Hastings and chamberlain, both men of honor and of great power. The one by long succession from his ancestry, the other by his office and the king's favor. These two, not bearing each other so much love, as hatred both unto the queen's party, in this point accorded together with the Duke of Gloucester, that they would utterly remove from the king's company all his mother's friends, under the name of their enemies. Upon this concluded, the Duke of Gloucester understanding that the lords which at that time were about the king intended to bring him up to his coronation, accompanied with such power of their friends, that it should be hard for him to bring his purpose to pass, without the gathering and great assembly of people and in manner of open war, whereof the end he wished was dubious, and in which the king being on their side, his part should have the face and name of a rebellion; he secretly therefore, by divers means, caused the queen to be persuaded and brought in mind, that it neither were needed, and also should be jeopardous, the king to come up

strong. For whereas now every lord loved other, and none other thing studied upon, but about the coronation and honor of the king; if the lords of her kindred should assemble in the king's name many people, they should give the lords, atwixt whom and them had been sometime debate, to fear and suspect, lest they should gather these people, not for the king's safeguard, whom no man impugned, but for their destruction, having more regard to their old variance, than their new atonement. For which cause they should assemble on the other party many people again for their defense, whose power she wist well stretched far. And thus should all the realm fall on a roar. And of all the hurt that thereof should ensue, which was likely not to be little, and the most harm there like to fall where she least would, all the world would put her and her kindred in the wrong, and say that they had unwisely, and untruly also, broken the amity and peace that the king her husband so prudently made between his kin and hers in his deathbed, and which the other party faithfully observed.

The queen being in this wise persuaded, such word sent unto her son, and unto her brother being about the king, and over that the Duke of Gloucester himself, and other lords the chief of his band, wrote unto the king so reverently and to the queen's friends there so lovingly, that they nothing earthly mistrusting, brought the king up in great haste, not in good speed, with a sober company. Now was the king on his way to London gone from Northampton, when these Dukes of Gloucester and Buckingham came thither. Where remained behind, Lord Rivers, the king's uncle, intending on the morrow to follow the king, and be with him at Stony Stratford [eleven] miles thence, early ere he departed. So was there made that night much friendly cheer between these dukes and Lord Rivers a great while. But incontinent after they were openly with great courtesy departed, and Lord Rivers lodged, the dukes secretly, with a few of their most privy friends, set them down in council wherein they spent a great part of the night. And at their rising in the dawning of the day, they sent about privily to their servants in their inns and lodgings about, giving them commandment to make themselves shortly ready, for their lords were to horse. Upon which messages, many of their folk were attendant when many of Lord Rivers' servants were unready. Now had these dukes taken also into their custody the keys of the inn, that none should pass forth without their license. And over this in the highway toward Stony Stratford where the king lay, they had bestowed certain of their folk, that should send back again, and compel to return, any man that were gotten out of Northampton toward Stony Stratford, till they should give other license. For as much as the dukes themselves intended, for the show of their diligence, to be the first that should that day attend upon the king's Highness out of that town; thus bore they folk in hand. But when Lord Rivers understood the gates closed, and the ways on every side beset, neither his servants nor himself suffered to go out, perceiving well so great a thing without his knowledge not begun for naught, comparing this manner present with this last night's cheer, in so few hours so great a change marvellously misliked. Howbeit since he could not get away, and keep himself close he would not, lest he should seem to hide himself for some secret fear of his own fault, whereof he saw no such cause in himself; he determined upon the surety of his own conscience, to go boldly to them, and inquire what this matter might mean. Whom as soon as they saw, they began to quarrel with him, and say that he intended to set distance between the king and them, and to bring them to confusion, but it should not lie in his power. And when he began (as he was a very well spoken man) in goodly wise to excuse himself, they tarried not the end of his answer, but shortly took him and put him in ward, and that done, forthwith went to horseback, and took the way to Stony Stratford where they found the king with his company ready to leap on horseback and depart forward, to leave that lodging for them, because it was too straight for both companies. And as soon as they came in his presence, they alighted down with all their company about them. To whom the Duke of Buckingham said, "Go afore, gentlemen and yeomen, keep your rooms." And thus in a goodly array they came to the king, and on their knees in very humble wise saluted his Grace, which received them in very joyous and amiable manner, nothing earthly knowing nor mistrusting as yet. But even by and by in his presence they picked a quarrel with Lord Richard Gray, the king's other brother by his mother, saying that he, with the Lord Marquis his brother and Lord Rivers his uncle, had compassed to rule the king and the realm, and to set variance among the states, and to subdue and destroy the noble blood of the realm. Toward the accomplishing whereof, they said that the Lord Marquis had

entered into the Tower of London, and thence taken out the king's treasure, and sent men to the sea. All which things these dukes wist well were done for good purposes and necessary by the whole council at London, saving that somewhat they must say. Unto which words the king answered, "What my brother Marquis has done I cannot say. But in good faith I dare well answer for my uncle Rivers and my brother here, that they be innocent of any such matters."

"Yea, my liege," quoth the Duke of Buckingham, "they have kept their dealing in these matters far from the knowledge of your good Grace." And forthwith they arrested Lord Richard and Sir Thomas Vaughan, knight, in the king's presence, and brought the king and all back unto Northampton, where they took again further counsel. And there they sent away from the king whom it pleased them, and set new servants about him, such as liked better them than him. At which dealing he wept and was nothing content, but it booted not. And at dinner the Duke of Gloucester sent a dish from his own table to Lord Rivers, praying him to be of good cheer, all should be well enough. And he thanked the duke and prayed the messenger to bear it to his nephew Lord Richard with the same message for his comfort, who he thought had more need of comfort, as one to whom such adversity was strange. But himself had been all his days inured therewith, and therefore could bear it the better. But for all this comfortable courtesy of the Duke of Gloucester he sent Lord Rivers and Lord Richard with Sir Thomas Vaughan into the North country into divers places to prison, and afterward all to Pontefract, where they were in conclusion beheaded.

In this wise the Duke of Gloucester took upon himself the order and governance of the young king, whom with much honor and humble reverence he conveyed upward toward the city. But anon the tidings of this matter came hastily to the queen, a little before the midnight following, and that in the sorest wise, that the king her son was taken, her brother, her son and her other friends arrested, and sent no man knew whither, to be done with God wot what. With which tidings the queen in great fright and heaviness, bewailing her child's reign, her friends' mischance, and her own misfortune, damning the time that ever she dissuaded the gathering of power about the king, got herself in all the haste possible with her younger son and her daughters out of the palace of Westminster in which she then lay, into the sanctuary, lodging herself and her company there in the abbott's place.

Now came there one, in likewise not long after midnight, from the lord chamberlain unto the Archbishop of York then Chancellor of England, to his place not far from Westminster. And for that he showed his servants that he had tidings of so great importance, that his master gave him in charge not to forbear his rest, they letted not to wake him, nor he to admit this messenger in to his bedside. Of whom he heard that these dukes were gone back with the king's Grace from Stony Stratford unto Northampton. "Notwithstanding, sir," quoth he, "my lord sends your Lordship word that there is no fear. For he assures you that all shall be well."

"I assure him," quoth the archbishop, "be it as well as it will, it will never be so well as we have seen it." And thereupon by and by after the messenger departed, he caused in all haste all his servants to be called up, and so with his own household about him, and every man weaponed, he took the Great Seal with him, and came yet before day unto the queen. About whom he found much heaviness, rumble, haste and business, carriage and conveyance of her stuff into sanctuary, chests, coffers, packs, fardels, trusses, all on men's backs, no man unoccupied, some lading, some going, some discharging, some coming for more, some breaking down the walls to bring in the next way, and some yet drew to them that helped to carry a wrong way. The queen herself sat alone alow on the rushes all desolate and dismayed, whom the archbishop comforted in the best manner he could, showing her that he trusted the matter was nothing so sore as she took it for. And that he was put in good hope and out of fear by the message sent him from the lord chamberlain. "Ah, woe worth him," quoth she, "for he is one of them that laboreth to destroy me and my blood."

"Madame," quoth he, "be ye of good cheer. For I assure you if they crown any other king than your son, whom they now have with them, we shall on the morrow crown his brother whom you have here with you. And here is the Great Seal, which in likewise as that noble prince your husband delivered it unto me, so here I deliver it unto you, to the use and behoof of your son." And therewith he betook her the Great Seal, and departed home again, yet in the dawning of the day. By which time he might in his chamber window see all the Thames full of boats of the Duke of Gloucester's servants, watching that

no man should go to sanctuary, nor none could pass unsearched. Then was there great commotion and murmur as well in other places about, as specially in the city, the people diversely divining upon this dealing. And some lords, knights, and gentlemen either for favor of the queen, or for fear of themselves, assembled in sundry companies, and went flockmeal in harness; and many also, for that they reckoned this demeanor attempted not so specially against the other lords, as against the king himself in the disturbance of his coronation. But then by and by the lords assembled together at ———. Toward which meeting, the Archbishop of York fearing that it would be ascribed (as it was indeed) to his overmuch lightness, that he so suddenly had yielded up the Great Seal to the queen, to whom the custody thereof nothing pertained, without especial commandment of the king, secretly sent for the seal again, and brought it with him after the customary manner. And at this meeting Lord Hastings, whose truth toward the king no man doubted nor needed to doubt, persuaded the lords to believe that the Duke of Gloucester was sure and fastly faithful to his prince, and that Lord Rivers and Lord Richard with the other knights were, for matters attempted by them against the Dukes of Gloucester and Buckingham, put under arrest for their surety, not for the king's jeopardy; and that they were also in safeguard, and there no longer should remain, than till the matter was, not by the dukes only, but also by all the other lords of the king's council, indifferently examined, and by other discretions ordered, and either judged or appeased. But one thing he advised them beware, that they judged not the matter too quickly, ere they knew the truth, nor turning their private grudges into the common hurt, irritating and provoking men into anger, and disturbing the king's coronation, toward which the dukes were coming up, that they might peradventure bring the matter so far out of joint, that it should never be brought in frame again. . . .

With these persuasions of Lord Hastings, whereof part himself believed, of part he knew the contrary, these commotions were somewhat appeased. But specially by that that the Dukes of Gloucester and Buckingham were so near, and came so shortly on with the king, in none other manner, with no other voice or semblance, than to his coronation, causing the fame to be blown about, that these lords and knights which were taken had contrived the destruction of the Dukes of Gloucester and Buckingham, and of other noble blood of the realm, to the end that themselves would alone demean and govern the king at their pleasure. And for the colorable proof thereof, such of the dukes' servants as rode with the carts of their stuff that were taken (among which stuff no marvel though some were harness, which at the breaking up of that household must needs either be brought away or cast away) they showed unto the people all the way as they went, "Lo, here be the barrels of harness that these traitors had privily conveyed in their carriage to destroy the noble lords withal." This device, albeit that it made the matter to wise men more unlikely, well perceiving that the intenders of such a purpose would rather have had their harness on their backs than have bound them up in barrels, yet much part of the common people were therewith very well satisfied, and said it were alms to hang them.

When the king approached near to the city, Edmund Sha, goldsmith, then mayor, with William White and John Mathew sheriffs, and all the other aldermen in scarlet, with five hundred horse of the citizens in violet, received him reverently at Hornsey, and riding from thence, accompanied him into the city, which he entered the fourth day of May, the first and last year of his reign. But the Duke of Gloucester bore him in open sight so reverently to the prince, with all semblance of lowliness, that from the great obloquy in which he was so late before, he was suddenly fallen in so great trust, that at the council next assembled, he was made the only man chosen and thought most meet to be protector of the king and his realm, so that (were it destiny or were it folly) the lamb was betaken to the wolf to keep. . . .

Now all were it so that the protector so sore thirsted for the finishing of that he had begun, that thought every day a year till it were achieved, yet durst he no further attempt as long as he had but half his prey in his hand; well witting that if he deposed the one brother, all the realm would fall to the other, if he either remained in sanctuary, or should haply be shortly conveyed to his further liberty. Wherefore incontinent at the next meeting of the lords at the council, he proposed unto them, that it was a heinous deed of the queen, and proceeding of great malice toward the king's councilors, that she should keep in sanctuary the king's brother from him, whose special pleasure and comfort were to

have his brother with him. And that by her done to no other intent, but to bring all the lords in obloquy and murmur of the people. As though they were not to be trusted with the king's brother, that by the assent of the nobles of the land were appointed, as the king's nearest friends, to the tuition of his own royal person. "The prosperity whereof standeth," quoth he, "not all in keeping from enemies or ill viand, but partly also in recreation and moderate pleasure; which he cannot in this tender youth take in the company of ancient persons, but in the familiar conversation of those that be neither far under nor far above his age, and natheless of estate convenient to accompany his noble majesty. Wherefore with whom rather than with his own brother? And if any man think this consideration (which I think no man thinketh that loveth the king) let him consider that sometimes without small things greater cannot stand. And verily it redoundeth greatly to the dishonor both of the king's highness and of all us that be about his Grace, to have it run in every man's mouth, not in this realm only, but also in other lands (as evil words walk far) that the king's brother should be fain to keep sanctuary. . . .

"Wherefore me thinketh it were not worst to send unto the queen, for the redress of this matter, some honorable trusty man, such as both tendereth the king's weal, and the honor of his council, and is also in favor and credence with her. For all which considerations, none seemeth to me more meetly than our reverend father here present, my Lord Cardinal, who may in this matter do most good of any man, if it please him to take the pain. Which I doubt not of his goodness he will not refuse, for the king's sake and ours, and wealth of the young duke himself, the king's most honorable brother, and after my sovereign lord himself, my most dear nephew; considered that thereby shall be ceased the slanderous rumor and obloquy now going and the hurts avoided that thereof might ensue, and much rest and quiet grow to all the realm. And if she be perchance so obstinate, and so precisely set upon her own will, that neither his wise and faithful advertisement can move her, nor any man's reason content her; then shall we by my advice, by the king's authority, fetch him out of that prison, and bring him to his noble presence, in whose continual company he shall be so well cherished and so honorably entreated, that all the world shall, to our honor and her reproach, perceive that it was only malice, frowardness, or folly, that caused her to keep him there. This is my mind in this matter for this time, except any of your lordships anything perceive to the contrary. For never shall I by God's grace so wed myself to my own will, but that I shall be ready to change it upon your better advice."

When the protector had said, all the council affirmed that the motion was good and reasonable, and to the king and the duke his brother honorable, and a thing that should cease great murmur in the realm, if the mother might be by good means induced to deliver him. Which thing the Archbishop of York, whom they all agreed also to be thereto most convenient, took upon him to move her, and therein to do his uttermost devoir. Howbeit if she could be in no wise entreated with her good will to deliver him, then thought he and such others as were of the spirituality present, that it were not in any wise to be attempted to take him out against her will. For it would be a thing that should turn to the great grudge of all men, and high displeasure of God, if the privilege of that holy place should now be broken. . . . "And therefore," quoth the Archbishop of York, "God forbid that any man should, for anything earthly, enterprise to break the immunity and liberty of that sacred sanctuary, that has been the safeguard of so many a good man's life. And I trust," quoth he, "with God's grace, we shall not need it. But for any manner need, I would not we should do it. I trust that she shall be with reason contented, and all things in good manner obtained. And if it happen that I bring it not so to pass, yet shall I toward it so far forth do my best, that you shall all well perceive that no lack of my devoir, but the mother's dread and womanish fear shall be the let."

"Womanish fear, nay, womanish frowardness," quoth the Duke of Buckingham. "For I dare take it upon my soul, she well knows she need no such thing to fear, either for her son or for herself. For as for her, here is no man that will be at war with women. Would God some of the men of her kin were women too, and then should all be soon in rest. Howbeit there is none of her kin the less loved, for that they be her kin, but for their own evil deserving. And natheless if we loved neither her nor her kin, yet were there no cause to think that we should hate the king's noble brother, to whose Grace we ourself be of kin. . . . And we all (I think) content, that both be with her, if she come thence and bide in such place where they may with their honor be. . . .

"And if no body may be taken out of sanctuary that says he will bide there; then if a child will take sanctuary, because he fears to go to school, his master must let him alone. And as simple as that sample is, yet is there less reason in our case, than in that. For therein though it be a childish fear, yet is there at the leastwise some fear. And herein is there none at all. And verily I have often heard of sanctuary men, but I never heard before of sanctuary children. And therefore as for the conclusion of my mind, whoso may have deserved to need it, if they think it for their surety, let them keep it. But he can be no sanctuary man, that neither has wisdom to desire it, nor malice to deserve it, whose life or liberty can by no lawful process stand in jeopardy. And he that taketh one out of sanctuary to do him good, I say plainly that he breaketh no sanctuary."

When the duke had done, the temporal men wholly, and good part of the spiritual also, thinking no earthly hurt meant toward the young babe, condescended in effect, that if he were not delivered, he should be fetched. . . . And the Lord Cardinal, leaving the protector with the council in the star chamber, departed into the sanctuary to the queen, with divers other lords with him, were it for the respect of his honor, or that she should by presence of so many perceive that his errand was not one man's mind, or were it for that the protector intended not in this matter to trust any one man alone, or else that if she finally was determined to keep him, some of that company had haply secret instruction incontinent, maugre his mind, to take him and to leave her no respite to convey him, which she was likely to mind after this matter broken to her, if her time would in any wise serve her.

When the queen and these lords were come together in presence, the Lord Cardinal showed unto her that it was thought unto the protector and unto the whole council, that her keeping of the king's brother in that place was the thing which highly sounded, not only to the great rumor of the people and their obloquy, but also to the importable grief and displeasure of the king's royal majesty. To whose grace it were as singular comfort to have his natural brother in company, as it was their both dishonor, and all theirs and hers also, to suffer him in sanctuary. As though the one brother stood in danger and peril of the other. And he showed her that the council therefore had sent him unto her, to require her the delivery of him, that he might be brought unto the king's presence at his liberty, out of that place which they reckoned as a prison. And there should he be demeaned according to his estate. And she in this doing should both do great good to the realm, pleasure to the council and profit to herself, succor to her friends that were in distress, and over that (which he wist well she specially tendered) not only great comfort and honor to the king, but also to the young duke himself, whose both great welfare it were to be together. . . .

"My lord," quoth the queen, "I say not nay, but that it were very convenient that this gentleman whom you require were in the company of the king his brother. And in good faith me thinks it were as great commodity to them both, as for yet awhile, to be in the custody of their mother, the tender age considered of the elder of them both, but specially the younger, which besides his infancy that also needs good looking to, has a while been so sore diseased, vexed with sickness, and is so newly rather a little mended than well recovered, that I dare put no person earthly in trust with his keeping but myself only. . . .

"Wherefore here intend I to keep him, since man's law serves the guardian to keep the infant. The law of nature will the mother keep her child. God's law privileges the sanctuary, and the sanctuary my son, sith I fear to put him in the protector's hands that has his brother already, and were, if both failed, inheritor to the crown. The cause of my fear hath no man to do to examine. And yet fear I no further than the law fears which, as learned men tell me, forbids every man the custody of them, by whose death he may inherit less land than a kingdom. I can no more, but whosoever he be that breaketh this holy sanctuary; I pray God shortly send him need of sanctuary, when he may not come to it. For taken out of sanctuary would I not my mortal enemy were."

The Lord Cardinal perceiving that the queen waxed ever the longer the farther off, and also that she began to kindle and chafe, and speak sore biting words against the protector, and such as he neither believed, and was also loath to hear, he said unto her for a final conclusion, that he would no longer dispute the matter. But if she were content to deliver the duke to him and to the other lords there present, he durst lay his own body and soul both in pledge, not only for his surety but also for his estate. . . .

The queen with these words stood a good while in a great study. And for as much her seemed the cardinal more ready to depart, than some of the remnant, and the protector himself ready at hand, so that she verily thought she could not keep him there, but that he should incontinent be taken thence: and to convey him elsewhere, neither had she time to serve her, nor place determined, nor persons appointed, all things unready this message came on her so suddenly, nothing less looking for than to have him fetched out of sanctuary, which she thought to be now beset in such places about, that he could not be conveyed out untaken, and partly as she thought it might fortune her fear to be false, so well she wist it was either needless or bootless: wherefore if she should needs go from him, she deemed it best to deliver him. And over that, of the cardinal's faith she nothing doubted, nor of some other lords neither, whom she saw there. Which as she feared lest they might be deceived; so was she well assured they would not be corrupted. Then thought she it should yet make them the more wary to look to him, and the more circumspectly to see to his surety, if she with her own hands betook him to them of trust. And at the last she took the young duke by the hand, and said unto the lords, "My lord," quoth she, "and all my lords, I neither am so unwise to mistrust your wits, nor so suspicious to mistrust your troths. Of which thing I propose to make you such a proof, as if either or both lacked in you, might turn both me to great sorrow, the realm to much harm, and you to great reproach. For lo, here is," quoth she, "this gentleman, whom I doubt not but I could here keep safe if I would, whatsoever any man say. And I doubt not also but there be some abroad so deadly enemies unto my blood, that if they wist where any of it lay in their own body, they would let it out. We have also had experience that the desire of a kingdom knows no kindred. The brother hath been the brother's bane. And may the nephews be sure of their uncle? Each of these children is the other's defense while they be asunder, and each of their lives lies in the other's body. Keep one safe and both be sure, and nothing for them both more perilous, than to be both in one place. . . . Farewell, my own sweet son, God send you good keeping, let me kiss you once yet ere you go, for God knows when we shall kiss together again." And therewith she kissed him, and blessed him, turned her back and wept and went her way, leaving the child weeping as fast. When the Lord Cardinal and these other lords with him, had received this young duke, they brought him into the star chamber where the protector took him in his arms and kissed him with these words, "Now welcome, my lord, even with all my very heart." And he said in that of likelihood as he thought. Thereupon forthwith they brought him to the king his brother into the bishop's palace at [St.] Paul's, and from thence through the city honorably into the Tower, out of which after that day they never came abroad.

When the protector had both the children in his hands, he opened himself more boldly, both to certain other men, and also chiefly to the Duke of Buckingham. Although I know that many thought that this duke was privy to all the protector's counsel, even from the beginning, and some of the protector's friends said that the duke was the first mover of the protector to this matter, sending a privy messenger unto him, straight after King Edward's death. But others again, which knew better the subtle wit of the protector, deny that he ever opened his enterprise to the duke, until he had brought to pass the things before rehearsed. But when he had imprisoned the queen's kinsfolk, and gotten both her sons into his own hands, then he opened the rest of his purpose with less fear to them whom he thought meet for the matter, and specially to the duke; who being won to his purpose, he thought his strength more than half increased. The matter was broken unto the duke by subtle folks, and such as were their craft masters in the handling of such wicked devices; who declared unto him, that the young king was offended with him for his kinsfolk's sakes, and that if he were ever able, he would revenge them. Who would prick him forward thereunto, if they escaped (for they would remember their imprisonment) or else if they were put to death, without doubt the young king would be careful for their deaths, whose imprisonment was grievous unto him. And that with repenting the duke should nothing avail; for there was no way left to redeem his offense by benefits; but he should sooner destroy himself than save the king, who with his brother and his kinsfolk he saw in such places imprisoned, as the protector might with a beck destroy them all; and that it were no doubt but he would do it indeed, if there were

any new enterprise attempted. And that it was likely that as the protector had provided privy guards for himself, so had he spies for the duke, and trains to catch him, if he should be against him, and that peradventure from them whom he least suspected. For the state of things and the dispositions of men were then such, that a man could not well tell whom he might trust, or whom he might fear. These things and such like, being beaten into the duke's mind, brought him to that point, that where he had repented the way that he had entered, yet would he go forth in the same; and since he had once begun, he would stoutly go through. And therefore to this wicked enterprise, which he believed could not be avoided, he bent himself and went through; and determined that since the common mischief could not be amended, he would turn it as much as he might to his own commodity.

Then it was agreed that the protector should have the duke's aid to make him king, and that the protector's only lawful son should marry the duke's daughter, and that the protector should grant him the quiet possession of the Earldom of Hereford, which he claimed as his inheritance and could never obtain in King Edward's time. Besides these requests of the duke, the protector of his own mind promised him a great quantity of the king's treasure and of his household stuff. And when they were thus at a point between themselves, they went about to prepare for the coronation of the young king, as they would have it seem. And that they might turn both the eyes and minds of men from perceiving of their drifts other where, the lords, being sent for from all parts of the realm, came thick to that solemnity. But the protector and the duke, after they had set the Lord Cardinal, the Archbishop of York then lord chancellor, the Bishop of Ely, Lord Stanley, and Lord Hastings, then lord chamberlain, with many other noble men, to commune and devise about the coronation in one place; as fast were they in another place contriving the contrary, and to make the protector king. To which council, albeit there were admitted very few, and they very secret; yet began there, here and there about, some manner of muttering among the people, as though all should not long be well, though they neither wist what they feared nor wherefore; were it that before such great things men's hearts of a secret instinct of nature misgive them, as the sea without wind swelleth of himself sometime before a tempest; or were it that some one man, haply somewhat perceiving, filled many men with suspicion, though he showed few men what he knew. . . . Little and little all folk withdrew from the Tower, and drew to Crosby's place in Bishopsgate street where the protector kept his household. The protector had the resort, the king in manner desolate. While some for their business made suit to them that had the doing, some were by their friends secretly warned, that it might haply turn them to no good, to be too much attendant about the king without the protector's appointment; who removed also divers of the prince's old servants from him, and set new about him. Thus many things coming together partly by chance, partly of purpose, caused at length, not common people only that wave with the wind, but wise men also and some lords even to mark the matter and muse thereon: so generally that Lord Stanley, that was after Earl of Derby, wisely mistrusted it, and said unto Lord Hastings, that he much misliked these two several councils. "For while we," quoth he, "talk of one matter in the one place, little wot we whereof they talk in the other place."

"My lord," quoth Lord Hastings, "on my life never doubt you. For while one man is there which is never thence, never can there be things once minded that should sound amiss toward me, but it should be in mine ear ere it were well out of their mouths." This meant he by Catesby, which was of his near secret council, and whom he very familiarly used, and in his most weighty matters put no man in so special trust, reckoning himself to no man so dear, since he well wist there was no man to him so much beholden as was this Catesby, which was a man well learned in the laws of this land, and by the special favor of the lord chamberlain in good authority and much rule bore in all the county of Leicester where the lord chamberlain's power chiefly lay. . . . In whom, if Lord Hastings had not put so special trust, Lord Stanley and he had departed with divers other lords, and broken all the dance, for many ill signs that he saw, which he now construed all to the best. So surely thought he that there could be no harm toward him in that council intended where Catesby was. And of truth the protector and the Duke of Buckingham made very good semblance unto Lord Hastings, and kept him much in company. And undoubtedly the protector loved him well, and loath was to have lost him, saving for fear lest his life should have quelled their purpose. For which cause he moved

Catesby to prove with some words cast out afar off, whither he could think it possible to win Lord Hastings into their party. But Catesby, whither he assayed him or assayed him not, reported unto them, that he found him so fast, and heard him speak so terrible words, that he durst no further inquire. . . .

Whereupon soon after, that is to wit, on Friday the [13th] day of [June] many lords assembled in the Tower, and there sat in council devising the honorable solemnity of the king's coronation. . . . These lords so sitting together communing of this matter, the protector came in among them, first about nine o'clock, saluting them courteously, and excusing himself that he had been from them so long, saying merrily that he had been asleep that day. And after a little talking with them, he said unto the Bishop of Ely, "My lord, you have very good strawberries at your garden in Holborn, I require you let us have a mess of them."

"Gladly, my lord," quoth he, "would God I had some better thing as ready to your pleasure as that." And therewith in all haste he sent his servant for a mess of strawberries.

The protector set the lords fast in communing, and thereupon praying them to spare him for a little while departed thence. And soon, after one hour, between ten and eleven, he returned into the chamber among them, all changed, with a wonderful sour angry countenance, knitting the brows, frowning and fretting and gnawing on his lips, and so sat him down in his place; all the lords much dismayed and sore marvelling of this manner of sudden change, and what thing should him ail. Then when he had sat still a while, thus he began: "What were they worthy to have, that compass and imagine the destruction of me, being so near of blood unto the king and protector of his royal person and his realm?"

At this question, all the lords sat sore astonied, musing much by whom this question should be meant, of which every man wist himself clear. Then the lord chamberlain, as he that for the love between them thought he might be boldest with him, answered and said, that they were worthy to be punished as heinous traitors, whatsoever they were. And all the others affirmed the same. "That is," quoth he, "yonder sorceress my brother's wife and other with her," meaning the queen. At these words many of the other lords were greatly abashed that favored her. But Lord Hastings was in his mind better content, that it was moved by her, than by any other whom he loved better. Albeit his heart somewhat grudged, that he was not afore made of counsel in this matter, as he was of the taking of her kindred, and of their putting to death, who were by his assent before devised to be beheaded at Pontefract, this self-same day, in which he was not aware that it was by others devised, that himself should the same day be beheaded at London. Then said the protector, "Ye shall all see in what wise that sorceress and that other witch of her counsel, Shore's wife, with their affinity, have by their sorcery and witchcraft wasted my body." And therewith he plucked up his doublet sleeve to his elbow upon his left arm, where he showed a werish withered arm and small, as it was never other. And thereupon every man's mind sore misgave them, well perceiving that this matter was but a quarrel. For well they wist, that the queen was too wise to go about any such folly. And also if she would, yet would she of all folk least make Shore's wife of counsel, whom of all women she most hated, as that concubine whom the king her husband had most loved. And also no man was there present, but well knew that his arm was ever such since his birth.

Natheless the lord chamberlain (which from the death of King Edward kept Shore's wife, on whom he somewhat doted in the king's life, saving, as it is said, he that while forbore her of reverence towards his king, or else of a certain kind of fidelity to his friend) answered and said, "Certainly, my lord, if they have so heinously done, they be worthy heinous punishment."

"What," quoth the protector, "thou servest me, I ween, with ifs and with ands; I tell thee they have so done, and that I will make good on thy body, traitor!" And therewith as in a great anger, he clapped his fist upon the board a great rap. At which token given, one cried, "Treason!" without the chamber. Therewith a door clapped, and in came there rushing men in harness as many as the chamber might hold. And anon the protector said to Lord Hastings, "I arrest thee, traitor."

"What, me, my lord?" quoth he.

"Yea thee, traitor," quoth the protector. And another let fly at Lord Stanley who shrank at the stroke and fell under the table, or else his head had been cleft to the teeth: for as shortly as he shrank, yet ran the blood about his ears. Then were they all quickly bestowed in divers chambers, except the lord chamberlain, whom the protector bade, "Speed and shrive him apace, for by saint Paul," quoth he, "I will not to dinner till I see thy head off." It booted him not to ask why, but heavily he took a priest at

adventure, and made a short shrift, for a longer would not be suffered, the protector made so much haste to dinner, which he might not go to till this were done for saving of his oath. So was he brought forth into the green beside the chapel within the Tower, and his head laid down upon a long log of timber, and there stricken off. . . .

A marvellous case is it to hear, either the warnings of that he should have avoided, or the tokens of that he could not avoid. For the self night next before his death, Lord Stanley sent a trusty secret messenger unto him at midnight in all haste, requiring him to rise and ride away with him, for he was disposed utterly no longer to bide; he had so fearful a dream, in which he thought that a boar with his tusks so razed them both by the heads, that the blood ran about both their shoulders. And forasmuch as the protector gave the boar for his cognizance, this dream made so fearful an impression in his heart, that he was thoroughly determined no longer to tarry, but had his horse ready, if Lord Hastings would go with him to ride so far yet the same night, that they should be out of danger ere day. "Eh, good lord," quoth Lord Hastings to this messenger, "leaneth my lord thy master so much to such trifles, and has such faith in dreams, which either his own fear fantasies or do rise in the night's rest by reason of his day thoughts? Tell him it is plain witchcraft to believe in such dreams; which if they were tokens of things to come, why thinketh he not that we might be as likely to make them true by our going if we were caught and brought back (as friends fail fleers), for then had the boar a cause likely to raze us with his tusks, as folks that fled for some falsehood, wherefore either is there no peril; nor none there is indeed; or if any be, it is rather in going than biding. And if we should needs cost fall in peril one way or other; yet had I liefer that men should see it were by other men's falsehood, than think it were either our own fault or faint heart. And therefore go to thy master, man, and commend me to him, and pray him be merry and have no fear: for I ensure him I am as sure of the man that he woteth of, as I am of my own hand."

"God send grace, sir," quoth the messenger, and went his way.

Certain is it also, that in riding toward the Tower, the same morning in which he was beheaded, his horse twice or thrice stumbled with him almost to falling; which thing albeit each man wot well daily happens to them to whom no such mischance is toward, yet has it been, of an old rite and custom, observed as a token often times notably foregoing some great misfortune. . . . The same morning ere he was up, came a knight unto him, as it were of courtesy to accompany him to the council, but of truth sent by the protector to haste him thitherward. . . . This knight, when it happed the lord chamberlain by the way to stay his horse, and commune a while with a priest whom he met in the Tower street, broke his tale and said merrily to him, "What, my lord, I pray you come on, whereto talk you so long with that priest, you have no need of a priest yet." And therewith he laughed upon him, as though he would say, ye shall have soon. But so little wist the other what he meant, and so little mistrusted, that he was never merrier nor never so full of good hope in his life; which self thing is often seen a sign of change. But I shall rather let anything pass me, than the vain surety of man's mind so near his death. Upon the very Tower wharf, so near the place where his head was off so soon after, there met he with one Hastings, a pursuivant of his own name. And of their meeting in that place, he was put in remembrance of another time, in which it had happened them before to meet in like manner together in the same place. At which other time the lord chamberlain had been accused unto King Edward, by Lord Rivers the queen's brother, in such wise that he was for the while (but it lasted not long) far fallen into the king's indignation, and stood in great fear of himself. And forasmuch as he now met this pursuivant in the same place, that jeopardy so well passed, it gave him great pleasure to talk with him thereof. . . . And therefore he said, "Ah, Hastings, art thou remembered when I met thee here once with an heavy heart?"

"Yea, my lord," quoth he, "that remember I well, and thanked be God they got no good, nor ye no harm thereby."

"Thou wouldst say so," quoth he, "if thou knewest as much as I know, which few know else as yet and more shall shortly." That meant he by the lords of the queen's kindred that were taken before, and should that day be beheaded at Pontefract, which he well wist, but nothing ware that the axe hung over his own head. "In faith, man," quoth he, "I was never so sorry, nor never stood in so great dread in my life, as I did when thou and I met here. And lo, how the world is turned, now stand mine enemies in the danger (as thou mayst hap to hear more hereafter) and I never

in my life so merry nor never in so great surety." Oh good God, the blindness of our mortal nature; when he most feared, he was in good surety: when he reckoned himself surest, he lost his life, and that within two hours after. . . . Now flew the fame of this lord's death swiftly through the city, and so forth further about like a wind in every man's ear. But the protector immediately after dinner, intended to set some color upon the matter, sent in all haste for many substantial men out of the city into the Tower. And at their coming, himself with the Duke of Buckingham, stood harnessed in old ill-faring briganders, such as no man should ween that they would vouchsafe to have put upon their backs, except that some sudden necessity had constrained them. And then the protector showed them, that the lord chamberlain, and others of his conspiracy, had contrived to have suddenly destroyed him and the duke, there that same day in the council. And what they intended further was as yet not well known. Of which their treason he never had knowledge before ten o'clock the same forenoon. Which sudden fear drove them to put on for their defense such harness as came next to hand. And so had God helped them, that the mischief turned upon them that would have done it. And this he required them to report. Every man answered him fair, as though no man mistrusted the matter which of truth no man believed. Yet for the further appeasing of the people's mind, he sent immediately after dinner in all haste, one herald of arms, with a proclamation to be made through the city in the king's name, containing that Lord Hastings, with divers other of his traitorous purpose, had before conspired that same day to have slain the lord protector and the Duke of Buckingham sitting in the council, and after to have taken upon them to rule the king and the realm at their pleasure, and thereby to pillage and spoil whom they list uncontrolled. And much matter was there in the proclamation devised, to the slander of the lord chamberlain, as that he was an evil counsellor to the king's father, enticing him to many things highly redounding to the diminishing of his honor, and to the universal hurt of his realm, by his evil company, sinister procuring, and ungracious example, as well in many other things as in the vicious living and inordinate abusion of his body both with many other, and also specially with Shore's wife; who was one also of his most secret counsel of this heinous treason, with whom he lay nightly, and namely the night last passed next before his death so that it was the less marvel, if ungracious living brought him to an unhappy ending. . . .

Now was this proclamation made within two hours after that he was beheaded, and it was so curiously indited, and so fair written in parchment in so well a set hand, and therewith of itself so long a process, that every child might well perceive that it was prepared before. For all the time between his death and the proclaiming could scant have sufficed unto the bare writing alone, all had it been but in paper and scribbled forth in haste at adventure. So that upon the proclaiming thereof, one that was schoolmaster of [St.] Paul's of chance standing by, and comparing the shortness of the time with the length of the matter, said unto them that stood about him, "Here is a gay goodly cast foul cast away for haste." And a merchant answered him, that it was written by prophecy.

Now then by and by . . . the protector sent into the house of Shore's wife (for her husband dwelled not with her) and spoiled her of all that ever she had, above the value of two or three thousand marks, and sent her body to prison. And when he had a while laid unto her, for the manner sake, that she went about to bewitch him, and that she was of counsel with the lord chamberlain to destroy him: in conclusion, when that no color could fasten upon these matters, then he laid heinously to her charge, the thing that herself could not deny, that all the world wist was true, and that natheless every man laughed at to hear it then so suddenly so highly taken, that she was naught of her body. And for this cause (as a goodly continent prince, clean and faultless of himself, sent out of heaven into this vicious world for the amendment of men's manners) he caused the Bishop of London to put her to open penance, going before the cross in procession upon a Sunday with a taper in her hand. In which she went in countenance and pace demure so womanly, and albeit she were out of all array save her kirtle only: yet went she so fair and lovely, namely while the wondering of the people cast a comely red in her cheeks (of which she before had most missed) that her great shame won her much praise among those that were more amorous of her body than curious of her soul. And many good folk also, that hated her living, and glad were to see sin corrected, yet pitied they more her penance, than rejoiced therein, when they considered that the protector procured it, more of a corrupt intent than any virtuous affection.

This woman was born in London, worshipfully friended, honestly brought up, and very well married, saving somewhat too soon, her husband an honest citizen, young and goodly and of good substance. But forasmuch as they were coupled ere she were well ripe, she not very fervently loved, for whom she never longed, which was haply the thing that the more easily made her incline unto the king's appetite when he required her. Howbeit the respect of his royalty, the hope of gay apparel, ease, pleasure, and other wanton wealth, was able soon to pierce a soft, tender heart. But when the king had abused her, anon her husband (as he was an honest man, and one that could his good, not presuming to touch a king's concubine) left her up to him altogether. When the king died, the lord chamberlain took her, which in the king's day, albeit he was sore enamored upon her, yet he forebore her; either for reverence, or for a certain friendly faithfulness. Proper she was and fair; nothing in her body that you would have changed, but if you would have wished her somewhat higher. Thus say they that knew her in her youth. Albeit some that now see her (for yet she liveth) deem her never to have been well visaged. Whose judgment seemeth me somewhat like as though men should guess the beauty of one long before departed, by her scalp taken out of the charnel house; for now is she old, lean, withered, and dried up, nothing left but shrivelled skin and hard bone. . . . Yet delighted not men so much in her beauty, as in her pleasant behavior. For a proper wit had she, and could both read well and write, merry in company, ready and quick of answer, neither mute nor full of babble, sometimes taunting without displeasure and not without disport. The king would say that he had three concubines, who in three diverse properties diversely excelled. One the merriest, another the wiliest, the third the holiest harlot in his realm, as one whom no man could get out of the church lightly to any place, but it were to his bed.

The other two were somewhat greater personages, and natheless of their humility content to be nameless, and to forebear the praise of those properties: but the merriest was this Shore's wife in whom the king therefore took special pleasure. For many he had, but her he loved whose favor to say the truth (for sin it were to believe the devil), she never abused to any man's hurt, but to many a man's comfort and relief: where the king took displeasure she would mitigate and appease his mind:

where men were out of favor, she would bring them in his grace. For many that had highly offended, she obtained pardon. Of great forfeitures she got men remission. And finally in many weighty suits she stood many men in great stead, either for none, or very small rewards, and those rather gay than rich; either for that she was content with the deed itself well done, or for that she delighted to be sued unto, and to show what she was able to do with the king, or for that wanton women and wealthy be not always covetous. I doubt not some shall think this woman too slight a thing to be written of and set among the remembrances of great matters; which they shall specially think, that haply shall esteem her only by that they now see her. But meseemeth the chance so much the more worthy to be remembered, in how much she is now in the more beggarly condition, unfriended and worn out of acquaintance, after good substance, after as great favor with the prince, after as great suit and seeking to with all those that those days had business to speed, as many other men were in their times, which be now famous, only by the infamy of their ill deeds. Her doings were not much less, albeit they be much less remembered, because they were not so evil. For men use if they have an evil turn, to write it in marble: and whoso doth us a good turn, we write it in dust, which is not worst proved by her: for at this day she beggeth of many at this day living that at this day had begged if she had not been. . . .

Now when the lord chamberlain, and these other lords and knights were thus beheaded and rid out of the way, then thought the protector, that while men mused what the matter meant, while the lords of the realm were about him out of their own strengths, while no man wist what to think nor whom to trust, ere ever they should have space to dispute and digest the matter and make parties, it were best hastily to pursue his purpose, and put himself in possession of the crown, ere men could have time to devise any ways to resist. But now was all the study, by what means this matter being of itself so heinous, might be first broken to the people, in such wise that it might be well taken. To this counsel they took divers, and such as they thought meetly to be trusted, likely to be induced to the part, and able to stand them in stead, either by power or policy. Among whom, they made of counsel Edmund Sha, knight, then Mayor of London, who, upon trust of his own advancement, whereof he was of a proud heart highly desirous, should frame

the city to their appetite. Of spiritual men they took such as had wit, and were in authority among the people for opinion of their learning, and had no scrupulous conscience. Among these they had Ralph Sha, clerk, brother to the mayor, and friar Penker, provincial of the Augustinian friars, both doctors of divinity, both great preachers, both of more learning than virtue, of more fame than learning. For they were before greatly esteemed among the people, but after that never. Of these two the one had a sermon in praise of the protector before the coronation, the other after, both so full of tedious flattery, that no man's ears could abide them. Penker in his sermon so lost his voice that he was fain to leave off and come down in the midst. Doctor Sha by his sermon lost his honesty, and soon after his life, for very shame of the world, into which he durst never after come abroad. . . . But certain is it, that Doctor Sha was of counsel in the beginning, so much so that they determined that he should first break the matter in a sermon at Paul's Cross, in which he should, by the authority of his preaching, incline the people to the protector's ghostly purpose. But now was all the labor and study in the devising of some convenient pretext, for which the people should be content to depose the prince and accept the protector for king. In which, divers things they devised. But the chief thing and the weightiest of all that invention rested in this, that they should allege bastardy, either in King Edward himself, or in his children, or both. So that he should seem disabled to inherit the crown by the Duke of York, and the prince by him. To lay bastardy in King Edward sounded openly to the rebuke of the protector's own mother, who was mother to them both; for in that point could be no other color, but to pretend that his own mother was an adulteress which notwithstanding, to further this purpose, he letted not; but natheless he would that point should be less, and more favorably, handled, not even fully plain and directly, but that the matter should be touched aslope craftily, as though men spared in that point to speak all the truth for fear of his displeasure. But the other point concerning the bastardy that they devised to surmise in King Edward's children, that would he should be openly declared and enforced to the uttermost. The color and pretext whereof cannot be well perceived, but if we first repeat you some things long before done about King Edward's marriage.

After that King Edward the Fourth had

deposed King Henry the Sixth, and was in peaceable possession of the realm, determining himself to marry, as it was requisite both for himself and for the realm, he sent over in embassy the Earl of Warwick with other noblemen in his company unto Spain, to entreat and conclude a marriage between King Edward and the king's daughter of Spain. . . . Now happed it that in the mean season, there came to make a suit, by petition to the king, dame Elizabeth Gray who was after his queen, at that time a widow born of noble blood, specially by her mother, who was Duchess of Bedford ere she married Lord Woodville her father. . . . Whom when the king beheld and heard her speak, as she was both fair, of a good favor, moderate of stature, well made and very wise: he not only pitied her, but also waxed enamored on her, and taking her afterward secretly aside, began to enter in talking familiarly. Whose appetite when she perceived, she virtuously denied him. But that did she so wisely, and with so good manner, and words so well set, that she rather kindled his desire than quenched it. And finally, after many a meeting, much wooing, and many great promises, she well espied the king's affection toward her so greatly increased, that she durst somewhat the more boldly say her mind, as to him whose heart she perceived more firmly set than to fall off for a word. And in conclusion she showed him plain that as she wist herself too simple to be his wife, so thought she herself too good to be his concubine. The king, much marvelling of her constancy, as he who had not been wont elsewhere to be so stiffly said nay, so much esteemed her continence and chastity that he set her virtue in the stead of possession and riches, and thus, taking counsel of his desire, determining in all possible haste to marry her. And after he was thus appointed, and had between them twain ensured her; then asked he counsel of his other friends, and that in such manner, as they might easily perceive it booted not greatly to say nay. Notwithstanding the Duchess of York his mother was so sore moved therewith, that she dissuaded the marriage as much as she possibly might. . . .

The duchess . . . nothing appeased, and seeing the king so set thereon that she could not pull him back, so highly she disdained it, that under pretext of her duty to God, she devised to disturb this marriage, and rather to help that he should marry one dame Elizabeth Lucy, whom the king had also not long before gotten with child. Wherefore the king's mother objected openly against his marriage,

as it were in discharge of her conscience, that the king was sure to dame Elizabeth Lucy and her husband before God. By reason of which words, such obstacle was made in the matter, that either the bishops durst not, or the king would not, proceed to the solemnization of this wedding, till these same were clearly purged, and the truth well and openly testified. Whereupon dame Elizabeth Lucy was sent for. And albeit that she was by the king's mother and many others put in good comfort, to affirm that she was ensured unto the king: yet when she was solemnly sworn to say the truth, she confessed that they were never ensured. Howbeit she said his Grace spoke so loving words unto her, that she verily hoped he would have married her, and that if it had not been for such kind words she would never have shown such kindness to him, to let him so kindly get her with child. This examination solemnly taken, when it was clearly perceived that there was no impediment, the king, with great feast and honorable solemnity, married dame Elizabeth Gray and her crowned queen who was his enemy's wife, and many times had prayed full heartily for his loss. In which God loved her better, than to grant her her boon. . . .

Now then as I began to show you, it was by the protector and his council concluded, that this Doctor Sha should, in a sermon at Paul's Cross, signify to the people, that neither King Edward himself, nor the Duke of Clarence, were lawfully begotten, nor were not the very children of the Duke of York; but gotten unlawfully by other persons by the adultery of the duchess their mother. And that also dame Elizabeth Lucy was verily the wife of King Edward, and so the prince and all his children bastards that were gotten upon the queen. According to this device, Doctor Sha the Sunday after at Paul's Cross in a great audience (as always assembled great number to his preaching), he took for his theme *spuria vitulamina non agent radices altas.* That is to say, bastard slips shall never take deep root. . . . And when he had laid for the proof and confirmation of this sentence, certain examples taken out of the Old Testament and other ancient histories, then began he to descend into the praise of the lord Richard late Duke of York, calling him father to the lord protector, and declared the title of his heirs unto the crown, to whom it was after the death of King Henry the Sixth entailed by authority of parliament. Then showed he that this very right heir of his body lawfully begotten, was only the lord protector. For he declared then that King Edward was never lawfully married unto the queen, but was before God husband unto dame Elizabeth Lucy, and so his children bastards. And besides that, neither King Edward himself, nor the Duke of Clarence, among those that were secret in the household, were reckoned very surely for the children of the noble duke. . . .

Now was it before devised, that in the speaking of these words, the protector should have come in among the people to the sermonward, to the end that those words meeting with his presence, might have been taken among the hearers, as though the Holy Ghost had put them in the preacher's mouth, and should have moved the people even there to cry, "King Richard, King Richard," that it might have been after said, that he was specially chosen by God and in manner by miracle. But this device failed either by the protector's negligence, or the preacher's overmuch diligence. For while the protector found by the way tarrying lest he should prevent those words, and the doctor fearing that he should come ere his sermon could come to those words hasted his matter thereto; he was come to them and past them, and entered into other matters ere the protector came. Whom when he beheld coming, he suddenly left the matter, with which he was in hand, and without any deduction thereunto, out of all order, and out of all frame, began to repeat those words again, "This is that very noble prince, the special patron of knightly prowess, which as well in all princely behavior, as in the lineaments and favor of his visage, represents the very face of the noble Duke of York his father. . . ." While these words were in speaking, the protector accompanied with the Duke of Buckingham, went through the people into the place where the doctors commonly stand in the upper story, where he stood to hearken the sermon. But the people were so far from crying "King Richard," that they stood as they had been turned into stones, for wonder of this shameful sermon. . . .

Then on the Tuesday following this sermon there came unto the Guild Hall in London the Duke of Buckingham, accompanied with divers lords and knights, more than haply knew the message that they brought. And there in the east end of the hall where the mayor keeps the hustings, the mayor and all the aldermen being assembled about him, all the commons of the city gathered before them, after silence commanded upon great pain in the protector's name, the duke stood up, and (as he was neither unlearned, and of nature marvellously well spoken) he said unto the people with a clear and a loud voice in this manner of wise.

"Friends, for the zeal and hearty favor that we bear you, we be come to break unto you, of a matter right great and weighty, and no less weighty, than pleasing to God and profitable to all the realm; nor to no part of the realm more profitable, than to you the citizens of this noble city. . . . I am not so proud to look therefore, that ye should reckon my words of as great authority as the preachers of the word of God, namely a man so cunning and so wise . . . so good and virtuous that he would not say the thing which he wist he should not say, in the pulpit . . . which honorable preacher ye well remember substantially declared unto you at Paul's Cross on Sunday last passed, the right and title that the most excellent prince Richard, Duke of Gloucester, now protector of this realm, hath unto the crown and kingdom of the same. For as the worshipful man proudly made open unto you, the children of King Edward the Fourth were never lawfully begotten, forasmuch as the king (living his very wife dame Elizabeth Lucy) was never lawfully married unto the queen their mother, whose blood, saving that he set his voluptuous pleasure before his honor, was fully unmeetly to be matched with his, and the mingling of whose bloods together, hath been the effusion of great part of the noble blood of this realm. . . . For these causes, I say, before remembered, that is to wit, for lack of other issue lawfully coming of the late noble prince Richard Duke of York, to whose royal blood the crown of England and of France is by the high authority of parliament entailed, the right and title of the same is, by the just course of inheritance according to the common law of this land, devolved and come unto the most excellent prince the lord protector as to the very lawfully begotten son of the fore-remembered noble Duke of York. Which thing well considered, and the great knightly prowess pondered, with manifold virtues which in his noble person singularly abound, the nobles and commons also of this realm, and specially of the north parts, not willing any bastard blood to have the rule of the land . . . have condescended and fully determined to make humble petition unto the most puissant prince the lord protector, that it may like his Grace, at our humble request, to take upon him the guiding and governance of this realm, to the wealth and increase of the same, according to his very right and just title. . . . Yet shall he to our petition in that behalf the more graciously incline if ye, the worshipful citizens of this the chief city of this realm, join with us the nobles in our said request. Which for your own weal we doubt not but ye will, and natheless I heartily pray you so to do, whereby you shall do great profit to all this realm beside in choosing them so good a king, and unto yourselves special commodity, to whom his majesty shall ever after bear so much the more tender favor, in how much he shall perceive you the more prone and benevolently minded toward his election. Wherein, dear friends, what mind you have, we require you plainly to show us."

When the duke had said, and looked that the people whom he hoped that the mayor had framed before, should, after this proposition made, have cried, "King Richard, King Richard," all was hushed and mute, and not one word answered thereunto. Wherewith the duke was marvellously abashed, and taking the mayor nearer to him, with others that were about him privy to that matter, said unto them softly, "What meaneth this, that this people be so still?"

"Sir," quoth the mayor, "perchance they perceive you not well."

"That shall we mend," quoth he, "if that will help." And by and by somewhat louder, he rehearsed them the same matter again in other order and other words, so well and ornately, and natheless so evidently and plain, with voice, gesture and countenance so comely and so convenient, that every man much marvelled that heard him, and thought that they never had in their lives heard so evil a tale so well told. But were it for wonder or fear, or that each looked that other should speak first; not one word was there answered of all the people that stood before, but all was as still as the midnight. . . . Whereupon the duke rounded unto the mayor and said, "This is a marvellous obstinate silence." And therewith he turned unto the people again with these words: "Dear friends, we come to move you to that thing which peradventure we not so greatly needed, but that the lords of this realm and the commons of other parts might have sufficed, saving that we such love bore you, and so much set by you, that we would not gladly do without you that thing in which to be partners is your weal and honor which, as it seems, either you see not or weigh not. Wherefore we require you give us answer one or other, whither you be minded as all the nobles of the realm be, to have this noble prince now protector to be your king or not." At these words the people began to whisper

among themselves secretly, that the voice was neither loud nor distinct, but as it were the sound of a swarm of bees, till at the last in the nether end of the hall, a bushment of the duke's servants . . . and others belonging to the protector, with some apprentices and lads that thrust into the hall among the press, began suddenly at men's backs to cry out as loud as their throats would give, "King Richard, King Richard," and threw up their caps in token of joy. And they that stood before, cast back their heads marvelling thereof, but nothing they said. And when the duke and the mayor saw this manner, they wisely turned it to their purpose. And said it was a goodly cry and a joyful to hear, every man with one voice, no man saying nay.

"Wherefore friends," quoth the duke, "since that we perceive it is all your whole minds to have this noble man for your king, whereof we shall make his Grace so effectual report, that we doubt not but it shall redound unto your great weal and commodity; we require ye that ye tomorrow go with us and we with you unto his noble Grace, to make our humble request unto him in manner before remembered. . . ."

Then on the morrow after, the mayor with all the aldermen and chief commoners of the city in their best manner apparelled, assembling themselves together resorted unto Baynard's castle where the protector lay. To which place repaired also according to their appointment the Duke of Buckingham, with divers noblemen with him, beside many knights and other gentlemen. And thereupon the duke sent word unto the lord protector, of being there of a great and honorable company, to move a great matter unto his Grace. Whereupon the protector made difficulties to come out unto them, but if he first knew some part of their errand, as though he doubted and partly distrusted the coming of such number unto him so suddenly, without any warning or knowledge, whither they came for good or harm. . . . And thereupon the Duke of Buckingham first made humble petition unto him, on behalf of them all, that his Grace would pardon them and license them to purpose unto his Grace the intent of their coming. . . . When the duke had this leave and pardon to speak, then waxed he bold to show him their intent and purpose, with all the causes moving them thereunto as ye before have heard, and finally to beseech his Grace, that it would like him of his accustomed goodness and zeal unto the realm . . . to set his gracious hands to the redress and amendment thereof, by taking upon him the crown and governance of this realm, according to his right and title lawfully descended unto him. . . .

When the protector had heard the proposition, he looked very strangely thereat, and answered that, all were it that he partly knew the things by them alleged to be true; yet such entire love he bore unto King Edward and his children, that so much more regarded his honor in other realms about, than the crown of any one, of which he was never desirous, that he could not find in his heart in this point to incline to their desire. . . . But when he saw there was no other way, but either he must take it or else he and his both go from it, he said unto the lords and commons: "Since we perceive well that all the realm is so set, whereof we be very sorry that they will not suffer in any wise King Edward's line to govern them, whom no man earthly can govern against their wills, and we well also perceive, that no man is there, to whom the crown can by so just title appertain as to our self, as very right heir lawfully begotten of the body of our most dear father Richard late Duke of York, to which title is now joined your election, the nobles and commons of this realm, which we of all titles possible take for most effectual: we be content and agree favorably to incline to your petition and request, and according to the same, here we take upon us the royal estate, preeminence and kingdom of the two noble realms, England and France. . . ."

With this there was a great shout, crying, "King Richard, King Richard!" And then the lords went up to the king (for so was he from that time called) and the people departed, talking diversely of the matter every man as his fancy gave him. . . .

Now fell there mischiefs thick. And as the thing evil gotten is never well kept, through all the time of his reign, never ceased there cruel death and slaughter, till his own destruction ended it. But as he finished his time with the best death, and the most righteous, that is to wit his own; so began he with the most piteous and wicked, I mean the lamentable murder of his innocent nephews, the young king and his tender brother. Whose death and final misfortune has natheless so far come in question, that some remain yet in doubt, whether they were in his days destroyed or no. . . . But in the mean time for this present matter, I shall rehearse you the dolorous end of those babes, not after every way that I have heard, but after that way that I have so heard by such men and by such means, as me thinks it were hard but it should be true. King Richard after his coronation, taking his way to Gloucester to visit, in his new honor, the town of which he bore the name of his old, devised as he rode to fulfill that thing which he before had intended. . . . Whereupon he sent one John Green, whom he specially trusted, unto Sir Robert Brackenbury, constable of the Tower, with a letter and credence also, that the same Sir Robert should in any wise put the two children to death. This John Green did his errand unto Brackenbury . . . who plainly answered that he would never put them to death to die therefore, with which answer John Green returning recounted the same to King Richard at Warwick yet in his way. Wherewith he took such displeasure and thought, that the same night, he said unto a secret page of his, "Ah, whom shall a man trust? Those that I have brought up myself, those that I had thought would most surely serve me, even those fail me, and at my commandment will do nothing for me."

"Sir," quoth his page, "there lyeth one on your pallet without, that I dare well say, to do your Grace pleasure, the thing were right hard that he would refuse," meaning by this Sir James Tyrell, who was a man of right goodly personage, and for nature's gifts, worthy to have served a much better prince. . . . The man had an high heart, and sore longed upward, not rising yet so fast as he had hoped. . . . Upon this page's words King Richard arose (for this communication had he sitting at the draught, a convenient carpet for such a council) and came out into the pallet chamber, on which he found in bed Sir James and Sir Thomas Tyrell, of person like and brethren of blood, but nothing of kin in conditions. Then said the king merely to them, "What, sirs, be ye in bed so soon?" and calling up Sir James, broke to him secretly his mind in this mischievous matter. In which he found him nothing strange. Wherefore on the morrow he sent him to Brackenbury with a letter, by which he was commanded to deliver Sir James all the keys of the Tower for one night, to the end he might there accomplish the king's pleasure, in such thing as he had given him commandment. After which letter delivered and the keys received, Sir James appointed the night next ensuing to destroy them, devising before and preparing the means. The prince, as soon as the protector left that name and took himself as king, had it shown unto him, that he should not reign, but his uncle should have the crown. At which word the prince sore abashed, began to sigh and said: "Alas, I would my uncle would let me have my life yet, though I lose my kingdom." Then he that told him the tale, used him with good words, and put him in the best comfort he could. But forthwith was the prince and his brother both shut up, and all others removed from them, only one called Black Will or William Slaughter excepted, set to serve them and see them sure. After which time the prince never tied his points, nor ought wrought of himself, but with that young babe his brother, lingered in thought and heaviness till this traitorous death delivered them of that wretchedness. For Sir James Tyrell devised that they should be murdered in their beds. To the execution whereof, he appointed Miles Forest, one of the four that kept them, a fellow fleshed in murder before time. To him he joined one John Dighton, his own horsekeeper, a big broad square strong knave. Then all the others being removed from them, this Miles Forest and John Dighton, about midnight (the silly children lying in their beds) came into the chamber, and suddenly lapped them up among the clothes, so bewrapped them and entangled them, keeping down by force the featherbed and pillows hard unto their mouths, that within a while smothered and stifled, their breath failing, they gave up to God their innocent souls into the joys of heaven, leaving to the tormentors their bodies dead in the bed. Which after that the wretches perceived, first by the struggling with the pains of death, and after long lying still, to be thoroughly dead, they laid their bodies naked out upon the bed, and fetched Sir James to see them. Which upon the sight of them, caused those murderers to bury them at the stair foot, meetly deep in the ground under a great heap of stones. Then rode Sir James in great haste to King Richard, and showed him all the manner of the murder, who gave him great thanks and, as some say, there made him knight. But he allowed not, as I have heard, the burying in so vile a corner, saying that he would have them buried in a better place, because they were a king's sons. Lo, the honorable courage of a king! Whereupon they say that a priest of Sir Robert Brackenbury took up the bodies again, and secretly interred them in such place, as by the occasion of his death, who only knew it, could never since come to light. Very truth it is and well known, that at such time as Sir James Tyrell was in the Tower, for treason committed against the most famous prince King Henry the Seventh, both Dighton and he were examined, and confessed the murder in manner above written, but whither the bodies were removed they could nothing tell.

And thus as I have learned of them that much knew and little cause had to lie, were these two noble princes, these innocent tender children, born of most royal blood brought up in great wealth, likely long to live to reign and rule in the realm, by traitorous tyranny taken, deprived of their estate, shortly shut up in prison, and privily slain and murdered, their bodies cast God wot where by the cruel ambition of their unnatural uncle and his dispiteous tormentors. Which things on every part well pondered, God never gave this world a more notable example, neither in what unsurety standeth this wordly weal, or what mischief worketh the proud enterprise of an high heart, or finally what wretched end ensueth such dispiteous cruelty. For first to begin with the ministers, Miles Forest at Saint Martin's piecemeal rotted away. Dighton indeed yet walks on alive in good possibility to be hanged ere he die. But Sir James Tyrell died at Tower Hill, beheaded for treason. King Richard himself, as ye shall hereafter hear, slain in the field, hacked and hewed of his enemies' hands, harried on horseback dead, his hair in despite torn and togged like a cur dog. And the mischief that he took, within less than three years of the mischief that he did. And yet all the meantime spent in much pain and trouble outward, much fear and anguish and sorrow within. For I have heard by credible report of such as were secret with his chamberers, that after this abominable deed done, he never had quiet in his mind, he never thought himself sure. Where he went abroad, his eyes whirled about, his body privily fenced, his hand ever on his dagger, his countenance and manner like one always ready to strike again, he took ill rest at night, lay long waking and musing, sore wearied with care and watch, rather slumbered than slept, troubled with fearful dreams, suddenly sometimes started up, leaped out of his bed and ran about the chamber, so was his restless heart continually tossed and tumbled with the tedious impression and stormy remembrance of his abominable deed.

Now had he outward no long time in rest. For hereupon soon after began the conspiracy, or rather good confederation, between the Duke of Buckingham and many other gentlemen against him. . . . And surely the occasion of their variance is of divers men diversely reported. Some have I heard say, that the duke a little before the coronation among other things, required of the protector the Duke of Hereford's lands, to which he pretended himself just inheritor. And forasmuch as the title which he claimed by inheritance, was somewhat interlaced with the title to the crown by the line of King Henry before deprived; the protector conceived such indignation, that he rejected the duke's request with many spiteful and minatory words. Which so wounded his heart with hatred and mistrust, that he never after could endure to look aright on King Richard, but ever feared his own life. . . . But men say that he was of truth not well at ease, and that both to King Richard well known, and not ill taken nor any demand of the duke's uncourteously rejected, but he both with great gifts and high behests, in most loving and trusty manner departed at Gloucester. But soon after his coming home to Brecknock, having there in his custody, by the commandment of King Richard, Doctor Morton, Bishop of Ely, who as ye before heard was taken in the council at the Tower, waxed with him familiar. Whose wisdom abused his pride to his own deliverance and the duke's destruction.

ANONYMOUS

From The Praise of King Richard the Third[1]

That princes are naturally ambitious, and that ambition makes them to effect their desires, rather than to affect the equity of their designs may more truly than safely be avowed. For all of them, I think, were the record of their actions indifferent, might be taxed of this vice. But this excuse clears not the accused; yet it testifies that princes err against nature, if they aspire not. We hold (not without reason) that if the bill of the plaintiff be stuffed with frivolous assertions, that the complaint savoureth more of malice than of wrong. Why should not the same axiom be a motive to clear this wronged prince, whose accusers lay to his charge the anguish his mother felt, when he came into the world? Than which accusation what can be more frivolous, it being a punishment hereditary to all women, from the first? His being toothed as soon as born seems to me rather a blessing, than any imputation, as being a presage of his future worthiness, and as all nurses will confess, an ease of much pain and danger. But he was crook-backed, lame, ill-shapen, ill-favored. I might impute that fault to nature, but that I rather think it her bounty, for the being wholly attentive to his mind, neglected his form, so that she infused a straight mind in a crooked body, wherein she showed her careful providence. For oftentimes, the care to keep those parts well formed, with-draws men's minds from better actions, and drowns them in effeminate curiosity. His lameness turned to his glory; for with those imperfect limbs he performed actions most perfectly valiant.

How rightly his father claimed, his brother obtained the scepter, is sufficiently known, and therefore superfluous and impertinent. . . . But

[1] This essay, excerpted from William Cornwallis' *Essayes of Certain Paradoxes* (2nd imp., enlarged, London, 1617), is the earliest published defense of Richard. W. Gordon Zeeveld has suggested in "A Tudor Defense of Richard III," *PMLA,* **LV** (1940), that it dates from the early sixteenth century and is a direct reply to that attack attributed to More but more probably written by Morton.

to dilate how variable and inconstant the people of those times were shall be more necessary and effectual, that knowing their inconstancy, their traditions (like themselves) may the less be believed, so light-headed, so foolish, so irreligious, as their opinion (for what else are the thoughts of ignorance but opinion?) made them break their oath to their prince [Henry VI], and to such a prince as they did not shame to dislike, only because he was too good. Him they abandoned, deposed, after restored; not as desiring . . . but only that it stood with the liking of Warwick, the child of their love. If then they were such (as indeed they were), and that those relations we have must come from that people, it were better (I think) to bury their traditions, than refute their objections, were not our age, apt to err, infected with this folly. . . .

Never was he noted all the life of King Edward to thirst after the kingdom; never denied he any commandment of his prince, but performed all his employments discreetly, valiantly, successfully. The suspicion of helping his brother Clarence to his end was but a suspicion, since the King's old displeasure, awaked by a new prophecy, was undoubtedly the cause; if otherwise (when he after repented) he would have misliked of Gloucester, it being natural to sin; but unnatural, to ease others of their crimes. For the killing of the heir of the house of Lancaster at Tewkesbury (if so) seems to me rather the effect of love to his brother, than cruelty to the prince; for he was an enemy, yea, the chief and principal enemy of the contrary faction. Yet it cannot be proved the action of Richard, but that it was an act wished by the King to be done, and executed in both their presences, by the Duke of Clarence, the Marquis Dorset, the Lord Hastings and others.

The death of Henry the VI in the Tower can no way belong to him, since the same reason that cleareth his brother fitteth him; he being able, if desiring his death, to have effected it by a more unworthy hand. And indeed this accusation hath no other proof, than a malicious affirmation. For many (more truly) did suppose that he died of mere melancholy and grief, when he had heard of the overthrow of his friends and slaughter of his son. But if it were true, though it spots him with blood, yet it confirms his love to his prince; which love was so coldly requited, as might have moved a true lover of rewards more than of virtue, to have altered his endeavors; whether it were a jealousy of the nobility of his blood, or of the height of his spirit, whether the abundance of affection to be led by a woman, or that he was defective in all brotherly affection, certain it is, he rather employed him than rewarded his employments. Contrary, the Queen's kindred, daily rising, merely without desert, but that they were of her kindred; and their baseness being thus suddenly exalted, not only plucking from him promotions, due to his deserts, but envying the Duke and contending with him; how insupportable it must have been to so magnanimous a spirit, whose memory bears witness of their unworthiness, his own worth any like spirit may imagine.

Thus continued this unequal contention until the King, sent for before the great King of Kings, to make an account of his greatness, left his body, to testify the world's folly in contending for worlds, when one little part of the earth must contain them. His successor at that time very young, was wholly possessed by the mother's blood, whom the now Protector had great reason to fear, being ever his mortal enemy, and now most strong, by being most nearly allied to this prince. Therefore jealous of his own preservation, of the safety of the commonweal, and of the ancient nobility, with great reason and justice he executed them, whom, if he had suffered to live, were likely enough to have been the destruction of him, it, and them. But the deed accomplished, stirred up no little fear in the Queen-mother and her faction; for the Queen's taking sanctuary with her younger son Richard Duke of York, without any cause that he knew, drove Gloucester to suppose that they doubted of their right, and put him in possibility of obtaining his own. Wherein by ambitious Buckingham he was assisted, who then related to him afresh the unlawful marriage of his brother, that being unlawful, consequently his children were bastards, and so undoubtedly the crown was lawfully his. . . . Were it not common, every day's issue, it were admirable to note the impudence of man, who at this instant condemns actions which himself would instantly accom-

plish were he permitted by occasion. The Queen-mother's fear, his own right, Buckingham's aid, and his own jealousy to erect a prince, too young to govern himself, much less others, but was likely to be governed by his mother, and her kindred, the Protector's mortallest enemies, men of mean birth, not inured to government, such as were likely to destroy the ancient peers, to fortify their new nobility, could not but draw a true discerning spirit, to favor himself, to protect the ancient nobility, to defend the people from being wasted and oppressed by the ambition and tyranny of new inexperienced statists, and to respect his own preservation, rather than others. For well he saw he could not live, unless he were a king; that there was no safety, but in sovereignty. . . .

The state being thus in labor with innovation, the peers in council about their infant King's coronation, all busy, yet dissenting in their business; in a council held at the Tower, Hastings Lord Chamberlain was apprehended, and no sooner apprehended but executed. The not leisurely proceeding by form of law may seem to plead Hastings' innocence, the Protector's cruelty. But they that consider the nature of the people of that time, apt to sedition, greedy of innovation, and likely to be glad of so pitiful a color (for Hastings was a man grown very popular) will hold the Protector in that action very judicial, and, if guilty of any thing, of discretion and policy. But could Hastings be innocent, whom Commines reporteth to be a pensioner of the French King, Lewis the XI? . . . Or was he fit to be a statesman or councillor . . . who not only enticed his master, but accompanied him in all sensuality; who in the deflowering of men's wives, and such other his unprincelike actions, was his perpetual attendant, and sometimes (as it is thought) would begin to him? Doctor Sha's sermon not a little illustrates the malice of his accusers. For I think, no man that is discreet will imagine this prince so indiscreet, as to have witness that he commanded that sermon, and gave instructions what should be said. Then how do our chroniclers report it for truth, were not their malice greater than either their truth or their judgment? But they are Historians, and must be believed.

Alas, poor men, how would they be believed, whose greatest authorities . . . are built upon the notable foundation of hear-say? . . . But it is not mentioned, that Sha ever executed this action, with alleging him to be the cause. It is likely indeed, that Sha being ambitious, gaping after preferment, supposing some such intent in the Protector (as he had a reaching head) was bold to set his rhetoric to sale, to publish his fancies; but seeing his hopes vanish into smoke, and his expectation deluded, seeing the Protector neither rewarded nor regarded his rhetoric, he soon after languished and died, a just example to teach theologians so boldly to intermeddle with princes' affairs before they be commanded. For (doubtless) had the Protector set him a work, he would have paid him his hire. But if it were so, that he commanded the sermon (as that is yet unproved), was that an offense to make the people so publicly partakers of his right; yea, to prostitute his cause to their judgments? For charging his mother with adultery was a matter of no such great moment, since it is no wonder in that sex. And surely he had more reason to adventure her fame than his kingdom, because of two evils it is wisdom to choose the least. If it were true, it was no injustice to punish it, and could be expected from him; but true justice, who was so impartial, that he would not spare his own mother? If untrue, good faith, he was therein to blame, and her innocence the more meritorious; but certain it is, the people approved his right, for he was crowned with such consent, and so great applause both of peers and people, that if we will judge by the outward behavior (the only mark our judgments may or can level at), we must determine them so contented, as no actions which might testify the satisfaction of their minds were omitted. Surely, if ever the injudicial multitude did any thing judicially, it was in receiving this prince, whom his chief disgracers cannot but acknowledge for valiant. Then who was more meet to restrain domestic, to subdue foreign seditions? . . .

He was neither luxurious, nor an epicure, not given to any riot, nor to excess, neither in apparel nor play; for had he been touched with any of these vices, doubtless they who object lesser crimes would not have omitted these. Then (without question) he was largely interested in virtues, their contraries; but those (through malice) are either not registered, or if registered so infamed, as if all his virtues had a vicious intent. Yet to acknowledge the virtues of the vicious is such a right, that what historian willingly omitteth them, therein becometh vicious himself. . . . For, otherwise, had he lived to have left issue to have succeeded him, such might have been his and their merits, that fame would have been no more injurious to him than to his predecessors the fourth Henry and Edward, whose reigns were

polluted with much more royal blood; for he omitted nothing that in wisdom or true policy, might secure himself, or establish peace of good laws in this kingdom.

His statutes are extant; what can be found in them not becoming a king? What, not befitting the service of God? The worship of religion? The good of his country? Yea, I have heard of some, accounted both good lawyers and good statists, that in those three years of his government, there were more good statutes for the public weal enacted, than in thirty years before. He was no taxer of the people, no oppressor of the commons, though he came to manage an estate whose treasure was exceedingly exhausted; no suppressor of his subjects, to satisfy either licentious humors, or to enrich light-headed flatterers. . . .

This, the charge and commandment that he gave presently after his coronation to the lords and gentlemen (whom he sent home into their counties), that they should in their counties see justice duly administered and impartially (that no wrong, nor extortion should be done to his subjects), doth testify; this his laws, and all his actions approve; yet neither the care of his country, his laws, nor actions are thought to be sufficient to plead his equity and innocence. For malicious credulity rather embraceth the partial writings of indiscreet chroniclers, and witty play-makers, than his laws and actions, the most innocent and impartial witnesses. . . .

To justify his adversaries' accusation, in this time chanced the death of his two young nephews in the Tower, whose deaths promising quiet to him, and wholly imposed upon him, how truly I have reason to doubt because his accusers are so violent and impudent. . . . But if it were so, that their deaths were by him contribed and commanded, the offense was to God, not to the people; for the depriving them of their lives freed the people from dissension. And how could he demonstrate his love more amply, than to adventure his soul for their quiet? But who knoweth, whether it were not God's secret judgment to punish the father's transgression in the children? And if it be so, complain of their fate, not Richard's cruelty. . . .

For him there was no remedy but this one. Then if for this action he ought to be condemned, it is for indiscretion in the managing; for as safely might he have had the realm's general consent, in disposing of their lives as of their kingdom. Had he held a secret execution best he might have effected it more secretly, but he rather chose a middle way, content to let the people know it, holding their knowledge equal with their consents. And it should seem, the people (though they were at that time very factious) yet approved thereof, for we find not that in any action, either inward or outward, they showed any dislike. . . .

Let us yet further clear this wronged prince. It is constantly affirmed (say our chroniclers) that he first noised, after contrived the death of his wife, and that it was bruited before it was effected, thereby with her sorrows to confirm the report. . . . Certain it is (but uncertain that the King caused it), that such a rumor there was, and that it made a great impression in the Queen, deeming (as women are ever fearful) this prophetical relation to be the forerunner of her end; which bewailing to her husband, he sought with all kindness to remove that melancholy fantasy. What more could he do to testify his love, to cure her passions? But how absurd is it to think or imagine that the King contrived her death? Where if he had pleased to marry elsewhere (for that is made the cause) he might and would have used a more safe means by a divorce. . . .

After her death, being desirous to reconcile himself to all such as held themselves offended . . . he labored to win the one sort with benefits and rewards, and freely pardoned the other's misbehaviors and offenses. . . . The end and scope of this reconciliation was to unite himself in marriage with his niece, a contract (no doubt) inconvenient, and prohibited the vulgar; but amongst statesmen it is like to produce infinite good, both to prince and people. . . . It is granted that this desire of marriage was mentioned by this king, in respect of the public peace, to make satisfaction to the mother in exalting the daughter, for the ejecting of the sons, and to avoid the effusion of much of the people's blood, which was likely to be spilt if his niece should marry elsewhere. . . . For well he knew the headstrong obstinacy of this people could hardly be kept in awe by a man, therefore impossible to be restrained by children; this made him dispossess them of their kingdom, and (peradventure) of their lives, for had they been suffered to live, they would ever have been the firebrands of new seditions; and therefore he thought it more convenient, they should be quenched with their own bloods than with the bloods of infinite numbers of the people. Yet to make satisfaction for this wrong (if it were a wrong to deprive the disturbers of the common good), he was contented and much labored to marry their sister, his niece, but he

is therefore adjudged ill. Why? Because his accusers would be reputed good, though (without doubt) he was a good prince, and they all, or the most part of all, evil, fantastic and seditious people. . . .

About the time of the plotting of this marriage, the judicial Buckingham (not thinking himself sufficiently regarded), grew discontent, and got the Prince's favor to retire himself into the country; where (no doubt) his fantastic melancholy would soon have vanished . . . had not the prisoner corrupted the jailer, namely Morton, Bishop of Ely (committed by King Richard to his custody), who finding this Duke discontented, more desirous to inflame his griefs, than to redress them, with his fiery wit so wrought upon the Duke's combustible matter, that suddenly he brought him to kindle a fire of rebellion, and to take up arms against his sovereign. This King Richard soon hearing, he prosecuted him as an enemy, and so labored . . . that within a while he took his head from his body, for being no better able to advise him in his proceedings. . . .

But, to return to our defamed king, had not his mercy exceeded his cruelty, his safety had been better secured, and his name not so much subject to obloquy, for though he cut off the head of a mighty conspirator, yet he suffered the conspiracy to take so deep root, that in the end the branches thereof overtopped his glory, and overshadowed his greatness. For the Countess of Richmond laboring in her son's right, daily enticed and inveigled many to be of her faction; to strengthen which the more, it was plotted between the two mothers to join the two dissenting houses in unity by a marriage. This practice the King well knew; yet mercy, love, lenity so prevailed with him, that he only sought to prevent that conjunction by uniting his brother's daughter with himself, and inflicting no other punishment on the Countess, but only the committing of her to the custody of her husband. Would a cruel bloodthirsty prince have done so? Could any thing have been performed with more mildness and lenity? . . . With no less merciful gentleness he used her husband, and that at such time as her son had already landed and made claim to the kingdom, for he only took his son the Lord Strange as an hostage, and then suffered him to go into the country to levy his forces. So far was he from blood and cruelty, as, though he knew his alliance to the contrary faction, a motive sufficient to make him (as indeed he did) incline to their aid, though he might justly suspect him, and could not have wanted color to have beheaded him (as being father-in-law to his competitor), yet he only detained his son in his camp, and when he had assured notice of his father's disloyal revolt, yet he suffered the hostage of his loyalty to live, an evidence effectual enough to testify that he desired rather to settle than to overthrow the quiet of this land; that he labored to win the hearts of his subjects rather with meekness than cruelty. . . .

But now the heir of Lancaster being come to challenge the crown, what did the King? Did his spirits fail him? Was his magnanimous courage daunted? No, he then gathered new spirit, he new steeled his courage, he withstood him with the height of fortitude, protesting rather to die valiantly than to live less than a king. With what a Roman-like spirit did he resist fortune? Being overthrown, how heroically did he encounter with death? This our detracting chroniclers cannot but acknowledge, for so high, so powerful was his magnanimity, that in spite of malice it prevaileth, and like the sun breaketh through the misty clouds of his adversaries' slanders. . . . Surely he did courageously and valiantly withstand his enemies, with great expedition rallying his forces, and performing all things with wonderful celerity, he went to encounter the disturbers of his quiet.

It is reported, that the night before the day of the battle, he dreamed a most dreadful and horrible dream, which by our chroniclers is interpreted to be a testimony of his wicked and tyrannous life. Did not Caesar, before he attained the Empire, dream that he knew his own mother carnally? Had not both Dion and Brutus the figures of terrible spirits represented unto them, the night before their end? And yet these were reputed good men, and lovers and protectors of their country, and because King Richard dreamed with some terror, must his life of necessity be evil? O vain! O frivolous objection! But they hold this dream to be a compunction of his conscience. Happy prince to have so indiscreet slanderers; for how could they more truly witness his integrity, since only they who reverence and fear God are endowed with that inquiring conscience, which censureth their actions? For they who are given over to a reprobate sense are insensible of that good angel, which seeketh by telling us our faults, to make us repent our sins past, and to be wary, lest we commit any more.

Surely, I think, his conscience (like a glass) presented before him the figures of all his actions, which he faithfully examining, humbly craved pardon for his misdeeds; and so having made atonement with God, like a devout penitentiary settled his mind, he went with alacrity to the bloody court, where the cause of his life was to be tried, where his sword being his advocate, pleaded most valiantly. In all which tumult, he failed neither in discretion nor in execution, but boldly encouraged his soldiers, both by word and example. . . .

But now (both battles being joined) what did this valiant King? Did he only stand to give directions to others? No, he did rigorous execution with his sword upon his enemies. Did he, when he perceived some of his subjects disloyally to revolt, and that his forces were put to the worst, think upon yielding or flight? Though by some of his faithfullest servants he was counseled to fly, and for that purpose presented with a horse of wonderful speed, yet he would not, for having been inured to conquest, he scorned to yield. Having been a king, he would not die a vassal; and therefore because the garland was a crown, the prize of a kingdom; victory, majesty, and perpetual renown the reward, this lion-hearted King courageously charging his spear, ran into the battalion of his adversaries, where with his own hand he slew the stout Sir William Brandon, standard bearer of his enemy. He overthrew the strong and valiant Sir John Cheney, and singled out his competitor, who being the most heroic and valiant prince of those times, yet had doubtless been slain, had not he been rescued by Sir William Stanley, who came happily with three thousand men to his rescue, who on all sides encompassing King Richard, so assailed him, that though he did more than a man, though his sword acted wonders, yet being oppressed by so great a multitude, he was there manfully slain, not overcome, for he conquered the betrayers of men in danger, passion and fear.

Thus lost he both kingdom and life, but nothing diminished his interior virtues. . . . Yet neither can his blood redeem him from injurious tongues, nor the reproach offered his body be thought cruel enough, but that we must still make him more cruelly infamous in pamphlets and plays. Compare him now, judicious reader, impartially with other princes; judge truly of all their actions, their form of government, and their statutes and ordinances, the upholders, the strength, the sinews of government; and thou shalt find him as innocent of cruelty, extortion and tyranny as the most, as wise, politic and valiant as any. If so, censure him his actions, his ordinances, according to their deserts, and this treatise of mine as a charitable well wishing to a scandalized and defamed king.

From English History [1]

Richard, Duke of Gloucester, at the self same time that his brother King Edward departed this life, was in Yorkshire, unto whom William Hastings his chamberlain sent from London trusty messengers in post to certify him of his brother's death, and from himself to signify, that the king at his death had committed to him only, wife, children, goods, and all that ever he had, and therefore to exhort him, that he would with all convenient speed repair unto Prince Edward into Wales, and come with him to London to undertake the government. When Richard had intelligence hereof, he began to be kindled with an ardent desire of sovereignty; but for that there was no cause at all whereby he might bring the same to pass that could carry any color of honesty, so much as in outward show and appearance, he . . . sent most loving letters to Elizabeth the queen, comforting her with many words, and promising . . . to increase the credit of his carefulness and natural affection towards his brother's children, calling together unto York the honorable and worshipful of the country thereabout, he commanded all men to swear obedience unto Prince Edward; himself was the first that took the oath, which soon after he was the first to violate. . . . These things done, having gathered no small force of armed men, he prepared to set forward when time should serve. Prince Edward, being but a child in years not able to rule himself, lay the same time within his principality at Ludlow, under the tuition of his uncle Anthony, Earl Rivers; Thomas Vaughan, chief of his chamber; and Richard Gray, knight. Elizabeth the queen, and Thomas, Marquis Dorset, her son by John Gray her former husband, who was at London, advised these men by often messages to conduct the prince forthwith to London, that after the funeral of his father solemnized, he might, after the manner of his ancestors, be crowned king. They according to the queen's and mar-

quis's commandment took their journey not long after toward London. Richard also hastened thither, whom Henry, Duke of Buckingham met at Northampton, with whom the Duke of Gloucester had long conference. . . .

And thus when they had taken counsel Richard made haste unto the prince, who journeyed on before with a small train, and was now come to Stony Stratford . . . when he, together with Henry the duke, guarded with a band of soldiers, overtook the prince and received him into his rule and government; but he apprehended Anthony and Thomas Vaughan, and divers others, whom after he had taken supposing that they would not assent to his intent and purpose, he sent back to be kept in ward at Pontefract castle.

But when the fame of so outrageous and horrible fact came to London, all men were wonderously amazed, and in great fear, but especially Elizabeth the queen was much dismayed, and determined forthwith to fly; for, suspecting even then that there was no plain dealing, to the intent she might deliver her other children from the present danger, she conveyed herself with them and the marquis into the sanctuary at Westminster. . . . But Lord Hastings who bore privy hatred to the marquis and others of the queen's side, who for that cause had exhorted Richard to take upon him the government of the prince, when he saw all in uproar and that matters fell out otherwise than he had intended, repenting therefore that which he had done, called together unto [St.] Paul's church such friends as he knew to be right careful for the life, dignity, and estate of Prince Edward, and conferred with them what best was to be done. Here divers of them who were most offended with this late fact of Richard Duke of Gloucester, adjudged it meet with all speed to procure the liberty of Prince Edward, whom they accounted as utterly oppressed and wronged by force and violence. . . .

Not long after arrived Duke Richard and Henry with the prince, and lodged at the Bishop

[1] Sir Henry Ellis, ed., *Camden Society Publications*, **XXIX** (London, 1844).

of London's house beside [St.] Paul's, where their will was the prince should remain till other matters might be put in readiness. Then did Duke Richard assume the government wholly; but it grieved him spitefully that he might not receive into his tuition, without some great stir, his brother's other son Richard Duke of York, whom his mother kept in sanctuary; for, except he might get them both together into his power and custody, he utterly despaired to compass that which he longed for. . . .

And so it was agreed that Thomas Archbishop of Canterbury, Henry Duke of Buckingham, John Lord Howard, and sundry other grave men should deal in that cause, who repairing unto the sanctuary began to persuade the queen with many fair words and persuasions that she would return with her children into the palace, unto whom they gave both private and public assurance; but the woman, foreseeing in a sort within herself the thing that followed forthwith after, could not be moved with any persuasions to commit herself to the credit of Duke Richard, which when they understood, finally they demanded to be delivered to them her son Richard only, which they obtained hardly after many fair promises. And so was the innocent child pulled out of his mother's arms.

Richard having by this means obtained almost his heart's desire, conveyed his nephews from the Bishop of London's house unto the Tower; and yet all this caused no suspicion, for that the usage is at the king's coronation for the whole assembly to come out from thence solemnly, and so proceed to Westminster. . . .

But in the meantime perceiving that William Lord Hastings was most vehement and earnest to have Prince Edward once crowned king, who chiefly amongst all nobility was, for his bountifulness and liberality, much beloved of the common people, bearing great sway among all sorts of men and persons of best reputation, whether it were that he feared his power, or despaired it possible to draw him to his side and opinion, he determined to rid the man out of the way before his purpose should be discovered to the residue, whom he did not yet fully trust. Wherefore, burning with rage incredible to bring to effect the thing which in mind was resolved, he drew a plot for Lord Hastings as followeth: he placed privily in a chamber adjoining to that where himself and other lords sat usually in council a sort right ready to do a mischief, giving them in charge that when he should give a sign they should suddenly rush out, and, compassing about them who should sit with him, to lay hands specially upon William Lord Hastings, and kill him forthwith. This train thus laid, about the day before the ides of June he commanded to be sent for specially by name Thomas Rotherham Archbishop of York, John Morton Bishop of Ely, Henry Duke of Buckingham, Thomas Lord Stanley, William Lord Hastings, John Lord Howard, and many others whom he trusted to find faithful either for fear or benefit. The residue of the nobility, together with John Russell Bishop of Lincoln, Lord Chancellor of England, whom his will was not to have present at such an outrageous and foul spectacle, he commanded to be the same day at Westminster hall, with other magistrates, to proclaim the day of Prince Edward's coronation. But the nobles who were called came well early all into the Tower as to deliberate of the whole matter. Here, when the doors were shut, while they thus alone without testimony of any other than only God, had good will to consult of the most weighty affairs, Richard Duke of Gloucester, who thought of nothing but tyranny and cruelty, spoke unto them in this sort: "My lords, I have procured you all to be called hither this day for that only cause that I might show unto you in what great danger of death I stand; for by the space of a few days by past neither night nor day can I rest, drink, nor eat, wherefore my blood by little and little decreases, my force fails, my breath shortens, and all the parts of my body do above measure, as you see (and with that he showed them his arm), fall away; which mischief verily proceeds in me from that sorceress Elizabeth the queen, who with her witchcraft has so enchanted me that by the annoyance thereof I am dissolved." To these sayings when no man gave answer, as making little to the purpose, William Lord Hastings, who hated not Duke Richard, and was wont to speak all things with him very freely, answered, that the queen deserved well both to be put to open shame, and to be duly punished, if it might appear that by use of witchcraft she had done him any harm. To these Richard replied: "I am undone (I say) by that very woman's sorcery." Whereunto William made the same answer that before. Then Richard, to give a sign for them who were without laid privily for the nonce, spoke with more shrill voice: "What then, William, if by thine own practices I be brought to destruction?" He had scarce uttered these words when as they to whom charge was committed in that behalf issued, and with open assault apprehended all at once William Lord Hastings, both the Bishops of York and Ely, and also Lord Stanley. These three last were cast there into several prisons; but William Lord Hastings had scarce leisure to make his confession before his head was struck from his shoulders. . . .

When these things were done, Richard, knowing then for certain that there was no cause why he should any further dissemble the matter, sent his letters of warrant to the keeper of Pontefract castle to behead in haste Anthony Lord Rivers, Richard Gray, and Thomas Vaughan, which was done soon after. . . .

And so the man, being blind with covetousness of reigning, whom no foul fact could now hold back, after that he had resolved not to spare the blood of his own house, supposing also all regard of honor was to be rejected, devised and bethought himself of such a sleight as follows. He had secret conference with one Ralph Sha, a divine of great reputation as then among the people, to whom he uttered, that his father's inheritance ought to descend to him by right, as the eldest of all the sons which Richard his father Duke of York had begotten of Cecily his wife; for as much as it was manifest enough, and that by apparent argument, that Edward, who had before reigned, was a bastard, that is, not begotten of a right and lawful wife; praying the said Sha to instruct the people thereof in a sermon at Paul's Cross, whereby they might once in the end acknowledge their true liege lord. And said that he greatly required the same, because he esteemed it more meet to neglect his mother's honor and honesty than to suffer so noble a realm to be polluted with such a race of kings. This Ralph, whether dazed with fear, or bereft his wits, promised to follow, and obey his commandment. But when the day came, Duke Richard, who, under the color of serving another turn, had made himself mighty, came in royal manner, with a great guard of men armed, unto the church of St. Paul, and there was attentively present at the sermon. . . . But there is a common report that King Edward's children were in that sermon called bastards, and not King Edward, which is void of all truth; for Cecily, King Edward's mother, as is before said, being falsely accused of adultery, complained afterward in sundry places to right many noble men, whereof some yet live, of that great injury which her son Richard had done her. . . .

Thus Richard, without assent of the com-

monalty, by might and will of certain noblemen of his faction, enjoined the realm, contrary to the law of God and man; who, not long after, having established all things at London according to his own fancy, took his journey to York, and first he went straight to Gloucester, where the while he tarried the heinous guilt of wicked conscience did so fret him every moment that he lived in continual fear, for the expelling whereof by any kind of mean he determined by death to dispatch his nephews, because so long as they lived he could never be out of hazard; wherefore he sent warrant to Robert Brackenbury, lieutenant of the Tower of London, to procure their death with all diligence, by some convenient means. . . . But the lieutenant of the Tower at London after he had received the king's horrible commission was astonished with the cruelty of the fact, and fearing lest if he should obey the same might at one time or other turn to his own harm, did therefore defer the doing thereof in hope that the king would spare his own blood, or their tender age, or alter that heavy determination. But any one of those points was so far from taking place, seeing that the mind therein remained immovable, as that when King Richard understood the lieutenant to make delay of that which he had commanded, he anon committed the charge of hastening that slaughter unto another, that is to say James Tyrell, who, being forced to do the king's commandment, rode sorrowfully to London, and, to the worst example that hath been almost ever heard of, murdered those babes of the issue royal. This end had Prince Edward and Richard his brother; but with what kind of death these innocent children were executed it is not certainly known. But King Richard, delivered by this fact from his care and fear, kept the slaughter not long secret, who, within few days after, permitted the rumor of their death to go abroad, to the intent (as we may well believe) that after the people understood no issue male of King Edward to be now left alive, they might with better mind and good will bear and sustain his government. . . .

But hard it is to alter the natural disposition of one's mind, and suddenly to exterp the thing therein settled by daily conversation. And so, whether it were for that cause, or (as the bruit commonly goeth) because he now repented of his evil deeds he began afterward to take on hand a certain new form of life, and to give the show and countenance of a good man, whereby he might be accounted more righteous, more mild, better affected to the commonalty, and more liberal especially toward the poor; and so first might merit pardon for his offenses at God's hand; then after appease partly the envy of man, and procure himself good will, he began many works as well public as private, which (being prevented by death before his time) he perfected not. He founded a college at York of an hundred priests. Also he began now to give ear to the good admonition of his friends. But anon after it appeared evident that fear, which seldom causeth continuance of dutiful dealing, made King Richard so suddenly good, for as much as the bountifulness of the man being but counterfeit waxed cold again quickly; by reason whereof all his proposed practices began straight way to come to naught. For first he lost Edward his only son the third month after he had been made Prince of Wales; after that a conspiracy was contrived against him by means of Henry Duke of Buckingham, which, though it were by one of the conspirators discovered before it grew great, yet was he troubled in suppressing thereof. . . .

Therefore the duke . . . having gotten fit occasion to talk of the matter, demanded of King Richard that part of the Earl of Hereford's patrimony that to him by right of inheritance was due. To this King Richard, who supposed that matter to have been now forgotten, is reported to have answered forthwith in great rage, "What now, Duke Henry, will you challenge unto you that right of Henry the Fourth whereby he wickedly usurped the crown, and so make open for yourself the way thereunto?" Which King Richard's answer settled deep into the duke's breast, who from that time forth, moved much with ire and indignation, began to devise by what means he might thrust out that ungrateful man from the royal seat for whose cause he had right often done many things against his own conscience otherwise than before God he lawfully might. The duke, thus affected, accompanied King Richard not long after as he journeyed toward York unto Gloucester, from thence with his consent he repaired into Wales, where a great part of his livings lay. Here the while of his tarry, provoked partly by fresh memory of the late received injury, partly repenting that hitherto of himself he had not resisted King Richard's evil enterprise, but much had furthered the same, he resolved to separate himself from him (though indeed he should so have done in the beginning), and to bring to pass the thing which he had long revolved in

mind: and so he began to discover his intent to John, Bishop of Ely, whom (as we have before remembered) he had in Brecknock castle. The bishop suspecting treason, demanded why he went on about that matter, and prayed to do him no harm; afterward when he understood his just cause of hatred, which King Richard had well deserved long ago, he refused not to confer of the conspiracy. Then the duke unfolded all things to the Bishop of Ely, and discovered himself wholly, showing how he had devised the means whereby both the blood of King Edward and of Henry the Sixth that yet was remaining, being conjoined by affinity, might be restored to the dominion due unto both their progeny. The means was this, that Henry Earl of Richmond . . . might be sent for in all haste possible, and assisted with all that they might do, so that he would promise before by solemn oath, that after he had once obtained the kingdom he would take to wife Elizabeth, King Edward's eldest daughter.

The Bishop of Ely allowed as well the Duke's device as the manner of performing the same, and procured one Reginald Bray, servant to Margaret, Earl Henry's mother, who had married Thomas Lord Stanley, to come unto the duke into Wales, and his pleasure known to return speedily unto Margaret, and certify her of all things which had been deliberated betwixt him and the duke concerning common safety. This truly was the matter from which dissension sprang betwixt the king and the duke, and whereupon the conspiracy was made against him. But the common report was otherwise; for the multitude said that the duke did the less dissuade King Richard from usurping the kingdom, by means of so many mischievous deeds, upon the intent that he afterward, being hated both of God and man, might be expelled from the same, and so himself be called by the commons to that dignity, whereunto he aspired by all means possible, and that therefore he had at the last stirred up war against King Richard. . . .

Richard in the meantime having intelligence what covenants the confederates in Brittany had made amongst themselves, and how they had all escaped into France by the conduct of Earl Henry . . . determined to prevent by another way that Earl Henry should not come unto the kingdom by marriage of his niece Elizabeth. And because, in comparison of the horrible facts which blinded with desire of sovereignty, he had before enterprised, all other things that he should do afterward seemed in his estimation but small matters . . . there came therefore into his mind matter the most wicked to be spoken, and the foulest to be committed, that ever was heard of. For while he revolved with himself how great heap of mischief was imminent if Henry should be advanced by marriage of his niece . . . he therefore determined, by all means possible, to reconcile unto him Elizabeth the queen, that she might yield herself and her daughters into his hands, and Henry by that means defrauded from the affinity of his niece; and if it were not possible to salve the sores imminent otherwise, and that by hap it might fortune his wife to die, then he would rather marry his niece himself than by the affinity aforesaid to danger the state, as though by his fall the ruin of the realm must needs follow. And so he sent into the sanctuary often messengers unto the queen . . . promising mountains both unto her and her son Thomas the marquis to put the woman in passing great hope. The messengers being grave men, though at the first by reducing to memory the slaughter of her sons they somewhat wounded the queen's mind, and that her grief seemed scarce able to be comforted, yet they assailed her by so many means, and so many fair promises, that without much ado they began to mollify her (for so mutable is that sex), in so much that the woman heard them willingly, and finally said she would yield herself unto the king; and so not very long after, forgetting injuries, forgetting her faith and promise given to Margaret, Henry's mother, she first delivered her daughters into the hands of King Richard; then after by secret messengers advised the marquis her son, who was at Paris, to forsake Earl Henry, and with all speed convenient to return into England, where he should be sure to be called of the king unto high promotion. When the queen was thus qualified, King Richard received all his brother's daughters out of sanctuary into the court.

The only matter now remaining was to acquit himself of marriage, which he adjudged best for him to do by all means possible; but this savage and cruel mind of his was no little feared from so great and outrageous fact, for that (as we have before mentioned) he had of late counterfeited to be a good man, and therefore was afeared lest by the untimely death of his wife he should hinder the good opinion which he believed the people had conceived upon him. But the wicked intent won the mastery in the man wayward from all righteousness; for first he forbore to lie with her, and

withal began to complain much unto many noblemen of his wife's unfruitfulness, for that she brought him forth no children, and that chiefly did he lament with Thomas Rotherham, Archbishop of York, because he was a grave and good man, whom he had a little before let out of prison (who thereupon gathered and supposed it would come to pass that the queen should not long live, and foreshowed the same to divers [of] his friends). Then after he procured a rumor (uncertain from whom) to be spread abroad of the queen his wife's death, that either the woman being brought in great dolor, by report and fame of the matter, might fall into sickness, or else that he might thereby take a proof if the same should happen afterward whether the people would lay the blame thereof unto his charge. But when the queen heard of such terrible rumors dispersed already of her own death, supposing that her days were at an end, she went unto her husband very pensive and sad, and with many tears demanded of him what cause there was why he should determine her death. Hereunto the king, lest he might seem hard-hearted if he should show unto his wife no sign of love, kissing her, made answer lovingly, and comforting her, bade her be of good cheer. But the queen, whether she were dispatched with sorrowfulness, or poison, died within few days after, and was buried at Westminster. This is Anne, that one of the daughters of Richard Earl of Warwick who was sometime covenanted to Prince Edward, son to King Henry the Sixth. The king, thus loosed from the bond of matrimony, began to cast an eye upon Elizabeth his niece, and to desire her in marriage; but because both the young lady herself, and all others, did abhor the wickedness so detestable, he determined therefore to do every thing by leisure, for so much especially as he was overwhelmed with pinching cares on every hand; for that some man of name passed over daily unto Henry, others favored secretly the partners of the conspiracy. Amongst these principally was Thomas Stanley, William his brother, Gilbert Talbot, and others innumerable, whose inward mind though Richard was ignorant of, yet he trusted never one of them all, and Thomas Stanley least of all others, because he had in marriage Henry's mother, as the matter itself made manifest show; for when he at that time would have gone into his country, for his pleasure as he said, but indeed that he might be ready to receive Earl Henry as a friend at his coming, the king forbade him, and would not suffer him to depart before he had left George Lord Strange, his son, as a pledge in the court. . . .

In the meantime King Richard, hearing that the enemy drew near, came first to the place of fight, a little beyond Leicester (the name of that village is Bosworth), and there, pitching his tents, refreshed his soldiers that night from their travail, and with many words exhorted them to the fight to come. It is reported that King Richard had that night a terrible dream; for he thought in his sleep that he saw horrible images as it were of evil spirits haunting evidently about him, as it were before his eyes, and that they would not let him rest; which vision truly did not so much strike into his breast a sudden fear, as replenish the same with heavy cares: for forthwith after, being troubled in mind, his heart gave him thereupon that the event of the battle following would be grievous, and he did not buckle himself to the conflict with such liveliness of courage and countenance as before, which heaviness that it should not be said he showed as appalled with fear of his enemies, he reported his dream to many in the morning. . . .

The next day after King Richard, furnished thoroughly with all manner of things, drew his whole host out of their tents, and arrayed his van, stretching it forth of a wonderful length, so full replenished both with footmen and horsemen that to the beholders afar off it gave a terror for the multitude, and in the front were placed his archers, like a most strong trench and bulwark; of these archers he made leader John Duke of Norfolk. After this long van followed the king himself, with a choice force of soldiers. In the meantime Henry, being departed back from the conference with his friends, began to take better heart, and without any tarry encamped himself nigh his enemies, where he rested all night, and well early in the morning commanded the soldiers to arm themselves, sending withal to Thomas Stanley, who was now approached the place of fight, midway betwixt the two battles, that he would come to with his forces, to set the soldiers in array. He answered that the earl should set his own folks in order, while he should come to him with his army well appointed. . . . He [Henry] made a slender van for the small number of his people; before the same he placed archers, of whom he made captain John Earl of Oxford; in the right wing of the van he placed Gilbert Talbot to defend the same; in the left verily he sat John Savage; and himself, trusting to the aid of Thomas Stanley, with one troop of horsemen,

and a few footmen did follow. . . . There was a marsh betwixt both hosts, which Henry of purpose left on the right hand, that it might serve his men instead of a fortress, by the doing thereof also he left the sun upon his back; but when the king saw the enemy pass the marsh, he commanded his soldiers to give charge upon them. They making suddenly great shouts assaulted the enemy first with arrows, who were nothing faint unto the fight but began also to shoot fiercely; but when they came to hand-strokes the matter then was dealt with blades. In the meantime the Earl of Oxford, fearing lest his men in fighting might be environed of the multitude, commanded in every rank that no soldiers should go above ten feet from the standards; which charge being known, when all men had thronged thick together, and stayed awhile from fighting, the adversaries were therewith afeared, supposing some fraud, and so they all forbore the fight a certain space, and that verily did many with right good will, who rather coveted the king dead than alive, and therefore fought faintly. . . .

While the battle continued thus hot on both sides betwixt the vans, King Richard understood, first by spies where Earl Henry was afar off with small force of soldiers about him; then after drawing near he knew it perfectly by evident signs and tokens that it was Henry; wherefore, all inflamed with ire, he struck his horse with the spurs, and ran out of the one side without the van against him. Henry perceived King Richard come upon him, and because all his hope was then in valiancy of arms, he received him with great courage. King Richard at the first brunt killed certain, overthrew Henry's standard, together with William Brandon the standard bearer, and matched also with John Cheney a man of much fortitude . . . but the king with great force drove him to the ground, making way with weapon on every side. But yet Henry abode the brunt longer than ever his own soldiers would have weened, who were now almost out of hope of victory, when lo William Stanley with three thousand men came to the rescue: then truly in a very moment the residue all fled, and King Richard alone was killed fighting manfully in the thickest press of his enemies. . . . The report is that King Richard might have sought to save himself by flight; for they who were about him, seeing the soldiers even from the first stroke to lift up their weapons feebly and faintly, and some of them to depart the field privily, suspected treason, and exhorted him to fly, yea and when the matter began manifestly to quail, they brought him swift horses; but he, who was not ignorant that the people hated him, out of hope to have any better hap afterward, is said to have answered, that that very day he would make end either of war or life, such great fierceness and such huge force of mind he had: wherefore, knowing certainly that that day would either yield him a peaceable and quiet realm from thenceforth or else perpetually bereave him the same, he came to the field with the crown upon his head, that thereby he might either make a beginning or end of his reign. . . .

Henry, after the victory obtained, gave forthwith thanks unto Almighty God for the same; then after, replenished with joy incredible, he got himself unto the next hill, where, after he had commended his soldiers, and commanded to cure the wounded, and to bury them that were slain, he gave unto nobility and gentlemen immortal thanks, promising that he would be mindful of their benefits, all which meanwhile the soldiers cried, "God save King Henry, God save King Henry!" and with heart and hand uttered all the show of joy that might be; which when Thomas Stanley did see, he set King Richard's crown, found among the spoil in the field, upon his head. . . . In the mean-

time the body of King Richard naked of all clothing, and laid upon horseback with the arms and legs hanging down on both sides, was brought to the abbey of Franciscan monks at Leicester, a miserable spectacle in good sooth, but not unworthy for the man's life, and there was buried two days after without any pomp or solemn funeral. He reigned two years and so many months, and one day over. He was little of stature, deformed of body, one shoulder being higher than the other, a short and sour countenance, which seemed to savor of mischief, and utter evidently craft and deceit. The while he was thinking of any matter, he did continually bite his nether lip, as though that cruel nature of his did rage against itself in that little carcass. Also he was wont to be ever with his right hand pulling out of the sheath to the middle, and putting in again, the dagger which he did always wear. Truly he had a sharp wit, provident and subtle, apt both to counterfeit and dissemble; his courage also high and fierce, which failed him not in the very death, which, when his men forsook him, he rather yielded to take with the sword, than by foul flight to prolong his life, uncertain what death perchance soon after by sickness or other violence to suffer.

From The Chronicle of the Abbey of Croyland[1]

For awhile the councillors of the king, now deceased, were present with the queen at Westminster, and were naming a certain day, on which the eldest son of King Edward (who at this time was in Wales) should repair to London for the ceremonial of his coronation, there were various contentions among some of them, what number of men should be deemed a sufficient escort for a prince of such tender years, to accompany him upon his journey. Some were for limiting a greater, some a smaller number, while others again . . . would have it to consist of whatever number his faithful subjects should think fit to summon. Still, the ground of these differences was the same in each case; it being the most ardent desire of all who were present, that this prince should succeed his father in all his glory. The more prudent members of the council, however, were of the opinion that the guardianship of so youthful a person, until he should reach the years of maturity, ought to be utterly forbidden to his uncles and brothers by the mother's side. This, however, they were of opinion, could not be so easily brought about, if it should be allowed those of the queen's relatives who held the chief places about the prince, to bring him up for the solemnization of the coronation, without an escort of a moderate number of horse. The advice of Lord Hastings, the Captain of Calais, at last prevailed; who declared that he himself would fly thither with all speed, rather than await the arrival of the new king, if he did not come attended by a moderate escort. For he was afraid lest, if the supreme power should fall into the hands of the queen's relations, they would exact a most signal vengeance for the injuries which had been formerly inflicted on them by that same lord; in consequence of which, there had long existed extreme ill-will

[1] From *Ingulph's Chronicle of the Abbey of Croyland*, Henry T. Riley, ed., Bohn's Antiquarian Library (London, 1854).

between the said Lord Hastings and them. The queen most beneficially tried to extinguish every spark of murmuring and disturbance, and wrote to her son, requesting him, on his road to London not to exceed an escort of two thousand men. The same number was also approved of by the before-named lord; for, as it would appear, he felt fully assured that the Dukes of Gloucester and Buckingham, in whom he placed the greatest confidence, would not bring a smaller number with them.

The body of the deceased king being accordingly interred with all honor in due ecclesiastical form, in the new collegiate chapel of Windsor . . . all were most anxiously awaiting the day of the new king's coronation, which was to be the first Lord's day in the month of May, which fell this year on the fourth day of the said month. In the meantime, the Duke of Gloucester wrote the most soothing letters in order to console the queen, with promises that he would shortly arrive, and assurances of all duty, fealty, and due obedience to his king and lord Edward the Fifth, the eldest son of the deceased king, his brother, and of the queen. Accordingly, on his arrival at York with a becoming retinue, each person being arrayed in mourning, he performed a solemn funeral service for the king, the same being accompanied with plenteous tears. Constraining all the nobility of those parts to take the oath of fealty to the late king's son, he himself was the first of all to take the oath. On reaching Northampton, where the Duke of Buckingham joined him, there came thither for the purpose of paying their respects to him, Antony, Earl Rivers, the king's uncle, and Richard Grey, a most noble knight, and uterine brother to the king, together with several others who had been sent by the king, his nephew, to submit the conduct of everything to the will and discretion of his uncle, the Duke of Gloucester. On their first arrival, they were received with an especially cheerful and joyous countenance, and, sitting at supper at the duke's table, passed the whole time in very pleasant conversation. At last, Henry, Duke of Buckingham, also arrived there, and, as it was now late, they all retired to their respective lodgings.

When the morning, and as it afterwards turned out, a most disastrous one, had come, having taken counsel during the night, all the lords took their departure together, in order to present themselves before the new king at Stony Stratford, a town a few miles distant from Northampton; and now, lo and behold! when the two dukes had nearly arrived at the entrance of that town, they arrested the said Earl Rivers and his nephew Richard, the king's brother, together with some others who had come with them, and commanded them to be led prisoners into the north of England. Immediately after, this circumstance being not yet known in the neighbouring town, where the king was understood to be, they suddenly rushed into the place where the youthful king was staying, and in like manner made prisoners of certain others of his servants who were in attendance on his person. One of these was Thomas Vaughan, an aged knight and chamberlain of the prince before-named.

The Duke of Gloucester, however, who was the ringleader in this outbreak, did not omit or refuse to pay every mark of respect to the king, his nephew, in the way of uncovering the head, bending the knee, or other posture of the body required in a subject. He asserted that his only care was for the protection of his own person as he knew for certain that there were men in attendance upon the king who had conspired against both his own honor and his very existence. Thus saying, he caused proclamation to be made, that all the king's attendants should instantly withdraw from the town, and not approach any place to which the king might chance to come, under penalty of death. These events took place at Stony Stratford on Wednesday, on the last day of April. . . .

These reports having reached London on the following night, Queen Elizabeth betook herself, with all her children to the sanctuary at Westminster. In the morning you might have seen there the adherents of both parties, some sincerely, others treacherously, on account of the uncertainty of events, siding with the one party or the other. For some collected their forces at Westminster in the queen's name, others at London under the shadow of Lord Hastings, and took up their position there.

In a few days after this, the before-named dukes escorted the new king to London, there to be received with regal pomp; and, having placed him in the bishop's palace at Saint Paul's, compelled all the lords spiritual and temporal, and the mayor and aldermen of the city of London to take the oath of fealty to the king. This, as being a most encouraging presage of future prosperity, was done by all with the greatest pleasure and delight. A council being now held for several days, a discussion took place in Parliament about removing the king to some place where fewer restrictions should be imposed upon him. Some mentioned the Hospital of Saint John, and some Westminster, but the Duke of Buckingham suggested the Tower of London; which was at last agreed to by all, even those who had been originally opposed thereto. Upon this, the Duke of Gloucester received the same high office of Protector of the kingdom, which had been formerly given to Humphrey, Duke of Gloucester, during the minority of King Henry [VI]. He was accordingly invested with this authority, with the consent and good-will of all the lords, with power to order and forbid in every matter, just like another king, and according as the necessity of the case should demand. The feast of the Nativity of Saint John the Baptist being appointed as the day upon which the coronation of the king would take place without fail, all both hoped for and expected a season of prosperity for the kingdom. . . .

In the meanwhile, Lord Hastings, who seemed to wish in every way to serve the two dukes and to be desirous of earning their favor, was extremely elated at these changes to which the affairs of this world are so subject, and was in the habit of saying that hitherto nothing whatever had been done except the transferring of the government of the kingdom from two of the queen's blood to two more powerful persons of the king's; and this, too, effected without any slaughter, or indeed causing as much blood to be shed as would be produced by a cut finger. In the course, however, of a very few days after the utterance of these words, this extreme joy of his was supplanted by sorrow. For, the day previously, the Protector had, with singular adroitness, divided the council, so that one part met in the morning at Westminster, and the other at the Tower of London, where the king was. Lord Hastings, on the thirteenth day of the month of June, being the sixth day of the week, on coming to the Tower to join the council, was, by order of the Protector, beheaded. Two distinguished prelates, also, Thomas, Archbishop of York, and John, Bishop of Ely, being out of respect for their order held exempt from capital punishment, were carried prisoners to different castles in Wales. The three strongest supporters of the new king being thus removed without judgment or justice, and all the rest of his faithful subjects fearing the like treatment, the two dukes did thenceforth just as they pleased.

On the Monday following, they came with a great multitude by water to Westminster, armed with swords and staves, and compelled the Cardinal lord Archbishop of Canterbury, with many others, to enter the sanctuary, in order to appeal to the good feelings of the queen and prompt her to allow her son Richard, Duke of York, to come forth and proceed to the Tower, that he might comfort the king his brother. In words, assenting with many thanks to this proposal, she accordingly sent the boy, who was conducted by the lord Cardinal to the king in the Tower of London.

From this day, these dukes acted no longer in secret, but openly manifested their intentions. For, having summoned armed men, in fearful and unheard-of numbers, from the north, Wales, and all other parts then subject to them, the Protector Richard assumed the government of the kingdom, with the title of king, on the twentieth day of the aforesaid month of June; and on the same day, at the great Hall at Westminster, obtruded himself into the marble chair. The color for this act of usurpation, and his thus taking possession of the throne, was the following. It was set forth, by way of prayer, in an address in a certain roll of parchment, that the sons of King Edward were bastards, on the ground that he had contracted a marriage with one lady Eleanor Butler, before his marriage to Queen Elizabeth; added to which, the blood of his other brother, George, Duke of Clarence, had been attainted; so that, at the present time, no certain and uncorrupted lineal blood could be found of Richard, Duke of York, except in the person of the said Richard, Duke of Gloucester. For which reason, he was entreated, at the end of the said roll, on part of the lords and commons of the realm, to assume his lawful rights. However, it was at the time rumored that this address had been got up in the north, whence such vast numbers were flocking to London; although, at the same time, there was not a person but what very well knew who was the

sole mover at London of such seditious and disgraceful proceedings.

These multitudes of people, accordingly, making a descent from the north to the south, under the especial conduct and guidance of Sir Richard Ratcliffe; on their arrival at the town of Pontefract, by command of the said Richard Ratcliffe, and without any form of trial being observed, Antony, Earl Rivers, Richard Grey, his nephew, and Thomas Vaughan, an aged knight, were, in presence of these people, beheaded. This was the second innocent blood which was shed on the occasion of this sudden change.

After these events, Richard, Duke of Gloucester, having summoned Thomas, the Cardinal Archbishop of Canterbury, for the purpose, was on the sixth day of the month of July following, anointed and crowned king, at the conventual church of Saint Peter at Westminster, and, on the same day and place, his queen Anne, received the crown. From this day forward, as long as he lived, this man was styled King Richard, the Third of that name from the Conquest.

Being now desirous, with all speed, to show in the north, where in former years he had chiefly resided, the high and kingly station which he had by these means acquired, he entered the royal city of London, and passing through Windsor, Oxford, and Coventry, at length arrived at York. Here, on a day appointed for repeating his coronation in the metropolitan church, he also presented his only son, Edward, whom, on the same day, he had elevated to the rank of Prince of Wales, with the insignia of the golden wand, and the wreath upon the head. . . .

In the meantime, and while these things were going on, the two sons of King Edward beforenamed remained in the Tower of London, in the custody of certain persons appointed for that purpose. In order to deliver them from this captivity, the people of the southern and western parts of the kingdom began to murmur greatly, and to form meetings and confederacies. It soon became known that many things were going on in secret, and some in the face of all the world, for the purpose of promoting this object, especially on the part of those who, through fear, had availed themselves of the privileges of sanctuary and franchise. There was also a report that it had been recommended by those men who had taken refuge in the sanctuaries, that some of the king's daughters should leave Westminster, and go in disguise to the parts beyond sea; in order that, if any fatal mishap should befall the male children of the late king in the Tower, the kingdom might still, in consequence of the safety of the daughters, some day fall again into the hands of the rightful heirs. On this being discovered, the noble church of the monks at Westminster, and all the neighboring parts, assumed the appearance of a castle and fortress, while men of the greatest austerity were appointed by King Richard to act as the keepers thereof. The captain and head of these was one John Nesfeld, Esquire, who set a watch upon all the inlets and outlets of the monastery, so that not one of the persons there shut up could go forth, and no one could enter, without his permission.

At last, it was determined by the people in the vicinity of the city of London, throughout the counties of Kent, Essex, Sussex, Hampshire, Dorsetshire, Devonshire, Somersetshire, Wiltshire, and Berkshire as well as some others of the southern counties of the kingdom, to avenge their grievances before-stated; upon which, public proclamation was made, that Henry, Duke of Buckingham, who at this time was living at Brecknock in Wales, had repented of his former conduct, and would be the chief mover in this attempt, while a rumor was spread that the sons of King Edward before-named had died a violent death, but it was uncertain how. Accordingly, all those who had set on foot this insurrection, seeing that if they could find no one to take the lead in their designs, the ruin of all would speedily ensue, turned their thoughts to Henry, Earl of Richmond, who had been for many years living in exile in Brittany. To him a message was, accordingly, sent, by the Duke of Buckingham, by advice of the lord Bishop of Ely, who was then his prisoner at Brecknock, requesting him to hasten over to England as soon as he possibly could, for the purpose of marrying Elizabeth, the eldest daughter of the late king, and, at the same, together with her, taking possession of the throne.

The whole design of this plot, however, by means of spies, became perfectly well known to King Richard, who, as he exerted himself in the promotion of all his views in no drowsy manner, but with the greatest activity and vigilance, contrived that, throughout Wales, as well as in all parts of the marches thereof, armed men should be set in readiness around the said duke, as soon as ever he had set a foot from his home, to pounce upon all his property. . . .

Finding that he was placed in a position of extreme difficulty, and that he could in no direction find a safe mode of escape, he [Buckingham] first changed his dress, and then secretly left his people; but was at last discovered in the cottage of a poor man, in consequence of a greater quantity of provisions than usual being carried thither. Upon this, he was led to the city of Salisbury, to which place the king had come with a very large army, on the day of the commemoration of All Souls; and, notwithstanding the fact that it was the Lord's day, the duke suffered capital punishment in the public market-place of that city. . . .

Henry, Earl of Richmond, being unaware of these disturbances, had set sail with certain ships, and arrived with his adherents from Brittany, at the mouth of Plymouth harbor, where he came to anchor, in order to ascertain the real state of affairs. On news being at last brought him of the events which had happened, the death of the Duke of Buckingham, and the flight of his own supporters, he at once hoisted sail, and again put to sea. . . .

I shall pass . . . to the Parliament, which began to sit about the twenty-second day of January. At this sitting, Parliament confirmed the title, by which the king had in the preceding summer, ascended the throne; and although that Lay Court found itself [at first] unable to give a definition of his rights, when the question of the marriage [of Edward IV and Eleanor Butler] was discussed, still, in consequence of the fears entertained of the most persevering [of his adversaries], it presumed to do so, and did do so: while at the same time attainders were made of many lords and men of high rank, besides peers and commoners, as well as three bishops. . . .

During this last Parliament of the kingdom, and after frequent entreaties as well as threats had been made use of, Queen Elizabeth, being strongly solicited so to do, sent all her daughters from the sanctuary at Westminster beforementioned, to King Richard. . . .

However, in a short time after, it was fully seen how vain are the thoughts of a man who desires to establish his interests without the aid of God. For, in the following month of April, on a day not very far distant from the anniversary of King Edward, this only son of his, in whom all the hopes of the royal succession, fortified with so many oaths, were centred, was seized with an illness of but short duration, and died at Middleham Castle, in the year of our Lord, 1484, being the first of the reign of the said King Richard. On hearing the news of this at Nottingham, where they were then residing, you might have seen his father and mother in a state almost bordering on madness, by reason of their sudden grief. . . .

During this feast of the Nativity [1484], far too much attention was given to dancing and gaiety, and vain changes of apparel presented to Queen Anne and the lady Elizabeth, the eldest daughter of the late king, being of similar color and shape; a thing that caused the people to murmur and the nobles and prelates to wonder thereat; while it was said by many that the king was bent, either on the anticipated death of the queen taking place, or else, by means of a divorce, for which he supposed he had quite sufficient grounds, on contracting a marriage with the said Elizabeth. For it appeared that in no other way could his kingly power be established, or the hopes of his rival be put an end to.

In the course of a few days after this, the queen fell extremely sick, and her illness was supposed to have increased still more and more, because the king entirely shunned her bed, declaring that it was by the advice of his physicians that he did so. Why enlarge? About the middle of the following month, upon the day of the great eclipse of the sun, which then took place, Queen Anne, before-named, departed this life, and was buried at Westminster, with no less honors than befitted the interment of a queen.

The king's purpose and intention of contracting a marriage with his niece Elizabeth being mentioned to some who were opposed thereto, the king was obliged, having called a council together, to excuse himself with many words and to assert that such a thing had never once entered his mind. There were some persons, however, present at that same council, who very well knew the contrary. Those in especial who were unwilling that this marriage should take place, and to whose opinions the king hardly ever dared offer any opposition, were Sir Richard Ratcliffe and William Catesby, Esquire of his body. For by these persons the king was told to his face that if he did not abandon his intended purpose, and that, too, before the mayor and commons of the city of London, opposition would not be offered to him by merely the warnings of the voice; for all the people of the north, in whom he placed the greatest reliance, would rise in rebellion against him, and impute to him the death of the queen, the daughter and one of the heirs of the Earl of Warwick, through whom he had first gained his present high position; in order that he might, to the extreme

abhorrence of the Almighty, gratify an incestuous passion for his niece. Besides this, they brought to him more than twelve Doctors of Divinity, who asserted that the pope could grant no dispensation in the case of such a degree of consanguinity. It was supposed by many, that these men, together with others like them, threw so many impediments in the way, for fear lest, if the said Elizabeth should attain the rank of queen, it might at some time be in her power to avenge upon them the death of her uncle, Earl Antony, and her brother Richard, they having been the king's especial advisers in those matters. The king, accordingly followed their advice a little before Easter, in presence of the mayor and citizens of London, in the great hall of the Hospital of Saint John, by making the said denial in a loud and distinct voice; more, however, as many supposed, to suit the wishes of those who advised him to that effect, than in conformity with his own.

Rumors at length increasing daily that those who were in arms against the king were hastening to make a descent upon England, and the king being in doubt at what port they intended to effect a landing (as certain information thereon could be gained by none of his spies), he betook himself to the north. . . .

And then besides, the king, at this period, seemed especially to devote his attention to strengthening the southern parts of his kingdom. But it was all in vain: for, on the first day of August [1485] the enemy landed with a fair wind, and without opposition, at that most celebrated harbor, Milford Haven, near Pembroke.

On hearing of their arrival, the king rejoiced, or at least seemed to rejoice, writing to his adherents in every quarter that now the long wished-for day had arrived, for him to triumph with ease over so contemptible a faction, and thenceforth benefit his subjects with the blessings of uninterrupted tranquillity. . . .

In the meantime . . . the enemy hastening on and directing his steps night and day to meet the king, it became necessary to move the army, though its numbers were not yet fully made up, from Nottingham, and to come to Leicester. Here was found a number of warriors ready to fight on the king's side, greater than had ever been seen before in England collected together in behalf of one person. On the Lord's day before the feast of Bartholomew the Apostle, the king proceeded on his way, amid the greatest pomp, and wearing the crown on his head; being attended by John

Howard, Duke of Norfolk, and Henry Percy, Earl of Northumberland and other mighty lords, knights, and esquires, together with a countless multitude of the common people. On departing from the town of Leicester, he was informed by scouts where the enemy most probably intended to remain the following night; upon which, he encamped near the abbey of Mirival, at a distance of about eight miles from that town. . . .

At day-break on the Monday following there were no chaplains present to perform Divine service on behalf of King Richard, nor any breakfast prepared to refresh the flagging spirits of the king; besides which, as it is generally stated, in the morning he declared that during the night he had seen dreadful visions, and had imagined himself surrounded by a multitude of demons. He consequently presented a countenance which, always attenuated, was on this occasion more livid and ghastly than usual, and asserted that the issue of this day's battle to whichever side the victory might be granted, would prove the utter destruction of the kingdom of England. He also declared that it was his intention, if he should prove the conqueror, to crush all the supporters of the opposite faction; while, at the same time, he predicted that his adversary would do the same towards the well-wishers to his own party, in case the victory should fall to his lot. At length, the prince and knights on the opposite side now advancing at a moderate pace against the royal army, the king gave orders that Lord Strange . . . should be instantly beheaded. The persons, however, to whom this duty was entrusted, seeing that the issue was doubtful in the extreme, and that matters of more importance than the destruction of one individual were about to be decided, delayed the performance of this cruel order of the king, and leaving the man to his own disposal, returned to the thickest of the fight.

A battle of the greatest severity now ensuing between the two sides, the Earl of Richmond, together with his knights, made straight for King Richard: while the Earl of Oxford, who was next in rank to him in the whole army and a most valiant soldier, drew up his forces, consisting of a large body of French and English troops, opposite the wing in which the Duke of Norfolk had taken up his position. In the part where the Earl of Northumberland was posted, with a large and well-provided body of troops, there was no opposition made, as not a blow was given or received during the battle. At length a glorious victory was granted by heaven to the Earl of Richmond, now sole king, together with the crown, of exceeding value, which King Richard had previously worn on his head. For while fighting, and not in the act of flight, King Richard was pierced with numerous deadly wounds, and fell in the field like a brave and most valiant prince. . . .

From A Mirror for Magistrates[1]

From THE TRAGEDY OF LORD HASTINGS

From THE TRAGEDY OF LORD HASTINGS

Ascribed to John Dolman

To council chamber come, awhile we stayed
For him, without whom naught was done or
said.
At last he came, and courteously excused,
For he so long our patience had abused.
And pleasantly began to paint his cheer,
And said, My lord of Ely, would we had here
Some of the strawberries, whereof you have
store.
The last delighted me as nothing more.

Would, what so ye wish, I might as well
command,
My lord (quoth he) as those. And out of hand,
His servant sendeth to Ely place for them.
Out goeth from us the restless devil again.
Belike (I think) scarce yet persuaded full,
To work the mischief that thus madeth his
skull,
At last determined, of his bloody thought
And force ordained, to work the wile he
sought:

Frowning he enters, with so changed cheer,
As for mild May had chopped foul Januere.
And lowering on me with the goggle eye,
The whetted tusk, and furrowed forehead
high,
His crooked shoulder bristle-like set up,
With frothy jaws, whose foam he chawed and
supped,

With angry looks that flamed as the fire:
Thus 'gan at last to grunt the grimmest sire.

What earned they, who me, the kingdom's
stay,
Contrived have council, traitorously to slay?
Abashed all sat. I thought I might be bold,
For conscience clearness, and acquaintance old.
Their hire is plain quoth I. Be death the least,
To who so seeketh your grace so to molest.
Without stay: the queen, and the whore
Shore's wife,
By witchcraft (quoth he) seek to waste my
life.

Lo here the withered and bewitched arm,
That thus is spent by those two sorceress'
charm.
And bared his arm and showed his swinish skin.
Such cloaks they use, that seek to cloud their
sin.
But out alas, it serveth not for the rain.
To all the house the color was too plain.
Nature had given him many a maimed mark,
And it amongst, to note her monstrous work.

My doubtful heart distracted this reply.
For the one I cared not. The other nipped so
nigh
That wist I could not. But forthwith brake
forth.
If so it be, of death they are doubtless worth.
If, traitor? quoth he. Playest thou with ifs and
ands?
I'll on thy body avow it with these hands.
And therewithal he mightily bounced the
board.
In rushed his bill-men. One himself bestirred.

Laying at Lord Stanley whose brain he had
surely cleft
Had he not down beneath the table crept.
But Ely, York, and I, were taken straight.
Imprisoned they: I should no longer wait,
But charged was to shrive me, and shift with
haste.

[1] *A Mirror for Magistrates*, first printed in 1559, was a collection of moralistic accounts, called "tragedies," that portrayed the fall from eminence of well-known figures in English history. As in the following three excerpts, taken from the edition of 1563, the ghost of each character is conceived as narrating his own career, usually addressing himself to William Baldwin, a kind of general editor of the collection. Several editions of the *Mirror* were printed later in the century.

My lord must dine, and now midday was past.
The boar's first dish, not the boar's head should
be.
But Hastings' head the boarish beast would see.

Why stay I his dinner? Unto the chapel
joineth
A greenish hill, that body and soul oft twineth.
There on a block my head was stricken off.
As Baptist's head, for Herod's bloody gnoff.
Thus lived I Baldwin, thus died I, thus I fell.
This is the sum, which all at large to tell
Would volumes fill, whence yet these lessons
note
Ye noble lords, to learn and ken by rote.

From THE TRAGEDY OF RICHARD, DUKE
OF GLOUCESTER

Ascribed to Francis Seager

What heart so hard, but doth abhor to hear
The rueful reign of me the third Richard?
King unkindly called though I the crown did
wear,
Who entered by rigor, but right did not re-
gard,
By tyranny proceeding in killing King Edward,
Fifth of that name, right heir unto the crown,
With Richard his brother, princes of renown.

Of trust they were committed unto my gov-
ernance,
But trust turned to treason too truly it was
tried,
Both against nature, duty, and allegiance,
For through my procurement most shamefully
they died.
Desire of a kingdom forgetteth all kindred,
As after by discourse it shall be shewed here,
How cruelly these innocents in prison mur-
dered were.

The Lords and Commons all with one assent,
Protector made me both of land and king,
But I therewith alas was not content:
For minding mischief I meant another thing,
Which to confusion in short time did me
bring,
For I desirous to rule and reign alone,
Sought crown and kingdom, yet title had I
none.

* * *

Both God, nature, duty, allegiance all forgot,
This vile and heinous act unnaturally I con-
spired:
Which horrible deed done, alas, alas, God wot,
Such terrors me tormented, and so my spirits
fired
As unto such a murder and shameful deed
required,
Such broil daily felt I bleeding in my breast,
Whereby more and more, increased mine un-
rest.

My brother's children were right heirs unto
the crown
Whom nature rather bound to defend than
destroy,
But I not regarding their right nor my renown
My whole care and study to this end did em-
ploy,
The crown to obtain, and them both to put
down:
Wherein I God offended, provoking his just
ire,
For this my attempt and most wicked desire.

To cruel cursed Cain compare my careful case
Which did unjustly slay his brother just Abel,
And did not I in rage make run that rueful
race
My brother Duke of Clarence, whose death I
shame to tell
For that so strange it was, as it was horrible?
For sure he drenched was, and yet no water
near,
Which strange is to be told to all that shall it
hear.

The butt he was not whereat I did shoot,
But yet he stood between the mark and me:
For had he lived, for me it was no boot
To tempt the thing that by no means could be,
For I third was then of my brethren three:
But yet I thought the elder being gone,
Then needs must I bear the stroke alone.

Desire to rule made me alas to rue,
My fatal fall I could it not foresee,
Puffed up in pride, so haughty then I grew,
That none my peer I thought now could be,
Disdaining such as were of high degree:
Thus daily rising and pulling other down,
At last I shot how to win the crown.

And daily devising which was the best way
And mean how I might my nephews both de-
vour
I secretly then sent without further delay
To Brackenbury then lieutenant of the Tower,

Requesting him by letters to help unto his
    power,
For to accomplish this my desire and will,
And that he would secretly my brother's
    children kill.

He answered plainly with a flat nay,
Saying that to die he would not do that
    deed:
But finding then a proffer ready for my
    prey,
Well worth a friend (quoth I) yet in time of
    need.
James Tyrell hight his name, whom with all
    speed,
I sent again to Brackenbury, as you heard be-
    fore,
Commanding him deliver the keys of every
    door.

The keys he rendered, but partaker would not
    be
Of that flagitious fact. O happy man I say,
And as you heard before, he rather chose to
    die
Than on those silly lambs his violent hands to
    lay.
His conscience him pricked, his prince to be-
    tray:
O constant mind, that wouldst not condescend,
Thee may I praise, and myself discommend.

What though he refused, yet be sure you may,
That other were as ready to take in hand the
    thing,
Which watched and waited as duly for their
    prey,
As ever did the cat for the mouse-taking,
And how they might their purpose best to pass
    bring:
Where Tyrell he thought good to have no
    blood shed,
Caused them to be killed by smothering in
    their bed.

The wolves at hand were ready to devour
The silly lambs in bed whereas they lay
Abiding death and looking for the hour,
For well they wist, they could not scape away.
Ah, woe is me, that did them thus betray,
In assigning this vile deed to be done,
By Miles Forrest, and wicked John Dighton.

Who privily into their chamber stole,
In secret wise somewhat before midnight,
And 'gan the bed together tug and hale,
Bewrapping them alas in rueful plight,
Keeping them down, by force, by power, and
    might

With haling, tugging, turmoiling, torn and
    tossed,
Till they of force were forced yield the ghost.

Which when I heard, my heart I felt was eased
Of grudge, of grief, and inward deadly pain,
But with this deed the Nobles were displeased,
And said: O God, shall such a Tyrant reign,
That hath so cruelly his brother's children
    slain?
Which bruit once blown in the people's ears,
Their dolor was such, that they burst out in
    tears.

But what thing may suffice unto the bloody
    man,
The more he bathes in blood, the bloodier he
    is alway:
By proof I do this speak, which best declare
    it can,
Which only was the cause of this prince's de-
    cay.
The wolf was never greedier than I was of my
    prey,
But who so useth murder full well affirm I
    dare,
With murder shall be quit, ere he thereof be
    'ware.

And mark the sequel of this begun mischief
Which shortly after was cause of my decay,
For high and low conceived such a grief
And hate against me, which sought day by day,
All ways and means that possible they may,
On me to be revenged for this sin,
For cruel murdering unnaturally my kin.

Not only kin, but king, the truth to say,
Whom unkindly of kingdom I bereft,
His life also from him I wrought away,
With his brother's, which to my charge were
    left.
Of ambition behold the work and weft,
Provoking me to do this heinous treason,
And murder them against all right and reason.

After whose death thus wrought by violence,
The lords not liking this unnatural deed,
Began on me to have great diffidence,
Such burning hate 'gan in their hearts to breed,
Which made me doubt, and sore my danger
    dread:
Which doubt and dread proved not in vain,
By that ensued alas unto my pain.

For I supposing all things were as I wished,
When I had brought these silly babes to bane,
But yet in that my purpose for I missed:
For as the moon doth change after the wane,

So changed the hearts of such as I had ta'en
To be most rue, to troubles did me turn,
Such rage and rancor in boiling breasts do
     burn.

And suddenly a bruit abroad was blown,
That Buckingham the duke both stern and
     stout,
In field was ready, with divers to me known,
To give me battle if I durst come out:
Which daunted me and put me in great doubt,
For that I had no army then prepared,
But after that I little for it cared.

But yet remembering, that oft a little spark
Suffered doth grow unto a great flame,
I thought it wisdom wisely for to work,
Mustered then men in every place I came.
And marching forward daily with the same,
Directly towards the town of Salisbury,
Where I got knowledge of the duke's army.

And as I passed over Salisbury Down,
The rumor ran the duke was fled and gone,
His host dispersed beside Shrewsbury town,
And he dismayed was left there post alone,
Bewailing his chance and making great moan:
Towards whom I hasted with all expedition,
Making due search and diligent inquisition.

But at the first I could not of him hear,
For he was scaped by secret byways,
Unto the house of Humphrey Banister,
Whom he had much preferred in his days,
And was good lord to him in all assays:
Which he full ill requited in the end,
When he was driven to seek a trusty friend.

For it so happened to his mishap, alas,
When I no knowledge of the duke could hear,
A proclamation by my commandment was
Published and cried throughout every shire,
That whoso could tell where the duke were
A thousand mark should have for his pain.
What thing so hard but money can obtain?

But were it for money, meed or dread,
That Banister thus betrayed his guest,
Divers have diversely divined of this deed,
Some deem the worst, and some judge the best,
The doubt not dissolved nor plainly expressed,
But of the duke's death he doubtless was cause,
Which died without judgment or order of
     laws.

Lo this noble duke I brought thus unto bane,
Whose doings I doubted and had in great
     dread,
At Banister's house I made him to be ta'en,

And without judgment be shortened by the
     head,
By the Sheriff of Shropshire to Salisbury led.
In the market place upon the scaffold new
Where all the beholders did much his death
     rue.

And after this done I brake up my host,
Greatly applauded with this heavy hap,
And forthwith I sent to every sea coast
To foresee all mischiefs and stop every gap,
Before they should chance and light in my lap
Giving them in charge to have good regard
The sea coast to keep with good watch and
     ward.

Directing my letters unto every shrive,
With straight commandment under our name,
To suffer no man in their parts to arrive
Nor to pass forth out of the same,
As they tendered our favor, and 'void would
     our blame,
Doing therein their pain and industry,
With diligent care and vigilant eye.

And thus setting things in order as you hear,
To prevent mischiefs that might then betide,
I thought myself sure, and out of all fear,
And for other things began to provide:
To Nottingham castle straight did I ride,
Where I was not very long space,
Strange tidings came which did me sore amaze.

Reported it was, and that for certainty,
The Earl of Richmond landed was in Wales
At Milford Haven, with an huge army,
Dismissing his navy which were many sails:
Which at the first I thought fleeing tales.
But in the end did otherwise prove,
Which not a little did me vex and move.

Thus fawning Fortune began on me to frown,
And cast on me her scornful lowering look:
Then 'gan I fear the fall of my renown,
My heart it fainted, my sinews sore they shook,
This heavy hap a scourge for sin I took,
Yet did I not then utterly despair,
Hoping storms past, the weather should be
     fair.

And then with all speed possible I might,
I caused them muster throughout every shire,
Determining with the earl speedily to fight,
Before that his power much increased were,
By such as to him great favor did bear:
Which were no small number by true report
     made,
Daily repairing him for to aid.

Directing my letters to divers noblemen,
With earnest request their power to prepare,
To Nottingham castle where as I lay then,
To aid and assist me in this weighty affair:
Where straight to my presence did then repair,
John Duke of Norfolk, his eldest son also,
With the Earl of Northumberland and many
    other mo.

And thus being furnished with men and muni-
    tion,
Forward we marched in order of battle 'ray,
Making by scouts every way inquisition,
In what place the earl with his camp lay:
Towards whom directly we took then our
    way,
Evermore minding to seek our most avail,
In place convenient to give to him battle.

So long we labored, at last our armies met
In Bosworth plain beside Leicester town,
Where sure I thought the garland for to get,
And purchase peace, or else to lose my crown.
But fickle Fortune alas on me did frown,
For when I was encamped in the field,
Where most I trusted I soonest was beguiled.

The brand of malice thus kindling in my breast
Of deadly hate which I to him did bear,
Pricked me forward, and bade me not desist,
But boldly fight, and take at all no fear,
To win the field, and the earl to conquer:
Thus hoping glory great to gain and get,
My army then in order did I set.

Betide me life or death I desperately ran,
And joined me in battle with this earl so stout,
But Fortune so him favored that he the battle
    won.
With force and great power I was beset about,
Which when I did behold, in midst of the
    whole rout
With dint of sword I cast me on him to be
    revenged,
Where in the midst of them my wretched life
    I ended.

My body it was hurried and tugged like a dog,
On horseback all naked and bare as I was born.
My head, hands, and feet, down hanging like
    a hog,
With dirt and blood bespent, my corpse all too
    torn,
Cursing the day that ever I was born.
With grievous wounds bemangled most hor-
    rible to see
So sore they did abhor this my vile cruelty.

Lo here you may behold the due and just
    reward

Of tyranny and treason which God doth most
    detest,
For if unto my duty I had taken regard,
I might have lived still in honor with the best,
And had I not attempt the thing that I ought
    least.
But desire to rule alas did me so blind,
Which caused me to do against nature and
    kind.

Ah cursed caitiff, why did I climb so high,
Which was the cause of this my baleful thrall.
For still I thirsted for the regal dignity,
But hasty rising threateneth sudden fall,
Content yourselves with your estates all,
And seek not right by wrong to suppress,
For God hath promised each wrong to redress.

See here the fine and fatal fall of me,
And guerdon due for this my wretched deed,
Which to all princes a mirror now may be
That shall this tragical story after read,
Wishing them all by me to take heed,
And suffer right to rule as it is reason,
For time trieth out both truth and also treason.

From THE TRAGEDY OF JANE SHORE

Ascribed to Thomas Churchyard

What greater grief may come to any life,
Than after sweet to taste the bitter sour?
Or after peace to fall at war and strife,
Or after mirth to have a cause to lower?
Under such props false Fortune builds her
    bower,
Or sudden change her flitting frames be set,
Where is no way for to escape her net.

* * *

As long as life remained in Edward's breast,
Who was but I? Who had such friends at call?
His body was no sooner put in chest,
But well was he that could procure my fall:
His brother was mine enemy most of all,
Protector then, whose vice did still abound,
From ill to worse till death did him confound.

He falsely feigned, that I of counsel was
To poison him, which thing I never meant,
But he could set thereon a face of brass,
To bring to pass his lewd and false intent,
To such mischief this tyrant's heart was bent.
To God, nor man, he never stood in awe,
For in his wrath he made his will a law.

Lord Hastings' blood for vengeance on him
   cries,
And many more, that were too long to name:
But most of all, and in most woeful wise
I had good cause this wretched man to blame.
Before the world I suffered open shame,
Where people were as thick as is the sand,
I penance took with taper in my hand.

Each eye did stare, and look me in the face,
As I passed by, the rumors on me ran,
But patience then had lent me such a grace,
My quiet looks were praised of every man:
The shamefast blood brought me such color
   then,
That thousands said, which saw my sober
   cheer,
It is great ruth to see this woman here.

But what prevailed the people's pity there?
This raging wolf would spare no guiltless
   blood.
Oh wicked womb that such ill fruit did bear,
Oh cursed earth that yieldeth forth such mud,
The hell consume all things that did the good,
The heavens shut their gates against thy spirit
The world tread down thy glory under feet.

I ask of God a vengeance on thy bones,
Thy stinking corpse corrupts the air I know:
Thy shameful death no earthly wight bemoans,
For in thy life thy works were hated so,
That every man did wish thy overthrow:
Wherefore I may, though partial now I am,
Curse every cause whereof thy body came.

RAPHAEL HOLINSHED

From The First and Second Volumes of the Chronicles of England, Scotland, and Ireland[1]

Richard the third son, of whom we now intreat, was in wit and courage equal with either of them [Edward and Clarence], in body and prowess far under them both, little of stature, ill featured of limbs, crook-backed, his left shoulder much higher than his right, hard favored of visage, and such as is in states called warlie, in other men otherwise; he was malicious, wrathful, envious, and from afore his birth ever froward. It is for truth reported, that the duchess his mother had so much ado in her travail, that she could not be delivered of him uncut; and that he came into the world with the feet forward, as men be born outward, and (as the fame runneth also) not untoothed, whether men of hatred report above the truth, or else that nature changed her course in his beginning, which in the course of his life many things unnaturally committed. . . .

None evil captain was he in the war, as to which his disposition was more meetly than for peace. Sundry victories had he, and sometimes overthrows; but never on default as for his own person, either of hardiness or political order. Free was he called of dispense, and somewhat above his power liberal: with large gifts he got him unsteadfast friendship, for which he was fain to pill and spoil in other places, and got him steadfast hatred. He was close and secret, a deep dissembler, lowly of countenance, arrogant of heart, outwardly companionable where he inwardly hated, not letting to kiss whom he thought to kill: despiteous and cruel, not for evil will alway, but often for ambition, and either for the surety or increase of his estate.

Friend and foe was he much what indifferent; where his advantage grew, he spared no man's death whose life withstood his purpose. He

slew with his own hands King Henry the sixth, being prisoner in the Tower, as men constantly said, and that without commandment or knowledge of the king, which would undoubtedly (if he had intended that thing) have appointed that butcherly office to some other, than his own born brother. Some wise men also ween, that his drift covertly conveyed, lacked not in helping forth his brother of Clarence to his death: which he resisted openly, howbeit somewhat (as men deemed) more faintly than he that were heartily minded to his wealth. . . .

Then all the other being removed from them, this Miles Forrest and John Dighton, about midnight (the seely children lying in their beds) came into the chamber, and suddenly lapping them up among the clothes, so bewrapped them and entangled them, keeping down by force the feather-bed and pillows hard unto their mouths, that within a while, smothered and stifled, their breath failing, they gave up to God their innocent souls into the joys of heaven, leaving to the tormentors their bodies dead in the bed. Which after that the wretches perceived, first by the struggling with the pains of death, and after long lying still, to be thoroughly dead, they laid their bodies naked out upon the bed, and fetched Sir James to see them; which upon the sight of them caused those murderers to bury them at the stair foot, meetly deep in the ground, under a great heap of stones.

Then rode Sir James in great haste to King Richard, and shewed him all the manner of the murder; who gave him great thanks, and (as some say) there made him knight. But he allowed not (as I have heard) the burying in so vile a corner, saying, that he would have them buried in a better place, because they were a king's sons. Lo, the honorable courage

[1] London, 1587.

of a king. Whereupon they say, that a priest of Sir Robert Brackenbury's took up the bodies again, and secretly interred them in such place, as by the occasion of his death, which only knew it, could never since come to light. Very truth is it, and well known, that at such time as Sir James Tyrell was in the Tower, for treason committed against the most famous prince King Henry the seventh, both Dighton and he were examined, and confessed the murder in manner above written: but whither the bodies were removed, they could nothing tell. . . .

The fame went, that he had the same night [before Bosworth] a dreadful and terrible dream: for it seemed to him being asleep, that he did see diverse images like terrible devils, which pulled and haled him, not suffering him to take any quiet or rest. The which strange vision not so suddenly strake his heart with a sudden fear, but it stuffed his head and troubled his mind with many busy and dreadful imaginations. For incontinent after, his heart being almost damped, he prognosticated before the doubtful chance of the battle to come; not using the alacrity and mirth of mind and countenance as he was accustomed to do before he came toward the battle. And lest that it might be suspected that he was abashed for fear of his enemies, and for that cause looked so piteously; he recited and declared to his familiar friends in the morning his wonderful vision and fearful dream. . . .

[From the account of Richard's oration to his troops before the battle:] You see also, what a number of beggarly Britons and fainthearted Frenchmen be with him [Richmond] arrived to destroy us, our wives and children. Which imminent mischiefs and apparent inconveniences, if we will withstand and repel, we must live together as brethren, fight together like lions, and fear not to die together like men. And observing and keeping this rule and precept, believe me, the fearful hare never fled faster before the greedy greyhound, nor the silly lark before the sparrow hawk, nor yet the simple sheep before the ravenous wolf; than your proud bragging adversaries, astonied and amazed with the only sight of your manly visages, will flee, run, and skir out of the field. For if you consider and wisely ponder all things in your mind, you shall perceive, that we have manifest causes, and apparent tokens of triumph and victory.

And to begin with the earl of Richmond, captain of this rebellion, he is a Welsh milksop, a man of small courage, and of less experience in martial acts and feats of war, brought up by my mother's means, and mine, like a captive in a close cage in the court of Francis duke of Brittany; and never saw army, nor was exercised in martial affairs: by reason whereof he neither can, nor is able by his own will or experience to guide or rule an host. For in the wit and policy of the captain consisteth the chief adeption of the victory, and overthrow of the enemies. Secondarily fear not, but put away all doubts; for when the traitors and runnagates of our realm, shall see us with banner displayed come against them, remembering their oath, promise, and fidelity made unto us, as to their sovereign lord and anointed king; they shall be so pricked and stung in the bottom of their scrupulous consciences, that they for very remorse and dread of the divine plague, will either shamefully flee, or humbly submit themselves to our grace and mercy.

SIR FRANCIS BACON

From History of the Reign of King Henry VII[1]

After Richard, the third of that name, king in fact only, but tyrant both in title and regiment, and so commonly termed and reputed in all times since, was, by the divine revenge favoring the design of an exiled man, overthrown and slain at Bosworth field; there succeeded in the kingdom the Earl of Richmond, thenceforth styled Henry the Seventh. . . . Meanwhile the body of Richard, after many indignities and reproaches, the *diriges* and obsequies of the common people towards tyrants, was obscurely buried. For though the king of his nobleness gave charge unto the friars of Leicester to see an honorable interment to be given to it, yet the religious people themselves, being not free from the humors of the vulgar, neglected it; wherein nevertheless they did not them incur any man's blame or censure: no man thinking any ignominy or contumely unworthy of him, that had been the executioner of King Henry the Sixth, that innocent prince, with his own hands; the contriver of the death of the Duke of Clarence his brother; the murderer of his two nephews, one of them his lawful king in the present, and the other in the future, failing of him, and vehemently suspected to have been the poisoner of his wife, thereby to make vacant his bed, for a marriage within the degrees forbidden. Although he were a prince in military virtue approved, jealous of the honor of the English nation, and likewise a good law-maker, for the ease and solace of the common people; yet his cruelties and parricides, in the opinion of all men, weighed down his virtues and merits; and, in

the opinion of wise men, even those virtues themselves were conceived to be rather feigned and affected things to serve his ambition, than true qualities ingenerate in his judgment or nature. Therefore it was noted by men of great understanding, who seeing his after-acts, looked back upon his former proceedings, that even in the time of King Edward his brother he was not without secret trains and mines to turn envy and hatred upon his brother's government; as having an expectation and a kind of divination, that the king, by reason of his many disorders, could not be of long life, but was like to leave his sons of tender years; and then he knew well, how easy a step it was, from the place of a protector and first prince of the blood to the crown. Out of this deep root of ambition it sprung, that as well at the treaty of peace that passed between Edward the Fourth and Louis the Eleventh of France, concluded by interview of both kings at Picquigny, as upon all other occasions, Richard, then Duke of Gloucester, stood ever upon the side of honor, raising his own reputation to the disadvantage of the king his brother, and drawing the eyes of all, especially of the nobles and soldiers, upon himself; as if the king, by his voluptuous life and mean marriage, were become effeminate and less sensible of honor and reason of state than was fit for a king. And as for the politic and wholesome laws which were enacted in his time, they were interpreted to be but the brocage of an usurper, thereby to woo and win the hearts of the people, as being conscious to himself, that the true obligations of sovereignty in him failed, and were wanting.

[1] Ed. J. Rawson Lumby, rev. ed. (Cambridge University Press, 1892).

HORACE WALPOLE

From Historic Doubts on the Life and Reign of King Richard the Third[1]

There is a kind of literary superstition, which men are apt to contract from habit, and which makes them look on any attempt towards shaking their belief in any established characters, no matter whether good or bad, as a sort of profanation. They are determined to adhere to their first impressions, and are equally offended at any innovation, whether the person, whose character is to be raised or depressed, were patriot or tyrant, saint or sinner. No indulgence is granted to those who would ascertain the truth. The more the testimonies on either side have been multiplied, the stronger is the conviction; though it generally happens that the original evidence is wondrous slender, and that the number of writers have but copied one another; or, what is worse, have only added to the original, without any new authority. Attachment so groundless is not to be regarded; and in mere matters of curiosity, it were ridiculous to pay any deference to it. If time brings new materials to light, if facts and dates confute historians, what does it signify that we have been for two or three hundred years under an error? Does antiquity consecrate darkness? Does a lie become venerable from its age? . . .

The narrative [that of More] teems with improbabilities and notorious falsehoods, and is flatly contradicted by so many unquestionable facts, that if we have no other reason to believe the murder of Edward the Fifth and his brother, than the account transmitted to us, we shall very much doubt whether they ever were murdered at all.

[Here Walpole presents More's account.]

It is difficult to crowd more improbabilities and lies together than are comprehended in this short narrative. Who can believe if Richard meditated the murder, that he took no care to sift Brackenbury before he left London? Who can believe that he would trust so atro-

cious a commission to a letter? And who can imagine that on Brackenbury's non-compliance Richard would have ordered him to cede the government of the Tower to Tyrell for one night only, the purpose of which had been so plainly pointed out by the preceding message? And had such weak steps been taken, could the murder itself have remained a problem? And yet Sir Thomas More himself is forced to confess at the outset of this very narration, "that the deaths and final fortunes of the two young princes have nevertheless so far come in question, that some remained long in doubt, whether they were *in his days* destroyed or no." Very memorable words, and sufficient to balance More's own testimony with the most sanguine believers. . . . Sir Thomas goes on to affirm, "that he does not relate the story after every way that he had heard, but after that way that he had heard it by such men and such means, as he thought it hard but it should be true." This affirmation rests on the credibility of certain reporters, we do not know whom, but who we shall find were no credible reporters at all: for to proceed to the confutation. James Tyrell, a man in no secret trust with the king, and kept down by Catesby and Ratcliffe, is recommended as a proper person by a nameless page. In the first place Richard was crowned at York (after this transaction) September 8th. Edward the Fourth had not been dead four months, and Richard in possession of any power not above two months, and those very bustling and active: Tyrell must have been impatient indeed, if the page had had time to observe his discontent at the superior confidence of Ratcliffe and Catesby. It happens unluckily too, that great part of the time Ratcliffe was absent, Sir Thomas More himself telling us that Sir Richard Ratcliffe had the custody of the prisoners at Pontefract, and presided at their execution there. But a much more unlikely circumstance is, that James Tyrell, said to be knighted for this horrid service, was not only a knight be-

[1] London, 1768.

fore, but a great or very considerable officer of the crown; and in that situation had walked at Richard's preceding coronation. Should I be told that Sir Thomas More did not mean to confine the ill offices done to Tyrell by Ratcliffe and Catesby solely to the time of Richard's protectorate and regal power, but being all three attached to him when duke of Gloucester, the other two might have lessened Tyrell's credit with the duke even in the preceding reign; then I answer, that Richard's appointing him master of the horse on his accession had removed those disgusts, and left the page no room to represent him as ready through ambition and despondency to lend his ministry to assassination. Not indeed was the master of the horse likely to be sent to supersede the constable of the Tower for one night only. That very act was sufficient to point out what Richard desired to, and did, it seems, transact so covertly.

That Sir James Tyrell was and did walk as master of the horse at Richard's coronation cannot be contested. A most curious, invaluable, and authentic monument has lately been discovered, the coronation-roll of Richard the Third. Two several deliveries of parcels of stuff are there expressly entered, as made to "Sir James Tyrell, knight, master of the horse of our said sovereign lord the king." What now becomes of Sir Thomas More's informers, and of their narrative, which he thought hard but must be true?

I will go a step further, and consider the evidence of this murder, as produced by Henry the Seventh some years afterwards, when, instead of lamenting it, it was necessary for his majesty to hope it had been true; at least to hope the people would think so. On the appearance of Perkin Warbeck, who gave himself out for the second of the brothers, who was believed so by most people, and at least feared by the king to be so, he bestirred himself to prove that both the princes had been murdered by his predecessor. There had been but three actors, besides Richard who had commanded the execution, and was dead. These were Sir James Tyrell, Dighton, and Forest; and these were all the persons whose depositions Henry pretended to produce; at least of two of them, for Forest it seems had rotted piece-meal away; a kind of death unknown at present to the college. But there were some others, of whom no notice was taken; as the nameless page, Green, one Black Will or Will Slaughter who guarded the princes, the friar who buried them, and Sir Robert Brackenbury, who could not be quite ignorant of what

had happened: the latter was killed at Bosworth, and the friar was dead too. But why was no inquiry made after Green and the page? Still this silence was not so impudent as the pretended confession of Dighton and Sir James Tyrell. The former certainly did avow the fact, and was suffered to go unpunished wherever he pleased—undoubtedly that he might spread the tale. And observe these remarkable words of Lord Bacon, "John Dighton, who it seemeth *spake best for the king,* was forewith set at liberty." In truth, every step of this pretended discovery, as it stands in Lord Bacon, warns us to give no heed to it. Dighton and Tyrell agreed both in a tale, *as the king gave out.* Their confession therefore was not publicly made, as Sir James Tyrell was suffered to live; but was shut up in the Tower, and put to death afterwards for we know not what treason. What can we believe, but that Dighton was some low mercenary wretch hired to assume the guilt of a crime he had not committed, and that Sir James Tyrell never did, never would confess what he had not done; and was therefore put out of the way on a fictitious imputation? It must be observed too, that no inquiry was made into the murder on the accession of Henry the Seventh, the natural time for it, when the passions of men were heated, and when the Duke of Norfolk, Lord Lovel, Catesby, Ratcliffe, and the real abettors and accomplices of Richard, were attainted and executed. No mention of such a murder was made in the very act of parliament that attainted Richard himself, and which would have been the most heinous aggravation of his crimes.[2] And no prosecution of the supposed assassins was even thought of till eleven years afterwards, on the appearance of Perkin Warbeck. Tyrell is not named in the act of attainder to which I have had recourse; and such omissions cannot but induce us to surmise that Henry had never been certain of the deaths of the princes, nor ever interested himself to prove that both were dead, till he had great reason to believe that one of them was alive. Let me add, that if the confessions of Dighton and Tyrell were true, Sir Thomas More had no occasion to recur to the information of his unknown credible informers. If those confessions were not true, his informers were not creditable.

[2] There is a heap of general accusations alleged to have been committed by Richard *against Henry,* in particular of his having *shed infant's blood.* Was this sufficient specification of the murder of a king? Is it not rather a base way of insinuating a slander, of which no proof could be given? Was not it consonant to all Henry's policy of involving everything in obscure and general terms?

CHARLES DICKENS

From A Child's History of England[1]

From Chapter 24, ENGLAND UNDER EDWARD THE FIFTH

Being at last quite prepared, he [Richard] one day appeared unexpectedly at the council in the Tower, and appeared to be very jocular and merry, He was particularly gay with the Bishop of Ely: praising the strawberries that grew in his garden on Holborn Hill, and asking him to have some gathered that he might eat them at dinner. The Bishop, quite proud of the honor, sent one of his men to fetch some; and the Duke, still very jocular and gay, went out; and the council all said what a very agreeble duke he was! In a little time, however, he came back quite altered—not at all jocular—frowning and fierce—and suddenly said:

"What do those persons deserve who have compassed my destruction; I being the king's lawful, as well as natural, protector?"

To this strange question, Lord Hastings replied, that they deserved death, whosoever they were.

"Then," said the Duke, "I tell you that they are that sorceress my brother's wife"—meaning the Queen—"and that other sorceress, Jane Shore. Who, by witchcraft, have withered my body, and caused my arm to shrink as I now show you."

He then pulled up his sleeve and showed them his arm, which was shrunken, it is true, but which had been so, as they all very well knew, from the hour of his birth.

Jane Shore, being then the lover of Lord Hastings, as she had formerly been of the late King, that lord knew that he himself was attacked. So, he said, in some confusion, "Certainly, my lord, if they have done this, they be worthy of punishment."

"If?" said the Duke of Gloucester; "do you talk to me of ifs? I tell you that they *have* so done, and I will make it good upon thy body, thou traitor!"

With that, he struck the table a great blow with his fist. This was a signal to some of his people outside to cry "Treason!" They immediately did so, and there was a rush into the chamber of so many armed men that it was filled in a moment.

"First," said the Duke of Gloucester to Lord Hastings, "I arrest thee, traitor! And let him," he added to the armed men who took him, "have a priest at once, for by St. Paul I will not dine until I have seen his head off!"

Lord Hastings was hurried to the green by the Tower chapel, and there beheaded on a log of wood that happened to be lying on the ground. Then, the Duke dined with a good appetite, and after dinner summoning the principal citizens to attend him, told them that Lord Hastings and the rest had designed to murder both himself and the Duke of Buckingham, who stood by his side, if he had not providentially discovered their design. . . .

From Chapter 25, ENGLAND UNDER RICHARD THE THIRD

King Richard the Third was up betimes in the morning, and went to Westminster Hall. In the Hall was a marble seat, upon which he sat himself down between two great noblemen, and told the people that he began the new reign in that place, because the first duty of a sovereign was to adminster the laws equally to all, and to maintain justice. He then mounted his horse and rode back to the City, where he was received by the clergy and the crowd as if he really had a right to the throne, and really were a just man. The clergy and the crowd must have been rather ashamed of themselves in secret, I think, for being such poor-spirited knaves.

The new King and his Queen were soon crowned with a great deal of show and noise,

[1] *The Works of Charles Dickens*, Vol. XXVIII (New York, 1900).

which the people liked very much; and then the King set forth on a royal progress through his dominions. He was crowned a second time at York, in order that the people might have show and noise enough; and wherever he went was received with shouts of rejoicing—from a good many people of strong lungs, who were paid to strain their throats in crying, "God save King Richard!" The plan was so successful that I am told it has been imitated since, by other usurpers, in other progresses through other dominions.

While he was on this journey King Richard stayed a week at Warwick. And from Warwick he sent instructions home for one of the wickedest murders that ever was done—the murder of the two young princes, his nephews, who were shut up in the Tower of London.

Sir Robert Brackenbury was at that time Governor of the Tower. To him, by the hands of a messenger named John Green, did King Richard send a letter, ordering him by some means to put the two young princes to death. But Sir Robert—I hope because he had children of his own, and loved them—sent John Green back again, riding and spurring along the dusty roads, with the answer that he could not do so horrible a piece of work. The King, having frowningly considered a little, called to him Sir James Tyrrel, his master of the horse, and to him gave authority to take command of the Tower, whenever he would, for twenty-four hours, and to keep all the keys of the Tower during that space of time. Tyrrel, well knowing what was wanted, looked about him for two hardened ruffians, and chose John Dighton, one of his own grooms, and Miles Forest, who was a murderer by trade. Having secured these two assistants, he went, upon a day in August, to the Tower, showed his authority from the King, took the command for four-and-twenty hours, and obtained possession of the keys. And when the black night came he went creeping, creeping, like a guilty villain as he was, up the dark stone winding stairs, and along the dark stone passages, until he came to the door of the room where the two young princes, having said their prayers, lay fast asleep, clasped in each other's arms. And while he watched and listened at the door, he sent in those evil demons, John Dighton and Miles Forest, who smothered the two princes with the bed and pillows, and carried their bodies down the stairs, and buried them under a great heap of stones at the staircase foot. And when the day came, he gave up the command of the Tower, and restored the keys, and hurried away without once looking behind him; and Sir Robert Brackenbury went with fear and sadness to the princes' room, and found the princes gone forever. . . .

Richard knew full well that, let the Parliament say what it would, the Princess Elizabeth was remembered by people as the heiress of the house of York; and having accurate information, besides, of its being designed by the conspirators to marry her to Henry of Richmond, he felt that it would much strengthen him and weaken them to be beforehand with them, and marry her to his son. With this view he went to the Sanctuary at Westminster, where the late King's widow and her daughter still were, and besought them to come to Court, where (he swore by anything and everything) they should be safely and honorably entertained. They came, accordingly, but had scarcely been at Court a month when his son died suddenly—or was poisoned—and his plan was crushed to pieces.

In this extremity King Richard, always active, thought, "I must make another plan." And he made the plan of marrying the Princess Elizabeth himself, although she was his niece. There was one difficulty in the way: his wife, the Queen Anne, was alive. But, he knew (remembering his nephews) how to remove that obstacle, and he made love to the Princess Elizabeth, telling her he felt perfectly confident that the Queen would die in February. The Princess was not a very scrupulous young lady; for, instead of rejecting the murderer of her brothers with scorn and hatred, she openly declared she loved him dearly; and, when February came and the Queen did not die, she expressed her impatient opinion that she was too long about it. However, King Richard was not so far out in his prediction but that she died in March—he took good care of that—and then this precious pair hoped to be married. But they were disappointed; for the idea of such a marriage was so unpopular in the country that the King's chief counselors, Ratcliffe and Catesby, would by no means undertake to propose it, and the King was even obliged to declare in public that he had never thought of such a thing.

CLEMENTS R. MARKHAM

From Richard III, A Doubtful Verdict Reviewed[1]

The historical problem which the believers in the guilt of Richard III have to solve is the reconciliation of his general character with the special acts of which he is accused. It is incapable of solution. We are told, by the latest and best authority, Mr. Gairdner, that many of Richard's acts were dictated by charitable feelings or a sense of justice, that he had a great deal of native religious sentiment, that he made it his endeavor to prevent tyranny for the future, that he really studied his country's welfare, that there was nothing mean or paltry in his character, that his taste in buildings was magnificent and princely. He not only restored the property of attainted men to their families, but even gave pensions to the wives of traitors who were plotting against him in foreign countries. This is the picture of a generous and high-minded prince. Yet we are asked to believe that the same prince was a venomous hunchback from his birth, that he committed two peculiarly atrocious assassinations before he was nineteen, that he murdered his brother, poisoned his wife, waded through innocent blood to a usurped crown, and completed a career of diabolical wickedness by strangling two innocent children who were his nephews. The two pictures cannot well be true representations of the same person. The first is based on the chance admissions of enemies, and on the study of documents which are official in their character, and beyond the suspicion of bias. The second, therefore, seems to call for close scrutiny before it is accepted. At the first blush it has the aspect of an exaggerated caricature.

We must bear in mind that, on the death of Richard, there was a change of dynasty. Henry VII had no valid title to the throne. It was not only the new king's interest, but a necessity of his position, that he should cause grave charges to be brought against his predecessor, and that they should be accepted as true. Henry VII had the power and the will

to silence all comment. We know that he destroyed evidence in favor of his predecessor. Authors employed by him, and others who were anxious to please him and his successors, were alone permitted to write histories. Not a syllable was allowed to be uttered on the other side for 160 years. Bernard André, Archbishop Morton, and Polydore Virgil were actually in the pay or under the direct influence of Henry VII. John Rous and Robert Fabyan wrote during his reign, accepted his version of events and sought his favor. The Monk of Croyland Abbey, although he wrote during Henry's reign, is the sole writer with even a pretense to independence, for he did not write with a view to publication. Henry VII began the business of vilifying his predecessor very early in his reign. It was indeed a matter of the utmost moment to him, for he appears to have considered that a belief in the alleged crimes of Richard was essential to the security of his own position. . . .

By far the most important of the original authorities and the one on whose testimony all subsequent history has mainly been based, is Archbishop Morton. His narrative is contained in the "History of Richard III" attributed to Sir Thomas More, who was in Morton's household when a boy. This work first appeared in Hardyng's Chronicle, printed by Grafton in 1543. It was embodied in Hall's Chronicle and copied by Holinshed. Fourteen years after its publication another and somewhat different version was brought out by Rastell in 1557. Rastell was related to Sir Thomas More, and he alleged that his version was taken from a manuscript written in about 1513 in More's handwriting. . . . The history, as we have it, contains long speeches and dialogues which must have been fabricated by the writer. The title given by the publisher is misleading. It is not a "History of Richard III," but a very detailed narrative of events from the death of Edward IV to the accession of Richard, a period of less than three months. It must certainly have been written or dictated

[1] *English Historical Review,* **VI** (1891).

by Morton, for no one else could have been cognizant of some of the events. It ends abruptly at a point just before the date of Morton's flight from England. His personal knowledge ceased with his departure, and here the story suddenly comes to an end. He was personally acquainted with every detail that is related, and he possessed an exceptionally accurate memory. The errors and alterations of dates in the narrative must consequently have been made intentionally and with an object. The story of the murder of the princes at the end of the book cannot have been written by Morton, because it alludes to events which happened after 12 October 1500, the date of that prelate's death.

John Morton was born at Beer Regis in Dorsetshire, early in the fifteenth century. He began life as a lawyer, and became a master in chancery, increasing his income by taking orders. He took the Lancastrian side in the civil war, and fled to the continent with Queen Margaret in 1462. His fortunes were then at a low ebb, but they brightened when the earl of Warwick came to France to betray the cause of Edward IV. Morton attached himself to Warwick at Angers, went with him to England in 1470, escaped from Barnet to join Queen Margaret at Weymouth, and was with her at Tewkesbury. Obtaining a pardon from Edward, he was made Master of the Rolls, and became one of the greatest pluralists of the age. He was grasping and avaricious. He received a bribe from Louis XI for inducing his own sovereign to accept dishonorable terms of peace, and was further bought with a pension of 2,000 crowns a year. The contrast between the upright conduct of the duke of Gloucester on this occasion and his own baseness probably explains the wily priest's malignant hostility to Richard. Morton was made bishop of Ely in 1479. On the death of Edward IV he saw a wide opening for his ambition in the chances of a long minority. He was heart and soul in the conspiracy of Hastings and the Woodville faction against the protector. He brought Hastings to his death, but escaped himself. The incorrigible plotter was entrusted to the custody of the duke of Buckingham. By his cunning artifices he induced that weak nobleman to become a traitor. He led Buckingham to his death, but secured his own safety. He then joined Henry Tudor's conspiracy abroad, and it was doubtless through Morton's advice that the Welsh adventurer put forward a claim to the crown. Success at length attended the intriguer's schemes. Henry

VII made him chancellor and archbishop of Canterbury. After much importunity a cardinal's hat was obtained for him from the Borgian pope. He became enormously rich, and was one of the most odious instruments of Henry's extortions. In his old age he wrote or dictated this libel on King Richard III in the interests of his patron.

Such was the man who held the principal brief against our last Plantagenet. But Rastell assumed that this "History of Richard III" was composed by Sir Thomas More because a copy in his handwriting was found among his papers. The previous publication by Grafton proves that there were other copies abroad, differing slightly from each other, and there is no reason for assuming that the copy in More's handwriting was the original. Indeed there is evidence that it was not. Grafton's version contains a good deal at the end which is not in Rastell's narrative attributed to More. The latter ends abruptly, as if the whole had not been copied. The respect with which this production has been treated is entirely due to Sir Thomas More's reputed authorship. It is in reality an unscrupulous party pamphlet, and its authorship ought not to affect our judgment of its character. Yet the reply to any objection to statements contained in it has hitherto been that it was written by the good and virtuous Sir Thomas More, and therefore must be true.

If it was written by More, so much the worse for More's character for truth and decency. But internal evidence makes it certain that More did not write it. The author was an eyewitness at the deathbed of Edward IV. Morton was an eyewitness. But More was then a baby in arms, if indeed he was born. This settles the question. Sir Thomas made an incomplete copy of a work which was attracting a great deal of attention, and of which there were other copies in circulation, when he was a young man. The date of the copy is said by Rastell to be 1513. The actual compiler of the book, as we have it, is unknown. But the inspiration of the whole work, with the exception of the story of the murder of the young princes at the end, is undoubtedly from Archbishop Morton. It is not too much to say that the continued belief in the alleged crimes of Richard III is mainly due to the erroneous assumption that his chief accuser was Sir Thomas More. . . .[2]

---

[2] Markham's argument for Morton's authorship has been refuted by R. W. Chambers, "The Authorship of the 'History of Richard III,'" *Modern Language Review,* **XXIII** (1928), and in *The English Works of Sir Thomas More,* ed. W. E. Campbell (London, 1931). (Ed.).

The evidence on which the Tudor writers mainly rely for Richard's guilt, as regards the murder of his nephews, is the perpetration of numerous former crimes. We must, therefore, examine this evidence as it relates to each charge. The first concerns Richard's alleged deformity and the circumstances of his birth. Rous states that he was two years in his mother's womb, that he was born feet foremost, with hair down to his shoulders, with a complete set of teeth, and that his right shoulder was much higher than his left. Morton says that his left shoulder was higher than his right. Polydore Virgil says the shoulders were unequal. Fabyan and the Croyland monk do not say a word against Richard's personal appearance. The obvious fables, in these descriptions, throw just suspicion on all other statements from the same sources. The object of the Tudor historians, in commencing their grotesque caricature of an imaginary monster with these stories of his personal deformity, is apparent. They intended to make him detestable from the outset. They calculated that improbable crimes would be more readily believed, if the alleged perpetrator was a deformed hunchback born with teeth. They were right. . . . Richard was described as a hunchback, and made to commit several atrocious crimes, in order to prepare men's minds to receive, without incredulity, the story of the murder of his nephews. It was probably anticipated that this final draft on their powers of belief would be dishonored unless the alleged murderer had been steeped in crime from his infancy.

At the early age of eighteen Richard is accordingly accused of having committed a cowardly and inhuman murder in cold blood, after the battle of Tewkesbury. His accuser is the Italian who was the paid historian of Henry VII. Contemporary evidence is unanimous in contradicting this accusation. There was only one eyewitness who wrote an account of the battle. He said that young Edward of Lancaster "was taken fleeing to the townwards, and slain in the field." This was the plain truth. He fought bravely and fell in the retreat. The next writer, in order of time, was Warkworth, but he was not present. He wrote —"There was slain on the field, Prince Edward, which cried for succour to the duke of Clarence." Bernard André, the paid historian of Henry VII, and Comines say the same; that he fell on the field of battle. Fabyan, writing long afterwards to please Henry VII, is the first who started the story that young Edward

was taken prisoner and brought before the king. He added that Edward IV "strake him in the face with his gauntlet, on which the prince was by the king's servants incontinently slain." This story must be rejected as fabulous, because it contradicts all the contemporary accounts. But it no doubt suggested to Polydore Virgil a version which would be still more acceptable to his employer. This protégé of Pope Alexander VI conceived the idea of giving it a lurid Borgian coloring, better suited to the latitude of Urbino than to that of Tewkesbury. Instead of the king's servants, he substituted Clarence, Gloucester, and Hastings as the assassins. Holinshed added Dorset.

The question is whether Polydore Virgil repeated a tradition or invented a slander. Rous and Morton wrote with the object of bringing every charge they could collect against Richard. Yet they are silent about the murder of young Edward at Tewkesbury. If there had been a tradition of the sort, they must have known it, and would have eagerly repeated it. In the case of Morton this silence is a damning proof against Polydore Virgil. For Morton was actually present at Tewkesbury. If young Edward was murdered, he cannot have failed to be cognizant of the crime. Yet in a book prepared with the object of enumerating the alleged crimes of Richard he said nothing. He had no scruples. He repeated all he could think of, with the object of heaping opprobrium on Richard's memory, but there is not a hint about assassinating Edward of Lancaster. Morton's silence, under these circumstances, amounts to a proof that the story was not based on a tradition, but that it was a fabrication of the unscrupulous Italian. For if any one knew all the details of the battle of Tewkesbury at first hand, it was Morton. He was there. His silence explodes the fable. It also convicts Polydore Virgil of having fabricated an exceptionally foul slander. The evidence of such a man is worthless on any point in which he or his employer is personally interested. . . .

The charge against the duke of Gloucester that he murdered Henry VI is an insinuation rather than an accusation. Morton says, "as men constantly say," Polydore Virgil, "it was the continual report," Fabyan, "the common fame," Rous, "as many believe." We must, therefore, treat it, in the first instance, as a rumor only, and judge of it from probabilities. We are asked to believe that young Richard at the age of eighteen, when he had just won great military renown, arrived at the Tower in the evening of one day, with orders to proceed on active service early the next morning, that he found time to induce Lord Rivers, the constable, who was his political enemy, to deliver up charge to him, in order that he might assassinate a defenseless and feeble invalid with his own hand, a deed in which he was only remotely interested, and which might just as well have been perpetrated by any hired jailer; and that, although the act must have been done with the knowledge of Lord Rivers and his officials, and of Henry's numerous servants, yet there was never any certainty about it. Rivers, be it remembered, was Richard's enemy.

This grossly improbable story bears the evidence of its origin clearly marked. It was put forward in the reign and in the interests of Henry VII. It was a rumor manufactured by his paid writers. . . .

Other charges against Gloucester before his brother's death may be dismissed more summarily. He was said to have forced Lady Anne Neville to marry him immediately after he had murdered Edward of Lancaster, who was her husband. Edward was not her husband, and Gloucester did not murder him. On the other hand the two young cousins, Richard and Anne, were brought up together. Years before, at the inaugural feast of Archbishop Neville, they are mentioned as sitting at one table together. Their union was most natural. Anne was her husband's constant companion in every important crisis of his life, in sorrow and in joy, and there is good reason to believe that the marriage was a happy one. The malignant slander involved in the insinuation that Richard poisoned his wife, is due to the brain of the Italian priest, and is a peculiarly Borgian conception. Anne's illness was a lingering decline, during which she was assiduously cared for by her sorrowing husband and her physicians. The calumny that she was poisoned was merely an insinuation, but most of the Tudor calumnies take the form of insinuations. "It is a charge," wrote Sir Harris Nicholas, "which is deserving of attention for no other reason than as it affords a remarkable example of the manner in which ignorance and prejudice sometimes render what is called history more contemptible than a romance." But it is important as affording a further proof of the untrustworthiness of the authorities who made it, Polydore Virgil and Rous.

The most elaborate and detailed part of the indictment against Richard III refers to the so-called usurpation, including the period from his arrival in London to his coronation. The events of the interregnum had to be represented in such a way that it might appear that Henry Tudor was righteously superseding a tyrannical usurper. This was a matter of vital importance to the intruding dynasty. Accordingly much art was devoted to the preparation of a plausible story, while documents that would contradict it were carefully but not always effectually destroyed. The narrative of Richard's accession is mainly due to Morton. He was a leading actor in, and an eyewitness of, what he described. He was a very able and clever man, and he was intimately acquainted with the facts as they really happened. Consequently every mistake that is detected in his narrative, every date that is falsified, must have been inserted designedly, and with a special object.

Morton opens his case with the assumption that the duke of Gloucester had always intended to supplant his nephew. The truth is exactly the reverse of Morton's version. Gloucester's conduct was straightforward and loyal. After attending solemn obsequies of his brother in York Minster, he called on the nobility and gentry of Yorkshire to swear allegiance to his young nephew. When he arrived in London he ordered preparations to be made for his nephew's coronation, and he sent summonses to forty esquires to receive knighthood of the Bath on the occasion. He also caused the dresses to be got ready, which were to be worn by his nephew at the coronation. These preparations must have been well known to Morton who passed them over in silence, because they would tend to give a true impression, where he wanted to leave a false one. This state of things lasted for a month after the Protector Gloucester arrived in London with his nephew. On 5 June the protector had fixed the coronation for the 22nd. But now there came a change. On or about 8 June, Dr. Robert Stillington, bishop of Bath and Wells, revealed to the council the long concealed fact that Edward IV was married by the bishop to the Lady Eleanor Talbot, widow of a son of Lord Butler of Sudley, and daughter of the first earl of Shrewsbury, before he went through a secret marriage ceremony with Elizabeth Woodville, the widow of Sir John Grey. Dr. Stillington, when he performed the ceremony, had been strictly enjoined by the king not to reveal it. The Lady Eleanor afterwards retired to a convent at Norwich, where she died, and was buried in the church of the Carmelites.

Dr. Stillington was the second son of a

gentleman of good family, living on his own land at Acaster Selby in Yorkshire. He was a churchman of eminence, and in 1466 became bishop of Bath and Wells, and lord privy seal. In 1467 he was installed in the high office of lord chancellor, and delivered an eloquent and statesmanlike speech at the opening of parliament in May 1468. After holding the office of chancellor with dignity and credit for six years, he resigned owing to ill-health in 1473. If the Woodvilles had any knowledge of the first marriage, Bishop Stillington would be a source of anxiety and fear to them. We find that the duke of Clarence was attainted in February 1478, on a series of charges, most of them frivolous and none sufficiently serious to account for his death at the hands of his own brother. There must have been something behind. Mr. Gairdner has suggested that the execution of Clarence was due to his having discovered the secret. Certainly that would account for it. The influence of the Woodvilles was paramount, and it would then be a necessity of their continuance in power that Clarence should cease to live. It is very significant that, at the very time of Clarence's attainder, Bishop Stillington was arrested and imprisoned for "uttering words prejudicial to the king and his state." He was pardoned in the following June, 1478. All this points to the discovery of the first marriage by Clarence, and to the utterance of some imprudent speech by the bishop, which was expiated by imprisonment followed by renewed promises of silence.

Dr. Stillington appears to have been a pious and munificent bishop. He founded a collegiate chapel on his brother's land at Acaster, for a provost and fellows, and for free education in grammar, writing, and music. He was an able statesman and diplomatist, and a very loyal and faithful adherent of the white rose. His one fault was that he did not ensure his own destruction by proclaiming Edward's secret before that king's death. There was no urgent obligation to do so. But when the necessity arose, he was bound to come forward. Gloucester was only a child when his brother's matrimonial entanglements were formed, and knew nothing. He was eleven and a half when Elizabeth Woodville was taken into favour, and the Butler marriage was of a still earlier date.

The announcement of this previous marriage to the council, by Bishop Stillington, made it inevitable that the matter should be thoroughly sifted. The bishop "brought in instruments, proctors, and notaries of the law, with depositions of divers witnesses." The majority of the council must have seen at once that the illegitimate son of the late king could not succeed. Such a proceeding would inevitably be the precursor of innumerable troubles. The case was prepared to be laid before the parliament which was summoned to meet on 25 June. There was, however, a small but powerful minority in the council, led by Lord Hastings and Bishop Morton, to whom the prospect of losing the openings to their ambition offered by the succession of a minor was most distasteful. Both these statesmen had received bribes from Louis XI, and were not, therefore, men of scrupulous integrity. Hastings, indeed, had been guilty of the baseness of accepting bribes both from Louis and from the duke of Burgundy. These malcontents, with some others, commenced opposition, began to meet apart, and intrigued with the Woodville faction. The protector became alarmed and ordered troops up from York. The conspirators secretly issued a *supersedeas*, ordering the members of parliament not to come to London, so as to prevent any decision from being arrived at respecting the succession. Finally a plot was formed to seize the protector. It was probably a question of hours when, acting on a warning from Catesby, the protector arrested Lord Hastings, and broke up the conspiracy.

Morton relates these events with matchless cunning. His object was to instill a belief that Hastings worked against the Woodvilles throughout, and in concert with Gloucester, thus endeavouring to show that there was no conspiracy. In order to create this impression he gives two false dates. He makes young Richard leave sanctuary, to join his brother Edward, on 9 June. The true date was the 16th. He asserts that Lord Rivers was beheaded on 13 June, the very day of the arrest of Hastings, and he makes a great point of it, observing, as a striking coincidence, that Hastings suffered death on the selfsame day and about the selfsame hour as Rivers, whose execution he had approved. He knew this to be false. Rivers made his will on the 23rd, and was beheaded on the 25th. Morton had a motive for falsifying these dates. He wanted it to appear that Hastings was an enemy of the Woodville faction to the end, that he was a party to the removal of young Richard from sanctuary and to the execution of Rivers. But why? Clearly because Hastings was not an enemy of the Woodvilles to the end, because, with Morton and others, he had entered into conspiracy with them against the protector. It was important to conceal this because it justified the protector's action against Hastings, and Morton did so by resorting to a falsification of dates.

The astute prelate's minute description of the scene when Hastings was arrested on Friday, 13 June, is exceedingly clever. We have the reminiscences of an eyewitness, who was also a schemer so dealing with the facts as to leave false impressions, clothed in the semblance of veracious recollections. The tale of the strawberries is a masterly touch designed to give an air of reality to the scene. The withered arm is a fabrication intended to conceal the real charge made by the protector. That charge was contained in the proclamation of which Morton professes to give the substance. The seeker after truth would very much prefer the original text. But it was destroyed. Its destruction is a strong presumption in favour of the protector, and justifies the conclusion that the real charge was a serious one. It is incredible that Catesby merely revealed the nonsense about Jane Shore's sorcery. Morton has inserted this rubbish in order to conceal the real charge made by Gloucester. Morton further alleges that "Shore's wife was of all women the one the queen most hated," and that she was the mistress of Hastings. She was really the mistress of Dorset, the queen's son, and the motive for bringing in the queen's alleged hatred in this place is to conceal the real position of Jane Shore, which was that of a secret agent between the queen's party and Hastings. . . .

Morton next proceeds to misrepresent the title of King Richard III to the crown. The point is of great importance and merits close attention. The statement of Richard's title to the throne was drawn up and adopted by the Lords Spiritual and Temporal and Commons, between the 8th and the 25th of June. The document was afterwards embodied in an act of parliament, entitled the *Titulus Regius*, with which the writers employed by Henry VII must have been well acquainted. When Henry came to the throne he ordered this act to be repealed without quoting the preamble, with a view to its purport being concealed. He caused it to be destroyed, and threatened any one who kept a copy with fine and imprisonment during his pleasure. In spite of this threat the monk of Croyland told the truth, but his chronicle remained in manuscript. Henry's conduct affords a strong presumption that the title of King Richard was valid. For

he was not content with annulling the act. He granted an illusory pardon to Bishop Stillington, who was the principal witness to the truth of the main statement in the *Titulus Regius*. This was done with the object of keeping silence on the subject of the real offense, which was telling the truth. Henry then arrested him on another trumped-up charge, and kept him in close and solitary confinement in Windsor Castle until his death in June 1491.

These proceedings show the immense importance attached by Henry VII to a suppression of the truth relating to Richard's title to the crown. If the previous marriage of Edward IV with Lady Eleanor Butler had not been true, the falsehood would have been eagerly exposed, and there would have been no occasion to invent any other story. On the other hand, if this marriage really took place, the evidence would have been suppressed and another story would have been invented and promulgated. The evidence was suppressed, and a different tale was put forward. The conclusion is inevitable that the statement of a previous marriage of Edward IV with Lady Eleanor Butler was true.

By a mere accident the original draft of the *Titulus Regius* was not destroyed. It was discovered long afterwards among the Tower records. Its tenor was given by the Croyland monk, and it is printed more fully in Speede's History (1611). Richard's title rested on the evidence that Edward's children were illegitimate owing to the previous marriage with Lady Eleanor Butler, and that the children of Clarence were incapacitated by his attainder. It is certain, therefore, that this and this only was the statement made in inspired sermons and speeches at the time; for it was the official case of those who advocated Richard's accession. It is impossible that one ground for the claim should have been put forward officially, and another, which was not only different but contradictory, in the sermons and speeches directed to be made at the same time.

Now all this was perfectly well known to Morton and to Polydore Virgil when they concocted their stories. But they believed that the truth had been so effectually placed out of reach that it was safe for them to adopt what tale they chose. Their business was to conceal the truth. They, therefore, stated that Dr. Shaw preached a sermon on the Sunday before Richard's accession in which he calumniated the duchess of York by maintaining that all her sons were by some other man, except Richard who was the only son of the duke, her husband. The object was to throw the reader off the scent with regard to Edward's own connubial proceedings, by bringing an infamous and very absurd charge against his mother.

This is clearly the tale that Polydore Virgil was instructed to put into Dr. Shaw's mouth, and nothing more. For he alludes to the common report that Edward's children were called bastards by Dr. Shaw, and declares that the report was "voyd of all truthe." But Morton contradicts this. He also puts the slander about the duchess of York into Dr. Shaw's mouth, and he goes further, making the preacher tell another tale which would make bastards of Edward's children. According to Polydore Virgil the report that Dr. Shaw made bastards of Edward's children was "voyd of all truthe." According to Morton the preacher added that Edward was previously married to a woman named Lucy. It will be seen that these authorities contradict each other. Morton's introduction of the name of Elizabeth Lucy was a red herring drawn across the path. His great object was to conceal the name of Lady Eleanor Butler. The absurdity of Morton's story respecting the woman Lucy will be appreciated when we call to mind that she actually had two children by Edward IV. We are asked to believe that Dr. Shaw, in preaching a sermon in support of Richard's claim to the throne, put forward a statement which, if true, would make two children legitimate, whose legitimacy would at once bar any claim on the part of Richard. Such falsehoods alone discredit the authority of Polydore Virgil and Morton. There can now be no doubt that Dr. Shaw in his sermon, if indeed he ever preached it, simply explained to the people the contents of the petition stating Richard's title, which was about to be presented to him. We know that neither the duchess of York nor Elizabeth Lucy was mentioned in that petition.

Morton and Virgil are wholly unworthy of belief on any point relating to Richard III. One more instance of their misrepresentations may be given. They allege that the cause of the duke of Buckingham's discontent was the refusal of King Richard to grant him the moiety of the Bohun lands, that the duke's suit was rejected with many spiteful words, and that there was ever afterwards hatred and distrust between them. The truth is the exact opposite of this. Richard granted Buckingham's petition in the fullest and most generous manner, giving him the lands under the royal sign manual, and all the profits from the date of signature

until the formality was completed by authority of parliament. Of course Morton must have had an object in making this misleading statement. It was, no doubt, to conceal the true cause of Buckingham's discontent and subsequent treason; which were due to Morton's own deceitful and unscrupulous persuasions working on the weak mind of an ambitious and unprincipled nobleman. Assailed by the insidious flattery of this incorrigible intriguer he was hurried into a rash attempt which cost him his life.

The last charge against King Richard is that he intended to marry his illegitimate niece Elizabeth. It is unsustained by any evidence, and is contrary to all probability. Such a project would have stultified the act of parliament on which his title to the crown was based. The king was a politician and was not entirely bereft of his senses. But there is evidence that the scheme was favoured by the girl herself and by her mother, which accounts for the existence of the rumor. Their ages were suitable, the king being thirty-two and his niece in her twenty-first year; and in a letter to the duke of Norfolk, Elizabeth expressed a strong wish to become the wife of her uncle, who, she said, was "her only joy and maker in the world." But Richard himself can never have contemplated such a marriage. Directly the rumor reached his ears he publicly contradicted it. . . .

We now arrive at the main question round which all these accusations revolve, and to settle which they were invented. For, in attempting an impartial consideration of the question of the fate of King Edward's sons, it must always be remembered that the main argument against Richard rests upon the truth of his previous alleged crimes. This argument is destroyed if Richard was not a venomous hunchback born with teeth, if he was not a cold scheming villain who had already committed two atrocious murders, drowned his brother in a butt of malmsey, slandered his mother, poisoned his wife, and waded through the blood of innocent men to a usurped throne. A careful study of the evidence establishes the fact that these accusations are false, and that they were invented by the writers under a new dynasty in order to blacken the character of the last Plantagenet king, and to make the charge against him, that he murdered his nephews, more plausible. For it was a matter of the utmost moment to Henry VII, not only that the boys should have been put out of the way, but that it should be believed that the crime was perpetrated before his accession. . . .

We must approach the questions relating to the fate of the two young sons of Edward IV, without having constantly before our minds the grotesque caricature portrayed by the Tudor writers. Although it is not possible, especially at this distance of time, to account for the workings of any man's mind, or for the motives which may control his actions, it is yet necessary to consider this phase of the question with as much light as we can bring to bear on it. Edward IV always evinced unshaken love and affection for his young brother, and showed the most absolute confidence in him at the time of his death. Richard returned this affection with devoted loyalty. He had no love for the Woodville faction, but he must have felt some regard for his brother's children, being such a man as we believe he has now been shown to have been. This feeling of regard would decrease the strength of any motive producing a desire to put them out of the way for his own ends. But there was no such motive. The boys had been declared to be illegitimate by the unanimous voice of parliament. As claimants to the throne they had ceased to be dangerous. Excepting half a dozen Lancastrian exiles, and a few peers whose absence is accounted for by extreme age or youth or the calls of duty, the whole house of lords was at Richard's coronation. Even the Woodville faction had submitted, and was represented at the coronation by Viscount Lisle and the bishop of Salisbury. The mother of Henry Tudor bore the train of Richard's queen, and his uncle Lord Welles was also in attendance. There was absolutely no party for the illegitimate sons of Edward IV at the time of their alleged murder, and consequently no danger to be apprehended from them. If the story had put the murders after, or even just before, Buckingham's rising, it would be a little more plausible. But it placed them two or three months before the rising, when the king had not the shadow of a suspicion that any opposition was contemplated. There certainly was no motive for the crime.

It may, however, be argued that the workings of men's minds are inexplicable, and that Richard may have committed the crime from a motive which would seem insufficient to any reasonable man. To decide upon this proposition we can only turn to a consideration of his conduct as regards other persons in the same relationship and position as the two boys, and who might possibly give Richard trouble.

There were seven such persons; namely, the five daughters of Edward IV, and the two children of the duke of Clarence. The king treated his nieces with kindness and consideration as near relations, as soon as they came out of sanctuary, and were placed under his protection. The young earl of Warwick, son of Richard's elder brother Clarence, was a far more formidable rival than the sons of Edward. The former was incontestably legitimate, while the latter had been declared to be illegitimate by both houses of parliament. Richard knighted the earl of Warwick, made him a member of his household and of his council, and, on the death of his own son, he made Warwick his heir. It is alleged by Rous that he subsequently displaced the son of Clarence and put him in prison, substituting another nephew, the earl of Lincoln, as his heir. But this is disproved by the York records, where Warwick is shown to be still a member of the council with precedence before Lincoln, only four months previous to the battle of Bosworth. Warwick was still Richard's heir when the end came. We therefore know that Richard did not look upon the children of his elder brothers as enemies to be destroyed, but as relations to be cherished.

We find then that the two young sons of Edward IV went to reside in the royal lodgings in the Tower in June 1483. We have the evidence of Morton that Richard declared "he would so provide for them, and so maintain them in honorable estate as that all the realm ought and should be content." In the regulations of King Richard's household, dated 23 July, 1484, some months after the death of his own little son, it is ordained that "the children are to be together at one breakfast." That these children were of high rank is shown by the further order that no livery is to exceed the allowance "but only to my Lord" (Lincoln?) "and the children." These children were probably Edward, son of Clarence, and Edward and Richard, sons of Edward IV, the three nephews of the king who formed part of his household. When the realm was threatened with invasion, they would naturally be sent to places of safety; Warwick and Elizabeth to Sheriff Hutton, Edward and Richard to the Tower.

There are other circumstances which tend to confirm the belief that the king's nephews were alive and well during the whole period of his reign. It is barely credible that, if there had been foul play, the mother could have been induced by any promises to throw her remaining children on the protection of one who had already violated the most sacred ties as regards her two sons. It is, however, just possible that a weak and selfish woman, weary of confinement in sanctuary, might have been induced to come to terms with the murderer of her sons, in order to obtain a comfortable provision for herself and her daughters. But she did more than this: she sent to her other son Dorset, who was safe in France, advising him to return home and reconcile himself with the king. It is absolutely incredible that she could have done this, if her two sons had been foully murdered by this very king, or even if she did not know that they were alive and well. She remained on friendly terms with Richard until his death, and her daughters attended the festivities at his court. Still stronger evidence, in the same direction, is afforded by the letter to the duke of Norfolk, whether it was written by the king's niece Elizabeth, or by her mother as Mr. Gairdner suggests. Neither mother nor daughter could have spoken of Richard as "her only joy and maker in the world" or have said that she was "his in heart and thought," if he had just murdered the sons of one and the brothers of the other. The thing is quite impossible. If this letter was written, or if the queen dowager sent for Dorset from France, which is a fact, the two boys must have been alive and well.

There remain for consideration the rumors which are alleged to have prevailed during the reign of King Richard, to the effect that his nephews had been murdered. It is maintained that, as these rumors were generally believed, Richard must have been guilty, because if he had been innocent he would have taken some steps to disprove the rumors, and he took no such steps—or rather no such steps are recorded by his enemies. The points for investigation are whether such rumors actually existed, and if so, whether they were so general as to reach the king's ears, and make it advisable that anything should be done to refute them.

It is alleged that these rumors took shape during the king's progress to York, in the summer and autumn of 1483. It is nowhere alleged that they existed at any other time during Richard's reign. The authority for a rumor about the fate of the two boys in the summer of 1483 is the Croyland Chronicle; and there can be no doubt that the statement was made in good faith, although the writer may have been deceived. The statement is to the effect that the princes remaining in custody in the Tower, the people in the south and west of England

became anxious for their liberation, that meetings were held on the subject, and that proposals were made to arrange the escape of the daughters of Edward IV, so that, if anything happened to his sons, there might still be heirs of his body. It was also reported that the sons of Edward were dead, though it was not known by what violent means they met their ends. So far the Croyland Chronicle.

No doubt there were partisans of the defeated factions of Hastings and the Woodvilles who were ready to spread any rumors injurious to the king. The question is whether the rumors which reached the ears of the Croyland monk were ever generally credited by the people, so as to call for action from the government. Is it true that they led to loud murmurings from meetings and assemblages of the people in the south and west of England, such as would attract general notice? The only proof offered is that an officer named Nesfield was ordered to watch the approaches of the sanctuary at Westminster, and see that no one left it secretly. But this was a precaution which would have been taken under any circumstances. Polydore Virgil alleges that Richard himself spread a report that his nephews were dead. We know how much credit a statement from such a source deserves.

There is besides strong reason for rejecting the monk of Croyland's story. If the rumors had really existed, and if in consequence there were mutinous assemblages of the people pointing to an insurrectionary movement, the vigilant and energetic young king would have made all necessary preparations to meet the danger. Nothing is more certain in his history than that he was taken absolutely by surprise when he received tidings of an outbreak in Kent on October 11, 1483. No previous rumors can have reached him and they must have reached him if they had gained the popular ear. We must, therefore, conclude that there was no rumor that the young princes had been murdered. The Kentish outbreak was part of the plan for an insurrection, arranged by Buckingham and his friends.

Yet the story had certainly been told to the Croyland monk. If it had not reached him as a general rumor, it must have come direct from some malignant enemy of the king. Was there such a man lurking in the fen country round Croyland? We know that Morton had taken refuge in the Isle of Ely at this very time. If that unscrupulous intriguer was at the chronicler's elbow, the story is fully accounted for. The rumors mentioned in the Croyland

Chronicle probably originated with Morton when he was hiding in the fens, and ceased to exist when he sailed for Flanders. Morton and his slanders went abroad together. The rumors are heard of no more in England, but as soon as Morton reached the continent they reappeared with him. He left England in the autumn of 1483. In January 1484 the murder of the princes was alleged as a fact by the chancellor of France in addressing the States General at Tours. The chancellor may have been told this by some other Lancastrian exile, but it is more probable that it came from Morton. It was seized upon as a pretext for reviling the English king. Louis XI had hated Richard because he opposed the peace which the French king bought from his brother Edward, and because he disapproved of the consequent desertion of England's ally, the duke of Burgundy. The antipathy was inherited by his daughter, the lady of Beaujeu, who became regent on the death of Louis in August 1483. The calumnious insult to the king of England, uttered by the French chancellor, may not have reached Richard's government. If it did, it must have been apologized for or explained away, for some months afterwards, in July 1484, King Richard received an embassy from the French regency to treat of peace. The calumny originated from the spite of Morton, or some other outlawed malcontent, and not from any general rumor.

Fabyan, writing in the time of Henry VII, talked of a rumor and of its having been the common fame that Richard put his nephews to secret death. But this was really what Henry wanted to be "common fame," and no one dared to gainsay it. In the year after his accession the usurping Tudor ordered it to be given out that the boys were murdered by their uncle, and his paid writers had to repeat the statement. André said they were killed with a sword. Rous affirmed that they were put to death by some means unknown. Polydore followed Rous. At the same time both Morton and Polydore Virgil inadvertently furnish evidence that no general belief existed in Richard's reign that the boys were dead. The former says that it remained in doubt whether they were destroyed or not in Richard's days, and the latter mentions a rumor that they had escaped abroad. No question arose before King Richard's death. Many persons must have known that his nephews were alive and well treated. After Henry's accession those who knew the truth had a choice between silence and ruin, or even death. Among the mass of the people there was no knowledge of what had happened. Of course, many baseless rumors then became current. The statements accusing Richard, and the assertions that these rumors received popular credit during his reign, merely indicated what his successor wished to be believed on the subject. . . .[3]

It cannot, however, be doubted that the young princes were made away with. If King Richard was innocent, Henry Tudor must have been the criminal. After the battle of Bosworth, the lucky adventurer marched on London and seized the government. He then became responsible for the surviving members of the royal family of England, legitimate or otherwise. What did he do with them? There were Edward and Richard, illegitimate sons of Edward IV; there was Edward, the legitimate son of Clarence and rightful king of England; and there was John, the illegitimate son of Richard III. They all fell into his hands, and he alone became answerable for their lives. There is too much reason to believe that they all met with foul play at his hands.

In usurping the crown Henry Tudor found himself in a difficult position. His mother's claim was worthless in itself, and moreover it had not yet descended to him and never did, for she survived him. He wisely refrained from stating such a claim as this, although he alleged a vague hereditary right of some sort which he did not explain. There remained the right of conquest with the aid of French mercenaries, and he ventured to put it forward. But he soon saw that he would have to find some other prop to support his usurpation. Henry was certainly a man of great ability, with an acute but narrow mind. He was suspicious and a lover of mystery, and not naturally cruel. Indeed he showed natural affection when his own interests were not concerned, and he recoiled from crime. Yet he became capable of any foul deed if he deemed it necessary for his own security. But he meditated over a crime for months and even years, and stood trembling on the brink for a long time, before he summoned up courage to act. Even then he much preferred the forms of law, thinking that if he shared the deed with others, the guilt became less. All that was done by this subtle and cold-blooded tyrant was done deliberately.

Henry had the wisdom to perceive that, although his claim of conquest and vague as-

[3] Since Markham wrote there has appeared Dominic Mancini's *The Usurpation of Richard III*, ed. C. A. J. Armstrong (Oxford: The University Press, 1936), which provides contradictory evidence. (Ed.)

sertion of hereditary right might serve for a time, he must establish some better title to secure any stability for his throne. There was Elizabeth, the late king's niece, whose person he had secured. If she was made queen it might propitiate the powerful Yorkist party. But she was illegitimate. It is true that all evidence of the illegitimacy might be destroyed, but this would raise another difficulty, for her brothers would become legitimate also. Still he finally resolved upon this course. The act of parliament reciting Richard's title was expunged, and orders were given to destroy all traces of it. But this was not enough. There was other work to be done from which Henry long recoiled. Yet without its perpetration his marriage with Elizabeth would be worse than useless.

His first act, after assembling a so-called parliament of his outlawed adherents, was to pass an act of attainder against King Richard and his chief supporters. It is very significant that, although the late king is here reviled in general terms, he is not directly accused of the murder of his nephews. Henry got possession of the Tower at once. If the young princes had been missing, it is certain that the usurper would have promptly accused King Richard of having murdered them, in the act of attainder. But he did not do so. There can only be one explanation of this omission. The young princes were not missing.

Here then was Henry's great difficulty. This fully accounts for the long delay in marrying Elizabeth. He was afraid. He was ready to commit any crime with the forms of law. But a recourse to law was impossible in this case. Whatever he was to do, must be done in profound secrecy. Yet his timid and superstitious nature shrank from a crime, the responsibility of which he could not share with others. He hesitated for months. All evidence of the illegitimacy had been hidden out of sight. He long stood on the brink. At length he took the plunge. He married Elizabeth on 18 January, 1486, nearly five months after his accession. The die was then cast. It became a matter of life and death to Henry VII that the brothers of his wife should cease to exist.

We must now apply the same tests to Henry as we applied to Richard. Had Henry sufficient motive for the crime? It is impossible that a man in his position could have had a stronger motive. He had denied the illegitimacy and had thus made his wife's brothers his most formidable rivals. He dare not let them live, unless he relinquished all he had gained.

The second test we applied to Richard was his treatment of those persons who were in his power, and who might possibly threaten his position. Let us apply the same test to Henry. John of Gloucester, the illegitimate son of Richard III, fell into his hands. At first he received a maintenance allowance of 20*l.* a year. But he was soon thrown into prison, on suspicion of an invitation having reached him to come to Ireland. He never came out alive. This active well-disposed boy, as he is described in Rymer's "Foedera," fell a victim to the usurper's fears. The earl of Warwick was also in Henry's power. The tyrant hesitated for years before he made up his mind to commit another foul crime. But he finally put the unhappy youth to death, under circumstances of exceptional baseness and infamy. His next supposed danger was caused by the earl of Suffolk, another of King Richard's nephews. This ill-fated prince was delivered into Henry's hands under a promise that his life should be spared. He evaded the promise by enjoining his son to kill him. That son complied, and followed up the death of Suffolk by beheading five other descendants of the Plantagenet royal family. These Tudor kings cannot stand the tests we applied to Richard III, and which he passed unscathed. The conduct of Richard to the relations who were under his protection was that of a Christian king. The executions of which Henry VII and his son were guilty were an imitation of the policy of Turkish sultans.

If the young princes were in the Tower when Henry arrived, his conduct in analogous cases leaves no doubt of their fate. It was the fate of John of Gloucester, of Warwick, and of Suffolk. They may not have been made away with before Henry's marriage, nor for some months afterwards. The tyrant had the will but not the courage. He hesitated long, but, for reasons which will appear presently, it is likely that the boys were murdered, by order of Henry VII, between 16 June and 16 July, 1486.

Then, for the first time, the "common fame" was ordered to spread the report that King Richard "had put them under suer kepynge within the Tower in such wise that they never came abrode after," and that "King Richard put them unto secrete death." But Henry feared detection. The mother knew that this was false. If the boys were murdered in July 1486, that mother must soon have begun to feel uneasy. She was at Winchester with her daughter when her grandchild Arthur was born on 20 September, 1486, and was present at the christening. But she was in London later in the autumn, and before many months her suspicions must have been aroused. She must be silenced. Consequently, in February 1487, "it was resolved that the Lady Elizabeth, wife of King Edward IV, should lose and forfeit all her lands and possessions because she had voluntarily submitted herself and her daughters to the hands of King Richard. Whereat there was much wondering." She was ordered to reside in the nunnery of Bermondsey, where she died six years afterwards. Once she was allowed to appear at court on a state occasion. Lingard and Nicolas brought forward a negotiation with the king of Scots, in November 1487, in the course of which Henry proposed that James III should marry Elizabeth Woodville. If he suspected her, they argue, he would not have given her the opportunity of plotting against him as queen of Scotland. Although Henry may have momentarily entertained the idea of getting rid of a woman who knew too much, by this expatriation, he soon changed his mind. She was safer in his power, and the negotiations were broken off. The avowed pretext for her detention was not the real motive, for Henry had made grants of manors to her soon after his accession, when her conduct with regard to Richard was equally well known to him. The real reason was kept secret as well it might be. If the boys ceased to live in July 1486, it was high time for Henry to silence the awkward questions of the mother in the following February. He did so by condemning her to lifelong seclusion in a nunnery.

Years passed on. At length, in 1502 or thereabouts, the first detailed story of the murder of the two princes was put forward, after the execution of Sir James Tyrrel, and was subsequently published by Polydore Virgil. It was to the effect that King Richard sent a messenger to Sir R. Brackenbury, lieutenant of the Tower, with an order to procure the deaths of the princes, before he set out for York. Brackenbury deferred any action until Richard sent Sir James Tyrrel to the Tower, who murdered the children; "but with what kind of death they were executed is not certainly known." It is probable that further details were added afterwards, for a much more elaborate fable appeared in the history published by Rastell, and in Grafton. Here it is alleged that "at the time when Sir James Tyrrel and John Dighton were in prison for treason, they made a confession in August 1483, when on his way to Gloucester, King Richard sent one John Green with a letter to Sir Robert Brackenbury,

ordering him to put the boys to death." It will be observed that here the story of Polydore Virgil has been altered, the place where the king gave the order being changed from London to the road to Gloucester. Brackenbury refused, as in the former story, and Green returning reported his answer to Richard at Warwick. "The same night the king said to his secret page, who shall I trust to do my bidding?" The page replied that there was one without who would not refuse. This was Sir James Tyrrel, who was dispatched with a letter to Brackenbury to deliver to Sir James all the keys of the Tower for one night. The princes were in charge of Will Slater or Slaughter, called "Black Will." Tyrrel appointed one of the jailers named Miles Forest, "a fellow fleshed in murder aforetime," and John Dighton, his horsekeeper, to "commit the murders. Tyrrel caused the bodies to be buried at the stair foot, 'metely deep in the ground' under a great heap of stones." But the king caused their bodies to be removed to another place. Miles Forest, at St. Martin's le Grand, piecemeal rotted away. "Dighton lived at Calais long after, no less disdained than pointed at." The narrator concludes: "Thus as I have learned of them that much knew and little cause had to lie, were these two princes murdered." This last sentence is somewhat audacious. They "that much knew," if they ever existed outside the writer's imagination, had very strong cause to lie. The truth, if they knew it, would have been their ruin.

Such is the detailed accusation which was finally put forward. On the face of it there is no confession in this story. It is a concocted tale, and indeed this is admitted. It merely claims to be the most probable among several others which were based on various accounts of the alleged confession. If there ever was a confession, why should there be various accounts of it? It would certainly have been published if it was ever made, and the silence of Fabyan and Polydore Virgil is conclusive against the truth of the story of a confession. It is alleged that Tyrrel and Dighton both confessed. Yet Tyrrel was beheaded for another offense, and Dighton was rewarded with a residence at Calais. If the confessions had ever been made, Tyrrel and Dighton must have been tried and convicted for these atrocious murders, and duly punished. In point of fact Dighton was not arrested with Tyrrel. The names of those who were concerned in Tyrrel's business are given by the chroniclers, and that of Dighton is not one of them.

It is unnecessary to dwell on the absurdities and contradictions in the story itself. But it is worth while to refer to the contention of Sharon Turner and Lingard that the story must be true, on the grounds that the persons mentioned in it were rewarded by King Richard. They mention that Brackenbury and Tyrrel received several grants of land; Green was made receiver of the Isle of Wight and of Porchester, Dighton was appointed bailiff of the manor of Ayton, Forest was keeper of the wardrobe at Barnard's Castle. All this can easily be answered. Tyrrel and Brackenbury were Yorkist officers of rank, and such grants might have been made to them under any circumstances. As regards the others, either the grants were made previous to the alleged date of the murders, or there is no evidence to show whether they were made before or after, or in any way to connect them with the crime. The statement that Green held the receiverships of the Isle of Wight and Porchester is derived from an unsupported note by Strype, who gives no authority. A man named Dighton was made bailiff of Ayton, but there is nothing to show this appointment was made after the alleged date of the murder. Miles Forest is asserted to have been a jailer in the Tower who was a professional murderer, and rotted away piecemeal at St. Martin's le Grand. These statements are certainly false. Miles Forest was keeper of the wardrobe at Barnard's Castle in Durham, 244 miles from the Tower of London. There he lived with his wife and grown-up son Edward. There is not the slightest reason for believing that Forest entered upon his appointment after the date of the alleged murders, but much to disprove this assumption. He died in September 1484, and, as his wife and son received a pension for their lives, he must have been an old and faithful servant who had held the office for many years.

Dr. Lingard suggested that the pension was granted to the widow because Forest held the post for so *short* a time, assuming that he was one of the murderers in the story. This is certainly a very odd reason for granting a pension. Miles Forest was a responsible old official in a royal castle, living with his wife and grown-up son in the far north of England, where he died, and his family received a pension in acknowledgment of his long service. We are asked to believe that he was, at the same time, a notorious murderer who was a jailer in the Tower of London, and that he died in sanctuary at St. Martin's le Grand.

How Forest's name got into the story it is not possible, at this distance of time, to surmise. But the author was quite unscrupulous, and the above considerations justify the conclusion that Forest's name was used at haphazard. There was a desire to give names and other details in order to throw an air of verisimilitude over the fable. We see the same chance adoption of a name in the use of that of Dighton. He was not Tyrrel's horsekeeper, nor probably the actual murderer. But there was a John Dighton living at Calais when the story was made up, who was known to be connected, in some mysterious way, with the disappearance of the princes. So the author of the story hit upon his name to do duty as the groom who did the deed. The name of Forest was doubtless adopted owing to some similar chance. Neither Forest's nor Dighton's names occur in the authorized version as given by Polydore Virgil.

Henry at first only accused Tyrrel of the murders, but it seems likely that he subsequently put forward some further details. There is an indication of the Green episode in Polydore Virgil. It is, therefore, probable that it was sanctioned by Henry's authority, as well as the details respecting the interment of the bodies. All the rest about Dighton and Forest, and the way in which the crime was committed, is a fabrication based on the authorized story which is given in Polydore Virgil. The Italian was supplied with the statement sanctioned by the king, and he distinctly tells us that the mode of death was not divulged.

There remains a circumstantial story which may really have been connected with a secret tragedy. It has a very suspicious look of having been parodied out of something which actually happened. It is unlikely to have been pure invention. The fear of detection must have been always haunting Henry's mind. He would be tortured with the apprehension that the vague rumors he had set afloat against Richard were not credited; and this would be an inducement to promulgate a more detailed and circumstantial story. He could not and dared not accuse Tyrrel while he was alive for a reason which will appear directly, but as soon as he was dead it would be safe to do so. At the time when he got rid of Tyrrel his son Arthur had just died. The man's mind would be filled with fears of retributive justice. Then terror of detection would increase upon him. He would long to throw off suspicion from himself by something more decisive than vague rumor. The notion of imputing his own crime, in its real details, to his predecessor, is quite in keeping with the workings of a subtle and ingenious mind such as we know Henry's to have been. Hence Tyrrel, Green, Dighton, and Black Will may have been the accomplices of Henry VII, instead of Richard III. As soon as Tyrrel was disposed of, the circumstantial story might be divulged as his confession, merely substituting the name of Richard for that of Henry, and the name of Brackenbury for that of Digby.

With this clue to guide us, let us see what light can still be thrown on the dark question of the murders. Sir James Tyrrel of Gipping had been a knight of some distinction. He had been on a commission for executing the office of lord high constable under Edward IV. He had also been master of the horse, and was created a knight banneret at Berwick siege. King Richard made him master of the henchmen and conferred several favors on him. But he was not one of the good men and true who stood by their sovereign to the end. His name drops out of history during the last anxious months before Bosworth. He was no doubt a trimmer. But he could not escape the consequences of his long service under the Yorkist kings. Henry VII deprived him of his chamberlainship of the exchequer, and of his constableship of Newport, in order to bestow those appointments on his own friends. Tyrrel had to wait patiently in the cold shade. But he was ambitious and ready to do a great deal for the sake of the new king's favor. Here was a ready instrument for such a man as Henry Tudor.

The die had been cast. The usurper had married Elizabeth of York and entered upon the year 1486. There was a dark deed which must be done. Henry set out on a progress to York, leaving London in the middle of March. On the 11th of the same month John Green received, from the new king, a grant of a third of the manor of Benyngton in Hertfordshire. For this favor Green had, no doubt, to perform some secret service which, if satisfactorily executed, would be more fully rewarded. We know from the story what that service was. We also know from the story that Green did not succeed. Henry VII returned from his progress in June, only to find that Green had failed him in his need.

Then Henry (not Richard) may well have exclaimed, "Who shall I trust to do my bidding?" "Sir," quoth a secret councillor (called a page in the story), "there waiteth without one who I dare well say will do your grace's pleasure." So Tyrrel was taken into favor, and probably undertook to perform Henry's work with the understanding that he was to receive a sufficient reward. He became a knight of the king's body. On 16 June, 1486, Sir James Tyrrel, late of Gipping, received a general pardon. There is nothing extraordinary in this. It was an ordinary practice in those days to grant general pardons on various occasions. But it marks the date when Henry VII found "one without" who was ready to do his pleasure. Tyrrel, as the story tells us, was given a warrant to the lieutenant of the Tower, conferring on him the needful powers. The murders were then committed, as the story informs us, by William Slater or Slaughter, called "Black Will," with the aid of John Dighton. Slater was the jailer. Master John Dighton, however, was not Tyrrel's groom. He was a priest, and probably a chaplain in the Tower. He may have been only an accessory after the fact, in connection with the interments. The bodies, as we are told in the story, were buried at the stair foot, "metely deep in the ground," where they were discovered in July 1674. The tale about their removal and the death of the priest was no doubt inserted by Henry to prevent that discovery.

On 16 July, 1486, Sir James Tyrrel received a second general pardon. This would be very singular under ordinary circumstances, the second pardon having been granted within a month of the first. But it is not so singular when we reflect on what probably took place in the interval. There was a crime to be condoned which must be kept a profound secret. Thus we are able to fix the time of the murder of the two young princes, between 16 June and 16 July, 1486. One was fifteen and a half, the other twelve years of age.

Henry had at length found courage to commit the crime. He may have excused it to himself from the absolute necessity of his position. It had been perpetrated in profound secrecy. If the mother, brother, or sisters suspected anything, they could be silenced. They were absolutely at Henry's mercy. The mother was stripped of her property, immured in Bermondsey nunnery, and left dependent on her son-in-law for subsistence. She was effectually silenced. The marquis of Dorset, half-brother of the murdered boys, was committed to the Tower; but he succeeded in convincing the tyrant that there was nothing to fear from him, and he was eventually released. The eldest sister was Henry's wife and at his mercy—the wife of a man who, as his admirers mildly put it, "was not uxorious." She was within two months of her confinement, and doubtless for that reason her mother kept all misgivings to herself. Henry married the next sister Cecily, in that very year, to his old uncle Lord Welles, who would ensure her silence. The other sisters were still children. Others who knew much, and must have suspected more, had the choice between silence and ruin or death.

Yet the guilty tyrant could have known no peace. He must have been haunted by the fear of detection, however industriously he might cause reports to be spread, and histories to be written, in which his predecessor was charged with his crimes. Then there was the horror of having to deal with his accomplices. Here fortune favored him. Green died in the end of 1486, though hush-money seems to have been paid to "Black Will" for some time longer. John Dighton was presented by Henry VII with the living of Fulbeck near Grantham, in Lincolnshire, on 2 May 1487. But he was expected to live on the other side of the channel.

Sir James Tyrrel received ample recompense. He was appointed to the office of constable of Guisnes immediately after the date of his second general pardon. He was sent as ambassador to Maximilian, king of the Romans, to conclude a perpetual league and treaty. In 1487 he received a grant for life of the stewardship of Ogmore in Wales. In 1493 he was one of the commissioners for negotiating the treaty of Etaples with France. Henry, although he was obliged to reward his accomplices, was anxious to keep them on the other side of the channel as much as possible. Dighton had to reside at Calais. Tyrrel was induced to make an exchange, giving up his estates in Wales to the king, and receiving revenues from the county of Guisnes of equal value. In 1498 Henry still addressed him as his well-beloved and faithful councillor.

The long-sought pretext for getting rid of Tyrrel was ·found in 1502. The usurper dreaded the earl of Suffolk, King Richard's nephew, as a claimant to the crown. He heard that Tyrrel had favored the escape of the ill-fated young prince to Germany. Henry would naturally be terrified at the idea of Tyrrel taking the side of another claimant, and publicly denouncing his misdeeds. He ordered the arrest of his accomplice, but Tyrrel refused to surrender the castle of Guisnes. He was be-

sieged by the whole garrison of Calais. Treachery was then resorted to. Deceived by false promises, and the *pulchra verba* of Dr. Fox, lord privy seal, he unwisely put himself in the power of his enemies. He was safely locked up in a dungeon of the Tower, and beheaded without delay, on 6 May, 1502.

At length Henry could breathe freely. Of his accomplices only Dighton remained, who could be useful as a false witness. But the tyrant suffered for his crimes. The secret removal of his wife's brothers, and of young John of Gloucester, did not complete the catalogue. The earl of Warwick was the next victim; for he was a living reminder of his wife's illegitimacy. If Elizabeth had been legitimate, there would have been no danger to Henry from the existence of Warwick. That young prince would have been far removed from the succession. His wife's illegitimacy made her cousin the rightful heir, and hence another crime seemed necessary. Henry delayed its perpetration for years. At length he committed it, at the dictation of Ferdinand of Spain. But remorse gnawed the tyrant's heart. The Spanish ambassador noticed the change that had taken place in Henry's appearance since the murder of young Warwick. Don Pedro de Ayala had been in Scotland during the interval. The king had come to look many years older in a single month. Yet he contemplated another crime to make his position safe. He could not get the earl of Suffolk into his clutches without giving a solemn promise to spare his life. He evaded the promise by enjoining his son to commit the crime. Murderous designs thus occupied his mind on his deathbed.

Henry became haggard and restless. Prosperous and successful as the world deemed him, we may rely upon it that his crimes were not unpunished. His cowardly nature was peculiarly susceptible to the torturing pangs of remorse. He died, full of terrors, prematurely old and worn out, at the early age of fifty-two, on 21 April, 1509. He accumulated riches by plunder and extortion. He cleared his path of rivals. He established a despotic government. We are told that he inaugurated a new era— era of benevolences and star-chamber prosecutions. In all these things he was successful as the world counts success. As a slanderer he was pre-eminently successful. He succeeded in blackening the name of a far better man than himself for all time.

J. DOVER WILSON

A Note on *Richard III*[1]

Few readers of this review are likely to be also regular readers of the *British Medical Journal*. I therefore make no apologies for quoting in full the following letter which appeared in that periodical on 15 June 1956 and to which my attention was drawn by Dr. Bernard Brown, my own doctor:

Sir, A recent visit to a famous film prompted me to consider the strange case of King Richard III and the strawberries. The story, "as every schoolboy knows," is briefly as follows. Richard, riding to a meeting of the Privy Council, sees fine strawberries growing in the Bishop of Ely's garden in Holborn. On arrival at Westminster he asks the Bishop to send for a dish of them, and eats them before proceeding to business. A little later he pulls up his sleeve, disclosing his withered arm, accuses Hastings of bewitching him, and hustles him off to execution, swearing that he will not dine till Hastings's head is off.

This story is derived from the history by St. Thomas More, who had been a page to Cardinal Morton, the Bishop who owned the garden, and More must have heard the story from him. But in the form that has come down to us it does not make sense. If Richard really had a withered arm (unlikely in so great a warrior), everyone in the kingdom must have known it, and he could not have persuaded the Council that it was due to witchcraft. And what was the point of his demand for strawberries? Suppose now that Richard was allergic to strawberries and knew that he could produce an urticarial rash by eating them. The sudden appearance of the rash would be accepted as witchcraft

by most fifteenth-century minds, and it would be regarded as proof positive if the rash faded away just as Hastings died. Hence Richard's insistence on Hastings's death before dinner-time. More took down the story from Morton's lips many years later and mistook the nature of the change in Richard's arm, perhaps substituting "withered" for some such word as "tettered."

I am sure that this suggested version must have occurred to other medical men before now, but I have never heard it put forth. It will not appeal to the modern whitewashing school of historians, but it exactly fits the cynical audacity of the traditional character of Richard III as Shakespeare portrays it. I am, etc.

Coventry   J. Swift Joly

That Richard saw the Bishop's strawberry bed as he rode to the Council meeting is a fanciful addition to More's account; the meeting was held at the Tower and not at Westminster as Dr. Joly states;[2] it was Mistress Shore not her lover Hastings who was accused of witchcraft; and we may surmise but do not *know* that More had the story from Morton who had been his patron as a lad and the Bishop of Ely in question. But these are trifles. Dr. Joly has, I submit, discovered the point of an episode oddly pointless in the versions of both More and Shakespeare, and offered an explanation which is not only probable in itself but by furnishing a missing link between the two parts of the story seems to set the stamp of truth upon it. For one does not invent an episode which can only be understood when someone else has supplied the key to it.

Shakespeare endeavors, not very successfully, to make it work by suggesting that Richard's request for the strawberries is an expression of the geniality he affects when he first comes in. At least that appears to be the

[1] J. Dover Wilson, "A Note on *Richard III:* The Bishop of Ely's Strawberries," *Modern Language Review*, LII (1957). This article first appeared in the *Modern Language Review* . . . and is reprinted by permission of the General Editor and of the Modern Humanities Research Association.

[2] Ely Place, near the modern Holborn Circus, would not take a messenger on horseback long to reach from the Tower.

reason why after sending the Bishop out to dispatch a messenger to Ely Place he brings him back to remind us of the strawberries just before the infatuated Hastings utters the tribute to Richard's sincerity of character which begins

His grace looks cheerfully and smooth this morning;
There's some conceit or other likes him well.

More, from whom Shakespeare got the tale, does not of course need to make it work since he is writing not drama but a chronicle of events. Yet as one reads this passage in the *Historie* one cannot help wondering why More, or Morton if Morton was his informant, should have made such a point of this "messe of strawberries," if it had not at some time been recognized as an important move in the elaborate intrigue he was engaged in retailing with such wealth of detail.

In the play, for instance, Richard is only absent from the council for about fifteen lines which of course allows no time for the strawberries to take effect. More, on the other hand, is careful to tell us that he "came in among them, fyrst aboute ix. of the clock," went out again after asking for the strawberries and setting "the lordes faste in comoning," and then returned "after one hower, betwene .x. and .xi." And while Shakespeare makes him come in and go out with Buckingham, More suggests nothing of the kind. Thus according to the account in the *Historie* Richard had both an opportunity for taking his dose of strawberries in the privacy of his chamber and time for the rash to form before bursting upon the council with his tale of sorcery.

One last point. Neither More in his "description of Richarde the thirde" at the beginning of the *Historie* nor Shakespeare in Richard's soliloquy at the beginning of the play makes any reference to a withered arm. Indeed, as Dr. Joly hints, it is absurd to suppose so renowned and valiant a warrior, whose prowess is one of the themes of *3 Henry VI*, can have been thus incapacitated. It is only after the feast of strawberries that we are told anything is wrong with the arm. And though More says that when "he plucked vp hys doublet sleue to his elbow . . . he shewed a werish withered arme and small, as it was neuer other," and later that "no man was there present, but wel knew that his harme was euer such since his birth," these are the natural embroideries of a mythopoeic age when faced with phenomena that it can only explain as due to witchcraft.

A. R. MYERS

From The Character of Richard III[1]

"Shakespeare, the only history of England I ever read," the great Duke of Marlborough is said to have remarked; and Shakespeare's enormous influence in shaping subsequent concepts of fifteenth-century England is nowhere better illustrated than in the case of the character of Richard III. His picture is the more effective because it is so skilfully simple—the portrait of evil incarnate. Born a monster, before his time, hunchbacked, "not made to court an amorous looking-glass," Richard pretends loyalty to his father and his brother Edward only in order to further his own wicked ambitions. Under a cloak of virtue he kills one by one those who stand between him and the throne, whether it is a defenseless boy after the battle of Tewkesbury, a saintly old king in the Tower, or his own brother in the same fortress a few years later. On the death of Edward IV, so the Shakespearean version runs, Richard cunningly allays suspicion by protesting obsequious loyalty to his nephew, Edward V, whom he nevertheless shuts up in the Tower with his younger brother. After the beheading without trial of Rivers, Grey, Vaughan, and Hastings, Richard does not hesitate to have it publicly proclaimed that his nephews are bastards, and, in order to make Edward IV appear illegitimate too, does not even stop at accusing his own mother of adultery. By this time we are well prepared for his seizure of the throne, his murders of his nephews and his wife, and his attempt to marry his niece. But the avenging angel soon appears in the person of the "virtuous and holy" Henry Tudor, to whom all decent men quickly flock. Deserted by nearly all, lamented by none, "the son of Hell" falls at Bosworth, slain by the man whom Heaven has sent to restore justice, unity, and prosperity to England.

Incredible as this portrait of a total villain may seem to our generation, conscious of the complexity of human psychology, it is not merely a dramatist's creation. It is true that Shakespeare was the contemporary of dramatists fascinated by the triumph and downfall of evil men; but even in quite small details Shakespeare can be shown to be drawing on what was to be found in history books. It does not, however, require much investigation to see that the historical material on which he relied is open to serious objections. It was produced under a powerful dynasty which stood to gain by the character of Richard III being painted as black as possible; for if England was from 1483 to 1485 oppressed by a usurping tyrant, the invasion of Henry Tudor was not merely that of a landless adventurer with a weak claim to the throne but that of the gracious deliverer appointed by Providence. It is not surprising that the improbable picture of Richard as a diabolical monster, whose courage was his sole redeeming feature, should have provoked a violent reaction as soon as the last Tudor monarch was laid to rest, and the fears of a disputed succession and civil war had died away. In Sir George Buc's biography, written between 1605 and 1621, we have the first substantial defense of Richard III—no half-hearted apology but a vigorous rebuttal of every charge brought against him. This should logically have involved a condemnation of Henry VII; for if Richard III was not a usurper, then Henry was. Buc did argue that Perkin Warbeck was indeed one of the sons of Edward IV; but he also goes out of his way to say that he was not impugning the title of Henry VII, who is described as a wise and religious prince. This was prudent; for not only did James I claim the throne of England through a Tudor princess, but English people were already looking back on Elizabeth's reign as a golden age.

By the time of Horace Walpole there was no need for tenderness towards the reputation of Henry VII if one wished to defend Richard III; and in his *Historic Doubts* Walpole not only cleared Richard of all the principal accusations but suggested that it was Henry VII

[1] *History Today*, **IV** (1954). Reprinted by permission of *History Today* and Alec R. Myers.

who murdered the young king Edward V. Since then other writers, in a more detailed study of the evidence than that made by either Buc or Walpole, have taken a favorable view of Richard III, until the most complete vindication on a serious level was reached with the biography of Sir Clements R. Markham, published in 1906. With the vehemence and forensic skill of a defending counsel, he argued that all the evidence against Richard is tainted either because it was written by those who hated him or because it was composed to please the Tudors, whose interest it was to besmirch his character. Everything that Tudor writers say against Richard is therefore suspect; everything that they say in his favor can be accepted all the more readily as it comes from his foes; and where the evidence is not clear (which is often) Markham was fond of using a "must have been" to resolve the doubts in Richard's favor. As a result Richard stands forth, not as the villain of Tudor legend, but as a "gallant young hero" and almost a saint. He was, thought Markham, one of the best kings England has ever had, and his evil reputation is entirely due to "the accumulated garbage and filth of centuries of calumny." Not that Markham's book lacks its villain, but he turns out to be Henry VII. Cold, cunning, and merciless, an "adventurer who waded through the blood of innocent men to his usurped throne," he it was who murdered the princes in the Tower between June 16th and July 16th, 1486. He followed this up with the murder of other rivals, the intimidation of his wife, and the imprisonment of those who, like his mother-in-law, knew too much of his crimes; and he died, like the coward he was, "full of terrors, prematurely old and worn out" at the "early age" of fifty-two.

This is indeed a far cry from the Shakespearean Richard. What are we to believe when offered portraits of Richard which have scarcely anything in common except the name?

It must be acknowledged that Markham had some strong ground on which to build his case. First, there is the fact that there is not much strictly contemporary evidence for the character of Richard III; and it is possible to follow the growth of some stories against Richard which move further and further from such contemporary evidence as we have. For example, contemporary writers say nothing about the murder in cold blood of Edward of Lancaster by Richard and others after the battle of Tewkesbury. Perhaps in such a matter we can refuse to accept the silent smoothness of *The Arrivall of Edward IV*, an official Yorkist version intended as an apologia to foreign governments; but the same cannot be our reaction to a Lancastrian contemporary, John Warkworth, whose chronicle merely says: "And ther was slayne in the felde, Prynce Edward, which cryede for socoure to his brother-in-lawe, the Duke of Clarence." Warkworth's silence is the more remarkable because elsewhere he makes some adverse comments on the Yorkist leaders. A chronicle of Tewkesbury, in an account of the battle probably compiled soon afterwards, and in a spirit rather hostile to Edward IV, also merely states that Prince Edward was slain in the field. Moreover, the memoirs of Philippe de Comines say the same; and this is noteworthy since he almost certainly derived his information from Lancastrian refugees in Burgundy, who would not have been loath to indict the Yorkist leaders if there had been any accusation to make. Yet in spite of this consensus of contemporary opinion, we find sixteenth-century writers gradually building up a detailed charge against Richard. First, two London chronicles, Fabyan's Chronicle, completed in 1504, and the Great Chronicle, finished in 1512, say that Prince Edward was brought before Edward IV and killed by the king's attendants for impertinence. Then Polydore Vergil, an Italian who began his *Anglica Historia* at the request of Henry VII but ended it only in the reign of his son, added to this by naming Gloucester among the murderers. The influential Edward Hall, a zealous supporter of Henry VIII, took over Vergil's account, and made it more vivid with further details. Later writers largely copied Hall, and so we reach the Shakespearean picture of a captive but spirited youth struck down by Edward IV for his courageous words and stabbed to death by Gloucester and Clarence as he lies defenseless on the ground. . . . We see the construction of a detailed certainty of crime on a foundation of rumor which first appears some twenty years after Richard's death, and over thirty years after the incident described.

There are other elements in the Tudor picture of Richard which rest on sources open to serious criticism. The first descriptions of Richard's person come in John Rous's *Historia Regum Angliae*, written between 1489 and 1491 and dedicated to Henry VII. Here we are first informed that Richard was weak of body, deformed, with the right shoulder higher than the left, born with hair and teeth after two years in his mother's womb. Born a monster, he was destined to become like the scorpion which was ascendant at his birth. In contrast to this is Henry VII, who is said to have had an angelic countenance that won the love of all who beheld it. Yet the old chantry priest who could write this had only a few years earlier paid a fulsome tribute to Richard in which Rous stressed the king's legitimacy and praised his wise and virtuous rule.

With *The History of Henry VII* by Bernard André, an Austin friar whom Henry VII made royal historiographer and tutor to Prince Arthur, the legend took a long step forward. His account is not a history, but a portrait of two figures, the one of darkness, the other of light, black Richard and the angelic Richmond. And when we come to the *History of King Richard III* written by Sir Thomas More about 1513, Richard now appears as evil incarnate. Nevertheless, this work cannot be simply rejected as solely the propaganda of Cardinal Morton. The case for More's authorship has been pretty conclusively proved and it is unreasonable to do as Markham does and limit More's informants to Morton, who had been dead at least thirteen years. There were others who had taken part in public affairs while Richard was on the throne and were not only still alive when More wrote but were his friends, acquaintances or neighbors. But several of these persons, such as Bishop Fox or Christopher Urswick, were known opponents of Richard III, and others were burdened with a past which was better forgotten or modified in the reign of Henry VIII. In any case they were recalling events of between thirty and fifty years before; and there was little to be learnt of Richard III from books when More wrote. The short but mostly excellent account of the Yorkist period by the *Continuator of the Croyland Chronicle,* who had been a councillor of Edward IV, was composed in 1486; but it was unknown in More's day and remained unprinted until 1684. Moreover, it is questionable whether More regarded himself as writing history; his story is much more like a drama, unfolded in magnificent prose, for which fidelity to historical fact is scarcely relevant. It is possible that he took up and intensified the current legends about the monster Richard as a means of launching a discreet attack on the unscrupulous policies of the rulers of his own day. We know that, like his friend Erasmus, More was much concerned about the vital necessity of truly Christian princes in that age of powerful monarchies; and as a warning he may have wished to present Richard as a personified Vice in a Renaissance equivalent of a morality play. Certainly, the serious errors of fact, and the blanks left in the manuscript for the insertion of various dates and names, seem to indicate that More never revised his "Richard III" and did not intend it to be published as he left it. Yet it exercised enormous influence; it was embodied with only slight alterations in all subsequent chronicles of importance, such as those of Hall, Grafton, Holinshed and Stow, and formed the basis of much of Shakespeare's picture.

The history of Polydore Vergil, which was second only to More's biography in importance for shaping the Elizabethan view of Richard, makes a greater attempt at impartiality, and Vergil's picture of Richard is in various respects less hostile than that of More. Yet Vergil's work was much influenced by the fact that he had been called upon to produce an apologia for the House of Tudor and that it was necessary for an unpopular foreigner to be very circumspect to keep the favor of Henry VIII. . . . And as succeeding chroniclers used Vergil's history, bodily or as a basis, for those parts of the Yorkist reigns not touched upon by More, Vergil's accusations against Richard become very potent.

It is this peculiar characteristic of the sources for Richard's life—that all those which formed the Elizabethan picture of the king were written after his death under influences hostile to him—which somewhat mars Dr. Gairdner's important biography (first published in 1878, and revised in 1898). Gairdner was a great scholar who did much by his learning to clarify the picture of Richard III and to discredit some of the more extreme charges made against him. Yet Gairdner was by temperament and experience a conservative who revered tradition; and he recorded in the preface to his biography his view that "a minute study of the facts of Richard's life has tended more and more to convince me of the general fidelity of the portrait with which we have been made familiar by Shakespeare and Sir Thomas More." This result was reached because his "larger study of history in other periods" convinced him that "the attempt to discard tradition in the examination of original sources of history is, in fact, like the attempt to learn an unknown language without a teacher." Where there is no pressing reason to suspect tradition, historians should no doubt pay careful attention to it; but in this case to build on the assumption that the traditional view is essentially correct is to take for granted one of the very points in dispute. The problem of the character of Richard III is in large measure the problem of the validity of the Tudor traditions about him. Gairdner tried to be just and to base his narrative on documentary evidence; but his attitude is that of a prosecuting counsel rather than of a judge, always inclined to fill gaps in the evidence from Tudor tradition (especially More), and to assign bad motives for possibly creditable acts of Richard, because that tradition asserted him to be a villain. Thus, after admitting that the evidence for Richard murdering Prince Edward at Tewkesbury rests "on very slender testimony and that not strictly contemporary," he nevertheless accepts the traditional view of the matter; and Gloucester's foundation of chantries for his deceased father, brothers, and sisters, shortly after the death of Clarence, is interpreted as a sign of an uneasy conscience instead of being treated as a possibly sincere act of piety.

No more does the Elizabethan tradition of Richard's devouring ambition, fed by numerous crimes from an early age, rest on sure foundations. During the lifetime of Edward IV Richard seems, in contrast to Clarence and others, to have been conspicuous for his fidelity to his eldest brother. There is, for example, in Polydore Vergil's narrative, hostile to Richard though it was, no suggestion that Richard at that period cherished any designs on the crown; that suggestion entered the Tudor tradition only with More's biography. It is More, too, who first hinted that Richard had a hand in Clarence's death, and even More is careful to say that this is only rumor. We have seen that there is no contemporary evidence for Richard's participation in the death of Edward of Lancaster, and the same is true of Richard's reputed poisoning of his wife; even later writers either omit the charge altogether or report it as a rumor, not a proven fact. Rather stronger, though still unsatisfactory, is the evidence for Richard's alleged project to marry his niece. We need not reject the statement of the usually well-informed and moderate *Continuator of the Croyland Chronicle*, that a rumor spread just before the death of Queen Anne of Richard's intention to marry Elizabeth in order to thwart Henry Tudor. But the same writer records Richard's denial of any such intention, first in council and later in public, and it would not have been to the king's interest to contemplate such a match. His title to the crown would not have been strengthened by marrying a woman whom the law had declared a bastard; and to have repealed that declaration would have been to call into existence her right to the crown at his own expense. Moreover, if he had thought of such a marriage, it would not have been a criminal design as such a plan would be now. The union of an uncle and a niece was apparently almost unknown in England and generally abhorred there; but such marriages had been legalized by papal dispensations before Richard's time, and other princes of Latin Christendom were to make use of this device in later days.

But if this reminder that Richard was a man of the fifteenth century may work in his favor in this case, it may work against him in some other respects: We have to recall that it was an age of violence and civil war, and that scruples about murder would be unlikely to deter men brought up in such an atmosphere as Edward IV and his brothers had been from killing a rival king if it seemed in their interests to do so. Yorkist propaganda asserted that Henry VI died of pure displeasure and melancholy; but an investigation of his remains has indicated that he died a violent death. Moreover, contemporaries specifically mention Richard as implicated in the murder of Henry VI; these sources comprise not only London chroniclers, who might be expected to remember what rumors were current in London, and do not mention Gloucester in connection with the execution of Clarence, but also include writers such as Warkworth and Comines, who refrain from accusing Richard of any part in the death of Edward of Lancaster.

It is, however, not the death of Henry VI but the disappearance of the princes in the Tower which has gained for Richard the greatest condemnation—and the most strenuous defense. A thoroughgoing admirer of Richard such as Sir Clements Markham had no difficulty in showing the defects of Sir Thomas More's famous account; and if it stood alone, it might leave us unconvinced. But the report that Richard murdered his two nephews is found in a large number of sources, not only in England but overseas; and it is incredible to ascribe every rumor of such a deed to the malevolence and ubiquity of Bishop Morton and the diabolical cunning of Henry VII. And not only do a number of writers give this report (including a contemporary visitor to London, Dominico Mancini, whose narrative has been published since Markham wrote), but there is not so much as a hint in any source that the boys were in fact murdered by Henry VII. Markham would explain this by arguing that Henry VII ruthlessly suppressed all knowledge or even rumors of his crime, which was the more effectively cloaked by spreading the notion that it was Richard III who had done it. But apart from the fact that rumors of the death of the princes were current before the accession of Henry VII, this view does not fit in with what we know of the efficiency of early Tudor government. Even a modern totalitarian dictatorship finds it hard to keep locked up the skeletons in the cupboard; and in early Tudor England, with its slow communications and its army and police dependent for their working on the cooperation of the middle and upper classes, it was far more difficult to do so. If Henry VII's government was so efficient that it could suppress every report of the princes being still alive in 1485 and of their subsequent murder, it ought to have been able to produce a clearer and firmer story of their murder by Richard III than we actually have. If the princes were alive throughout the reign of Richard III, it is very hard to account for their permanent disappearance after the summer of 1483, and for Richard's failure to show them in public to scotch the rumors of their deaths. Moreover, the skeletons of the two boys discovered in the reign of Charles II at the foot of the staircase in the White Tower seem to support the reports of their murder by Richard. In 1933 the urn in Westminster Abbey containing these skeletons was opened, and the bones were medically examined by Professor W. Wright. In spite of some difficulties in the evidence which he did not discuss, he appears to be correct in his conclusion that the bones were consistent with the sizes and ages of the two princes in 1483. Besides these considerations it is perhaps of minor consequence that Markham's thesis necessitates a Henry VII as completely villainous as the Shakespearean Richard. Markham supposes, for example, that Elizabeth of York loathed her husband as the murderer of her brothers, and that her mother died in strict imprisonment because she discovered the truth. But there is evidence that Elizabeth of York and Henry VII had a mutual affection, and that he not only granted Elizabeth Wydeville a competence (since her estates had been confiscated by Richard) but made her godmother to Arthur, Prince of Wales, in preference to his own mother, and negotiated for her marriage to the King of Scots at a time when her imprisonment is alleged to have already begun.

If Henry VII is more satisfactorily explained,

not as a complete villain, but as a complex character, so is Richard III. He could, as Duke of Gloucester, make himself popular in the north by the better justice and greater order which he promoted in that wild region, so that the York records could lament his death as a great heaviness to the city; and yet he may have been involved in the murder of a defenseless old king. He could be brave, able, and resolute in campaign and battle; but he could be fearful for his own safety and ready to sweep out of his path those who seemed to threaten it. He could be honest and patriotic, as in the negotiations at Picquigny, when most of those around him were corrupt; but he could give way to a personal ambition which brought rebellion and civil war to his country once more. Above all, he could usurp the throne, but not because of long-planned villainy.

It is absurd to portray Richard scheming from his 'teens to gain the crown; for who could have foreseen the death of the splendidly built Edward IV at the age of forty and the royal minority without which there could have been for Richard no chance of the throne? In fact, he seems to have been outstandingly loyal to his brother Edward, in adversity as well as success. By the late king's will Richard was entrusted with the care of his heir and kingdom and Gloucester's first acts seem to show that he meant to care for his nephew as faithfully as he had served his father. But the Prince of Wales had hitherto been in the custody of the queen's kinsmen, the Wydevilles and Greys; and since they knew that, as upstarts, they were intensely disliked by the older nobility, and that the protection of Edward IV was now withdrawn, they tried to control the government through the new king. They sought to exclude the dukes of Gloucester and Buckingham, the leaders of the blood royal and the old nobility, from every position of influence. This policy alarmed the dukes, for even if no immediate harm should befall them, the new king would, if allowed to grow up under the tutelage of the queen's kinsmen, be led to favor their ambitions and share their dislikes. It was less than forty years since the previous duke of Gloucester, also uncle of the reigning monarch and also heir presumptive, had (so it was now generally believed) been murdered by the clique surrounding the then king. Equally alarmed by the actions of the queen's party were those who, like Lord Hastings, had been trusted councillors of Edward IV and now foresaw their exclusion from power. The confidence inspired by Richard's previous reputation and the widespread distrust felt for the queen's party combined to place him in a strong position when, with Buckingham, he determined to get his blow in first; and so he arrested the king's guardians —Rivers, Grey and Vaughan—at Stony Stratford on the way to the early coronation which the Wydeville party had planned to end Richard's influence in the government.

Once they were under lock and key, the queen had fled to sanctuary, and the rest of her kinsmen had scattered, Lord Hastings's attitude began to change. It did not suit him and others who had been influential in the government of Edward IV that power should go to rivals such as the duke of Buckingham, the earl of Northumberland, Lords Howard and Lovell, who had already given particular support to Richard and were now rewarded by him with fees and offices. In resentment Hastings began negotiations with the Wydeville party against this new danger. These rivalries confronted Gloucester with a very unpleasant choice. If he should try to come to terms with the queen's kindred, it would be hard to be sure of conciliating them, and the young king, after what had happened at Stony Stratford; and an alliance with Hastings and his group, even if it could be achieved, might lose him Buckingham's more valuable aid. After trying in vain to win over Hastings while remaining in league with Buckingham, Gloucester seems to have decided to make sure of his power, and of the further support of Buckingham, Howard, Northumberland, Lovell and their followers, by striking down Hastings and the queen's kindred. So Hastings was suddenly arrested in council at the Tower of London and beheaded without trial the same day (June 13th),[2] the queen was denounced as a conspirator against Richard, and the execution of Rivers, Grey and Vaughan was decided upon.

This coup d'etat may have solved Richard's immediate difficulties, but only at the cost of creating greater problems beyond—if he should remain loyal to his nephew; for the remaining

members of the queen's party would now be irreconcilable foes, and the young king might be permanently alienated. Gloucester seems to have been an impulsive man and he evidently decided to cut the knot by seizing the crown. There may have been some truth in Bishop Stillington's story of Edward IV's pre-contract with Lady Eleanor Butler, and Clarence is said to have already flung against Edward the taunt of bastardy. But there seems no adequate grounds for asserting that Edward IV was illegitimate; and to use a technical impediment to invalidate his marriage was not only unscrupulous but almost bound to weaken the Yorkist dynasty whose interests Richard had previously so strenuously defended. The charges were so widely disbelieved, and Richard's elevation to the throne was resented by so many of the nobility and gentry, that he started his reign on a dangerously narrow basis of power. This led him to shut up the princes closely in the Tower, for fear of demonstrations in their favor; but this act precipitated the very unrest he feared. The widespread movement in the important south of England for the liberation of the princes seems to have convinced Richard that he would not be safe until they were dead; and in his impulsive way he probably ordered their murder. But their disappearance increased his troubles instead of lessening them, and Buckingham, who had helped him to power, joined the coalition of queen's kinsmen, displaced adminstrators of Edward IV, and Lancastrians which rose against him.

The suppression of this rising averted the immediate peril; but the defection of Buckingham and his supporters reduced still further the unsure foundation of Richard's power, a basis rendered even more insecure by the death of his only son in April 1484, and of his wife in March, 1485. He tried hard to live down the past and gain support by his energy and devotion to his kingly duties. And in spite of later denigration it must be owned that during his brief reign he displayed many qualities which, if he had come to the throne in a more acceptable way, might have helped him to a long and successful reign. He showed zeal for trade and English interest abroad; he tried to repress disorder and promote justice; he made it easier for poor suitors to present their petitions to him and his council; he strove to make financial reforms and lessen the burden of royal demands for money; he instigated a land law (on uses) which foreshadowed an important reform of Henry VIII. His public

[2] On pp. 454–5 of vol. VI (1891) of the *English Historical Review,* Gairdner demolished Markham's contention (made in an article in the same volume) that Hastings was executed, not on the day of his arrest, but a week later after a regular trial; but as Markham nevertheless reasserted the same theory in his book of 1906, and this theory has been repeated since then by Markham's followers, it may be useful to cite a piece of evidence which does not seem to have been hitherto noticed in this connection. The *Inquisitio Post Mortem,* the usual official inquiry into the estates of a deceased tenant of the crown, was, of course, made by Richard's own officials; and it stated that Hastings died on June 13th.

policy in these matters, together with his tenderness to clerical privileges, his building of churches, his advocacy of morality among the people, and his patronage of learning, moved the clergy assembled in convocation to praise him for his "most noble and blessed disposition." He endeavored to win popular approval by his magnificent dress, his princely building, his care for heraldry and pageantry, his generous magnanimity towards the dependents of some of his fallen opponents, his many recorded acts of kindness to petitioners in distress. He seems to have met with some success in this endeavor; and we find the Bishop of St. David's writing to the Prior of Christ Church, Canterbury: "He contents the people wher he goys best that ever did prince; for many a poor man that hath suffred wrong many days have be relevyd and helpyd by hym . . . God hathe sent hym to us for the wele of us al." If he could have prolonged his reign to twenty years instead of two, he might have overlaid with success and good deeds the memory of his path to the throne. Had not King John survived the murder of his nephew and died many years later a specially protected son of the Church? But popular acclamation was a frail substitute for the support of the aristocracy and gentry, who had been so largely alienated that the many time-servers among his remaining adherents doubted his power to survive. This proved his undoing; for it must be recognized that what brought him to defeat and death at Bosworth Field was not the feeling of the nation at large, but the desertion of a few great nobles and their forces.

To the Elizabethans his death was the fitting and morally necessary end of a monster, after a whole lifetime of scheming villainy. The modern investigator is more likely to be impressed by the play of events on a complex nature, in an age of contradictions of character. If Edward IV had lived to the age of fifty, instead of dying at forty, Richard might have gone down in history as a very commendable character, with a possible share in the murder of Henry VI as the only conspicuous blemish. He might have been remembered as an able and energetic administrator, a brave and skillful soldier, a faithful brother and affectionate father, a kind and generous man of culture, and of music and architecture, a patron of learning and a devoted son of the Church. But the responsibilities and perils of an unexpected royal minority aroused in his nature the elements of fear, ambition and impulsive ruthlessness which led him further and further along the path of immediate expediency at the expense of duty and honor. Even then his will to be a successful and popular king might have enabled his considerable talents to re-establish his reputation, had he been granted time; it is now generally agreed that the portraits of him as king show an anxious and nervous man rather than a cruel or merciless one.[3] But time was not on his side and he was vouchsafed only two uneasy years; and as Bishop Stubbs rightly said, he owes "the general condemnation, with which his life and reign have been visited, to the fact that he left none behind him whose duty or whose care it was to attempt his vindication."

Yet even in Tudor days men sometimes dared to speak good of him, and not only in the north of England. In 1525 Cardinal Wolsey was pressing the mayor and aldermen of London for a benevolence. To their objection that this demand was contrary to a statute of Richard III the cardinal retorted: "I marvell that you speak of Richard the third, which was a usurper and a murtherer of his awne nephewes." The reply to this is noteworthy, and one sentence in it might serve as a partial epitaph on Richard III: "although he did evill, yet in his tyme wer many good actes made."

[3] As for the hunchback, the portraits of Richard do not show any deformity. A contemporary traveller, Nicolas von Poppelau, found Richard's appearance impressive though rather emaciated; but there is some evidence that one shoulder was slightly higher than the other.

The Daughter of Time[1]

CHAPTER I

Grant lay on his high white cot and stared at the ceiling. Stared at it with loathing. He knew by heart every last minute crack on its nice clean surface. He had made maps of the ceiling and gone exploring on them; rivers, islands, and continents. He had made guessing games of it and discovered hidden objects; faces, birds, and fishes. He had made mathematical calculations of it and rediscovered his childhood; theorems, angles, and triangles. There was practically nothing else he could do but look at it. He hated the sight of it.

He had suggested to The Midget that she might turn his bed around a little so that he could have a new patch of ceiling to explore. But it seemed that that would spoil the symmetry of the room, and in hospitals symmetry ranked just a short head behind cleanliness and a whole length in front of Godliness. Anything out of the parallel was hospital profanity. Why didn't he read? she asked. Why didn't he go on reading some of those expensive brand-new novels that his friends kept on bringing him?

"There are far too many people born into the world, and far too many words written. Millions and millions of them pouring from the presses every minute. It's a horrible thought."

"You sound constipated," said The Midget.

The Midget was Nurse Ingham, and she was in sober fact a very nice five-feet-two, with everything in just proportion. Grant called her The Midget to compensate himself for being bossed around by a piece of Dresden china which he could pick up in one hand. When he was on his feet, that is to say. It was not only that she told him what he might or might not do, but she dealt with his six-feet-odd with an off-hand ease that Grant found humiliating. Weights meant nothing, apparently, to The Midget. She tossed mattresses around with the absent-minded grace of a plate spinner. When she was off duty he was attended to by The Amazon, a goddess with arms like the limb of a beech tree. The Amazon was Nurse Darroll, who came from Gloucestershire and was homesick each daffodil season. (The Midget came from Lytham St. Anne's, and there was no daffodil nonsense about her.) She had large soft hands and large soft cow's eyes and she always looked very sorry for you, but the slightest physical exertion set her breathing like a suction-pump. On the whole Grant found it even more humiliating to be treated as a dead weight than to be treated as if he were no weight at all.

Grant was bed-borne, and a charge on The Midget and The Amazon, because he had fallen through a trap-door. This, of course, was the absolute in humiliation; compared with which the heavings of The Amazon and the light slingings of The Midget were a mere corollary. To fall through a trap-door was the ultimate in absurdity; pantomimic, bathetic, grotesque. At the moment of his disappearance from the normal level of perambulation he had been in hot pursuit of Benny Skoll, and the fact that Benny had careered round the next corner slap into the arms of Sergeant Williams provided the one small crumb of comfort in an intolerable situation.

Benny was now "away" for three years, which was very satisfactory for the lieges, but Benny would get time off for good behavior. In hospitals there was no time off for good behavior.

Grant stopped staring at the ceiling, and slid his eyes sideways at the pile of books on his bedside table; the gay expensive pile that The Midget had been urging on his attention. The top one, with the pretty picture of Valetta in unlikely pink, was Lavinia Fitch's annual account of a blameless heroine's tribulations. In view of the representation of the Grand Harbor on the cover, the present Valerie or

Angela or Cecile or Denise must be a naval wife. He had opened the book only to read the kind message that Lavinia had written inside.

The Sweat and the Furrow was Silas Weekley being earthy and spade-conscious all over seven hundred pages. The situation, to judge from the first paragraph, had not materially changed since Silas's last book: mother lying-in with her eleventh upstairs, father laid-out after his ninth downstairs, eldest son lying to the Government in the cow-shed, eldest daughter lying with her lover in the hay-loft, everyone else lying low in the barn. The rain dripped from the thatch, and the manure steamed in the midden. Silas never omitted the manure. It was not Silas's fault that its steam provided the only up-rising element in the picture. If Silas could have discovered a brand of steam that steamed downwards, Silas would have introduced it.

Under the harsh shadows and highlights of Silas's jacket was an elegant affair of Edwardian curlicues and Baroque nonsense, entitled *Bells on Her Toes*. Which was Rupert Rouge being arch about vice. Rupert Rouge always seduced you into laughter for the first three pages. About Page Three you noticed that Rupert had learned from that very arch (but of course not vicious) creature George Bernard Shaw that the easiest way to sound witty was to use that cheap and convenient method, the paradox. After that you could see the jokes coming three sentences away.

The thing with a red gun-flash across a night-green cover was Oscar Oakley's latest. Toughs talking out of the corners of their mouths in synthetic American that had neither the wit nor the pungency of the real thing. Blondes, chromium bars, breakneck chases. Very remarkably bunk.

The Case of the Missing Tin-Opener, by John James Mark, had three errors of procedure in the first two pages, and had at least provided Grant with a pleasant five minutes while he composed an imaginary letter to its author.

He could not remember what the thin blue book at the bottom of the pile was. Something earnest and statistical, he thought. Tsetse flies, or calories, or sex behavior, or something.

Even in that, you knew what to expect on the next page. Did no one, any more, no one in all this wide world, change their record now and then? Was everyone nowadays thirled to a formula? Authors today wrote so much to a pattern that their public expected it.

The public talked about "a new Silas Weekley" or "a new Lavinia Fitch" exactly as they talked about "a new brick" or "a new hairbrush." They never said "a new book by" whoever it might be. Their interest was not in the book but in its newness. They knew quite well what the book would be like.

It might be a good thing, Grant thought as he turned his nauseated gaze away from the motley pile, if all the presses of the world were stopped for a generation. There ought to be a literary moratorium. Some Superman ought to invent a ray that would stop them all simultaneously. Then people wouldn't send you a lot of fool nonsense when you were flat on your back, and bossy bits of Meissen wouldn't expect you to read them.

He heard the door open, but did not stir himself to look. He had turned his face to the wall, literally and metaphorically.

He heard someone come across to his bed, and closed his eyes against possible conversation. He wanted neither Gloucestershire sympathy nor Lancashire briskness just now. In the succeeding pause a faint enticement, a nostalgic breath of all the fields of Grasse, teased his nostrils and swam about his brain. He savored it and considered. The Midget smelt of lavender dusting powder, and The Amazon of soap and iodoform. What was floating expensively about his nostrils was L'Enclos Numéro Cinq. Only one person of his acquaintance used L'Enclos Number Five. Marta Hallard.

He opened an eye and squinted up at her. She had evidently bent over to see if he was asleep, and was now standing in an irresolute way—if anything Marta did could be said to be irresolute—with her attention on the heap of all too obviously virgin publications on the table. In one arm she was carrying two new books, and in the other a great sheaf of white lilac. He wondered whether she had chosen white lilac because it was her idea of the proper floral offering for winter (it adorned her dressing-room at the theatre from December to March), or whether she had taken it because it would not detract from her black-and-white chic. She was wearing a new hat and her usual pearls; the pearls which he had once been the means of recovering for her. She looked very handsome, very Parisian, and blessedly unhospital-like.

"Did I waken you, Alan?"

"No. I wasn't asleep."

"I seem to be bringing the proverbial coals," she said, dropping the two books alongside their despised brethren. "I hope you will find these more interesting than you seem to have found that lot. Didn't you even try a little teensy taste of our Lavinia?"

"I can't read anything."

"Are you in pain?"

"Agony. But it's neither my leg nor my back."

"What then?"

"It's what my cousin Laura calls 'the prickles of boredom.'"

"Poor Alan. And how right your Laura is." She picked a bunch of narcissi out of a glass that was much too large for them, dropped them with one of her best gestures into the wash-basin, and proceeded to substitute the lilac. "One would expect boredom to be a great yawning emotion, but it isn't, of course. It's a small niggling thing."

"Small nothing. Niggling nothing. It's like being beaten with nettles."

"Why don't you take up something?"

"Improve the shining hour?"

"Improve your mind. To say nothing of your soul and your temper. You might study one of the philosophies. Yoga, or something like that. But I suppose an analytical mind is not the best kind to bring to the consideration of the abstract."

"I did think of going back to algebra. I have an idea that I never did algebra justice, at school. But I've done so much geometry on that damned ceiling that I'm a little off mathematics."

"Well, I suppose it is no use suggesting jig-saws to someone in your position. How about cross-words? I could get you a book of them, if you like."

"God forbid."

"You could invent them, of course. I have heard that that is more fun than solving them."

"Perhaps. But a dictionary weighs several pounds. Besides, I always did hate looking up something in a reference book."

"Do you play chess? I don't remember. How about chess problems? White to play and mate in three moves, or something like that."

"My only interest in chess is pictorial."

"Pictorial?"

"Very decorative things, knights and pawns and whatnot. Very elegant."

"Charming. I *could* bring you along a set to play with. All right, no chess. You could do some academic investigating. That's a sort of mathematics. Finding a solution to an unsolved problem."

"Crime, you mean? I know all the case-histories by heart. And there is nothing more that can be done about any of them. Certainly not by someone who is flat on his back."

"I didn't mean something out of the files at the Yard. I meant something more—what's the word?—something classic. Something that has puzzled the world for ages."

"As what, for instance?"

"Say, the casket letters."

"Oh, *not* Mary Queen of Scots!"

"Why not?" asked Marta, who like all actresses saw Mary Stuart through a haze of white veils.

"I could be interested in a bad woman but never in a silly one."

"*Silly?*" said Marta in her best lower-register Electra voice.

"*Very* silly."

"Oh, Alan, how can you!"

"If she had worn another kind of headdress no one would ever have bothered about her. It's that cap that seduces people."

"You think she would have loved less greatly in a sunbonnet?"

"She never loved greatly at all, in any kind of bonnet."

Marta looked as scandalized as a lifetime in the theatre and an hour of careful make-up allowed her to.

"Why do you think that?"

"Mary Stuart was six feet tall. Nearly all out-sized women are sexually cold. Ask any doctor."

And as he said it he wondered why, in all the years since Marta had first adopted him as a spare escort when she needed one, it had not occurred to him to wonder whether her notorious level-headedness about men had something to do with her inches. But Marta had not drawn any parallels; her mind was still on her favorite queen.

"At least she was a martyr. You'll have to allow her that."

"Martyr to what?"

"Her religion."

"The only thing she was a martyr to was rheumatism. She married Darnley without the Pope's dispensation, and Bothwell by Protestant rites."

"In a moment you'll be telling me she wasn't a prisoner!"

"The trouble with you is that you think of her in a little room at the top of a castle, with bars on the window and a faithful old attendant to share her prayers with her. In actual fact she had a personal household of sixty persons. She complained bitterly when it was reduced to a beggarly thirty, and nearly died of chagrin when it was reduced to two male secretaries, several women, an embroiderer, and a cook or two. And Elizabeth had to pay for all that out of her own purse. For twenty years she paid, and for twenty years Mary Stuart hawked the crown of Scotland round Europe to anyone who would start a revolution and put her back on the throne that she had lost; or, alternatively, on the one Elizabeth was sitting on."

He looked at Marta and found that she was smiling.

"Are they a little better now?" she asked.

"Are what better?"

"The prickles."

He laughed.

"Yes. For a whole minute I had forgotten about them. That is at least one good thing to put down to Mary Stuart's account!"

"How do you know so much about Mary?"

"I did an essay about her in my last year at school."

"And didn't like her, I take it."

"Didn't like what I found out about her."

"You don't think her tragic, then."

"Oh, yes, very. But not tragic in any of the ways that popular belief makes her tragic. Her tragedy was that she was born a queen with the outlook of a suburban housewife. Scoring off Mrs. Tudor in the next street is harmless and amusing; it may lead you into unwarrantable indulgence in hire-purchase, but it affects only yourself. When you use the same technique on kingdoms the result is disastrous. If you are willing to put a country of ten million people in pawn in order to score off a royal rival, then you end by being a friendless failure." He lay thinking abut it for a little. "She would have been a wild success as a mistress at a girl's school."

"Beast!"

"I meant it nicely. The staff would have liked her, and all the little girls would have adored her. That is what I meant about her being tragic."

"Ah well. No casket letters, it seems. What else is there? The Man in the Iron Mask?"

"I can't remember who that was, but I couldn't be interested in anyone who was being coy behind some tin-plate. I couldn't be interested in anyone at all unless I could see his face."

"Ah, yes. I forgot your passion for faces. The Borgias had wonderful faces. I should think they would provide a little mystery or two for you to dabble in if you looked them up.

Or there was Perkin Warbeck, of course. Imposture is always fascinating. Was he or wasn't he? A lovely game. The balance can never come down wholly on one side or the other. You push it over and up it comes again, like one of those weighted toys."

The door opened and Mrs. Tinker's homely face appeared in the aperture surmounted by her still more homely and historic hat. Mrs. Tinker had worn the same hat since first she began to "do" for Grant, and he could not imagine her in any other. That she did possess another one he knew, because it went with something that she referred to as "me blue." Her "blue" was an occasional affair, in both senses, and never appeared at 19 Tenby Court. It was worn with a ritualistic awareness, and having been worn it was used in the event as a yardstick by which to judge the proceedings. ("Did you enjoy it, Tink? What was it like?" "Not worth putting on me blue for.") She had worn it to Princess Elizabeth's wedding, and to various other royal functions, and had indeed figured in it for two flashing seconds in a newsreel shot of the Duchess of Kent cutting a ribbon, but to Grant it was a mere report; a criterion of the social worth of an occasion. A thing was or was not worth putting on "me blue" for.

"I 'eard you 'ad a visitor," said Mrs. Tinker, "and I was all set to go away again when I thought the voice sounded familiar like, and I says to meself: 'It's only Miss Hallard,' I says, so I come in."

She was carrying various paper bags and a small tight bunch of anemones. She greeted Marta as woman to woman, having been in her time a dresser and having therefore no exaggerated reverence for the goddesses of the theatre world, and looked askance at the beautiful arrangement of lilac sprays that had blossomed under Marta's ministrations. Marta did not see the glance but she saw the little bunch of anemones and took over the situation as if it were something already rehearsed.

"I squander my vagabond's hire on white lilac for you, and then Mrs. Tinker puts my nose out of joint by bringing you the Lilies of the Field."

"Lilies?" said Mrs. Tinker, doubtfully.

"Those are the Solomon in all his glory things. The ones that toiled not neither did they spin."

Mrs. Tinker went to church only for weddings and christenings, but she belonged to a generation that had been sent to Sunday school. She looked with a new interest at the little handful of glory encased by her woollen glove.

"Well, now. I never knew that. Makes more sense that way, don't it? I always pictured them arums. Fields and fields of arums. Awful expensive, you know, but a bit depressing. So they was colored? Well, why can't they say so? What do they have to call them lilies for!"

And they went on to talk about translation, and how misleading Holy Writ could be ("I always wondered what bread on the waters was," Mrs Tinker said) and the awkward moment was over.

While they were still busy with the Bible, The Midget came in with extra flower vases. Grant noticed that the vases were designed to hold white lilac and not anemones. They were tribute to Marta; a passport to further communing. But Marta never bothered about women unless she had an immediate use for them; her tact with Mrs. Tinker had been mere *savoir faire*; a conditioned reflex. So The Midget was reduced to being functional instead of social. She collected the discarded narcissi from the wash-basin and meekly put them back into a vase. The Midget being meek was the most beautiful sight that had gladdened Grant's eyes for a long time.

"Well," Marta said, having finished her arrangement of the lilac and placed the result where he could see it, "I shall leave Mrs. Tinker to feed you all the titbits out of those paper bags. It couldn't be, could it, Mrs. Tinker darling, that one of those bags contains any of your wonderful bachelor's buttons?"

Mrs. Tinker glowed.

"You'd like one or two maybe? Fresh outa me oven?"

"Well, of course I shall have to do penance for it afterwards—those little rich cakes are death on the waist—but just give me a couple to put in my bag for my tea at the theatre."

She chose two with a flattering deliberation ("I like them a little brown at the edges"), dropped them into her handbag, and said: "Well, au revoir, Alan. I shall look in, in a day or two, and start you on a sock. There is nothing so soothing, I understand, as knitting. Isn't that so, nurse?"

"Oh, yes, indeed. A lot of my gentlemen patients take to knitting. They find it whiles away the time very nicely."

Marta blew him a kiss from the door and was gone, followed by the respectful Midget.

"I'd be surprised if that hussy is any better than she ought to be," Mrs. Tinker said, beginning to open the paper bags. She was not referring to Marta.

CHAPTER II

But when Marta came back two days later it was not with knitting needles and wool. She breezed in, very dashing in a Cossack hat worn at a casual rake that must have taken her several minutes at her mirror, just after lunch.

"I haven't come to stay, my dear. I'm on my way to the theatre. It's matinée day, God help me. Tea trays and morons. And we've all got to the frightful stage when the lines have ceased to have any meaning at all for us. I don't think this play is ever coming off. It's going to be like those New York ones that run by the decade instead of by the year. It's too frightening. One's mind just won't stay on the thing. Geoffrey dried up in the middle of the second act last night. His eyes nearly popped out of his head. I thought for a moment he was having a stroke. He said afterwards that he had no recollection of anything that happened between his entrance and the point where he came to and found himself half-way through the act."

"A black-out, you mean?"

"No. Oh, no. Just being an automaton. Saying lines and doing the business and thinking of something else all the time."

"If all reports are true that's no unusual matter where actors are concerned."

"Oh, in moderation, no. Johnny Garson can tell you how much paper there is in the house what time he is sobbing his heart out on someone's lap. But that's different from being 'away' for half an act. Do you realize that Geoffrey had turned his son out of the house, quarrelled with his mistress, and accused his wife of having an affair with his best friend all without being aware of it?"

"What *was* he aware of?"

"He says he had decided to lease his Park Lane flat to Dolly Dacre and buy that Charles the Second house at Richmond that the Latimers are giving up because he has got that Governor's appointment. He had thought about the lack of bathrooms and decided that the little upstairs room with the eighteenth-century Chinese paper would make a very good one. They could remove the beautiful paper and use it to decorate that dull little room downstairs at the back. It's full of Victorian panelling, the dull little room. He had also reviewed the drainage, wondered if he had enough money to take the old tiling off and replace it, and speculated as to what kind of cooking range they had in the kitchen. He had just decided to get rid of the shrubbery at the gate when he found himself face to face with me, on a stage, in the presence of nine hundred and eighty-seven people, in the middle of a speech. Do you wonder that his eyes popped? I see that you have managed to read at least one of the books I brought you—if the rumpled jacket is any criterion."

"Yes. The mountain one. It was a godsend. I lay for hours looking at the pictures. Nothing puts things in perspective as quickly as a mountain."

"The stars are better, I find."

"Oh, *no.* The stars merely reduce one to the status of an amoeba. The stars take the last vestige of human pride, the last spark of confidence, from one. But a snow mountain is a nice human-size yardstick. I lay and looked at Everest and thanked God that I wasn't climbing those slopes. A hospital bed was a haven of warmth and rest and security by comparison, and The Midget and The Amazon two of the highest achievements of civilization."

"Ah, well, here are some more pictures for you."

Marta up-ended the quarto envelope she was carrying, and spilled a collection of paper sheets over his chest.

"What is this?"

"Faces," said Marta, delightedly. "Dozens of faces for you. Men, women, and children. All sorts, conditions, and sizes."

He picked a sheet off his chest and looked at it. It was an engraving of a fifteenth-century portrait. A woman.

"Who is this?"

"Lucrezia Borgia. Isn't she a duck?"

"Perhaps, but are you suggesting that there was any mystery about her?"

"Oh, yes. No one has ever decided whether she was her brother's tool or his accomplice."

He discarded Lucrezia, and picked up a second sheet. This proved to be the portrait of a small boy in late-eighteenth-century clothes, and under it in faint capitals was printed the words: Louis XVII.

"Now there's a *beautiful* mystery for you," Marta said. "The Dauphin. Did he escape or did he die in captivity?"

"Where did you get all these?"

"I routed James out of his cubby-hole at the Victoria and Albert, and made him take me to a print shop. I knew he would know about that sort of thing, and I'm sure he has nothing to interest him at the V. and A."

It was so like Marta to take it for granted that a Civil Servant, because he happened also to be a playwright and an authority on por-

traits, should be willing to leave his work and delve about in print shops for her pleasure.

He turned up the photograph of an Elizabethan portrait. A man in velvet and pearls. He turned the back to see who this might be and found that it was the Earl of Leicester.

"So that is Elizabeth's Robin," he said. "I don't think I ever saw a portrait of him before."

Marta looked down on the virile fleshy face and said: "It occurs to me for the first time that one of the major tragedies of history is that the best painters didn't paint you till you were past your best. Robin must have been quite a man. They say Henry the Eighth was dazzling as a young man, but what is he now? Something on a playing card. Nowadays we *know* what Tennyson was like before he grew that frightful beard. I must fly. I'm late as it is. I've been lunching at the Blague, and so many people came up to talk that I couldn't get away as early as I meant to."

"I hope your host was impressed," Grant said, with a glance at the hat.

"Oh, yes. She knows about hats. She took one look and said 'Jacques Tous, I take it.'"

"She!" said Grant surprised.

"Yes. Madeleine March. And it was I who was giving her luncheon. Don't look so astonished: it isn't tactful. I'm hoping, if you must know, that she'll write me that play about Lady Blessington. But there was such a to-ing and fro-ing that I had no chance to make any impression on her. However, I gave her a wonderful meal. Which reminds me that Tony Bittmaker was entertaining a party of seven. Magnums galore. How do you imagine he keeps going?"

"Lack of evidence," Grant said, and she laughed and went away.

In the silence he went back to considering Elizabeth's Robin. What mystery was there about Robin?

Oh, yes. Amy Robsart, of course.

Well, he wasn't interested in Amy Robsart. He didn't care how she had fallen down stairs, or why.

But he spent a very happy afternoon with the rest of the faces. Long before he had entered the Force he had taken a delight in faces, and in his years at the Yard that interest had proved both a private entertainment and a professional advantage. He had once in his early days dropped in with his Superintendent at an identification parade. It was not his case, and they were both there on other business, but they lingered in the background and watched while a man and a woman, separately, walked down the line of twelve nondescript men, looking for the one they hoped to recognize.

"Which is Chummy, do you know?" the Super had whispered to him.

"I don't know," Grant had said, "but I can guess."

"You can? Which do you make it?"

"The third from the left."

"What is the charge?"

"I don't know. Don't know anything about it."

His chief had cast him an amused glance. But when both the man and the woman had failed to identify anyone and had gone away, and the line broke into a chattering group, hitching collars and settling ties preparatory to going back to the street and the world of everyday from which they had been summoned to assist the Law, the one who did not move was the third man from the left. The third man from the left waited submissively for his escort and was led to his cell again.

"Strewth!" the Superintendent had said. "One chance out of twelve, and you made it. That was good going. He picked your man out of the bunch," he said in explanation to the local Inspector.

"Did you know him?" the Inspector said, a little surprised. "He's never been in trouble before, as far as we know."

"No, I never saw him before. I don't even know what the charge is."

"Then what made you pick him?"

Grant had hesitated, analyzing for the first time his process of selection. It had not been a matter of reasoning. He had not said: "That man's face has this characteristic or that characteristic, therefore he is the accused person." His choice had been almost instinctive; the reason was in his subconscious. At last, having delved into his subconscious, he blurted: "He was the only one of the twelve with no lines on his face."

They had laughed at that. But Grant, once he had pulled the thing into the light, saw how his instinct had worked and recognized the reasoning behind it. "It sounds silly, but it isn't," he said. "The only adult entirely without face lines is the idiot."

"Freeman's no idiot, take it from me," the Inspector broke in. "A very wide-awake boy he is, believe me."

"I didn't mean that. I mean that the idiot is irresponsible. The idiot is the standard of irresponsibility. All those twelve men in that parade were thirty-ish, but only one had an irresponsible face. So I picked him at once."

After that it had become a mild joke at the Yard that Grant could "pick them at sight." And the Assistant Commissioner had once said teasingly: "Don't tell me that you believe that there is such a thing as a criminal face, Inspector."

But Grant had said no, he wasn't as simple as that. "If there was only one kind of crime, sir, it might be possible; but crimes being as wide as human nature, if a policeman started to put faces into categories he would be sunk. You can tell what the normal run of over-sexed women look like by a walk down Bond Street any day between five and six, and yet the most notorious nymphomaniac in London looks like a cold saint."

"Not so saintly of late; she's drinking too much these days," the A.C. had said, identifying the lady without difficulty; and the conversation had gone on to other things.

But Grant's interest in faces had remained and enlarged until it became a conscious study. A matter of case records and comparisons. It was, as he had said, not possible to put faces into any kind of category, but it was possible to characterize individual faces. In a reprint of a famous trial, for instance, where photographs of the principal actors in the case were displayed for the public's interest, there was never any doubt as to which was the accused and which the judge. Occasionally, one of the counsel might on looks have changed places with the prisoner in the dock—counsel were after all a mere cross-section of humanity, as liable to passion and greed as the rest of the world, but a judge had a special quality; an integrity and a detachment. So, even without a wig, one did not confuse him with the man in the dock, who had neither integrity nor detachment.

Marta's James, having been dragged from his "cubby-hole," had evidently enjoyed himself, and a fine selection of offenders, or their victims, kept Grant entertained until The Midget brought his tea. As he tidied the sheets together to put them away in his locker his hand came in contact with one that had slipped off his chest and had lain all the afternoon unnoticed on the counterpane. He picked it up and looked at it.

It was the portrait of a man. A man dressed in the velvet cap and slashed doublet of the late fifteenth century. A man about thirty-five or thirty-six years old, lean and clean shaven. He wore a rich jewelled collar, and was in the act of putting a ring on the little finger of his right hand. But he was not looking at the ring. He was looking off into space.

Of all the portraits Grant had seen this afternoon this was the most individual. It was as if the artist had striven to put on canvas something that his talent was not sufficient to translate into paint. The expression in the eyes—that most arresting and individual expression—had defeated him. So had the mouth: he had not known how to make lips so thin and so wide look mobile, so the mouth was wooden and a failure. What he had best succeeded in was the bone structure of the face: the strong cheekbones, the hollows below them, the chin too large for strength.

Grant paused in the act of turning the thing over, to consider the face a moment longer. A judge? A soldier? A prince? Someone used to great responsibility, and responsible in his authority. Someone too conscientious. A worrier; perhaps a perfectionist. A man at ease in a large design, but anxious over details. A candidate for gastric ulcer. Someone, too, who had suffered ill-health as a child. He had that incommunicable, that indescribable look that childhood suffering leaves behind it; less positive than the look on a cripple's face, but as inescapable. This the artist had both understood and translated into terms of paint. The slight fullness of the lower eyelid, like a child that has slept too heavily; the texture of the skin; the old-man look in a young face.

He turned the portrait over to look for a caption.

On the back was printed: *Richard the Third. From the portrait in the National Portrait Gallery. Artist Unknown.*

Richard the Third.

So that was who it was. Richard the Third. Crouchback. The monster of nursery stories. The destroyer of innocence. A synonym for villainy.

He turned the paper over and looked again. Was that what the artist had tried to convey when he had painted those eyes? Had what he had seen in those eyes been the look of a man haunted?

He lay a long time looking at that face; at those extraordinary eyes. They were long eyes, set close under the brows; the brows slightly drawn in that worried, over-conscientious frown. At first glance they appeared to be peering; but as one looked one found that they were in fact withdrawn, almost absent-minded.

When The Midget came back for his tray he was still staring at the portrait. Nothing like this had come his way for years. It made La Giaconda look like a poster.

The Midget examined his virgin teacup, put a practiced hand against the teapot's tepid cheek, and pouted. She had better things to do, she conveyed, than bring him trays for him to ignore.

He pushed the portrait at her.

What did she think of it? If that man were her patient what would be her verdict?

"Liver," she said crisply, and bore away the tray in heel-tapping protest, all starch and blond curls.

But the surgeon, strolling in against her draught, kindly and casual, had other views. He looked at the portrait, as invited, and said after a moment's interested scrutiny:

"Poliomyelitis."

"Infantile paralysis?" Grant said; and remembered all of a sudden that Richard III had a withered arm.

"Who is it?" the surgeon asked.

"Richard the Third."

"Really? That's interesting."

"Did you know that he had a withered arm?"

"Had he? I didn't remember that. I thought he was a hunchback."

"So he was."

"What I do remember is that he was born with a full set of teeth and ate live frogs. Well, my diagnosis seems to be abnormally accurate."

"Uncanny. What made you choose polio?"

"I don't quite know, now that you ask me to be definitive. Just the look of the face, I suppose. It's the look one sees on the face of a cripple child. If he was born hunchbacked that probably accounts for it and not polio. I notice the artist has left out the hump."

"Yes. Court painters have to have a modicum of tact. It wasn't until Cromwell that sitters asked for 'warts and all.'"

"If you ask me," the surgeon said, absent-mindedly considering the splint on Grant's leg, "Cromwell started that inverted snobbery from which we are all suffering today. 'I'm a plain man, I am; no nonsense about *me*.' And no manners, grace, or generosity, either." He pinched Grant's toe with detached interest. "It's a raging disease. A horrible perversion. In some parts of the States, I understand, it's as much as a man's political life is worth to go to some constituencies with his tie tied and his coat on. That's being stuffed-shirt. The beau ideal is to be one of the boys. That's looking very healthy," he added, referring to Grant's big toe, and came back of his own accord to the portrait lying on the counterpane.

"Interesting," he said, "that about the polio. Perhaps it really was polio, and that accounts for the shrunken arm." He went on considering it, making no movement to go. "Interesting, anyhow. Portrait of a murderer. Does he run to type, would you say?"

"There isn't a murder type. People murder for too many different reasons. But I can't remember any murderer, either in my own experience, or in case-histories, who resembled him."

"Of course he was *hors concours* in his class, wasn't he? He couldn't have known the meaning of scruple."

"No."

"I once saw Olivier play him. The most dazzling exhibition of sheer evil, it was. Always on the verge of toppling over into the grotesque, and never doing it."

"When I showed you the portrait," Grant said, "before you knew who it was, did you think of villainy?"

"No," said the surgeon, "no, I thought of illness."

"It's odd, isn't it? I didn't think of villainy either. And now that I know who it is, now that I've read the name on the back, I can't think of it as anything but villainous."

"I suppose villainy, like beauty, is in the eye of the beholder. Well, I'll look in again towards the end of the week. No pain to speak of now?"

And he went away, kindly and casual as he had come.

It was only after he had given the portrait further puzzled consideration (it piqued him to have mistaken one of the most notorious murderers of all time for a judge; to have transferred a subject from the dock to the bench was a shocking piece of ineptitude) that it occurred to Grant that the portrait had been provided as the illustration to a piece of detection.

What mystery was there about Richard III?

And then he remembered. Richard had murdered his two boy nephews, but no one knew how. They had merely disappeared. They had disappeared, if he remembered rightly, while Richard was away from London. Richard had sent someone to do the deed. But the mystery of the children's actual fate had never been solved. Two skeletons had turned up—under some stairs?—in Charles II's day, and had been buried. It was taken for granted that the skeletons were the remains of the young princes, but nothing had ever been proved.

It was shocking how little history remained with one after a good education. All he knew about Richard III was that he was the younger brother of Edward IV. That Edward was a blond six-footer with remarkable good looks and a still more remarkable way with women; and that Richard was a hunchback who usurped the throne on his brother's death in place of the boy heir, and arranged the death of that heir and his small brother to save himself any further trouble. He also knew that Richard had died at the battle of Bosworth yelling for a horse, and that he was the last of his line. The last Plantagenet.

Every schoolboy turned over the final page of Richard III with relief, because now at last the Wars of the Roses were over and they could get on to the Tudors, who were dull but easy to follow.

When The Midget came to tidy him up for the night Grant said: "You don't happen to have a history book, by any chance, do you?"

"A history book? No. What would I be doing with a history book." It was not a question, so Grant did not try to provide an answer. His silence seemed to fret her.

"If you really want a history book," she said presently, "you could ask Nurse Darroll when she brings your supper. She has all her school books on a shelf in her room and its quite possible she has a history among them."

How like The Amazon to keep her school books! he thought. She was still homesick for school as she was homesick for Gloucestershire every time the daffodils bloomed. When she lumbered into the room, bearing his cheese pudding and stewed rhubarb, he looked at her with a tolerance that bordered on the benevolent. She ceased to be a large female who breathed like a suction-pump and became a potential dispenser of delight.

Oh yes, she had a history book, she said. Indeed, she rather thought that she had two. She had kept all her school books because she had loved school.

It was on the tip of Grant's tongue to ask her if she had kept her dolls, but he stopped himself in time.

"And of course I loved history," she said. "It was my favorite subject. Richard the Lionheart was my hero."

"An intolerable bounder," Grant said.

"Oh, no!" she said, looking wounded.

"A hyperthyroid type," Grant said pitilessly. "Rocketing to and fro about the earth like a badly made firework. Are you going off duty now?"

"Whenever I've finished my trays."

"Could you find that book for me tonight?"

"You're supposed to be going to sleep, not staying awake over history books."

"I might as well read some history as look at the ceiling—which is the alternative. Will you get it for me?"

"I don't think I could go all the way up to the Nurses' Block and back again tonight for someone who is rude about the Lionheart."

"All right," he said. "I'm not the stuff that martyrs are made of. As far as I'm concerned Coeur-de-Lion is the pattern of chivalry, the chevalier sans peur et sans reproche, a faultless commander and a triple D.S.O. Now will you get the book?"

"It seems to me you've sore need to read a little history," she said, smoothing a mitred sheet-corner with a large admiring hand, "so I'll bring you the book when I come past. I'm going out to the pictures anyhow."

It was nearly an hour before she reappeared, immense in a camel-hair coat. The room lights had been put out and she materialized into the light of his reading-lamp like some kindly genie.

"I was hoping you'd be asleep," she said. "I don't really think you should start on these tonight."

"If there is anything that is likely to put me to sleep," he said, "it would be an English history book. So you can hold hands with a clear conscience."

"I'm going with Nurse Burrows."

"You can still hold hands."

"I've no patience with you," she said patiently and faded backwards into the gloom.

She had brought two books.

One was the kind of history book known as a Historical Reader. It bore the same relation to history as Stories from the Bible bears to Holy Writ. Canute rebuked his courtiers on the shore, Alfred burned the cakes, Raleigh spread his cloak for Elizabeth, Nelson took leave of Hardy in his cabin on the *Victory*, all in nice clear large print and one-sentence paragraphs. To each episode went one full-page illustration.

There was something curiously touching in the fact that The Amazon should treasure this childish literature. He turned to the fly-leaf to see if her name was there. On the fly-leaf was written:

Ella Darroll,
Form III
Newbridge High School

Newbridge,
Gloucestershire.
England
Europe,
The World
The Universe.

This was surrounded by a fine selection of colored transfers.

Did all children do that, he wondered? Write their names like that, and spend their time in class making transfers? He certainly had. And the sight of those squares of bright primitive color brought back his childhood as nothing had for many years. He had forgotten the excitement of transfers. That wonderfully satisfying moment when you began the peeling-off and saw that it was coming perfectly. The adult world held few such gratifications. A clean smacking drive at golf, perhaps, was the nearest. Or the moment when your line tightened and you knew that the fish had struck.

The little book pleased him so much that he went through it at his leisure. Solemnly reading each childish story. This, after all, was the history that every adult remembered. This was what remained in their minds when tonnage and poundage, and ship money, and Laud's Liturgy, and the Rye House Plot, and the Triennial Acts, and all the long muddle of schism and shindy, treaty and treason, had faded from their consciousness.

The Richard III story, when he came to it, was called *The Princes in the Tower*, and it seemed that young Ella had found the Princes a poor substitute for Coeur-de-Lion, since she had filled every small O throughout the tale with neat pencil shading. The two golden-haired boys who played together in the sunbeam from the barred window in the accompanying picture had each been provided with a pair of anachronistic spectacles, and on the blank back of the picture-page someone had been playing Naughts and Crosses. As far as young Ella was concerned the Princes were a dead loss.

And yet it was a sufficiently arresting little story. Macabre enough to delight any child's heart. The innocent children; the wicked uncle. The classic ingredients in a tale of classic simplicity.

It had also a moral. It was the perfect cautionary tale.

But the King won no profit from this wicked deed. The people of England were shocked by his cold-blooded cruelty and decided that they would no longer have him for King. They sent for a distant cousin of Richard's, Henry Tudor, who was living in France, to come and be crowned King in his stead. Richard died bravely in the battle which resulted, but he had made his name hated throughout the country and many deserted him to fight for his rival.

Well, it was neat but not gaudy. Reporting at its simplest.

He turned to the second book.

The second book was the School History proper. The two thousand years of England's story were neatly parcelled into compartments for ready reference. The compartments, as usual, were reigns. It was no wonder that one pinned a personality to a reign, forgetful that that personality had known and lived under other kings. One put them in pigeon-holes automatically. Pepys: Charles II. Shakespeare: Elizabeth. Marlborough: Queen Anne. It never crossed one's mind that someone who had seen Queen Elizabeth could also have seen George I. One had been conditioned to the reign idea from childhood.

However, it did simplify things when you were just a policeman with a game leg and a concussed spine hunting up some information on dead and gone royalties to keep yourself from going crazy.

He was surprised to find the reign of Richard III so short. To have made oneself one of the best-known rulers in all those two thousand years of England's history, and to have had only two years to do it in, surely augured a towering personality. If Richard had not made friends he had certainly influenced people.

The history book, too, thought that he had personality.

Richard was a man of great ability, but quite unscrupulous as to his means. He boldly claimed the crown on the absurd grounds that his brother's marriage with Elizabeth Woodville had been illegal and the children of it illegitimate. He was accepted by the people, who dreaded a minority, and began his reign by making a progress through the south, where he was well received. During this progress, however, the two young Princes who were living in the Tower, disappeared, and were believed to have been murdered. A serious rebellion followed, which Richard put down with great ferocity. In order to recover some of his

lost popularity he held a Parliament, which passed useful statutes against Benevolences, Maintenance, and Livery.

But a second rebellion followed. This took the form of an invasion, with French troops, by the head of the Lancaster branch, Henry Tudor. He encountered Richard at Bosworth, near Leicester, where the treachery of the Stanleys gave the day to Henry. Richard was killed in battle, fighting courageously, leaving behind him a name hardly less infamous than that of John.

What on earth were Benevolences, Maintenance, and Livery?

And how did the English like having the succession decided for them by French troops?

But, of course, in the days of the Roses, France was still a sort of semi-detached part of England; a country much less foreign to an Englishman than Ireland was. A fifteenth-century Englishman went to France as a matter of course; but to Ireland only under protest.

He lay and thought about that England. The England over which the Wars of the Roses had been fought. A green, green England; with not a chimney-stack from Cumberland to Cornwall. An England still unhedged, with great forests alive with game, and wide marshes thick with wild-fowl. An England with the same small group of dwellings repeated every few miles in endless permutation: castle, church, and cottages; monastery, church, and cottages; manor, church, and cottages. The strips of cultivation round the cluster of dwellings, and beyond that the greenness. The unbroken greenness. The deep-rutted lanes that ran from group to group, mired to bog in the winter and white with dust in the summer; decorated with wild roses or red with hawthorn as the seasons came and went.

For thirty years, over this green uncrowded land, the Wars of the Roses had been fought. But it had been more of a blood feud than a war. A Montague and Capulet affair; of no great concern to the average Englishman. No one pushed in at your door to demand whether you were York or Lancaster and to hale you off to a concentration camp if your answer proved to be the wrong one for the occasion. It was a small concentrated war; almost a private party. They fought a battle in your lower meadow, and turned your kitchen into a dressing-station, and then moved off somewhere or other to fight a battle somewhere else, and a few weeks later you would hear what had happened at that battle, and you would have a family row about the result because your wife was probably Lancaster and you were perhaps York, and it was all rather like following rival football teams. No one persecuted you for being a Lancastrian or a Yorkist, any more than you would be persecuted for being an Arsenal fan or a Chelsea follower.

He was still thinking of that green England when he fell asleep.

And he was not a whit wiser about the two young Princes and their fate.

CHAPTER III

"Can't you find something more cheerful to look at than that thing?" The Midget asked next morning, referring to the Richard portrait which Grant had propped up against the pile of books on his bed-side table.

"You don't find it an interesting face?"

"Interesting! It gives me the willies. A proper Dismal Desmond."

"According to the history books he was a man of great ability."

"So was Bluebeard."

"And considerable popularity, it would seem."

"So was Bluebeard."

"A very fine soldier, too," Grant said wickedly, and waited. "No Bluebeard offers?"

"What do you want to look at that face for? Who was he anyway?"

"Richard the Third."

"Oh, well, I ask you!"

"You mean that's what you expected him to look like."

"Exactly."

"Why?"

"A murdering brute, wasn't he?"

"You seem to know your history."

"Everyone knows that. Did away with his two little nephews, poor brats. Had them smothered."

"Smothered?" said Grant, interested. "I didn't know that."

"Smothered with pillows." She banged his own pillows with a fragile vigorous fist, and replaced them with speed and precision.

"Why smothering? Why not poison?" Grant inquired.

"Don't ask me. I didn't arrange it."

"Who said they were smothered?"

"My history book at school said it."

"Yes, but whom was the history book quoting?"

"Quoting? It wasn't quoting anything. It was just giving facts."

"Who smothered them, did it say?"

"A man called Tyrrel. Didn't you do any history, at school?"

"I attended history lessons. It is not the same thing. Who was Tyrrel?"

"I haven't the remotest. A friend of Richard's."

"How did anyone know it was Tyrrel?"

"He confessed."

"*Confessed?*"

"After he had been found guilty, of course. Before he was hanged."

"You mean that this Tyrrel was actually hanged for the murder of the two Princes?"

"Yes, of course. Shall I take that dreary face away and put up something gayer? There were quite a lot of nice faces in that bundle Miss Hallard brought you yesterday."

"I'm not interested in nice faces. I'm interested only in dreary ones; in 'murdering brutes' who are 'men of great ability.'"

"Well, there's no accounting for tastes," said The Midget inevitably. "And *I* don't have to look at it, thank goodness. But in my humble estimation it's enough to prevent bones knitting, so help me it is."

"Well, if my fracture doesn't mend you can put it down to Richard III's account. Another little item on that account won't be noticed, it seems to me."

He must ask Marta when next she looked in if she too knew about this Tyrrel. Her general knowledge was not very great, but she had been educated very expensively at a highly approved school and perhaps some of it had stuck.

But the first visitor to penetrate from the outside world proved to be Sergeant Williams; large and pink and scrubbed-looking; and for a little Grant forgot about battles long ago and considered wide boys alive today. Williams sat planted on the small hard visitors' chair, his knees apart and his pale blue eyes blinking like a contented cat's in the light from the window, and Grant regarded him with affection. It was pleasant to talk shop again; to use that elliptical, allusive speech that one uses only with another of one's trade. It was pleasant to hear the professional gossip, to talk professional politics; to learn who was on the mat and who was on the skids.

"The Super sent his regards," Williams said

as he got up to go, "and said if there was anything he could do for you to let him know."
His eyes, no longer dazzled by the light, went
to the photograph propped against the books.
He leant his head sideways at it. "Who's the
bloke?"

Grant was just about to tell him when it
occurred to him that here was a fellow policeman. A man as used, professionally, to faces
as he was himself. Someone to whom faces
were of daily importance.

"Portrait of a man by an unknown fifteenth-
century painter," he said. "What do you make
of it?"

"I don't know the first thing about painting."

"I didn't mean that. I meant what do you
make of the subject?"

"Oh. Oh, I see." Williams bent forward and
drew his bland brows into a travesty of
concentration. "How do you mean: make of
it?"

"Well, where would you place him? In the
dock or on the bench?"

Williams considered for a moment, and
then said with confidence: "Oh, on the bench."

"You would?"

"Certainly. Why? Wouldn't you?"

"Yes. But the odd thing is that we're both
wrong. He belongs in the dock."

"You surprise me," Williams said, peering
again. "Do you know who he was, then?"

"Yes. Richard the Third."

Williams whistled.

"So that's who it is, is it! Well, well. The
Princes in the Tower, and all that. The original
Wicked Uncle. I suppose, once you know,
you can see it, but off-hand it wouldn't occur
to you. I mean, that he was a crook. He's the
spit of old Halsbury, come to think of it, and
if Halsbury had a fault at all it was that he
was too soft with the bastards in the dock.
He used to lean over backwards to give them
the benefit in his summing-up."

"Do you know how the Princes were murdered?"

"I don't know a thing about Richard III except that his mother was two years conceiving
him."

"What! Where did you get that tale?"

"In my school history, I suppose."

"You must have gone to a very remarkable
school. Conception was not mentioned in any
history book of mine. That is what made
Shakespeare and the Bible so refreshing as
lessons; the facts of life were always turning
up. Did you ever hear of a man called Tyrrel?"

"Yes; he was a con man on the P. & O. boats.
Drowned in the *Egypt*."

"No; I mean, in history."

"I tell you, I never knew any history except
1066 and 1603."

"What happened in 1603?" Grant asked, his
mind still on Tyrrel.

"We had the Scots tied to our tails for
good."

"Better than having them at our throats
every five minutes. Tyrrel is said to be the
man who put the boys out of the way."

"The nephews? No, it doesn't ring a bell.
Well, I must be getting along. Anything I
can do for you?"

"Did you say you were going to Charing
Cross Road?"

"To the Phoenix, yes."

"You could do something for me."

"What is that?"

"Go into one of the bookshops and buy me
a History of England. An adult one. And a
Life of Richard III, if you can find one."

"Sure, I'll do that."

As he was going out he encountered The
Amazon, and looked startled to find anything
as large as himself in nurse's uniform. He murmured a good-morning in an abashed way,
cast a questioning glance at Grant, and faded
into the corridor.

The Amazon said that she was supposed to
be giving Number Four her blanket bath but
that she had to look in to see if he was convinced.

"Convinced?"

About the nobility of Richard Coeur-de-
Lion.

"I haven't got around to Richard the First
yet. But keep Number Four waiting a few
moments longer and tell me what you know
about Richard III."

"Ah, those poor lambs!" she said, her great
cow's eyes soft with pity.

"Who?"

"Those two precious little boys. It used to
be my nightmare when I was a kiddie. That
someone would come and put a pillow over
my face when I was asleep."

"Is that how it was done: the murder?"

"Oh, yes. Didn't you know? Sir James Tyrrel rode back to London when the court was
at Warwick, and told Dighton and Forrest to
kill them, and then they buried them at the
foot of some stairs under a great mound of
stones."

"But it doesn't say that in the book you lent
me."

"Oh, that book is just history-for-exams, if you know what I mean. You don't get really interesting history in swot books like that."

"And where did you get the juicy gossip about Tyrrel, may one ask?"

"It isn't gossip," she said, hurt. "You'll find it in Sir Thomas More's history of his time. And you can't find a more respected or trustworthy person in the whole of history than Sir Thomas More, now can you?"

"No. It would be bad manners to contradict Sir Thomas."

"Well, that's what Sir Thomas says, and, after all, he was alive then and knew all those people to talk to."

"Dighton and Forrest?"

"No, of course not. But Richard, and the poor Queen, and those."

"The Queen? Richard's Queen?"

"Yes."

"Why 'poor'?"

"He led her an awful life. They say he poisoned her. He wanted to marry his niece."

"Why?"

"Because she was the heir to the throne."

"I see. He got rid of the two boys, and then wanted to marry their eldest sister."

"Yes. He couldn't marry either of the boys, you see."

"No, I suppose even Richard the Third never thought of that one."

"So he wanted to marry Elizabeth so as to feel safer on the throne. Actually, of course, she married his successor. She was Queen Elizabeth's grandmother. It always used to please me that Elizabeth was a little bit Plantagenet. I never was very fond of the Tudor side. Now I must go, or Matron will be here on her round before I have Number Four tidied up."

"That would be the end of the world."

"It would be the end of *me*," she said, and went away.

Grant took the book she had left him off the pile again, and tried to make head or tail of the Wars of the Roses. He failed. Armies marched and counter-marched. York and Lancaster succeeded each other as victors in a bewildering repetition. It was as meaningless as watching a crowd of dodgem cars bumping and whirling at a fair.

But it seemed to him that the whole trouble was implicit, the germ of it sown, nearly a hundred years earlier, when the direct line was broken by the deposition of Richard II. He knew all about that because he had in his youth seen *Richard of Bordeaux* [2] at the New Theatre; four times he had seen it. For three generations the usurping Lancasters had ruled England: Richard of Bordeaux's Henry unhappily but with fair efficiency, Shakespeare's Prince Hal with Agincourt for glory and the stake for zeal, and his son in half-witted muddle and failure. It was no wonder if men hankered after the legitimate line again, as they watched poor Henry VI's inept friends frittering away the victories in France while Henry nursed his new foundation of Eton and besought the ladies at court to cover up their bosoms.

All three Lancasters had had an unlovely fanaticism which contrasted sharply with the liberalism of the Court which had died with Richard II. Richard's live-and-let-live methods had given place, almost overnight, to the burning of heretics. For three generations heretics had burned. It was no wonder if a less public fire of discontent had begun to smolder in the heart of the man in the street.

Especially since there, before their eyes, was the Duke of York. Able, sensible, influential, gifted, a great prince in his own right, and by blood the heir of Richard II. They might not desire that York should take the place of poor silly Henry, but they did wish that he would take over the running of the country and clean up the mess.

York tried it, and died in battle for his pains, and his family spent much time in exile or sanctuary as a result.

But when the tumult and the shouting was all over, there on the throne of England was the son who had fought alongside him in that struggle, and the country settled back happily under that tall, flaxen, wenching, exceedingly beautiful but most remarkably shrewd young man, Edward IV.

And that was as near as Grant would ever come to understanding the Wars of the Roses.

He looked up from his book to find Matron standing in the middle of the room.

"I did knock," she said, "but you were lost in your book."

She stood there, slender and remote; as elegant in her way as Marta was; her white-cuffed hands clasped loosely in front of her narrow waist; her white veil spreading itself in imperishable dignity; her only ornament the small silver badge of her diploma. Grant wondered if there was anywhere in this world a more

[2] *Richard of Bordeaux* (London, 1933), by Gordon Daviot —a pseudonym of Elizabeth Mackintosh. (Ed.)

unshakable poise than that achieved by the Matron of a great hospital.

"I've taken to history," he said. "Rather late in the day."

"An admirable choice," she said. "It puts things in perspective." Her eye lighted on the portrait and she said: "Are you York or Lancaster?"

"So you recognize the portrait."

"Oh, yes. When I was a probationer I used to spend a lot of time in the National. I had very little money and very sore feet, and it was warm in the Gallery and quiet and it had plenty of seats." She smiled a very little, looking back from her present consequence to that young, tired, earnest creature she had been. "I liked the Portrait Gallery best because it gave one the same sense of proportion that reading history does. All those Importances who had made such a to-do over so much in their day. All just names. Just canvas and paint. I saw a lot of that portrait in those days." Her attention went back to the picture. "A most unhappy creature," she said.

"My surgeon thinks it is poliomyelitis."

"Polio?" She considered it. "Perhaps. I hadn't thought of it before. But to me it has always seemed to be intense unhappiness. It is the most desperately unhappy face that I have ever encountered—and I have encountered a great many."

"You think it was painted later than the murder, then?"

"Oh, yes. Obviously. He is not a type that would do anything lightly. A man of that calibre. He must have been well aware of how —heinous the crime was."

"You think he belonged to the type who can't live with themselves any more."

"What a good description! Yes. The kind who want something badly, and then discover that the price they have paid for it is too high."

"So you don't think he was an out-and-out villain?"

"No; oh, no. Villains don't suffer, and that face is full of the most dreadful pain."

They considered the portrait in silence for a moment or two.

"It must have seemed like retribution, you know. Losing his only boy so soon after. And his wife's death. Being stripped of his own personal world in so short a time. It must have seemed like Divine justice."

"Would he care about his wife?"

"She was his cousin, and they had known each other from childhood. So whether he loved her or not, she must have been a com-panion for him. When you sit on a throne I suspect that companionship is a rare blessing. Now I must go and see how my hospital is getting on. I have not even asked the question that I came to ask. Which was how you felt this morning. But it is a very healthy sign that you have interest to spare for a man dead these four hundred years."

She had not moved from the position in which he had first caught sight of her. Now she smiled her faint, withdrawn smile, and with her hands still clasped lightly in front of her belt-buckle moved towards the door. She had a transcendental repose. Like a nun. Like a queen.

CHAPTER IV

It was after luncheon before Sergeant Williams reappeared, breathless, bearing two fat volumes.

"You should have left them with the porter," Grant said. "I didn't mean you to come sweating up here with them."

"I had to come up and explain. I had only time to go to one shop, but it's the biggest in the street. That's the best history of England they have in stock. It's the best there is anywhere, they say." He laid down a severe-looking sage-green tome, with an air of taking no responsibility for it. "They had no separate history of Richard III. I mean, no life of him. But they gave me this." This was a gay affair with a coat of arms on the wrapper. It was called *The Rose of Raby*.

"What is this?"

"She was his mother, it seems. The Rose in question, I mean. I can't wait: I'm due at the Yard in five minutes from now and the Super will flay me alive if I'm late. Sorry I couldn't do better. I'll look in again, first time I'm passing, and if these are no good I'll see what else I can get."

Grant was grateful and said so.

To the sound of Williams' brisk departing footsteps he began his inspection of the "best history of England there is." It turned out to be what is known as a "constitutional" history; a sober compilation lightened with improving illustrations. An illumination from the Luttrell Psalter decorated the husbandry of the fourteenth century, and a contemporary map of London bisected the Great Fire. Kings and queens were mentioned only incidentally. Tanner's Constitutional History was concerned only with social progress and political evolution; with the Black Death, and the invention of printing, and the use of gunpowder, and the formation of the Trade Guilds, and so forth. But here and there Mr. Tanner was forced, by a horrid germaneness, to mention a king or his relations. And one such germaneness occurred in connection with the invention of printing.

A man called Caxton came out of the Weald of Kent as draper's apprentice to a future Lord Mayor of London, and then went to Bruges with the twenty marks his master left him in his will. And when, in the dreary autumn rain of the Low Countries, two young refugees from England fetched up on those low shores, in very low water, it was the successful merchant from the Weald of Kent who gave them succor. The refugees were Edward IV and his brother Richard; and when in the turn of the wheel Edward came back to rule England, Caxton came too, and the first books printed in England were printed for Edward IV and written by Edward's brother-in-law.

He turned the pages and marvelled how dull information is deprived of personality. The sorrows of humanity are no one's sorrows, as newspaper readers long ago found out. A *frisson* of horror may go down one's spine at wholesale destruction but one's heart stays unmoved. A thousand people drowned in floods in China are news: a solitary child drowned in a pond is tragedy. So Mr. Tanner's account of the progress of the English race was admirable but unexciting. But here and there where he could not avoid the personal his narrative flowered into a more immediate interest. In extracts from the Pastons' letters, for instance. The Pastons had a habit of sandwiching scraps of history between orders for salad oil and inquiries as to how Clement was doing at Cambridge. And between two of those domesticities appeared the small item that the two little York boys, George and Richard, were living in the Pastons' London lodgings, and that their brother Edward came every day to see them.

Surely, thought Grant, dropping the book for a moment on the counterpane and staring up at the now invisible ceiling, surely never before can anyone have come to the throne of England with so personal an experience of the ordinary man's life as Edward IV and his brother Richard. And perhaps only Charles II after them. And Charles, even in poverty and

flight, had always been a King's son; a man apart. The two little boys who were living in the Pastons' lodgings were merely the babies of the York family. Of no particular importance at the best of times, and at the moment when the Paston letter was written without a home and possibly without a future.

Grant reached for The Amazon's history book to find out what Edward was about in London at that date, and learned that he was collecting an army. "London was always Yorkist in temper, and men flocked with enthusiasm to the banner of the youthful Edward," said the history book.

And yet young Edward, aged eighteen, idol of a capital city and on the way to the first of his victories, found time to come every day to see his small brothers.

Was it now, Grant wondered, that the remarkable devotion of Richard to his elder brother was born. An unwavering life-long devotion that the history books not only did not deny but actually used in order to point the moral. "Up to the moment of his brother's death Richard had been in all vicissitudes his loyal and faithful helpmeet, but the opportunity of a crown proved too much for him." Or in the simpler words of the Historical Reader: "He had been a good brother to Edward but when he saw that he might become King greed hardened his heart."

Grant took a sideways look at the portrait and decided that the Historical Reader was off the beam. Whatever had hardened Richard's heart to the point of murder had not been greed. Or did the Historical Reader mean greed for power? Probably. Probably.

But surely Richard must have had all the power that mortal man could wish. He was the King's brother, and rich. Was that short step further so important that he could murder his brother's children to achieve it?

It is an odd set-up altogether.

He was still mulling it over in his mind when Mrs. Tinker came in with fresh pajamas for him and her daily précis of the newspaper headlines. Mrs. Tinker never read past the third headline of a report unless it happened to be a murder, in which case she read every word and bought an evening paper for herself on the way home to cook Tinker's supper.

Today the gentle burble of her comment on a Yorkshire arsenic-and-exhumation case flowed over him unbroken until she caught sight of the morning paper lying in its virgin condition alongside the books on the table. This brought her to a sudden halt.

"You not feelin' so good today?" she asked in a concerned way.

"I'm fine, Tink, fine. Why?"

"You 'aven't as much as opened your paper. That's 'ow my sister's gel started her decline. Not takin' no notice of what was in the paper."

"Don't you worry. I'm on the up-grade. Even my temper has improved. I forgot about the paper because I've been reading history stories. Ever heard of the Princes in the Tower?"

"*Everyone's* 'eard of the Princes in the Tower."

"And do you know how they met their end?"

"Course I do. He put a pillow on their faces when they was asleep."

"Who did?"

"Their wicked uncle. Richard the Third. You didn't ought to think of things like that when you're poorly. You ought to be reading something nice and cheerful."

"Are you in a hurry to get home, Tink, or could you go round by St. Martin's Lane for me?"

"No, I've plenty of time. Is it Miss Hallard? She won't be at the theatre till six-about."

"No, I know. But you might leave a note for her and she'll get it when she comes in."

He reached for his scribbling pad and pencil and wrote:

"For the love of Mike find me a copy of Thomas More's history of Richard III."

He tore off the page, folded it and scribbled Marta's name on it.

"You can give it to old Saxton at the stage-door. He'll see that she gets it."

"If I can get near the stage-door what with the stools for the queue," Mrs. Tinker said; in comment rather than in truth. "That thing's going to run for ever."

She put the folded paper carefully away in the cheap pseudo-leather handbag with the shabby edges that was as much a part of her as her hat. Grant had, Christmas by Christmas, provided her with a new bag; each of them a work of art in the best tradition of English leather-working, an article so admirable in design and so perfect in execution that Marta Hallard might have carried it to luncheon at the Blague. But that was the last he had ever seen of any of them. Since Mrs. Tinker regarded a pawnshop as one degree more disgraceful than prison, he absolved her from any suspicion of cashing in on her presents. He deduced that the handbags were safely laid away in a drawer somewhere, still wrapped up in the original tissue paper. Perhaps she took them out to show people sometimes, sometimes perhaps just to gloat over; or perhaps the knowledge that they were there enriched her, as the knowledge of "something put by for my funeral" might enrich another. Next Christmas he was going to open this shabby sack of hers, this perennial satchel *à toute faire*, and put something in the money compartment. She would fritter it away, of course, in small unimportances; so that in the end she would not know what she had done with it; but perhaps a series of small satisfactions scattered like sequins over the texture of everyday life was of greater worth than the academic satisfaction of owning a collection of fine objects at the back of a drawer.

When she had gone creaking away, in a shoes-and-corset concerto, he went back to Mr. Tanner and tried to improve his mind by acquiring some of Mr. Tanner's interest in the human race. But he found it an effort. Neither by nature nor by profession was he interested in mankind in the large. His bias, native and acquired, was towards the personal. He waded through Mr. Tanner's statistics and longed for a king in an oak tree, or a broom tied to a mast-head, or a Highlander hanging on to a trooper's stirrup in a charge. But at least he had the satisfaction of learning that the Englishman of the fifteenth century "drank water only as a penance." The English laborer of Richard III's day was, it seemed, the admiration of the continent. Mr. Tanner quoted a contemporary, writing in France.

The King of France will allow no one to use salt, but what is bought of himself at his own arbitrary price. The troops pay for nothing, and treat the people barbarously if they are not satisfied. All growers of vines must give a fourth to the King. All the towns must pay the King great yearly sums for his men-at-arms. The peasant live in great hardship and misery. They wear no woollen. Their clothing consists of little short jerkins of sackcloth, no trowse but from the knees up, and legs exposed and naked. The women all go barefoot. The people eat no meat, except the fat of bacon in their soup. Nor are the gentry much better off. If an accusation is brought against them they are examined in private, and perhaps never more heard of.

In England it is very different. No one can abide in another man's house without his leave. The King cannot put on taxes, nor alter the laws, nor make new ones. The English never drink water except for penance. They eat all sorts of flesh and fish. They are clothed throughout in good woollens, and are provided with all sorts of household goods. An Englishman cannot be sued except before the ordinary judge.

And it seemed to Grant that if you were very hard up and wanted to go to see what your Lizzie's first-born looked like it must have been reassuring to know that there was shelter and a hand-out at every religious house, instead of wondering how you were going to raise the train fare. That green England he had fallen asleep with last night had a lot to be said for it.

He thumbed through the pages on the fifteenth century, looking for personal items; for individual reports that might, in their single vividness, illumine the scene for him as a "spot" lights the desired part of a stage. But the story was distressingly devoted to the general. According to Mr. Tanner, Richard III's only Parliament was the most liberal and progressive within record; and he regretted, did the worthy Mr. Tanner, that his private crimes should have militated against his patent desire for the common weal. And that seemed to be all that Mr. Tanner had to say about Richard III. Except for the Pastons, chatting indestructibly through the centuries, there was a dearth of human beings in this record of humanity.

He let the book slide off his chest, and searched with his hand until he found *The Rose of Raby*.

Chapter V

The Rose of Raby proved to be fiction; but it was at least easier to hold than Tanner's Constitutional History of England. It was, moreover, the almost-respectable form of historical fiction which is merely history-with-conversation, so to speak. An imaginative biography rather than an imagined story. Evelyn Payne-Ellis, whoever she might be, had provided portraits and a family tree, and had made no attempt, it seemed, to what he and his cousin Laura used to call in their childhood "write forsoothly." There were no "by our Ladys," no "nathelesses" or "varlets." It was an honest affair according to its lights.

And its lights were more illuminating than Mr. Tanner.

Much more illuminating.

It was Grant's belief that if you could not find out about a man, the next best way to arrive at an estimate of him was to find out about his mother.

So until Marta could provide him with the sainted and infallible Thomas More's personal account of Richard, he would do very happily with Cecily Nevill, Duchess of York.

He glanced at the family tree, and thought that if the two York brothers, Edward and Richard, were, as kings, unique in their experience of ordinary life they were no less unique in their Englishness. He looked at their breeding and marvelled. Nevill, Fitzalan, Percy, Holland, Mortimer, Clifford and Audley, as well as Plantagenet. Queen Elizabeth (who made it her boast) was all English if one counted the Welsh streak as English. But among all the half-bred monarchs who had graced the throne between the Conquest and Farmer George—half-French, half-Spanish, half-Danish, half-Dutch, half-Portuguese—Edward IV and Richard III were remarkable in their home-bred quality.

They were also, he noted, as royally bred on their mother's side as on their father's. Cecily Nevill's grandfather was John of Gaunt, the first of the Lancasters; third son of Edward III. Her husband's two grandfathers were two other sons of Edward III. So three of Edward III's five sons had contributed to the making of the two York brothers.

"To be a Nevill" said Miss Payne-Ellis "was to be of some importance since they were great landowners. To be a Nevill was almost certainly to be handsome, since they were a good-looking family. To be a Nevill was to have personality, since they excelled in displays of both character and temperament. To unite all three Nevill gifts, in their finest quality, in one person was the good fortune of Cecily Nevill, who was the sole Rose of the north long before that north was forced to choose between White Roses and Red."

It was Miss Payne-Ellis's contention that the marriage with Richard Plantagenet, Duke of York, was a love match. Grant received her theory with a skepticism bordering on scorn until he noticed the results of that marriage. To have a yearly addition to the family was not, in the fifteenth century, evidence of anything but fertility. And the long family produced by Cecily Nevill to her charming husband augured nothing nearer love than cohabitation. But in a time when the wife's rôle was to stay meekly at home and see to her still-room, Cecily Nevill's constant travellings about in her husband's company were surely remarkable enough to suggest an abnormal pleasure in that company. The extent and constancy of that travel was witnessed to by the birthplaces of her children. Anne, her first, was born at Fotheringhay, the family home in Northhamptonshire. Henry, who died as a baby, at Hatfield. Edward at Rouen, where the Duke was on active service. Edmund and Elizabeth also at Rouen. Margaret at Fotheringhay. John, who died young, at Neath in Wales. George in Dublin (and could it be, wondered Grant, that that accounted for the almost Irish perverseness of the ineffable George?). Richard at Fotheringhay.

Cecily Nevill had not sat at home in Northhamptonshire waiting for her lord and master to visit her when it seemed good to him. She had accompanied him about the world of their inhabiting. There was a strong presumption in favor of Miss Payne-Ellis's theory. At the very canniest reckoning it was patently a very successful marriage.

Which perhaps accounted for the family devotion of those daily visits of Edward to his small brothers in the Pastons' lodgings. The York family, even before its tribulations, was a united one.

This was borne out unexpectedly when, spurting the pages from under his thumb, he came on a letter. It was a letter from the two elder boys, Edward and Edmund, to their father. The boys were at Ludlow Castle, undergoing their education, and on a Saturday in Easter week, taking advantage of a courier who was going back, they burst out in loud complaint of their tutor and his "odiousness" and begged their father to listen to the tale of the courier, William Smyth, who was fully charged with the details of their oppression. This S.O.S. was introduced and ended in respectful padding, the formality of which was a little marred by their pointing out that it was nice of him to send the clothes but that he had forgotten their breviary.

The conscientious Miss Payne-Ellis had given the reference for this letter (one of the Cotton manuscripts, it appeared) and he thumbed more slowly, in search of more. Factual evidence was a policeman's meat.

He could not find any, but he came on a family tableau which held him for a moment.

The Duchess moved out into the thin sharp sunlight of a London December morning, and stood on the steps to watch them go: her husband, her brother, and her son. Dirk and his nephews brought the horses into the courtyard, scattering the pigeons and the fussing sparrows from the cobbles. She watched her husband mount, equable and deliberate as always, and thought that for all the emotion he showed he might be riding down to Fotheringhay to look at some new rams instead of setting out on a campaign. Salisbury, her brother, was being Nevill and temperamental; a little conscious of the occasion and living up to it. She looked at them both and smiled in her mind at them. But it was Edmund who caught at her heart. Edmund at seventeen, very slender, very untried, very vulnerable. Flushed with pride and excitement at this setting-out to his first campaigning. She wanted to say to her husband: "Take care of Edmund," but she could not do that. Her husband would not understand; and Edmund, if he were to suspect, would be furious. If Edward, only a year older, was commanding an army of his own on the borders of Wales at this very minute, then he, Edmund, was more than old enough to see a war at first-hand.

She glanced behind her at the three younger children who had come out in her wake; Margaret and George, the two solid fair ones, and behind them, a pace in the rear as always, her changeling baby, Richard; his dark brows and brown hair making him look like a visitor. Good-natured untidy Margaret watched with all the moist-eyed emotion of fourteen; George in a passionate envy and wild rebellion that he was only eleven and of no consequence in this martial moment. Thin little Richard showed no excitement at all, but his mother thought that he vibrated like a softly tapped drum.

The three horses moved out of the courtyard in a clatter of slipping hooves and jingling accoutrements, to join the servants waiting for them in the roadway, and the children called and danced and waved them out of the gate.

And Cecily, who in her time had seen so many men, and so many of her family, go off to war, went back to the house with an unaccustomed weight at her bosom. Which of them, said the voice in her unwilling mind, which of them was it who was not coming back?

Her imagination did not compass anything so horrible as the fact that none of them was coming back again. That she would never see any one of them again.

That before the year was ended her husband's severed head, crowned for insult with a paper crown, would be nailed above the Micklegate Bar in York, and the heads of her brother and her son on the two other gates.

Well, that might be fiction, but it was an illuminating glimpse of Richard. The dark one in a blond family. The one who "looked like a visitor." The "changeling."

He abandoned Cecily Nevill for the moment, and went hunting through the book for her son Richard. But Miss Payne-Ellis seemed not to be greatly interested in Richard. He was merely the tail-end of the family. The magnificent young creature who flourished at the other end was more to her taste. Edward was much to the fore. With his Nevill cousin Warwick, Salisbury's son, he won the battle of Towton, and, with the memory of Lancastrian ferocity still fresh and his father's head still nailed to the Micklegate Bar, gave evidence of that tolerance that was to be characteristic of him. There was quarter at Towton for all who asked. He was crowned King of England in Westminster Abbey (and two small boys, home from exile in Utrecht, were created respectively Duke of Clarence and Duke of Gloucester). And he buried his father and his brother Edmund with great magnificence in the church at Fotheringhay (though it was Richard, aged thirteen, who convoyed that sad procession from Yorkshire, through the bright glory of five July days, to Northamptonshire; nearly six years after he had stood on the steps of Baynard's Castle in London to watch them ride away).

It was not until Edward had been King for some time that Miss Payne-Ellis allowed Richard to come back into the story. He was then being educated with his Nevill cousins at Middleham, in·Yorkshire.

As Richard rode into the shadow of the keep, out of the broad sunlight and flying winds of Wensleydale, it seemed to him that there was an atmosphere of strangeness about the place. The guards were talking in loud excitement in the gatehouse and seemed abashed at his presence. From their sudden silence he rode on into a silent court that should have been bustling with activity at this hour of the day. It would soon be supper time, and both habit and hunger brought all the inhabitants of Middleham home from their various occupations, as they were bringing him back from his hawking, for the evening meal. This hush, this desertion, was unusual. He walked his horse to the stables, but there was no one there to give it to. As he unsaddled he noticed a hardridden bay in the next stall; a horse that did not belong to Middleham; a horse so tired that he had not eaten up and his head hung in a despondent beaten way between his knees.

Richard wiped his horse down and rugged him, brought him some hay and fresh water, and left him; wondering about that beaten horse and the uncanny silence. As he paused in the doorway he could hear voices in the distance of the great hall; and debated whether he should go there and investigate before going upstairs to his own quarters. As he hesitated a voice from the stairs above him said: "Z-z-zt!"

He looked up to see his cousin Anne's head peering over the banisters, her two long fair plaits hanging down like bell-ropes.

"Richard!" she said, half whispering. "Have you heard?"

"Is something wrong?" he asked. "What is it?"

As he moved up to her she grabbed his hand and dragged him upwards towards their schoolroom in the roof.

"But what is it?" he asked, leaning back in protest against her urgency. "What has happened? Is it something so awful that you can't tell me here!"

She swept him into the schoolroom and shut the door.

"It's Edward!"

"Edward? Is he ill?"

"No! *Scandal!*"

"Oh," said Richard, relieved. Scandal and Edward were never far apart. "What is it? Has he a new mistress?"

"Much worse than that! Oh, much, *much* worse. He's married."

"Married?" said Richard, so unbelieving that he sounded calm. "He can't be."

"But he is. The news came from London an hour ago."

"He can't be married," Richard insisted. "For a King marriage is a long affair. A matter of contracts, and agreements. A matter for Parliament, even, I think. What made you think he had got married?"

"I don't *think*," Anne said, out of patience

at this sober reception of her broadside. "The whole family is raging together in the Great Hall over the affair."

"Anne! have you been listening at the door?"

"Oh, don't be so righteous. I didn't have to listen very hard, anyhow. You could hear them on the other side of the river. He has married Lady Grey!"

"Who is Lady Grey? Lady Grey of Groby?"

"Yes."

"But he can't. She has two children and she's quite old."

"She is five years older than Edward, and she is wonderfully beautiful—so I overhear."

"When did this happen?"

"They've been married five months. They got married in secret down in Northampton-shire."

"But I thought he was going to marry the King of France's sister."

"So," said Anne in a tone full of meaning, "did my father."

"Yes; yes, it makes things very awkward for him, doesn't it; after all the negotiating."

"According to the messenger from London he is throwing fits. It isn't only the making him look a fool. It seems she has cohorts of relations and he hates every one of them."

"Edward must be possessed." In Richard's hero-worshipping eyes everything Edward did had always been right. This folly, this undeniable, this inexcusable folly, could come only from possession.

"It will break my mother's heart," he said. He thought of his mother's courage when his father and Edmund had been killed, and the Lancastrian army was almost at the gates of London. She had not wept nor wrapped herself in protective veils of self-pity. She had arranged that he and George should go to Utrecht, as if she were arranging for them to go away to school. They might never see each other again, but she had busied herself about warm clothes for their winter voyage across the Channel with a calm and dry-eyed practicality.

How would she bear this; this further blow? This destructive folly. This shatter-ing foolishness.

"Yes," said Anne, softening. "Poor Aunt Cecily. It is monstrous of Edward to hurt everyone so. Monstrous."

But Edward was still the infallible. If Edward had done wrong it was because he was ill, or possessed, or bewitched. Edward still

had Richard's allegiance; his heart-whole and worshipping allegiance.

Nor in after years was that allegiance—an adult allegiance of recognition and ac-ceptance—ever less than heart-whole.

And then the story went on to Cecily Nevill's tribulation, and her efforts to bring some kind of order into the relations between her son Edward, half-pleased, half-ashamed, and her nephew Warwick, wholly furious. There was also a long description of that indestructibly virtuous beauty with the famous "gilt" hair, who had succeeded where more complaisant beauties had failed; and of her enthroning at Reading Abbey (led to the throne by a silently protesting Warwick, who could not but note the large array of Woodvilles, come to see their sister Elizabeth acknowledged Queen of England).

The next time Richard turned up in the tale he was setting out from Lynn without a penny in his pocket, in a Dutch vessel that happened to be in the harbor when it was needed. Along with him was his brother Edward, Edward's friend Lord Hastings, and a few followers. None of them had anything except what they stood up in, and after some argument the ship's captain agreed to accept Edward's fur-lined cape as fare.

Warwick had finally decided that the Woodville clan was more than he could stom-ach. He had helped to put his cousin Edward on the throne of England; he could just as easily unseat him. For the achievement of this he had the help of the whole Nevill brood; and, incredibly, the active assistance of the ineffable George. Who had decided that fall-ing heir to half the lands of Montague, Nevill, and Beauchamp, by marrying Warwick's other daughter Isabel, was a better bet than being loyal to his brother Edward. In eleven days Warwick was master of a surprised England, and Edward and Richard were squelching through the October mud between Alkmaar and The Hague.

From then on, Richard was always in the background of the story. Through that dreary winter in Bruges. Staying with Margaret in Bur-gundy—for that kind moist-eyed Margaret who had stood on the steps of Baynard's Castle with himself and George to watch their father ride away was now the very new Duchess of Bur-gundy. Margaret, kind Margaret, was saddened and dismayed—as many people in future were to be saddened and dismayed—by George's in-explicable conduct, and set herself to missionary work what time she got together funds for her two more admirable brothers.

Not even Miss Payne-Ellis's interest in the magnificent Edward allowed her to conceal that the real work of outfitting the ships hired with Margaret's money was done by Richard; a Richard not yet eighteen. And when Edward with an absurd handful of followers found himself once more camped in an English meadow, facing George with an army, it was Richard who went over to George's camp and talked the Margaret-weakened George into alliance again and so left the road to London open to them.

Not, Grant thought, that this last was any great achievement. George could obviously be talked into anything. He was the born missionee.

Chapter VI

He had not nearly exhausted *The Rose of Raby* and the illicit joys of fiction when, next morning about eleven, a parcel arrived from Marta containing the more respectable entertainment of history as recorded by the sainted Sir Thomas.

With the book was a note in Marta's large sprawling writing on Marta's stiff expensive notepaper.

Have to send this instead of bringing it. Frantically busy. Think I have got M.M. to the sticking point re Blessington. No T. More in any of the bookshops, so tried Public Library. Can't think why one never thinks of Public Libraries. Probably because books expected to be soupy. Think this looks quite clean and unsoupy. You get fourteen days. Sounds like a sentence rather than a loan. Hope this interest in Crouchback means that the prickles are less nettlish. Till soon.

                                        Marta.

The book did indeed look clean and unsoupy, if a little elderly. But after the light going of *The Rose* its print looked unexciting and its solid paragraphs forbidding. Nevertheless he attacked it with interest. This was, after all, where Richard III was concerned, "the horse's mouth."

He came to the surface an hour later, vaguely puzzled and ill at ease. It was not that the

matter surprised him; the facts were very much what he had expected them to be. It was that this was not how he had expected Sir Thomas to write.

He took ill rest at nights, lay long and waking and musing; sore wearied with care and watch, he slumbered rather than slept. So was his restless heart continually tossed and tumbled with the tedious impression and stormy remembrance of his most abominable deeds.

That was all right. But when he added that "this he had from such as were secret with his chamberers" one was suddenly repelled. An aroma of backstair gossip and servants' spying came off the page. So that one's sympathy tilted before one was aware of it from the smug commentator to the tortured creature sleepless on his bed. The murderer seemed of greater stature than the man who was writing of him.

Which was all wrong.

Grant was conscious too of the same unease that filled him when he listened to a witness telling a perfect story that he knew to be flawed somewhere.

And that was very puzzling indeed. What could possibly be wrong with the personal account of a man revered for his integrity as Thomas More had been revered for four centuries?

The Richard who appeared in More's account was, Grant thought, one that Matron would have recognized. A man highly-strung and capable of both great evil and great suffering. "He was never quiet in his mind, never thought himself secure. His eyes whirled about, his body was privily fenced, his hand ever on his dagger, his countenance and manner like one always ready to strike again."

And of course there was the dramatic, not to say hysterical, scene that Grant remembered from his schooldays; that every schoolboy, probably remembered. The council scene in the Tower before he laid claim to the crown. Richard's sudden challenge to Hastings as to what was the proper fate for a man who plotted the death of the Protector of the Kingdom. The insane claim that Edward's wife and Edward's mistress (Jane Shore) were responsible for his withered arm by their sorcery. The smiting of the table in his rage, which was the signal for his armed satellites to burst in and arrest Lord Hastings, Lord Stanley, and John Morton, Bishop of Ely. The rushing of Hastings down into the courtyard and his beheading on a handy log of wood after bare time to confess himself to the first priest who could be found.

That was certainly the picture of a man who would act first—in fury, in fear, in revenge—and repent afterwards.

But it seemed that he was capable of more calculated iniquity. He caused a sermon to be preached by a certain Dr. Shaw, brother of the Lord Mayor, at Paul's Cross, on June 22, on the text: "Bastard slips shall take no root." Wherein Dr. Shaw maintained that both Edward and George were sons of the Duchess of York by some unknown man, and that Richard was the only legitimate son of the Duke and Duchess of York.

This was so unlikely, so inherently absurd, that Grant went back and read it over again. But it still said the same thing. That Richard had traduced his mother, in public and for his own material advantage, with an unbelievable infamy.

Well, Sir Thomas More said it. And if anyone should know it would be Thomas More. And if anyone should know how to pick and choose between the credibilities in the reporting of a story it ought to be Thomas More, Lord Chancellor of England.

Richard's mother, said Sir Thomas, complained bitterly of the slander with which her son had smirched her. Understandably, on the whole, Grant thought.

As for Dr. Shaw, he was overcome with remorse. So much so that "within a few days he withered and consumed away."

Had a stroke, probably, Grant considered. And little wonder. To have stood up and told that tale to a London crowd must have taken some nerve.

Sir Thomas's account of the Princes in the Tower was the same as The Amazon's, but Sir Thomas's version was more detailed. Richard had suggested to Robert Brackenbury, Constable of the Tower, that it might be a good thing if the Princes disappeared, but Brackenbury would have no part in such an act. Richard therefore waited until he was at Warwick, during his progress through England after his coronation, and then sent Tyrrel to London with orders that he was to receive the keys of the Tower for one night. During that night two ruffians, Dighton and Forrest, one a groom and one a warder, smothered the two boys.

At this point The Midget came in with his lunch and removed the book from his grasp; and while he forked the shepherd's pie from plate to mouth he considered again the face of the man in the dock. The faithful and patient small brother who had turned into a monster.

When The Midget came back for his tray he said: "Did you know that Richard III was a very popular person in his day? Before he came to the throne, I mean."

The Midget cast a baleful glance at the picture.

"Always was a snake in the grass, if you ask me. Smooth, that's what he was: smooth. Biding his time."

Biding his time for what? he wondered, as she tapped away down the corridor. He could not have known that his brother Edward would die unexpectedly at the early age of forty. He could not have foreseen (even after a childhood shared with him in uncommon intimacy) that George's on-goings would end in attainder and the debarring of his two children from the succession. There seemed little point in "biding one's time" if there was nothing to bide for. The indestructibly virtuous beauty with the gilt hair had, except for her incurable nepotism, proved an admirable Queen and had provided Edward with a large brood of healthy children, including two boys. The whole of that brood, together with George and his son and daughter, stood between Richard and the throne. It was surely unlikely that a man busy with the administration of the North of England, or campaigning (with dazzling success) against the Scots, would have much spare interest in being "smooth."

What then had changed him so fundamentally in so short a time?

Grant reached for *The Rose of Raby* to see what Miss Payne-Ellis had had to say about the unhappy metamorphosis of Cecily Nevill's youngest son. But that wily author had burked the issue. She had wanted the book to be a happy one, and to have carried it to its logical conclusion would have made it unredeemed tragedy. She had therefore wound it up with a fine resounding major chord by making her last chapter the coming-out of young Elizabeth, Edward's eldest child. This avoided both the tragedy of Elizabeth's young brothers and the defeat and death of Richard in battle.

So the book ended with a Palace party, and a flushed and happy young Elizabeth, very magnificent in a new white dress and her first pearls, dancing the soles out of her slippers like the princesses in the fairy-tale. Richard and Anne, and their delicate little son, had come up from Middleham for the occasion. But neither George nor Isabel was there. Isabel had died in childbirth years ago, obscurely and as far as George was concerned unmourned. George too had died obscurely, but with that perverseness that was so peculiarly George's, had by that very obscurity won for himself imperishable fame.

George's life had been a progression from one spectacular piece of spiritual extravagance to the next. Each time, his family must have said: Well, that at last is the summit of frightfulness; even George cannot think of anything more fantastic than that. And each time George had surprised them. There was no limit to George's antic capacity.

The seed was perhaps sown when, during his first backsliding in the company of his father-in-law, Warwick had created him heir to the poor crazy puppet-King, Henry VI, whom Warwick had dumped back on the throne to spite his cousin Edward. Both Warwick's hopes of seeing his daughter a Queen and George's royal pretensions had gone down the drain on that night when Richard had gone over to the Lancastrian camp and talked to George. But the taste of importance had perhaps proved too much for a natural sweettooth. In the years to come the family were always heading George off from unexpected vagaries, or rescuing him from his latest caper.

When Isabel died he had been certain that she had been poisoned by her waiting woman, and that his baby son had been poisoned by another. Edward, thinking the affair important enough to be tried before a London court, sent down a writ; only to find that George had tried them both at a petty sessions of his own magistrates and hanged them. The furious Edward, by way of rapping him over the knuckles, had two members of George's household tried for treason; but instead of taking the hint George declared that this was just judicial murder, and went about saying so in loud tones and a fine blaze of lèse-majesté.

Then he decided that he wanted to marry the richest heiress in Europe; who was Margaret's step-daughter, young Mary of Burgundy. Kind Margaret thought that it would be nice to have her brother in Burgundy, but Edward had arranged to back Maximilian of Austria's suit, and George was a continual embarrassment.

When the Burgundy intrigue came to nothing, the family hoped for a little peace. After all, George owned half the Nevill lands and had no need to marry again either for fortune or children. But George had a new scheme for marrying Margaret, the sister of James III of Scotland.

At last his *folie de grandeur* graduated from secret negotiation undertaken on his own behalf with foreign courts to open display of the Lancastrian act of Parliament which had declared him heir to the throne after Henry VI. This, inevitably, landed him before another Parliament, and a much less amenable one.

The trial was chiefly remarkable for a flaming and wordy row between the two brothers, Edward and George, but when the expected attainder was passed, there was a pause. Depriving George of his standing was one thing: desirable and indeed necessary. But executing him was something else again.

As the days went by without sentence being carried out, the Commons sent a reminder. And next day it was announced that George, Duke of Clarence, had died in the Tower.

"Drowned in a butt of malmsey," said London. And what was merely a Cockney's comment on a drunkard's end passed into history and made the undeserving George immortal.

So George was not at that party at Westminster, and the emphasis in Miss Payne-Ellis's final chapter was not on Cecily Nevill as the mother of sons, but on Cecily Nevill the grandmother of a fine brood. George might have died discredited, on a dried-leaf heap of worn-out friendships, but his son, young Warwick, was a fine upstanding boy, and little Margaret at ten was already showing signs of the traditional Nevill beauty. Edmund, dead in battle at seventeen, might seem a wanton waste of young life, but there to balance it was the delicate baby whom she had never thought to rear; and he had a son to follow him. Richard in his twenties still looked as though one could break him in two, but he was as tough as a heather root, and perhaps his fragile-looking son would grow up to be as resilient. As for Edward, her tall blond Edward, his beauty might be blurring into grossness and his amiability into sloth, but his two small sons and his five girls had all the character and good looks of their combined ancestry.

As a grandmother she could look on that crowd of children with a personal pride, and as a Princess of England she could look on them with assurance. The crown was safe in the York line for generations to come.

If anyone, looking in a crystal ball at that party, had told Cecily Nevill that in four years not only the York line but the whole Plantagenet dynasty would have gone for ever, she would have held it to be either madness or treason.

But what Miss Payne-Ellis had not sought to gloss over was the prevalence of the Wood-ville clan in a Nevill-Plantagenet gathering.

She looked round the room and wished that her daughter-in-law Elizabeth had been blessed either with a less generous heart or with fewer relations. The Woodville match had turned out far more happily than any-one had dared to hope; Elizabeth had been an admirable wife; but the by-products had not been so fortunate. It was perhaps inevitable that the governorship of the two boys should have gone to her eldest brother; and Rivers, if a little nouveau riche in his liking for display and a little too obviously am-bitious, was a cultured creature and an ad-mirable person to have the boys in charge during their schoolroom days at Ludlow. But as for the rest: four brothers, seven sisters, and two sons by her first husband, were really too many by half to have brought into the marriage market in her wake.

Cecily looked across the laughing mêlée of the children's blind man's buff to the grown-ups standing round the supper table. Anne Woodville married to the Earl of Essex's heir. Eleanor Woodville married to the Earl of Kent's heir. Margaret Woodville married to the Earl of Arundel's heir. Catherine Woodville married to the Duke of Bucking-ham. Jacquette Woodville to Lord Strange. Mary Woodville to Lord Herbert's heir. And John Woodville, disgracefully, to the Dowager of Norfolk who was old enough to be his grandmother. It was good that new blood should strengthen the old families—new blood had always seeped in—but it was not good that it should come suddenly and in a flood from one particular source. It was like a fever in the political blood of the country; a foreign introduction, difficult to be assimilated. Unwise and regrettable.

However. There were long years ahead in which that influx could be assimilated. This new sudden power in the body politic would cease to be so concentrated, would spread out, would settle down, would cease to be dangerous and upsetting. Edward for all his amiability had a shrewd common sense; he would keep the country on an even keel as he had kept it for nearly twenty years. No one had run England with a more despotic power or a lighter hand than her acute, lazy, woman-loving Edward.

It would be all right eventually.

She was about to rise and join them in their discussion of sweetmeats—they must not think that she was being critical or aloof—when her granddaughter Elizabeth came breathless and laughing out of the scrimmage and swept into the seat beside her.

"I am much too old for this sort of thing," she said between her gasps, "and it is ruinous to one's clothes. Do you like my dress, grandmother? I had to coax it out of Father. He said my old tawny satin would do. The one I had when Aunt Margaret came from Burgundy to visit us. That is the worst of having a father who notices what women wear. He knows too much about one's ward-robe. Did you hear that the Dauphin has jilted me? Father is in a pet, but I am so happy. I lighted ten candles to St. Catherine. It took all I had left of my allowance. I don't want to leave England. I want never to leave England ever. Can you arrange that for me, grandmother?"

Cecily smiled and said that she would try.

"Old Ankaret, who tells fortunes, says that I am to be a Queen. But since there is no prince to marry me I do not see how that may be." She paused, and added in a smaller voice: "She said Queen of England. But I expect she was just a little tipsy. She is very fond of hippocras."

It was unfair, not to say inartistic, of Miss Payne-Ellis to hint at Elizabeth's future as the wife of Henry VII if as author she was not prepared to face the unpleasantness that lay between. To presuppose in her readers a knowledge of Elizabeth's marriage to the first Tudor king, was also to presuppose their awareness of her brothers' murder. So that a dark reminding shadow fell across the festive scene with which she had chosen to end her story.

But on the whole, Grant thought, she had made a good enough job of the story, judging by what he had read of it. He might even go back sometime and read the bits he had skipped.

CHAPTER VII

Grant had switched off his bedside light that night, and was half asleep, when a voice in his mind said, "But Thomas More was Henry the Eighth."

This brought him wide awake. He flicked the light on again.

What the voice had meant, of course, was not that Thomas More and Henry the Eighth were one and the same person, but that, in that business of putting personalities into pigeon-holes according to reigns, Thomas More belonged to the reign of Henry the Eighth.

Grant lay looking at the pool of light that his lamp threw on the ceiling, and reckoned. If Thomas More was Henry VIII's Chancellor, then he must have lived through the whole of Henry VII's long reign as well as Richard III's. There was something wrong somewhere.

He reached for More's *History of Richard III*. It had as preface a short life of More which he had not bothered to read. Now he turned to it to find out how More could have been both Richard III's historian and Henry VIII's Chancellor. How old was More when Richard succeeded?

He was five.

When that dramatic council scene had taken place at the Tower, Thomas More had been five years old. He had been only eight when Richard died at Bosworth.

Everything in that history had been hearsay.

And if there was one word that a policeman loathed more than another it was hearsay. Especially when applied to evidence.

He was so disgusted that he flung the precious book on to the floor before he remembered that it was the property of a Public Library and his only by grace and for fourteen days.

More had never known Richard III at all. He had indeed grown up under a Tudor administration. That book was the Bible of the whole historical world on the subject of Richard III—it was from that account that Holinshed had taken his material, and from that that Shakespeare had written his—and except that More believed what he wrote to be true it was of no more value than what the soldier said. It was what his cousin Laura called "snow on their boots." A "gospel-true" event seen by someone other than the teller. That More had a critical mind and an admirable integrity did not make the story acceptable evidence. A great many otherwise admirable minds had accepted that story of the Russian troops passing through Britain. Grant had dealt too long with the human intelligence to accept as truth someone's report of someone's report of what that someone remembered to have seen or been told.

He was disgusted.

At the first opportunity he must get an actual contemporary account of the events of Richard's short reign. The Public Library could have Sir Thomas More back tomorrow and be damned to their fourteen days. The fact that Sir Thomas was a martyr and a Great Mind did not cut any ice at all with him, Alan Grant. He, Alan Grant, had known Great Minds so uncritical that they would believe a story that would make a con man blush for shame. He had known a great scientist who was convinced that a piece of butter muslin was his great-aunt Sophia because an illiterate medium from the back streets of Plymouth told him so. He had known a great authority on the Human Mind and Its Evolution who had been taken for all he had by an incurable knave because he "judged for himself and not on police stories." As far as he, Alan Grant, was concerned there was nothing so uncritical or so damn-silly as your Great Mind. As far as he, Alan Grant, was concerned Thomas More was washed out, cancelled, deleted; and he, Alan Grant, was beginning from scratch again tomorrow morning.

He was still illogically fuming when he fell asleep and he woke fuming.

"Do you know that your Sir Thomas More knew nothing about Richard III at all?" he said, accusing, to The Amazon the moment her large person appeared in the doorway.

She looked startled, not at his news but at his ferocity. Her eyes looked as if they might brim with tears at another rough word.

"But of *course* he knew!" she protested. "He *lived* then."

"He was eight when Richard died," Grant said, relentless. "And all he knew was what he had been told. Like me. Like you. Like Will Rogers of blessed memory. There is nothing hallowed at all about Sir Thomas More's history of Richard III. It's a damned piece of hearsay and a swindle."

"Aren't you feeling so well this morning?" she asked anxiously. "Do you think you've got a temperature?"

"I don't know about a temperature, but my blood pressure's away up."

"Oh dear, dear," she said, taking this literally. "And you were doing so very well. Nurse Ingham will be so distressed. She has been boasting about your good recovery."

That The Midget should have found him a subject for boasting was a new idea to Grant, but it was not one that gave him any gratification. He resolved to have a temperature in earnest if he could manage it, just to score off The Midget.

But the morning visit of Marta distracted him from this experiment in the power of mind over matter.

Marta, it seemed, was pluming herself on his mental health very much as The Midget was pluming herself on his physical improvement. She was delighted that her pokings-about with James in the print shop had been so effective.

"Have you decided on Perkin Warbeck, then?" she asked.

"No. Not Warbeck. Tell me: what made you bring me a portrait of Richard III? There's no mystery about Richard, is there?"

"No. I suppose we took it as illustration to the Warbeck story. No, wait a moment. I remember. James turned it up and said: 'If he's mad about faces, there's one for him!' He said: 'That's the most notorious murderer in history, and yet his face is in my estimation the face of a saint.'"

"A saint!" Grant said; and then remembered something. "'Over-conscientious,'" he said.

"What?"

"Nothing. I was just remembering my first impressions of it. Is that how it seemed to you: the face of a saint?"

She looked across at the picture, propped up against the pile of books. "I can't see it against the light," she said, and picked it up for a closer scrutiny.

He was suddenly reminded that to Marta, as to Sergeant Williams, faces were a professional matter. The slant of an eyebrow, the set of a mouth, was just as much an evidence of character to Marta as to Williams. Indeed she actually made herself faces to match the characters she played.

"Nurse Ingham thinks he's dreary. Nurse Darroll thinks he's a horror. My surgeon thinks he's a polio victim. Sergeant Williams thinks he's a born judge. Matron thinks he's a soul in torment."

Marta said nothing for a little. Then she said: "It's odd, you know. When you first look at it you think it a mean, suspicious face. Even cantankerous. But when you look at it a little longer you find that it isn't like that at all. It is quite calm. It is really quite a gentle face. Perhaps that is what James meant by being saint-like."

"No. No, I don't think so. What he meant was the subservience to conscience."

"Whatever it is, it *is a face*, isn't it! Not just a collection of organs for seeing, breathing, and eating with. A wonderful face. With very little alteration, you know, it might be a portrait of Lorenzo the Magnificent."

"You don't suppose that it *is* Lorenzo and that we're considering the wrong man altogether?"

"Of course not. Why should you think that?"

"Because nothing in the face fits the facts of history. And pictures have got shuffled before now."

"Oh, yes, of course they have. But that is Richard all right. The original—or what is supposed to be the original—is at Windsor Castle. James told me. It is included in Henry VIII's inventory, so it has been there for four hundred years or so. And there are duplicates at Hatfield and Albury."

"It's Richard," Grant said resignedly. "I just don't know anything about faces. Do you know anyone at the B.M.?"

"At the British Museum?" Marta asked, her attention still on the portrait. "No, I don't think so. Not that I can think of at the moment. I went there once to look at some Egyptian jewellery, when I was playing Cleopatra with Geoffrey—did you ever see Geoffrey's Antony? it was superlatively genteel—but the place frightens me rather. Such a garnering of the ages. It made me feel the way the stars make you feel: small and no-account. What do you want of the B.M.?"

"I wanted some information about history written in Richard III's day. Contemporary accounts."

"Isn't the sainted Sir Thomas any good, then?"

"The sainted Sir Thomas is nothing but an old gossip," Grant said with venom. He had taken a wild dislike to the much-admired More.

"Oh, dear. And the nice man at the Library seemed so reverent about him. The Gospel of Richard III according to St. Thomas More, and all that."

"Gospel nothing," Grant said rudely. "He was writing down in a Tudor England what someone had told him about events that happened in a Plantagenet England when he himself was five."

"Five years old?"

"Yes."

"Oh, dear. Not exactly the horse's mouth."

"Not even straight from the course. Come to think of it, it's as reliable as a bookie's tips would be. He's on the wrong side of the rails altogether. If he was a Tudor servant he was on the laying side where Richard III was concerned."

"Yes. Yes, I suppose so. What do you want to find out about Richard, when there is no mystery to investigate?"

"I want to know what made him tick. That is a more profound mystery than anything I have come up against of late. What changed him almost overnight? Up to the moment of his brother's death he seems to have been entirely admirable. And devoted to his brother."

"I suppose the supreme honor must always be a temptation."

"He was Regent until the boy came of age. Protector of England. With his previous history, you would think that would have been enough for him. You would have thought, indeed, that it would have been very much his cup of tea: guardian of both Edward's son and the kingdom."

"Perhaps the brat was unbearable, and Richard longed to 'larn' him. Isn't it odd how we never think of victims as anything but white innocents. Like Joseph in the Bible. I'm sure he was a quite intolerable young man, actually, and long overdue for that pushing into the pit. Perhaps young Edward was just sitting up and begging to be quietly put down."

"There were two of them," Grant reminded her.

"Yes, of course. Of course there isn't an explanation. It was the ultimate barbarism. Poor little woolly lambs! Oh!"

"What was the 'Oh' for?"

"I've just thought of something. Woolly lambs made me think of it."

"Well?"

"No, I won't tell you in case it doesn't come off. I must fly."

"Have you charmed Madeleine March into agreeing to write the play?"

"Well, she hasn't actually signed a contract yet, but I think she is sold on the idea. Au revoir, my dear. I shall look in soon again."

She went away, sped on her way by a blushing Amazon, and Grant did not remember anything about woolly lambs until the woolly lamb actually turned up in his room next evening. The woolly lamb was wearing horn-rimmed spectacles, which in some odd way emphasized the resemblance instead of detracting from it. Grant had been dozing, more at peace with the world than he had been for some time; history was, as Matron had pointed out, an excellent way of acquiring a sense of perspective. The tap at his door was so tentative that he had decided that he had imagined it. Taps on hospital doors are not apt to be tentative. But something made him say: "Come in!" and there in the opening was something that was so unmistakably Marta's woolly lamb that Grant laughed aloud before he could stop himself.

The young man looked abashed, smiled nervously, propped the spectacles on his nose with a long thin forefinger, cleared his throat, and said:

"Mr. Grant? My name is Carradine. Brent Carradine. I hope I haven't disturbed you when you were resting."

"No, no. Come in, Mr. Carradine. I am delighted to see you."

"Marta—Miss Hallard, that is—sent me. She said I could be of some help to you."

"Did she say how? Do sit down. You'll find a chair over there behind the door. Bring it over."

He was a tall boy, hatless, with soft fair curls crowning a high forehead and a much too big tweed coat hanging unfastened round him in negligent folds. American-wise. Indeed, it was obvious that he was in fact American. He brought over the chair, planted himself on it with the coat spread round him like some royal robe and looked at Grant with kind brown eyes whose luminous charm not even the horn-rims could dim.

"Marta—Miss Hallard, that is—said that you wanted something looked up."

"And are you a looker-upper?"

"I'm doing research, here in London. Historical research, I mean. And she said something about your wanting something in that line. She knows I work at the B.M. most mornings. I'd be very pleased, Mr. Grant, to do anything I can to help you."

"That's very kind of you; very kind indeed. What is it that you are working on? Your research, I mean."

"The Peasants' Revolt."

"Oh, Richard II."

"Yes."

"Are you interested in social conditions?"

The young man grinned suddenly in a very unstudent-like way and said: "No, I'm interested in staying in England."

"And can't you stay in England without doing research?"

"Not very easily. I've got to have an alibi. My pop thinks I should go into the family business. It's furniture. Wholesale furniture. You order it by mail. Out of a book. Don't misunderstand me, Mr. Grant: it's very good furniture. Lasts for ever. It's just that I can't take much interest in furnishing-units."

"And, short of Polar exploration, the British Museum was the best hideaway you could think of."

"Well, it's warm. And I really do like history. I majored in it. And—well, Mr. Grant, if you really want to know, I just had to follow Atlanta Shergold to England. She's the dumb blonde in Marta's—I mean: in Miss Hallard's play. I mean she *plays* the dumb blonde. She's not at all dumb, Atlanta."

"No, indeed. A very gifted young woman indeed."

"You've seen her?"

"I shouldn't think there is anyone in London who hasn't seen her."

"No, I suppose not. It does go on and on, doesn't it? We didn't think—Atlanta and me —that it would run for more than a few weeks, so we just waved each other goodbye and said: See you at the beginning of the month! It was when we found that it was going on indefinitely that I just had to find an excuse to come to England."

"Wasn't Atlanta sufficient excuse?"

"Not for my pop! The family are very snooty about Atlanta, but Pop is the worst of the bunch. When he can bring himself to mention her he refers to her as 'that young actress acquaintance of yours.' You see, Pop is Carradine the Third, and Atlanta's father is very much Shergold the First. A little grocery store on Main Street, as a matter of fact. And the salt of the earth, in case you're interested. And of course Atlanta hadn't really done very much, back in the States. I mean, on the stage. This is her first big success. That is why she didn't want to break her contract and come back home. As a matter of fact it'll be quite a fight to get her back home at all. She says we never appreciated her."

"So you took to research."

"I had to think of something that I could do only in London, you see. And I had done some research at college. So the B.M. seemed to be what you call my cup of tea. I could enjoy myself and yet show my father that I was really working, both at the same time."

"Yes. It's as nice an alibi as ever I met with. Why the Peasants' Revolt, by the way?"

"Well, it's an interesting time. And I thought it would please Pop."

"Is *he* interested in social reform, then?"

"No, but he hates kings."

"Carradine the Third?"

"Yes, it's a laugh, isn't it? I wouldn't put it past him to have a crown in one of his safe deposit boxes. I bet he takes out the parcel every now and then and sneaks over to Grand Central and tries it on in the men's washroom. I'm afraid I'm tiring you, Mr. Grant; gabbing on about my own affairs like this. I didn't come for that. I came to——"

"Whatever you came for, you're manna straight from heaven. So relax, if you're not in a hurry."

"I'm never in a hurry," the young man said, unfolding his legs and laying them out in front of him. As he did it his feet, at the far extremity of his long limbs, touched the bedside table and shook the portrait of Richard III from its precarious position, so that it dropped to the floor.

"Oh, pardon me! That was careless of me. I haven't really got used to the length of my legs yet. You'd think a fellow would be used to his growth by twenty-two, wouldn't you?" He picked up the photograph, dusted it carefully with the cuff of his sleeve, and looked at it with interest. "Richardus III. Ang. Rex.," he read aloud.

"You're the first person to have noticed that background writing," Grant said.

"Well, I suppose it isn't visible unless you look into it. You're the first person I ever met who had a king for a pin-up."

"No beauty, is he?"

"I don't know," said the boy slowly. "It's not a bad face, as faces go. I had a prof at college who looked rather like him. He lived on bismuth and glasses of milk so he had a slightly jaundiced outlook on life, but he was the kindest creature imaginable. Is it about Richard that you wanted information?"

"Yes. Nothing very abstruse or difficult. Just to know what the contemporary authority is."

"Well, that should be easy enough. It isn't very far from my own time. I mean my research period. Indeed, the modern authority for Richard II—Sir Cuthbert Oliphant[3]— stretches over both. Have you read Oliphant?" Grant said that he had read nothing but school books and Sir Thomas More.

"More? Henry VIII's Chancellor?"

"Yes."

"I take it that that was a bit of special pleading!"

---

[3] Sir Cuthbert Oliphant is in reality Sir Charles Oman, author of *The Great Revolt of 1381* (Oxford, 1906) and *The History of England from the accession of Richard II to the death of Richard III (1377–1485)* (London, 1906). (Ed.)

"It read to me more like a party pamphlet," Grant said, realizing for the first time that that was the taste that had been left in his mouth. It had not read like a statesman's account; it had read like a party throw-away.

No, it had read like a columnist. Like a columnist who got his information below-stairs.

"Do you know anything about Richard III?"

"Nothing except that he croaked his nephews, and offered his kingdom for a horse. And that he had two stooges known as the Cat and the Rat."

"What!"

"You know: 'The Cat, the Rat, and Lovel Our Dog, Rule all England under a Hog.'"

"Yes, of course. I'd forgotten that. What does it mean, do you know?"

"No, I've no idea. I don't know that period very well. How did you get interested in Richard III?"

"Marta suggested that I should do some academic investigating, since I can't do any practical investigating for some time to come. And because I find faces interesting she brought me portraits of all the principals. Principals in the various mysteries she suggested, I mean. Richard got in more or less by accident, but he proved the biggest mystery of the lot."

"He did? In what way?"

"He is the author of the most revolting crime in history, and he has the face of a great judge; a great administrator. Moreover he was by all accounts an abnormally civilized and well-living creature. He actually *was* a good adminstrator, by the way. He governed the North of England and did it excellently. He was a good staff officer and a good soldier. And nothing is known against his private life. His brother, perhaps you know, was—bar Charles II—our most wench-ridden royal product."

"Edward IV. Yes, I know. A six-foot hunk of male beauty. Perhaps Richard suffered from a resentment at the contrast. And that accounts for his willingness to blot out his brother's seed."

This was something that Grant had not thought of.

"You're suggesting that Richard had a suppressed hate for his brother?"

"Why suppressed?"

"Because even his worst detractors admit that he was devoted to Edward. They were together in everything from the time that Richard was twelve or thirteen. The other

brother was no good to anyone. George."

"Who was George?"

"The Duke of Clarence."

"Oh. Him! Butt-of-malmsey Clarence."

"That's the one. So there were just the two of them—Edward and Richard I mean. And there was a ten-year gap in their ages. Just the right difference for hero worship."

"If I were a hunchback," young Carradine said musingly, "I sure would hate a brother who took my credit and my women and my place in the sun."

"It's possible," Grant said after an interval. "It's the best explanation I've come on so far."

"It mightn't have been an overt thing at all, you know. It mightn't have even been a conscious thing. It may just have all boiled up in him when he saw the chance of a crown. He may have said—I mean his blood may have said: 'Here's my chance! All those years of fetching and carrying and standing one pace in the rear, and no thanks for them. Here's where I take my pay. Here's where I settle accounts.'"

Grant noticed that by sheer chance Carradine had used the same imagined description of Richard as Miss Payne-Ellis. Standing one pace in the rear. That is how the novelist had seen him, standing with the fair, solid Margaret and George, on the steps of Baynard's Castle watching their father go away to war. One pace in the rear, "as usual."

"That's very interesting, though, what you say about Richard being apparently a good sort up to the time of the crime," Carradine said, propping one leg of his horn-rims with a long forefinger in his characteristic gesture. "Makes him more of a person. That Shakespeare version of him, you know, that's just a caricature. Not a man at all. I'll be very pleased to do any investigating you want, Mr. Grant. It'll make a nice change from the peasants."

"The Cat and the Rat instead of John Ball and Wat Tyler."

"That's it."

"Well, it's very nice of you. I'd be glad of anything you can rake up. But at the moment all I pine for is a contemporary account of events. They must have been country-rocking events. I want to read a contemporary's account of them. Not what someone heard-tell about events that happened when he was five, and under another régime altogether."

"I'll find out who the contemporary historian is. Fabyan, perhaps. Or is he Henry VII? Anyway, I'll find out. And meanwhile perhaps you'd like a look at Oliphant. He's the modern authority on the period, or so I understand."

Grant said that he would be delighted to take a look at Sir Cuthbert.

"I'll drop him in when I'm passing tomorrow—I suppose it'll be all right if I leave him in the office for you?—and as soon as I find out about the contemporary writers I'll be in with the news. That suit you?"

Grant said that that was perfect.

Young Carradine went suddenly shy, reminding Grant of the woolly lamb which he had quite forgotten in the interest of this new approach to Richard. He said goodnight in a quiet smothered way, and ambled out of the room followed by the sweeping skirts of his topcoat.

Grant thought that, the Carradine fortune apart, Atlanta Shergold looked like being on a good thing.

CHAPTER VIII

"*Well*," said Marta when she came again, "what did you think of my woolly lamb?"

"It was *very* kind of you to find him for me."

"I didn't have to find him. He's continually underfoot. He practically lives at the theatre. He must have seen *To Sea in a Bowl* five hundred times; when he isn't in Atlanta's dressing-room he's in front. I wish they'd get married, and then we might see less of him. They're not even living together, you know. It's all pure idyll." She dropped her "actress" voice for a moment and said: "They're rather sweet together. In some ways they are more like twins than lovers. They have that utter trust in each other; that dependence on the other half to make a proper whole. And they never have rows—or even quarrels, that I can see. An idyll, as I said. Was it Brent who brought you this?"

She poked the solid bulk of Oliphant with a doubtful finger.

"Yes, he left it with the porter for me."

"It looks very indigestible."

"A bit unappetizing, let us say. It is quite easily digested once you have swallowed it. History for the student. Set out in detailed fact."

"Ugh!"

"At least I've discovered where the revered

and sainted Sir Thomas More got his account of Richard."

"Yes? Where?"

"From one John Morton."

"Never heard of him."

"Neither did I, but that's our ignorance."

"Who was he?"

"He was Henry VII's Archbishop of Canterbury. And Richard's bitterest enemy."

If Marta had been capable of whistling, she would have whistled in comment.

"So *that* was the horse's mouth!" she said.

"That was the horse's mouth. And it is on that account of Richard that all the later ones were built. It is on that story that Holinshed fashioned his history, and on that story that Shakespeare fashioned his character."

"So it is the version of someone who hated Richard. I didn't know that. Why did the sainted Sir Thomas report Morton rather than someone else?"

"Whoever he reported, it would be a Tudor version. But he reported Morton, it seems, because he had been in Morton's household as a boy. And of course Morton had been very much 'on in the act,' so it was natural to write down the version of an eyewitness whose account he could have at first hand."

Marta poked her finger at Oliphant again. "Does your dull fat historian acknowledge that it is a biased version?"

"Oliphant? Only by implication. He is, to be honest, in a sad muddle himself about Richard. On the same page he says that he was an admirable administrator and general, with an excellent reputation, staid and good-living, very popular by contrast with the Woodville upstarts (the Queen's relations) and that he was 'perfectly unscrupulous and ready to wade through any depth of bloodshed to the crown which lay within his grasp.' On one page he says grudgingly: 'There are reasons for supposing that he was not destitute of a conscience' and then on a later page reports More's picture of a man so tormented by his own deed that he could not sleep. And so on."

"Does your dull fat Oliphant prefer his roses red, then?"

"Oh, I don't think so. I don't think he is consciously Lancastrian. Though now that I think of it he *is* very tolerant of Henry VII's usurpation. I can't remember his saying anywhere, brutally, that Henry hadn't a vestige of a shadow of a claim to the throne."

"Who put him there, then? Henry, I mean."

"The Lancastrian remnant and the upstart Woodvilles, backed, I suppose, by a country

revolted by the boys' murder. Apparently anyone with a spice of Lancastrian blood in their
veins would do. Henry himself was canny
enough to put 'conquest' first in his claim to
the throne, and his Lancaster blood second.
'De jure belli et de jure Lancastriae.' His
mother was the heir of an illegitimate son of
the third son of Edward III."

"All I know about Henry VII is that he was
fantastically rich and fantastically mean. Do
you know the lovely Kipling story [4] about his
knighting the craftsman not for having done
beautiful work but for having saved him the
cost of some scroll-work?"

"With a rusty sword from behind the arras.
You must be one of the few women who know
their Kipling."

"Oh, I'm a very remarkable woman in many
ways. So you are no nearer finding out about
Richard's personality than you were?"

"No. I'm as completely bewildered as Sir
Cuthbert Oliphant, bless his heart. The only
difference between us is that I know I'm bewildered and he doesn't seem to be aware of
it."

"Have you seen much of my woolly lamb?"

"I've seen nothing of him since his first visit,
and that's three days ago. I'm beginning to
wonder whether he has repented of his promise."

"Oh, no. I'm sure not. Faithfulness is his
banner and creed."

"Like Richard."

"Richard?"

"His motto was: 'Loyauté me lie.' Loyalty
binds me."

There was a tentative tap at the door, and
in answer to Grant's invitation, Brent Carradine appeared, hung around with topcoat
as usual.

"Oh! I seem to be butting in. I didn't know
you were here, Miss Hallard. I met the Statue
of Liberty in the corridor there, and she
seemed to think you were alone, Mr. Grant."

Grant identified the Statue of Liberty without difficulty. Marta said that she was in the
act of going, and that in any case Brent was
a much more welcome visitor than she was
nowadays. She would leave them in peace to
pursue their search for the soul of a murderer.

When he had bowed her politely to the
door Brent came back and sat himself down in
the visitors' chair with exactly the same air that

an Englishman wears when he sits down to his
port after the women have left the table.
Grant wondered if even the female-ridden
American felt a subconscious relief at settling
down to a stag party. In answer to Brent's
inquiry as to how he was getting on with
Oliphant, he said he found Sir Cuthbert ad-
mirably lucid.

"I've discovered who the Cat and the Rat
were, incidentally. They were entirely respectable knights of the realm: William Catesby
and Richard Ratcliffe. Catesby was Speaker of
the House of Commons, and Ratcliffe was one
of the Commissioners of Peace with Scotland.
It's odd how the very sound of words makes
a political jingle vicious. The Hog of course
was Richard's badge. The White Boar. Do
you frequent our English pubs?"

"Sure. They're one of the things I think you
do better than us."

"You forgive us our plumbing for the sake
of the beer at the Boar."

"I wouldn't go as far as to say I forgive it.
I discount it, shall we say?"

"Magnanimous of you. Well, there's something else you've got to discount. That theory
of yours that Richard hated his brother because of the contrast between his beauty and
Richard's hunchbacked state. According to
Sir Cuthbert, the hunchback is a myth. So is
the withered arm. It appears that he had no
visible deformity. At least none that mattered.
His left shoulder was lower than his right,
that was all. Did you find out who the contemporary historian is?"

"There isn't one."

"None at *all!*"

"Not in the sense that you mean it. There
were writers who were contemporaries of
Richard, but they wrote after his death. For
the Tudors. Which puts them out of court.
There is a monkish chronicle in Latin somewhere that is contemporary, but I haven't been
able to get hold of it yet. One thing I have
discovered though: that account of Richard
III is called Sir Thomas More's not because he
wrote it but because the manuscript was found
among his papers. It was an unfinished copy
of an account that appears elsewhere in finished
form."

"Well!" Grant considered this with interest.
"You mean it was More's own manuscript
copy?"

"Yes. In his own writing. Made when he was
about thirty-five. In those days, before printing
was general, manuscript copies of books were
the usual thing."

[4] Rudyard Kipling, "The Wrong Thing," in *Rewards and
Fairies*. (Ed.)

"Yes. So, if the information came from John Morton, as it did, it is just likely that the thing was written by Morton."

"Yes."

"Which would certainly account for the—the lack of sensibility. A climber like Morton wouldn't be at all abashed by backstairs gossip. Do you know about Morton?"

"No."

"He was a lawyer turned churchman, and the greatest pluralist on record. He chose the Lancastrian side and stayed with it until it was clear that Edward IV was home and dried. Then he made his peace with the York side and Edward made him Bishop of Ely. And vicar of God knows how many parishes besides. But after Richard's accession he backed first the Woodvilles and then Henry Tudor and ended up with a cardinal's hat as Henry VII's Archbishop of ——"

"Wait a minute!" said the boy, amused. "Of *course* I know Morton. He was Morton of 'Morton's Fork.' 'You can't be spending much so how about something for the King; you're spending such a lot you must be very rich so how about something for the King.' "

"Yes. That's Morton. Henry's best thumbscrew. And I've just thought of a reason why he might have a personal hatred for Richard long before the murder of the boys."

"Yes?"

"Edward took a large bribe from Louis XI to make a dishonorable peace in France. Richard was very angry about that—it really was a disgraceful affair—and washed his hands of the business. Which included refusing a large cash offer. But Morton was very much in favor both of the deal and the cash. Indeed he took a pension from Louis. A very nice pension it was. Two thousand crowns a year. I don't suppose Richard's outspoken comments went down very well, even with good gold for a chaser."

"No. I guess not."

"And of course there would be no preferment for Morton under the straight-laced Richard as there had been under the easygoing Edward. So he would have taken the Woodville side, even if there had been no murder."

"About that murder—" the boy said; and paused.

"Yes?"

"About that murder—the murder of those two boys—isn't it odd that no one talks of it?"

"How do you mean: no one talks of it?"

"These last three days I've been going through contemporary papers: letters and what not. And no one mentions them at all."

"Perhaps they were afraid to. It was a time when it paid to be discreet."

"Yes; but I'll tell you something even odder. You know that Henry brought a Bill of Attainder against Richard, after Bosworth. Before Parliament, I mean. Well, he accuses Richard of cruelty and tyranny but doesn't even mention the murder."

"What!" said Grant, startled.

"Yes, you may well look startled."

"Are you sure!"

"Quite sure."

"But Henry got possession of the Tower immediately on his arrival in London after Bosworth. If the boys were missing it is incredible that he should not publish the fact immediately. It was the trump card in his hand." He lay in surprised silence for a little. The sparrows on the window-sill quarrelled loudly. "I can't make sense of it," he said. "What possible explanation can there be for his omission to make capital out of the fact that the boys were missing?"

Brent shifted his long legs to a more comfortable position. "There is only one explanation," he said. "And that is that the boys weren't missing."

There was a still longer silence this time, while they stared at each other.

"Oh, no, it's nonsense," Grant said. "There must be some obvious explanation that we are failing to see."

"As what, for instance?"

"I don't know. I haven't had time to think."

"I've had nearly three days to think, and I still haven't thought up a reason that will fit. *Nothing* will fit the facts except the conclusion that the boys were alive when Henry took over the Tower. It was a completely unscrupulous Act of Attainder; it accused Richard's followers—the loyal followers of an anointed King fighting against an invader—of treason. Every accusation that Henry could possibly make with any hope of getting away with it was put into that Bill. And the very worst he could accuse Richard of was the usual cruelty and tyranny. The boys aren't even mentioned."

"It's fantastic."

"It's unbelievable. But it is fact."

"What it means is that there was *no contemporary accusation at all.*"

"That's about it."

"But—but wait a minute. Tyrrel was *hanged* for the murder. He actually confessed to it before he died. Wait a minute." He reached for Oliphant and sped through the pages looking for the place. "There's a full account of it here somewhere. There was no mystery about it. Even the Statue of Liberty knew about it."

"*Who?*"

"The nurse you met in the corridor. It was Tyrrel who committed the murder and he was found guilty and confessed before his death."

"Was that when Henry took over in London, then?"

"Wait a moment. Here it is." He skimmed down the paragraph. "No, it was in 1502." He realized all of a sudden what he had just said, and repeated in a new, bewildered tone: "In—1502."

"But—but—but that was——"

"Yes. Nearly twenty years afterwards."

Brent fumbled for his cigarette case, took it out, and then put it hastily away again.

"Smoke if you like," Grant said. "It's a good stiff drink I need. I don't think my brain can be working very well. I feel the way I used to feel as a child when I was blindfolded and whirled round before beginning a blind-man's-buff game."

"Yes," said Carradine. He took out a cigarette and lighted it. "Completely in the dark, and more than a little dizzy."

He sat staring at the sparrows.

"Forty million school books can't be wrong," Grant said after a little.

"Can't they?"

"Well, can they!"

"I used to think so, but I'm not so sure nowadays."

"Aren't you being a little sudden in your skepticism?"

"Oh, it wasn't this that shook me."

"What then?"

"A little affair called the Boston Massacre. Ever heard of it?"

"Of course."

"Well, I discovered quite by accident, when I was looking up something at college, that the Boston Massacre consisted of a mob throwing stones at a sentry. The total casualties were four. I was brought up on the Boston Massacre, Mr. Grant. My twenty-eight-inch chest used to swell at the very memory of it. My good red spinach-laden blood used to seethe at the thought of helpless civilians mowed down by the fire of British troops. You can't imagine what a shock it was to find that all it added up to in actual fact was a brawl that wouldn't get more than local reporting in a clash between police and strikers in any American lock-out."

As Grant made no reply to this, he squinted his eyes against the light to see how Grant was taking it. But Grant was staring at the ceiling as if he were watching patterns forming there.

"That's partly why I like to research so much," Carradine volunteered; and settled back to staring at the sparrows.

Presently Grant put his hand out, wordlessly, and Carradine gave him a cigarette and lighted it for him.

They smoked in silence.

It was Grant who interrupted the sparrows' performance.

"Tonypandy," he said.

"How's that?"

But Grant was still far away.

"After all, I've seen the thing at work in my own day, haven't I?" he said, not to Carradine but to the ceiling. "It's Tonypandy."

"And what in heck is Tonypandy?" Brent asked. "It sounds like a patent medicine. Does your child get out of sorts? Does the little face get flushed, the temper short, and the limbs easily tired? Give the little one Tonypandy, and see the radiant results." And then, as Grant made no answer: "All right, then; keep your Tonypandy. I wouldn't have it as a gift."

"Tonypandy," Grant said, still in that sleep-walking voice, "is a place in the South of Wales."

"I knew it was some kind of physic."

"If you go to South Wales you will hear that, in 1910, the Government used troops to shoot down Welsh miners who were striking for their rights. You'll probably hear that Winston Churchill, who was Home Secretary at the time, was responsible. South Wales, you will be told, will never forget Tonypandy!"

Carradine had dropped his flippant air.

"And it wasn't a bit like that?"

"The actual facts are these. The rougher section of the Rhondda Valley crowd had got quite out of hand. Shops were being looted and property destroyed. The Chief Constable of Glamorgan sent a request to the Home Office for troops to protect the lieges. If a Chief Constable thinks a situation serious enough to ask for the help of the military a Home Secretary has very little choice in the matter. But Churchill was so horrified at the possibility of the troops coming face to face with a crowd of rioters and having to fire on them, that he stopped the movement of the troops and sent instead a body of plain, solid Metropolitan Police, armed with nothing but their rolled-up mackintoshes. The troops were kept in reserve, and all contact with the rioters was made by unarmed London police. The only bloodshed in the whole affair was a bloody nose or two. The Home Secretary was severely criticized in the House of Commons incidentally for his 'unprecedented intervention.' That was Tony-pandy. That is the shooting down by troops that Wales will never forget."

"Yes," Carradine said, considering. "Yes. It's almost a parallel to the Boston affair. Someone blowing up a simple affair to huge proportions for a political end."

"The point is not that it is a parallel. The point is that *every single man* who was there knows that the story is nonsense, and yet it has never been contradicted. It will never be overtaken now. It is a completely untrue story grown to legend while the men who knew it to be untrue looked on and said nothing."

"Yes. That's very interesting; very. History as it is made."

"Yes. History."

"Give me research. After all, the truth of anything at all doesn't lie in someone's account of it. It lies in all the small facts of the time. An advertisement in a paper. The sale of a house. The price of a ring."

Grant went on looking at the ceiling, and the sparrows' clamor came back into the room.

"What amuses you?" Grant said, turning his head at last and catching the expression on his visitor's face.

"This is the first time I've seen you look like a policeman."

"I'm feeling like a policeman. I'm *thinking* like a policeman. I'm asking myself the question that every policeman asks in every case of murder: Who benefits? And for the first time it occurs to me that the glib theory that Richard got rid of the boys to make himself safer on the throne is so much nonsense. Supposing he had got rid of the boys. There were still the boys' five sisters between him and the throne. To say nothing of George's two: the boy and girl. George's son and daughter were barred by their father's attainder; but I take it that an attainder can be reversed, or annulled, or something. If Richard's claim was shaky, all those lives stood between him and safety."

"And did they all survive him?"

"I don't know. But I shall make it my business to find out. The boys' eldest sister certainly did because she became Queen of England as Henry's wife."

"Look, Mr. Grant, let's you and I start at the very beginning of this thing. Without history books, or modern versions, or anyone's opinion about anything. Truth isn't in accounts but in account books."

"A neat phrase," Grant said, complimentary. "Does it mean anything?"

"It means everything. The real history is written in forms not meant as history. In Wardrobe accounts, in Privy Purse expenses, in personal letters, in estate books. If someone, say, insists that Lady Whoosit never had a child, and you find in the account book the entry: 'For the son born to my lady on Michaelmas eve: five yards of blue ribbon, fourpence halfpenny' it's a reasonably fair deduction that my lady had a son on Michaelmas eve."

"Yes. I see. All right, where do we begin?"

"You're the investigator. I'm only the looker-upper."

"Research Worker."

"Thanks. What do you want to know?"

"Well, for a start, it would be useful, not to say enlightening, to know how the principals in the case reacted to Edward's death. Edward IV, I mean. Edward died unexpectedly, and his death must have caught everyone on the hop. I'd like to know how the people concerned reacted."

"That's straightforward and easy. I take it you mean what they did and not what they thought."

"Yes, of course."

"Only historians tell you what they thought. Research workers stick to what they did."

"What they did is all I want to know. I've always been a believer in the old saw that actions speak louder than words."

"Incidentally, what does the sainted Sir Thomas say that Richard did when he heard that his brother was dead?" Brent wanted to know.

"The sainted Sir Thomas (alias John Morton) says that Richard got busy being charming to the Queen and persuading her not to send a large bodyguard to escort the boy prince from Ludlow; meanwhile cooking up a plot to kidnap the boy on his way to London."

"According to the sainted More, then, Richard meant from the very first to supplant the boy."

"Oh, yes."

"Well, we shall find out, at least, who was where and doing what, whether we can deduce their intentions or not."

"That's what I want. Exactly."

"Policeman," jibed the boy. " 'Where were you at five P.M. on the night of the fifteenth inst?' "

"It works," Grant assured him. "It works."

"Well, I'll go away and work too. I'll be in again as soon as I have got the information you want. I'm very grateful to you, Mr. Grant. This is a lot better than the Peasants."

He floated away into the gathering dusk of the winter afternoon, his train-like coat giving an academic sweep and dignity to his thin young figure.

Grant switched on his lamp, and examined the pattern it made on the ceiling as if he had never seen it before.

It was a unique and engaging problem that the boy had dropped so casually into his lap. As unexpected as it was baffling.

What possible reason could there be for that lack of contemporary accusation?

Henry had not even needed proof that Richard was himself responsible. The boys were in Richard's care. If they were not to be found when the Tower was taken over, then that was far finer, thicker mud to throw at his dead rival than the routine accusations of cruelty and tyranny.

Grant ate his supper without for one moment being conscious either of its taste or its nature.

It was only when The Amazon, taking away his tray, said kindly: "Come now, that's a very good sign. Both rissoles all eaten up to the last crumb!" that he became aware that he had partaken of a meal.

For another hour he watched the lamp-pattern on the ceiling, going over the thing in his mind; going round and round it looking for some small crack that might indicate a way into the heart of the matter.

In the end he withdrew his attention altogether from the problem. Which was his habit when a conundrum proved too round and smooth and solid for immediate solution. If he slept on the proposition it might, tomorrow, show a facet that he had missed.

He looked for something that might stop his mind from harking back to that Act of Attainder, and saw the pile of letters waiting to be acknowledged. Kind, well-wishing letters from all sorts of people; including a few old lags. The really likable old lags were an outmoded type, growing fewer and fewer daily. Their place had been taken by brash young thugs with not a spark of humanity in their egocentric souls, as illiterate as puppies and as pitiless as a circular saw. The old professional burglar was apt to be as individual as the member of any other profession, and as little vicious. Quiet little domestic men, interested in family holidays and the children's tonsils; or odd bachelors devoted to cage-birds, or second-hand bookshops, or complicated and infallible betting systems. Old-fashioned types.

No modern thug would write to say that he was sorry that a "busy" was laid aside. No such idea would ever cross a modern thug's mind.

Writing a letter when lying on one's back is a laborious business, and Grant shied away from it. But the top envelope on the pile bore the writing of his cousin Laura, and Laura would become anxious if she had no answer at all from him. Laura and he had shared summer holidays as children, and had been a little in love with each other all through one Highland summer, and that made a bond between them that had never been broken. He had better send Laura a note to say that he was alive.

He read her letter again, smiling a little; and the waters of the Turlie sounded in his ears and slid under his eyes, and he could smell the sweet cold smell of a Highland moor in winter, and he forgot for a little that he was a hospital patient and that life was sordid and boring and claustrophobic.

Pat sends what would be his love if he were a little older or just a little younger. Being nine, he says: "Tell Alan I was asking for him," and has a fly of his own invention waiting to be presented to you when you come on sick leave. He is a little in disgrace at the moment in school, having learned for the first time that the Scots sold Charles the First to the English and having decided that he can no longer belong to such a nation. He is therefore, I understand, conducting a one-man protest strike against all things Scottish, and will learn no history, sing no song, nor memorize any geography pertaining to so deplorable a country. He announced going to bed last night that he has decided to apply for Norwegian citizenship.

Grant took his letter pad from the table and wrote in pencil:

Dearest Laura,
    Would you be unbearably surprised to learn that the Princes in the Tower survived Richard III?

As ever
Alan

P.S. I am nearly well again.

CHAPTER IX

"Do you know that the Bill attainting Richard III before Parliament didn't mention the murder of the Princes in the Tower?" Grant asked the surgeon next morning.

"Really?" said the surgeon. "That's odd, isn't it?"

"Extremely odd. Can you think of an explanation?"

"Probably trying to minimize the scandal. For the sake of the family."

"He wasn't succeeded by one of his family. He was the last of his line. His successor was the first Tudor. Henry VII."

"Yes, of course. I'd forgotten. I was never any good at history. I used to use the history period to do my home algebra. They don't manage to make history very interesting in schools. Perhaps more portraits might help." He glanced up at the Richard portrait and went back to his professional inspection. "That is looking very nice and healthy, I'm glad to say. No pain to speak of now?"

And he went away, kindly and casual. He was interested in faces because they were part of his trade, but history was just something that he used for other purposes; something that he set aside in favor of algebra under the desk. He had living bodies in his care, and the future in his hands; he had no thought to spare for problems academic.

Matron, too, had more immediate worries. She listened politely while he put his difficulty to her, but he had the impression that she might say: "I should see the almoner about it if I were you." It was not her affair. She looked down from her regal eminence at the great hive below her buzzing with activity, all of it urgent and important; she could hardly be expected to focus her gaze on something more than four hundred years away.

He wanted to say: "But you of all people should be interested in what can happen to royalty; in the frailness of your reputation's worth. Tomorrow a whisper may destroy you." But he was already guiltily conscious that to hinder a Matron with irrelevances was to lengthen her already lengthy morning round without reason or excuse.

The Midget did not know what an Attainder was, and made it clear that she did not care.

"It's becoming an obsession with you, that thing," she said, leaning her head at the portrait. "It's not healthy. Why don't you read some of those nice books?"

Even Marta, to whose visit he had looked forward so that he could put this odd, new proposition to her and see her reaction, even Marta was too full of wrath with Madeleine March to pay any attention to him.

"After practically promising me that she would write it! After all our get-together and my plans for when this endless thing finally comes to an end. I had even talked to Jacques about clothes! And now she decides that she must write one of her awful little detective stories. She says she must write it while it is fresh—whatever that is."

He listened to Marta's grieving with sympathy—good plays were the scarcest commodity in the world and good playwrights worth their weight in platinum—but it was like watching something through a window. The fifteenth century was more actual to him this morning than any on-goings in Shaftesbury Avenue.

"I don't suppose it will take her long to write her detective book," he said comfortingly.

"Oh, no. She does them in six weeks or so. But now that she's off the chain how do I know that I'll ever get her on again? Tony Savilla wants her to write a Marlborough play for him, and you know what Tony is when he sets his heart on something. He'd talk the pigeons off the Admiralty Arch."

She came back to the Attainder problem, briefly, before she took her leave.

"There's sure to be some explanation, my dear," she said from the door.

Of *course* there's an explanation, he wanted to shout after her, but what is it? The thing is against all likelihood and sense. Historians say that the murder caused a great revulsion of feeling against Richard, that he was hated for the crime by the common people of England, and that was why they welcomed a stranger in his place. And yet when the tale of his wrongdoing is placed before Parliament there is no mention of the crime.

Richard was dead when that complaint was drawn up, and his followers in flight or exile; his enemies were free to bring against him any charge they could think of. And *they had not thought of that spectacular murder.*

Why?

The country was reputedly ringing with the scandal of the boys' disappearance. The very recent scandal. And when his enemies collected his alleged offenses against morality and the State they had not included Richard's most spectacular piece of infamy.

Why?

Henry needed every small featherweight of advantage in the precarious newness of his accession. He was unknown to the country at large and he had no right by blood to be where he was. But he hadn't used the overwhelming advantage that Richard's published crime would have given him.

Why?

He was succeeding a man of great reputation, known personally to the people from the Marches of Wales to the Scots border, a man universally liked and admired until the disappearance of his nephews. And yet he omitted to use the one real advantage he had against Richard, the unforgivable, the abhorred thing.

Why?

Only The Amazon seemed concerned about the oddity that was engaging his mind; and she not out of any feeling for Richard but because her conscientious soul was distressed at any possibility of mistake. The Amazon would go all the way down the corridor and back again to tear off a page in a loose-leaf calendar that someone had forgotten to remove. But her instinct to be worried was less strong than her instinct to comfort.

"You don't need to worry about it," she said, soothing. "There'll be some quite simple explanation that you haven't thought of. It'll come to you sometime when you're thinking of something else altogether. That's usually how I remember where something I've mislaid is. I'll be putting the kettle on in the pantry, or counting the sterile dressings as Sister doles them out, and suddenly I'll think: 'Goodness, I left it in my burberry pocket.' Whatever the thing was, I mean. So you don't have to worry about it."

Sergeant Williams was in the wilds of Essex helping the local constabulary to decide who had hit an old shop-keeper over the head with a brass scale-weight and left her dead among the shoelaces and licorice all-sorts, so there was no help from the Yard.

There was no help from anyone until young Carradine turned up again three days later. Grant thought that his normal insouciance had a deeper tinge than usual; there was almost an air of self-congratulation about him. Being a well-brought-up child he inquired politely about Grant's physical progress, and having been reassured on that point he pulled some notes out of the capacious pocket of his coat and beamed through his horn-rims at his colleague.

"I wouldn't have the sainted More as a present," he observed pleasantly.

"You're not being offered him. There are no takers."

"He's way off the beam. Way off."

"I suspected as much. Let us have the facts. Can you begin on the day Edward died?"

"Sure. Edward died on April the 9th 1483. In London. I mean, in Westminster; which wasn't the same thing then. The Queen and the daughters were living there, *and* the younger boy, I think. The young Prince was doing lessons at Ludlow Castle in charge of the Queen's brother, Lord Rivers. The Queen's relations are very much to the fore, did you know? The place is just lousy with Woodvilles."

"Yes, I know. Go on. Where was Richard?"

"On the Scottish border."

"What!"

"Yes, I said: on the Scottish border. Caught away off base. But does he yell for a horse and go posting off to London? He does not."

"What did he do?"

"He arranged for a requiem mass at York, to which all the nobility of the North were summoned, and in his presence they took an oath of loyalty to the young Prince."

"Interesting," Grant said dryly. "What did Rivers do? The Queen's brother?"

"On the 24th of April he set out with the Prince for London. With two thousand men and a large supply of arms."

"What did he want the arms for?"

"Don't ask me. I'm only a research worker. Dorset, the elder of the Queen's two sons by her first marriage, took over both the arsenal and the treasure in the Tower and began to fit up ships to command the Channel. And Council orders were issued *in the name of Rivers and Dorset*—'avunculus Regis' and 'frater Regis uterinus' respectively—with no mention of Richard. Which was decidedly off-color when you remember—if you knew—that in his will Edward had appointed Richard guardian of the boy and Protector of the Kingdom in case of any minority. Richard alone, mind you, without a colleague."

"Yes, that is in character, at least. He must always have had complete faith in Richard. Both as a person and as an administrator. Did Richard come south with a young army too?"

"No. He came with six hundred gentlemen of the North, all in deep mourning. He arrived at Northampton on April the 29th. He had apparently expected to join up with the Ludlow crowd there; but that is report and you have only a historian's word for it. But the Ludlow procession—Rivers and the young Prince—had gone on to Stony Stratford without waiting for him. The person who actually met him at Northampton was the Duke of Buckingham with three hundred men. Do you know Buckingham?"

"We have a nodding acquaintance. He was a friend of Edward's."

"Yes. He arrived posthaste from London."

"With the news of what was going on."

"It's a fair deduction. He wouldn't bring three hundred men just to express his condolences. Anyhow a Council was held there and then—he had all the human material for a proper Council in his own train and Buckingham's, and Rivers and his three aides were arrested and sent to the North, while Richard went on with the young Prince to London. They arrived in London on the 4th of May."

"Well, that is very nice and clear. And what is clearest of all is that, considering time and distances, the sainted More's account of his writing sweet letters to the Queen to induce her to send only a small escort for the boy, is nonsense."

"Bunk."

"Indeed, Richard did just what one would expect him to do. He must of course have known the provisions of Edward's will. What his actions suggest is just what one would expect them to suggest; his own sorrow and his care for the boy. A requiem mass and an oath of allegiance."

"Yes."

"Where does the break in this orthodox pattern come? I mean: in Richard's behavior."

"Oh, not for a long time. When he arrived in London he found that the Queen, the younger boy, the daughters, and her first-marriage son, Dorset, had all bolted into sanctuary at Westminster. But apart from that things seem to have been normal."

"Did he take the boy to the Tower?"

Carradine riffled through his notes. "I don't remember. Perhaps I didn't get that. I was only—Oh, yes, here it is. No, he took the boy to the Bishop's Palace in St. Paul's Churchyard, and he himself went to stay with his mother at Baynard's Castle. Do you know where that was? I don't."

"Yes. It was the York's town house. It stood on the bank of the river just a little way west of St. Paul's."

"Oh. Well, he stayed there until June the 5th, when his wife arrived from the North and they went to stay in a house called Crosby Place."

"It is still called Crosby Place. It has been moved to Chelsea, and the window Richard put into it may not still be there—I haven't seen it lately—but the building is there."

"It is?" Carradine said, delighted. "I'll go and see it right away. It's a very domestic tale when you think of it, isn't it? Staying with his mother until his wife gets to town, and then moving in with her. Was Crosby Place theirs, then?"

"Richard had leased it, I think. It belonged to one of the Aldermen of London. So there is no suggestion of opposition to his Protectorship, or of change of plans, when he arrived in London."

"Oh, no. He was acknowledged Protector before he ever arrived in London."

"How do you know that?"

"In the Patent Rolls he is called Protector on two occasions—let me see—April 21st (that's less than a fortnight after Edward's death) and May the 2nd (that's two days before he arrived in London at all)."

"All right; I'm sold. And no fuss? No hint of trouble?"

"Not that I can find. On the 5th of June he gave detailed orders for the boy's coronation on the 22nd. He even had letters of summons sent out to the forty squires who would be made knights of the Bath. It seems it was the custom for the King to knight them on the occasion of his coronation."

"The 5th," Grant said musingly. "And he fixed the coronation for the 22nd. He wasn't leaving himself much time for a switch-over."

"No. There's even a record of the order for the boy's coronation clothes."

"And then what?"

"Well," Carradine said, apologetic, "that's as far as I've got. Something happened at a Council—on the 8th of June, I think—but the contemporary account is in the *Mémoires* of Philippe de Comines and I haven't been able to get hold of a copy so far. But someone has promised to let me see a copy of Mandrot's 1901 printing of it tomorrow. It seems that the Bishop of Bath broke some news to the Council on June the 8th. Do you know the Bishop of Bath? His name was Stillington."

"Never heard of him."

"He was a Fellow of All Souls, whatever that is, and a Canon of York, whatever *that* may be."

"Both learned and respectable, it appears."

"Well, we'll see."

"Have you turned up any contemporary historians—other than Comines?"

"Not any, so far, who wrote before Richard's death. Comines has a French bias but not a Tudor one, so he's more trustworthy than an Englishman writing about Richard under the Tudors would be. But I've got a lovely sample for you of how history is made. I found it when I was looking up the contemporary writers. You know that one of the things they tell about Richard III is that he killed Henry VI's only son in cold blood after the battle of Tewkesbury? Well, believe it or not, that story is made up out of whole cloth. You can trace it from the very time it was first told. It's the perfect answer to people who say there's no smoke without fire. Believe me, this smoke was made by rubbing two pieces of dry stick together."

"But Richard was just a boy at the time of Tewkesbury."

"He was eighteen, I think. And a very bonny fighter by all contemporary accounts. They were the same age, Henry's son and Richard. Well, *all* the contemporary accounts, of whatever complexion, are unanimous in saying that he was killed during the battle. Then the fun begins."

Carradine fluttered through his notes impatiently.

"Goldarn it, what did I do with it? Ah. Here we are. Now. Fabyan, writing for Henry VII, says that the boy was captured and brought before Edward IV, was struck in the face by Edward with his gauntlet and immediately slain by the King's servants. Nice? But Polydore Virgil goes one better. He says that the murder was done in person by George, Duke of Clarence, Richard, Duke of Gloucester, and William, Lord Hastings. Hall adds Dorset to the murderers. But that didn't satisfy Holinshed: Holinshed reports that it was Richard Duke of Gloucester who struck the first blow. How do you like that? Best quality Tonypandy, isn't it?"

"Pure Tonypandy. A dramatic story with not a word of truth in it. If you can bear to listen to a few sentences of the sainted More. I'll give you another sample of how history is made."

"The sainted More makes me sick at the stomach but I'll listen."

Grant looked for the paragraph he wanted, and read:

Some wise men also ween that his drift [that is, Richard's drift] covertly conveyed, lacked not in helping forth his brother Clarence to his death; which he resisted openly, howbeit somewhat, as men deemed, more faintly than he that were heartily minded to his weal. And they who deem thus think that he, long time in King Edward's life, forethought to be King in case that the King his brother (whose life he looked that evil diet should shorten) should happen to decease (as indeed he did) while his children were young. And they deem that for this intent he was glad of his brother Clarence's death, whose life must needs have hindered him so intending whether the same Clarence had kept true to his nephew the young King or enterprised to be King himself. But of all this point there is no certainty, and whoso divineth upon conjectures may as well shoot too far as too short.

"The mean, burbling, insinuating old bastard," said Carradine sweetly.

"Were you clever enough to pick out the one positive statement in all that speculation?"

"Oh, yes."

"You spotted it? That was smart of you. I had to read it three times before I got the one unqualified fact."

"That Richard protested openly against his brother George being put to death."

"Yes."

"Of course, with all that 'men say' stuff," Carradine observed, "the impression that is left is just the opposite. I told you, I wouldn't have the sainted More as a present."

"I think we ought to remember that it is John Morton's account and not the sainted More's."

"The sainted More sounds better. Besides, he liked the thing well enough to be copying it out."

Grant, the one-time soldier, lay thinking of the expert handling of that very sticky situation at Northampton.

"It was neat of him to mop up Rivers' two thousand without any open clash."

"I expect they preferred the King's brother to the Queen's brother, if they were faced with it."

"Yes. And of course a fighting man has a better chance with troops than a man who writes books."

"Did Rivers write books?"

"He wrote the first book printed in England. Very cultured, he was."

"Huh. It doesn't seem to have taught him not to try conclusions with a man who was a brigadier at eighteen and general before he was twenty-five. That's one thing that has surprised me, you know."

"Richard's qualities as a soldier?"

"No, his youth. I'd always thought of him as a middle-aged grouch. He was only thirty-two when he was killed at Bosworth."

"Tell me: when Richard took over the boy's guardianship, at Stony Stratford, did he make a clean sweep of the Ludlow crowd? I mean, was the boy separated from all the people he had been growing up with?"

"Oh, no. His tutor, Dr. Alcock, came on to London with him, for one."

"So there was no panic clearing-out of everyone who might be on the Woodville side; everyone who might influence the boy against him."

"Seems not. Just the four arrests."

"Yes. A very neat, discriminating operation altogether. I felicitate Richard Plantagenet."

"I'm positively beginning to like the guy. Well, I'm going along now to look at Crosby Place. I'm tickled pink at the thought of actually looking at a place he lived in. And tomorrow I'll have that copy of Comines, and let you know what he says about events in England in 1483, and what Robert Stillington, Bishop of Bath, told the Council in June of that year."

Chapter X

What Stillington told the Council on that summer day in 1483 was, Grant learned, that he had married Edward IV to Lady Eleanor Butler, a daughter of the first Earl of Shrewsbury, before Edward married Elizabeth Woodville.

"Why had he kept it to himself so long?" he asked when he had digested the news.

"Edward had commanded him to keep it secret. Naturally."

"Edward seems to have made a habit of secret marriages," Grant said dryly.

"Well, it must have been difficult for him, you know, when he came up against unassailable virtue. There was nothing for it but marriage. And he was so used to getting his own way with women—what with his looks and his crown—that he couldn't have taken very resignedly to frustration."

"Yes. That was the pattern of the Woodville marriage. The indestructibly virtuous beauty with the gilt hair, and the secret wedding. So Edward had used the same formula on a previous occasion, if Stillington's story was true. Was it true?"

"Well, in Edward's time, it seems, he was in turn both Privy Seal and Lord Chancellor, and he had been an ambassador to Brittany. So Edward either owed him something or liked him. And he, on his part, had no reason to cook up anything against Edward. Supposing he was the cooking sort."

"No, I suppose not."

"Anyway, the thing was put to Parliament so we don't have to take just Stillington's word for it."

"To Parliament!"

"Sure. Everything was open and above board. There was a very long meeting of the Lords at Westminster on the 9th. Stillington brought in his evidence and his witnesses, and a report was prepared to put before Parliament when it assembled on the 25th. On the 10th Richard sent a letter to the city of York asking for troops to protect and support him."

"Ha! Trouble at last."

"Yes. On the 11th he sent a similar letter to his cousin Lord Nevill. So the danger was real."

"It must have been real. A man who dealt so economically with that unexpected and very nasty situation at Northampton wouldn't be one to lose his head at a threat."

"On the 20th he went with a small body of retainers to the Tower—did you know that the Tower was the royal residence in London, and not a prison at all?"

"Yes, I knew that. It got its prison meaning only because nowadays being sent to the Tower has one meaning only. And of course because, being the royal castle in London, and the only strong keep, offenders were sent there for safe keeping in the days before we had His Majesty's Prisons. What did Richard go to the Tower for?"

"He went to interrupt a meeting of the conspirators, and arrested Lord Hastings, Lord Stanley, and one John Morton, Bishop of Ely."

"I thought we would arrive at John Morton sooner or later!"

"A proclamation was issued, giving details of the plot to murder Richard, but apparently no copy now exists. Only one of the conspirators was beheaded, and that one, oddly enough, seems to have been an old friend of both Edward and Richard. Lord Hastings."

"Yes, according to the sainted More he was rushed down to the courtyard and beheaded on the nearest log."

"Rushed nothing," said Carradine disgustedly. "He was beheaded a week later. There's a contemporary letter about it that gives the date. Moreover, Richard couldn't have done it out of sheer vindictiveness, because he granted Hastings' forfeited estates to his widow, and restored the children's right of succession to them—which they had automatically lost."

"No, the death of Hastings must have been inevitable," said Grant, who was thumbing through More's *Richard III*. "Even the sainted More says: 'Undoubtedly the Protector loved him well, and was loath to have lost him.' What happened to Stanley and to John Morton?"

"Stanley was pardoned—What are you groaning about?"

"Poor Richard. That was his death warrant."

"Death warrant? How could pardoning Stanley be his death warrant?"

"Because it was Stanley's sudden decision to go over to the other side that lost Richard the battle of Bosworth."

"You don't say."

"Odd to think that if Richard had seen to it that Stanley went to the block like his much-loved Hastings, he would have won the battle of Bosworth, there would never have been any Tudors, and the hunchbacked monster that appears in Tudor tradition would never have been invented. On his previous showing he would probably have had the best and most enlightened reign in history. What was done to Morton?"

"Nothing."

"Another mistake."

"Or at least nothing to signify. He was put into gentlemanly detention under the care of Buckingham. The people who did go to the block were the heads of the conspiracy that Richard had arrested at Northampton: Rivers and Co. And Jane Shore was sentenced to do penance."

"Jane Shore? What on earth has she got to do with the case? I thought she was Edward's mistress?"

"So she was. But Hastings inherited her from Edward, it seems. Or rather—let me see—Dorset did. And she was go-between between the Hastings side of the conspiracy and the Woodville side. One of Richard's letters existing today is about her. About Jane Shore."

"What about her?"

"His Solicitor-General wanted to marry her; when he was King, I mean."

"And he agreed?"

"He agreed. It's a lovely letter. More in sorrow than in anger—with a kind of twinkle in it."

" 'Lord, what fools these mortals be!' "

"That's it exactly."

"No vindictiveness there, either, it seems."

"No. Quite the opposite. You know, I know it isn't my business to think or draw deductions—I'm just the Research Worker—but it does strike me that Richard's ambition was to put an end to the York-Lancaster fight once and for all."

"What makes you think that?"

"Well, I've been looking at his coronation lists. It was the best-attended coronation on record, incidentally. You can't help being struck by the fact that practically nobody stayed away. Lancaster *or* York."

"Including the weather-cock Stanley, I suppose."

"I suppose so. I don't know them well enough to remember them individually."

"Perhaps you're right about his wanting a final end to the York-Lancaster feud. Perhaps his lenience with Stanley was due to that very thing."

"Was Stanley a Lancastrian, then?"

"No, but he was married to an abnormally rabid one. His wife was Margaret Beaufort, and the Beauforts were the reverse side, so to speak—the illegitimate side—of the Lancaster family. Not that her by-blow side worried her. *Or* her son."

"Who was her son?"

"Henry VII."

Carradine whistled, long and low.

"You actually mean to say that Lady Stanley was Henry's mother?"

"She was. By her first husband Edmund Tudor."

"But—but Lady Stanley had a place of honor at Richard's coronation. She carried the Queen's train. I noticed that because I thought it quaint. Carrying the train, I mean. In our country we don't carry trains. It's an honor, I take it."

"It's a thundering great honor. Poor Richard. Poor Richard. It didn't work."

"What didn't?"

"Magnanimity." He lay thinking about it while Carradine shuffled through his notes. "So Parliament accepted the evidence of Stillington."

"They did more. They incorporated it into an Act, giving Richard the title to the crown. It was called Titulus Regius."

"For a holy man of God, Stillington wasn't cutting a very glorious figure. But I suppose that to have talked sooner would have been to compass his own ruin."

"You're a bit hard on him, aren't you? There wasn't any need to talk sooner. No harm was being done anyone."

"What about Lady Eleanor Butler?"

"She died in a convent. She's buried in the Church of the White Carmelites at Norwich, in case you're interested. As long as Edward was alive no wrong was being done anyone. But when it came to the question of succession, then he *had* to talk, whatever kind of figure he cut."

"Yes. Of course you're right. So the children were proclaimed illegitimate, in open Parliament. And Richard was crowned. With all the nobility of England in attendance. Was the Queen still in sanctuary?"

"Yes. But she had let the younger boy join his brother."

"When was that?"

Carradine searched through his notes. "On June the 16th. I've put: 'At the request of the Archbishop of Canterbury. Both boys living at the Tower.'"

"That was after the news had broken. The news that they were illegitimate."

"Yes." He tidied his notes into some kind of neatness and put them away in the enormous pocket. "That seems to be all, to date. But here's the pay-off." He gathered his train from either side of him on to his knees with a gesture that both Marta and King Richard might have envied. "You know that Act, that Titulus Regius."

"Yes; what about it?"

"Well, when Henry VII came to the throne he ordered that the Act should be repealed, without being read. He ordered that the Act itself should be destroyed, and forbade any copies to be kept. Anyone who kept a copy was to be fined and imprisoned during his pleasure."

Grant stared in great astonishment.

"*Henry VII!*" he said. "Why? What possible difference could it make to him?"

"I haven't a glimmer of an idea. But I mean to find out before I'm much older. Meanwhile, here is something to keep you amused till the Statue of Liberty brings your British tea."

He dropped a paper on to Grant's chest.

"What is this?" Grant said, looking at the torn-out page of a note-book.

"It's that letter of Richard's about Jane Shore. I'll be seeing you."

Left alone by himself in the quiet, Grant turned over the page and read.

The contrast between the sprawling childish handwriting and the formal phrases of Richard's imagining was piquant in the extreme. But what neither the untidy modern script nor the dignified phrases could destroy was the flavor of the letter. The bouquet of good humor that came up from the page as a bouquet comes up from a good-humored wine. Translated into modern terms it said:

I hear to my great astonishment that Tom Lynom wants to marry Will Shore's wife. Apparently he is infatuated with her, and is quite determined about it. Do, my dear Bishop, send for him and see if you can talk some sense into his silly head. If you can't, and if there is no bar to their marriage from the Church's point of view, then I agree to it, but tell him to postpone the marriage till I am back in London. Meanwhile this will suffice to secure her release, on surety for her good behavior, and I suggest that you hand her over for the time being to the care of her father, or anyone else who seems good to you.

It was certainly, as young Carradine had said, "more in sorrow than in anger." Indeed, considering that it was written about a woman who had done him a deadly wrong, its kindness and good temper were remarkable. And this was a case where no personal advantage could come to him from magnanimity. The broadmindedness that had sought for a York-Lancaster peace might not have been disinterested; it would have been enormously to his advantage to have a united country to rule. But this letter to the Bishop of Lincoln was a small private matter, and the release of Jane Shore of no importance to anyone but the infatuated Tom Lynom. Richard had nothing to gain by his generosity. His instinct to see a friend happy was apparently greater than his instinct for revenge.

Indeed, his instinct for revenge seemed to be lacking to a degree that would be surprising in any red-blooded male, and quite astonishing in the case of that reputed monster Richard III.

CHAPTER XI

The letter lasted Grant very nicely until
The Amazon brought his tea. He listened to
the twentieth-century sparrows on his window-
sill and marvelled that he should be reading
phrases that formed in a man's mind more
than four hundred years ago. What a fantastic idea it would have seemed to Richard
that anyone would be reading that short, intimate letter about Shore's wife, and wondering
about him, four hundred years afterwards.

"There's a letter for you, now isn't that
nice?" The Amazon said, coming in with his
two pieces of bread-and-butter and a rock
bun.

Grant took his eyes from the uncompromis-
ing healthiness of the rock bun and saw that
the letter was from Laura.

He opened it with pleasure.

Dear Alan [said Laura]

Nothing (repeat: nothing) would surprise
me about history. Scotland has large monuments to two women martyrs drowned
for their faith, in spite of the fact that they
weren't drowned at all and neither was a
martyr anyway. They were convicted of
treason—fifth column work for the projected
invasion from Holland, I think. Anyhow on
a purely civil charge. They were reprieved
on their own petition by the Privy Council,
and the reprieve is in the Privy Council
Register to this day.

This, of course, hasn't daunted the Scottish collectors of martyrs, and the tale of
their sad end, complete with heart-rending
dialogue, is to be found in every Scottish
bookcase. Entirely different dialogue in each
collection. And the gravestone of one of the
women, in Wigtown churchyard, reads:

Murdered for owning Christ supreme
Head of his Church, and no more crime
But her not owning Prelacy
And not abjuring Presbytry
Within the sea tied to a stake
She suffered for Christ Jesus sake.

They are even a subject for fine Presbyterian
sermons, I understand—though on that point
I speak from hearsay. And tourists come and
shake their heads over the monuments with
their moving inscriptions, and a very profitable time is had by all.

All this in spite of the fact that the
original collector of the material, canvassing

the Wigtown district only forty years after
the supposed martyrdom and at the height
of the Presbyterian triumph, complains that
"many deny that this happened"; and couldn't
find any eyewitnesses at all.

It is very good news that you are con-
valescent, and a great relief to us all. If you
manage it well your sick leave can coincide
with the spring run. The water is very low
at the moment, but by the time you are
better it should be deep enough to please
both the fish and you.

> Love from us all,
> Laura.

P.S. It's an odd thing but when you tell
someone the true facts of a mythical tale
they are indignant not with the teller but
with you. They don't *want* to have their
ideas upset. It rouses some vague uneasiness
in them, I think, and they resent it. So they
reject it and refuse to think about it. If
they were merely indifferent it would be
natural and understandable. But it is much
stronger than that, much more positive.
They are annoyed.

Very odd, isn't it?

More Tonypandy, he thought.

He began to wonder just how much of the
school book which up to now had represented
British history for him was Tonypandy.

He went back, now that he knew a few facts,
to read the sainted More again. To see how
the relevant passages sounded now.

If, when he had read them merely by the
light of his own critical mind, they had seemed
to him curiously tattling, and in places absurd,
they now read plain abominable. He was what
Laura's small Pat was in the habit of calling
"scunnered." And he was also puzzled.

This was Morton's account. Morton the
eyewitness, the participant. Morton must have
known with minute accuracy what took place
between the beginning and end of June that
year. And yet there was no mention of Lady
Eleanor Butler; no mention of Titulus Regius.
According to Morton, Richard's case had been
that Edward was previously married to his
mistress Elizabeth Lucy. But Elizabeth Lucy,
Morton pointed out, had denied that she was
ever married to the King.

Why did Morton set up a ninepin just to
knock it down again?

Why the substitution of Elizabeth Lucy for
Eleanor Butler?

Because he could deny with truth that Lucy
was ever married to the King, but could not

do the same in the case of Eleanor Butler?

Surely the presumption was that it was very important to someone or other that Richard's claim that the children were illegitimate should be shown to be untenable.

And since Morton—in the handwriting of the sainted More—was writing for Henry VII, then that someone was presumably Henry VII. The Henry VII who had destroyed Titulus Regius and forbidden anyone to keep a copy.

Something Carradine had said came back into Grant's mind.

Henry had caused the Act to be repealed *without being read.*

It was so important to Henry that the contents of the Act should not be brought to mind that he had specially provided for its unquoted destruction.

Why should it be of such importance to Henry VII?

How could it matter to *Henry* what Richard's rights were? It was not as if he could say: Richard's claim was a trumped-up one, therefore mine is good. Whatever wretched small claim Henry Tudor might have was a Lancastrian one, and the heirs of York did not enter into the matter.

Then why should it have been of such paramount importance to Henry that the contents of Titulus Regius should be forgotten?

Why hide away Eleanor Butler, and bring in in her place a mistress whom no one ever suggested was married to the King?

This problem lasted Grant very happily till just before supper; when the porter came in with a note for him.

"The front hall says that young American friend of yours left this for you," the porter said, handing him a folded sheet of paper.

"Thank you," said Grant. "What do you know about Richard the Third?"

"Is there a prize?"

"What for?"

"The quiz."

"No, just the satisfaction of intellectual curiosity. What *do* you know about Richard III?"

"He was the first multiple murderer."

"Multiple? I thought it was two nephews?"

"No, oh, no. I don't know much history but I do know that. Murdered his brother, and his cousin, and the poor old King in the Tower, and then finished off with his little nephews. A wholesale performer."

Grant considered this.

"If I told you that he never murdered anyone at all, what would you say?"

"I'd say that you're perfectly entitled to your opinion. Some people believe the earth is flat. Some people believe the world is going to end in A.D. 2000. Some people believe that it began less than five thousand years ago. You'll hear far funnier things than that at Marble Arch of a Sunday."

"So you wouldn't even entertain the idea for a moment?"

"I find it entertaining all right, but not what you might call very plausible, shall we say? But don't let me stand in your way. Try it out on a better bombing range. You take it to Marble Arch one Sunday, and I'll bet you'll find followers aplenty. Maybe start a movement."

He made a gay sketchy half-salute with his hand and went away humming to himself; secure and impervious.

So help me, Grant thought, I'm not far off it. If I get any deeper into this thing I *will* be standing on a soapbox at Marble Arch.

He unfolded the message from Carradine, and read: "You said that you wanted to know whether the other heirs to the throne survived Richard. As well as the boys, I mean. I forgot to say: would you make out a list of them for me, so that I can look them up. I think it's going to be important."

Well, if the world in general went on its humming way, brisk and uncaring, at least he had young America on his side.

He put aside the sainted More, with its Sunday-paper accounts of hysterical scenes and wild accusations, and reached for the sober student's account of history so that he might catalogue the possible rivals to Richard III in the English succession.

And as he put down More-Morton, he was reminded of something.

That hysterical scene during the Council in the Tower which was reported by More, that frantic outburst on Richard's part against the sorcery that had withered his arm, had been against Jane Shore.

The contrast between the reported scene, pointless and repellent even to a disinterested reader, and the kind, tolerant, almost casual air of the letter that Richard had actually written about her, was staggering.

So help me, he thought again, if I had to choose between the man who wrote that account and the man who wrote that letter I'd take the man who wrote the letter, whatever either of them had done besides.

The thought of Morton made him postpone his listing of the York heirs until he had found out what eventually became of John Morton. It seemed that, having used his leisure as Buckingham's guest to organize a joint Woodville-Lancastrian effort (in which Henry Tudor would bring ships and troops from France and Dorset and the rest of the Woodville tribe would meet him with what English malcontents they could induce to follow them), he escaped to his old hunting ground in the Ely district, and from there to the continent. And did not come back until he came in the wake of a Henry who had won both Bosworth and a crown; being himself on the way to Canterbury and a cardinal's hat and immortality as Morton of "Morton's Fork." Almost the only thing that any schoolboy remembered about his master Henry VII.

For the rest of the evening Grant pottered happily through the history books, collecting heirs.

There was no lack of them. Edward's five, George's boy and girl. And if these were discounted, the first through illegitimacy and the second through attainder, there was another possible: his elder sister Elizabeth's boy. Elizabeth was Duchess of Suffolk, and her son was John de la Pole, Earl of Lincoln.

There was, too, in the family, a boy whose existence Grant had not suspected. It appeared that the delicate child at Middleham was not Richard's only son. He had a love-child; a boy called John. John of Gloucester. A boy of no importance in rank, but acknowledged and living in the household. It was an age when a bend sinister was accepted without grief. Indeed the Conqueror had made it fashionable. And conquerors from then on had advertised its lack of disadvantage. By way of compensation, perhaps.

Grant made himself a little *aide-mémoire*.

EDWARD	ELIZABETH	GEORGE	RICHARD
Edward, Prince of Wales	John de la Pole, Earl of Lincoln	Edward, Earl of Warwick	John of Gloucester
Richard, Duke of York		Margaret, Countess of Salisbury	
Elizabeth			
Cecily			
Anne			
Katherine			
Bridget			

He copied it out again for young Carradine's use, wondering how it could ever have occurred to anyone, Richard most of all, that the elimination of Edward's two boys would have kept him safe from rebellion. The place was what young Carradine would call just lousy with heirs. Swarming with focuses (or was it foci?) for disaffection.

It was brought home to him for the first time not only what a useless thing the murder of the boys would have been, but what a *silly* thing.

And if there was anything that Richard of Gloucester was not, beyond a shadow of a shadow of doubt, it was silly.

He looked up Oliphant to see what Oliphant had to say on this obvious crack in the story.

"It is strange," said Oliphant, "that Richard does not seem to have published any version of their deaths."

It was more than strange: it was incomprehensible.

If Richard had wanted to murder his brother's sons then he most certainly would have

done it expertly. They would have died of a fever, and their bodies would have been exposed to the public gaze as royal bodies habitually were, so that all men would know that they were in fact departed from this life.

No one can say that a man is incapable of murder—after long years on the Embankment Grant knew that only too well—but one can be sure to within one degree of the absolute when a man is incapable of silliness.

Oliphant had no doubts about the murder, nevertheless. Richard according to Oliphant was Richard the Monster. Perhaps when an historian was covering a field as large as the Middle Ages and the Renaissance he had no time to stop and analyze detail. Oliphant accepted the sainted More, even while he paused in flight to wonder at an oddity here and there. Not seeing that the oddities ate away at the very foundations of his theory.

Having Oliphant in his hand, he went on with Oliphant. On through the triumphal progress through England after the coronation.

Oxford, Gloucester, Worcester, Warwick. No dissentient voice was recorded on that tour. Only a chorus of blessing and thanksgiving. A rejoicing that good government was to be the order of the day for a lifetime to come. That, after all, Edward's sudden death had not condemned them to years of faction and a new civil struggle over the person of his son.

And yet it was during this triumphant, this unanimous acclamation, this universal hosanna, that (according to Oliphant, riding in the pocket of the sainted More) Richard sent Tyrrel back to London to make away with the boys who were doing lessons in the Tower. Between July 7th and 15th. At Warwick. In the very summer of his safety, in the heart of the York country on the borders of Wales, he planned the destruction of two discredited children.

It was a highly unlikely story.

He began to wonder whether historians were possessed of minds any more commonsensical than those Great Minds he had encountered, who had been so credulous.

He must find out without delay why, if Tyrrel did that job in 1485, he wasn't brought to book until twenty years afterwards. Where had he been in the meantime?

But Richard's summer was like an April day. Full of a promise that came to nothing. In the autumn he had to face that Woodville-Lancastrian invasion which Morton had cooked up before leaving these shores himself. The Lancastrian part of the affair did Morton proud: they came with a fleet of French ships and a French army. But the Woodville side could provide nothing better than sporadic little gatherings in widely separated centres: Guildford, Salisbury, Maidstone, Newbury, Exeter, and Brecon. The English wanted no part of Henry Tudor, whom they did not know, nor any part of the Woodvilles, whom they knew only too well. Even the English weather would have none of them. And Dorset's hope of seeing his half-sister Elizabeth queen of England as Henry Tudor's wife was washed away in Severn floods. Henry tried to land in the West, but found Devon and Cornwall up in indignant arms at the idea. He therefore sailed away to France again, to wait for a luckier day. And Dorset went to join in the growing crowd of Woodville exiles hanging round the French court.

So Morton's plan was washed away in autumn rain and English indifference, and Richard could be at peace for a little; but with the spring came a grief that nothing could wash away. The death of his son.

"The King is said to have shown signs of desperate grief; he was not such an unnatural monster as to be destitute of the feeling of a father," said the historian.

Nor of a husband, it seemed. The same marks of suffering were reported of him less than a year later, when Anne died.

And after that there was nothing but the waiting for the renewal of the invasion that had failed; the keeping of England in a state of defense, and the anxiety that that drain on the Exchequer brought him.

He had done what good he could. He had given his name to a model Parliament. He had made peace at last with Scotland and arranged a marriage between his niece and James III's son. He had tried very hard for a peace with France, but had failed. At the French court was Henry Tudor, and Henry Tudor was France's whiteheaded boy. It would be only a matter of time before Henry landed in England, this time with better backing.

Grant suddenly remembered Lady Stanley, that ardent Lancastrian mother of Henry. What part had Lady Stanley had in that autumn invasion that had put paid to Richard's summer?

He hunted through the solid print until he found it.

Lady Stanley had been found guilty of treasonable correspondence with her son.

But again Richard had proved too lenient for his own good, it seemed. Her estates were forfeit, but they were handed over to her husband. And so was Lady Stanley. For safe keeping. The bitter joke being that Stanley had almost certainly been as knowledgeable about the invasion as his wife.

Truly, the monster was not running according to form.

As Grant was falling asleep a voice said in his mind: "If the boys were murdered in July, and the Woodville-Lancastrian invasion took place in October, why didn't they use the murder of the children as a rallying call?"

The invasion had, of course, been planned before there was any question of murder; it was a full-dress affair of fifteen ships and five thousand mercenaries and must have taken a long time to prepare. But by the time of the rising the rumors of Richard's infamy must have been widespread if there were any rumors at all. Why had they not gone shouting his crime through England, so that the horror of it brought men flocking to their cause?

CHAPTER XII

"Cool off, cool off," he said to himself when he awoke next morning, "you're beginning to be partisan. That's no way to conduct an investigation."

So, by way of moral discipline, he became prosecutor.

Supposing that the Butler story was a frame-up. A story concocted with Stillington's help. Supposing that both Lords and Commons were willing to be hoodwinked in the hope of stable Government to come.

Did that bring one any nearer the murder of the two boys?

It didn't, did it?

If the story was false, the person to be got rid of was Stillington. Lady Eleanor had died in her convent long ago, so was not there to blow Titulus Regius to pieces any time she had a mind. But Stillington could. And Stillington evidently showed no difficulty in going on living. He survived the man he had put on the throne.

The sudden jar in the proceedings, the abrupt break in the pattern of the coronation preparation, was either wonderful stage-managing or just what one would expect if the thunderclap of Stillington's confession descended on unprepared ears. Richard was—what? Eleven? Twelve?—when the Butler contract was signed and witnessed; it was unlikely that he knew anything of it.

If the Butler story was an invention to oblige Richard, then Richard must have rewarded Stillington. But there was no sign of Stillington's being obliged with a cardinal's hat, or preferment, or office.

But the surest evidence that the Butler story was true lay in Henry VII's urgent need to destroy it. If it were false, then all he had to do to discredit Richard was to bring it into the open and make Stillington eat his words. Instead he hushed it up.

At this point Grant realized with disgust that he was back on the Defense side again. He decided to give it up. He would take to Lavinia Fitch, or Rupert Rouge, or some other of the fashionable authors lying in such expensive neglect on his table, and forget Richard Plantagenet until such time as young Carradine appeared to renew the inquisition.

He put the family-tree sketch of Cecily Nevill's grandchildren into an envelope and addressed it to Carradine, and gave it to The Midget to post. Then he turned down the portrait that was leaning against the books, so that he should not be seduced by that face which Sergeant Williams had placed, without hesitation, on the bench, and reached for Silas Weekley's *The Sweat and the Furrow.* Thereafter he went from Silas's steamy wrestlings to Lavinia's teacups, and from Lavinia's teacups to Rupert's cavortings in the *coulisses,* with a growing dissatisfaction, until Brent Carradine once more turned up in his life.

Carradine regarded him anxiously and said: "You don't look so bright as last time I saw you, Mr. Grant. You not doing so well?"

"Not where Richard is concerned, I'm not," Grant said. "But I've got a new piece of Tonypandy for you."

And he handed him Laura's letter about the drowned women who were never drowned.

Carradine read it with a delight that grew on him like slow sunlight coming out, until eventually he glowed.

"My, but that's wonderful. That's very superior, first growth, dyed-in-the-wool Tonypandy, isn't it? Lovely, lovely. You didn't know about this before? And you a Scotsman?"

"I'm only a Scot once removed," Grant pointed out. "No; I knew that none of these Covenanters died 'for their Faith,' of course; but I didn't know that one of them—or rather, two of them—hadn't died at all."

"They didn't die for their Faith?" Carradine repeated bewildered. "D'you mean that the *whole thing's* Tonypandy?"

Grant laughed. "I suppose it is," he said, surprised. "I never thought about it before. I've known so long that the 'martyrs' were no more martyrs than that thug who is going to his death for killing that old shop-keeper in Essex, that I've ceased to think about it. No one in Scotland went to his death for anything but civil crime."

"But I thought they were very holy people —the Covenanters, I mean."

"You've been looking at nineteenth-century pictures of conventicles. The reverent little gathering in the heather listening to the preacher; young rapt faces, and white hair blowing in the winds of God. The Covenanters were the exact equivalent of the I.R.A. in Ireland. A small irreconcilable minority, and as bloodthirsty a crowd as ever disgraced a Christian nation. If you went to church on Sunday instead of to a conventicle, you were liable to wake on Monday and find your barn burned or your horses hamstrung. If you were more open in your disapproval you were shot. The men who shot Archbishop Sharp in his daughter's presence, in broad daylight on a road in Fife, were the heroes of the movement. 'Men of courage and zeal for the cause of God,' according to their admiring followers. They lived safe and swaggering among their covenanting fans in the West for years. It was a 'preacher of the gospel' who shot Bishop Honeyman in an Edinburgh street. And they shot the old parish priest of Carsphairn on his own doorstep."

"It does sound like Ireland, doesn't it?" Carradine said.

"They were actually worse than the I.R.A. because there was a fifth column element in it. They were financed from Holland, and their arms came from Holland. There was nothing forlorn about their movement, you know. They expected to take over the Government any day, and rule Scotland. All their preaching was pure sedition. The most violent incitement to crime you could imagine. No modern Government could afford to be so patient with such a menace as the Government of the time were. The Covenanters were continually being offered amnesties."

"Well, well. And I thought they were fighting for freedom to worship God their own way."

"No one ever stopped them from worshipping God any way they pleased. What they were out to do was to impose their method of church government not only on Scotland but on England, believe it or not. You should read the Covenant some day. Freedom of worship was not to be allowed to anyone according to the covenanting creed—except the Covenanters, of course."

"And all those gravestones and monuments that tourists go to see——"

"All Tonypandy. If you ever read on a gravestone that John Whosit 'suffered death for his adherence to the Word of God and Scotland's Covenanted work of Reformation,' with a touching little verse underneath about 'dust sacrificed to tyranny,' you can be sure that the said John Whosit was found guilty before a properly constituted court, of a civil crime punishable by death and that his deed had nothing whatever to do with the Word of God." He laughed a little under his breath. "It's the final irony, you know, that a group whose name was anathema to the rest of Scotland in their own time should have been elevated into the position of saints and martyrs."

"I wouldn't wonder if it wasn't onomatopoeic," Carradine said thoughtfully.

"What?"

"Like the Cat and the Rat, you know."

"What are you talking about?"

"'Member you said, about that Cat and Rat lampoon, that rhyme, that the sound of it made it an offense?"

"Yes; made it venomous."

"Well, the word dragoon does the same thing. I take it that the dragoons were just the policemen of the time."

"Yes. Mounted infantry."

"Well, to me—and I suspect to every other person reading about it—dragoons sound dreadful. They've come to mean something that they never were."

"Yes, I see. Force majeure in being. Actually the Government had only a tiny handful of men to police an enormous area, so the odds were all on the Covenanters' side. In more ways than one. A dragoon (read policeman) couldn't arrest anyone without a warrant (he couldn't stable his horse without the owner's permission, if it comes to that), but there was nothing to hinder a Covenanter lying snug in the heather and picking off dragoons at his leisure. Which they did, of course. And now there's a whole literature about the poor ill-used saint in the heather with his pistol; and the dragoon who died in the course of his duty is a Monster."

"Like Richard."

"Like Richard. How have you been getting on with our own particular Tonypandy?"

"Well, I still haven't managed to find out why Henry was so anxious to hush up that Act as well as repeal it. The thing was hushed-up and for years it was forgotten, until the original draft turned up, just by chance, in the Tower records. It was printed in 1611. Speed printed the full text of it in his *History of Great Britain*."

"Oh. So there's no question at all about Titulus Regius. Richard succeeded as the Act says, and the sainted More's account is nonsense. There never was an Elizabeth Lucy in the matter."

"Lucy? Who's Elizabeth Lucy?"

"Oh, I forgot. You weren't on in that act. According to the sainted More, Richard claimed that Edward was married to one of his mistresses, one Elizabeth Lucy."

The disgusted look that the mention of the sainted More always caused on young Carradine's mild face made him look almost nauseated.

"That's nonsense."

"So the sainted More smugly pointed out."

"Why did they want to hide Eleanor Butler?" Carradine said, seeing the point.

"Because she really had married Edward, and the children really were illegitimate. And if the children really were illegitimate, by the way, then no one could rise in their favor and they were no danger to Richard. Have you noticed that the Woodville-Lancastrian invasion was in Henry's favor, and not in the boys' —although Dorset was their half-brother? And that was before any rumors of their non-existence could have reached him. As far as the leaders of the Dorset-Morton rebellion were concerned the boys were of no account. They were backing Henry. That way, Dorset would have a brother-in-law on the throne of England, and the Queen would be his half-sister. Which would be a nice reversal of form for a penniless fugitive."

"Yes. Yes, that's a point, all right; that about Dorset not fighting to restore his half-brother. If there had been a chance at all that England would have accepted the boy, he surely would have backed the boy. I'll tell you another interesting thing I found. The Queen and her daughters came out of sanctuary quite soon. It's your talking about her son Dorset that reminded me. She not only came out of sanctuary but settled down as if nothing had happened. Her daughters went to festivities at the Palace. And do you know what the pay-off is?"

"No."

"That was *after the Princes had been 'murdered.'* Yes, and I'll tell you something else. With her two boys done to death by their wicked uncle, she writes to her other son, in France—Dorset—and asks him to come home and make his peace with Richard, who will treat him well."

There was silence.

There were no sparrows to talk today. Only the soft sound of the rain against the window.

"No comment." Carradine said at last.

"You know," Grant said, "from the police point of view there is no case against Richard at all. And I mean that literally. It isn't that the case isn't good enough. Good enough to bring into court, I mean. There, quite literally, isn't any case against him at all."

"I'll say there isn't. Especially when I tell you that every single one of those people whose names you sent me were alive and prosperous, and *free*, when Richard was killed at Bosworth. They were not only free, they

were very well cared for. Edward's children not only danced at the Palace, they had pensions. He appointed one of the crowd his heir when his own boy died."

"Which one?"

"George's boy."

"So he meant to reverse the attainder on his brother's children."

"Yes. He had protested about his being condemned, if you remember."

"According to even the sainted More, he did. So all the heirs to the throne of England were going about their business, free and unfettered, during the reign of Richard III, the Monster."

"They were more. They were part of the general scheme of things. I mean, part of the family and the general economy of the realm. I've been reading a collection of York records by a man Davies. Records of the town of York, I mean; not the family. Both Young Warwick —George's son—and his cousin, young Lincoln, were members of the Council. The town addressed a letter to them. In 1485, that was. What's more, Richard knighted Young Warwick at the same time as he knighted his own son, at a splendid 'do' at York." He paused a long moment, and then blurted out: "Mr. Grant, do you want to write a book about this?"

"A book!" Grant said, astonished. "God forbid. Why?"

"Because I should like to write one. It would make a much better book than the Peasants."

"Write away."

"You see, I'd like to have something to show my father. Pop thinks I'm no good because I can't take an interest in furniture, and marketing, and graphs of sales. If he could actually handle a book that I had written he might believe that I wasn't so hopeless a bet after all. In fact, I wouldn't put it past him to begin to boast about me for a change."

Grant looked at him with benevolence.

"I forgot to ask you what you thought of Crosby Place," he said.

"Oh, fine, fine. If Carradine the Third ever sees it he'll want to take it back with him and rebuild it in the Adirondacks somewhere."

"If you write that book about Richard, he most certainly will. He'll feel like a part-owner. What are you going to call it?"

"The book?"

"Yes."

"I'm going to borrow a phrase from Henry Ford, and call it *History Is the Bunk*."

"Excellent."

"However, I'll have a lot more reading to

do and a lot more research, before I can start writing."

"Most assuredly you have. You haven't arrived yet at the real question."

"What is that?"

"Who *did* murder the boys."

"Yes, of course."

"If the boys were alive when Henry took over the Tower what happened to them?"

"Yes. I'll get on to that. I still want to know why it was so important to Henry to hush up the contents of Titulus Regius."

He got up to go, and then noticed the portrait that was lying on its face on the table. He reached over and restored the photograph to its original place, propping it with a concerned care against the pile of books.

"You stay there," he said to the painted Richard. "I'm going to put you back where you belong."

As he went out of the door, Grant said:

"I've just thought of a piece of history which is *not* Tonypandy."

"Yes?" said Carradine, lingering.

"The massacre of Glencoe."

"That really did happen?"

"That really did happen. And—Brent!"

Brent put his head back inside the door.

"Yes?"

"The man who gave the order for it was an ardent Covenanter."

CHAPTER XIII

Carradine had not been gone more than twenty minutes when Marta appeared, laden with flowers, books, candy, and good-will. She found Grant deep in the fifteenth century as reported by Sir Cuthbert Oliphant. He greeted her with an absentmindedness to which she was not accustomed.

"If your two sons had been murdered by your brother-in-law, would you take a handsome pension from him?"

"I take it that the question is rhetorical," Marta said, putting down her sheaf of flowers and looking round to see which of the already occupied vases would best suit their type.

"Honestly, I think historians are all mad. Listen to this:

The conduct of the Queen-Dowager is hard to explain; whether she feared to be

taken from sanctuary by force, or whether she was merely tired of her forlorn existence at Westminster, and had resolved to be reconciled to the murder of her sons out of mere callous apathy, seems uncertain.

"Merciful Heaven!" said Marta, pausing with a delft jar in one hand and a glass cylinder in the other, and looking at him in wild surmise.

"Do you think historians really *listen* to what they are saying?"

"Who was the said Queen-Dowager?"

"Elizabeth Woodville. Edward IV's wife."

"Oh, yes. I played her once. It was a 'bit.' In a play about Warwick the Kingmaker."

"Of course I'm only a policeman," Grant said. "Perhaps I never moved in the right circles. It may be that I've met only nice people. Where would one have to go to meet a woman who became matey with the murderer of her two boys?"

"Greece, I should think," Marta said. "*Ancient* Greece."

"I can't remember a sample even there."

"Or a lunatic asylum, perhaps. Was there any sign of idiocy about Elizabeth Woodville?"

"Not that anyone ever noticed. And she was Queen for twenty years or so."

"Of course the thing is farce, I hope you see," Marta said, going on with her flower arranging. "Not tragedy at all. 'Yes, I know he did kill Edward and little Richard, but he really is a rather charming creature and it is so bad for my rheumatism living in rooms with a north light.'"

Grant laughed, and his good temper came back.

"Yes, of course. It's the height of absurdity. It belongs to Ruthless Rhymes, not to sober history. That is why historians surprise me. They seem to have no talent for the *likeliness* of any situation. They see history like a peep-show; with two-dimensional figures against a distant background."

"Perhaps when you are grubbing about with tattered records you haven't time to learn about people. I don't mean about the people in the records, but just about People. Flesh and blood. And how they react to circumstances."

"How would you play her?" Grant asked, remembering that the understanding of motive was Marta's trade.

"Play who?"

"The woman who came out of sanctuary

and made friends with her children's murderer for seven hundred marks per annum and the right to go to parties at the Palace."

"I couldn't. There is no such woman outside Euripides or a delinquent's home. One could only play her as a rag. She'd make a very good burlesque, now I think of it. A take-off of poetic tragedy. The blank verse kind. I must try it sometime. For a charity matinée, or something. I hope you don't hate mimosa. It's odd, considering how long I've known you, how little I know of your likes and dislikes. Who invented the woman who became buddies with her sons' murderer?"

"No one invented her. Elizabeth Woodville did come out of sanctuary, and did accept a pension from Richard. The pension was not only granted, it was paid. Her daughters went to parties at the Palace and she wrote to her other son—her first-marriage son—to come home from France and make his peace with Richard. Oliphant's only suggestion as to the reason for this is that she was either frightened of being dragged out of sanctuary (did you ever know of anyone who was dragged out of sanctuary? The man who did that would be excommunicated—and Richard was a very good son of Holy Church) or that she was bored with sanctuary life."

"And what is your theory about so odd a proceeding?"

"The obvious explanation is that the boys were alive and well. No one at that time ever suggested otherwise."

Marta considered the sprays of mimosa. "Yes, of course. You said that there was no accusation in that Bill of Attainder. After Richard's death, I mean." Her eyes went from the mimosa to the portrait on the table and then to Grant. "You think, then, you really soberly think, as a policeman, that Richard didn't have anything to do with the boys' deaths."

"I'm quite sure that they were alive and well when Henry took over the Tower on his arrival in London. There is *nothing* that would explain his omission to make a scandal of it if the boys were missing. Can you think of anything?"

"No. No, of course not. It is quite inexplicable. I have always taken it for granted that there was a terrific scandal about it. That it would be one of the main accusations against Richard. You and my woolly lamb seem to be having a lovely time with history. When I suggested a little investigation to pass the time and stop the prickles I had no idea that I was contributing to the rewriting of history.

Which reminds me, Atlanta Shergold is gunning for you."

"For me? I've never even met her."

"Nevertheless she is looking for you with a gun. She says that Brent's attitude to the B.M. has become the attitude of an addict to his drug. She can't drag him away from it. If she takes him away from it physically, he spends the time harking back to it in his mind; so that she mightn't exist as far as he is concerned. He has even stopped sitting through *To Sea in a Bowl*. Do you see much of him?"

"He was here a few minutes before you came. But I don't expect to hear from him again for some days to come."

But in that he was wrong.

Just before supper-time the porter appeared with a telegram.

Grant put his thumb under the dainty Post Office lick on the flap and extracted two sheets of telegram. The telegram was from Brent.

Hell and damnation an awful thing has happened (stop) you know that chronicle in Latin I talked about (stop) the chronicle written by the monk at Croyland Abbey (stop) well I've just seen it and the rumor is there the rumor about the boys being dead (stop) the thing is written before Richard's death so we are sunk aren't we and I specially am sunk and that fine book of mine will never be written (stop) is anyone allowed to commit suicide in your river or is it reserved for the British

Brent

Into the silence the voice of the porter said: "It's reply-paid, sir. Do you want to send an answer?"

"What? Oh. No. Not right away. I'll send it down presently."

"Very good, sir," said the porter looking respectfully at the two sheets of telegram—in the porter's family a telegram was confined to one sheet only—and went away, not humming this time.

Grant considered the news conveyed with such trans-Atlantic extravagance in the matter of telegraphic communication. He read the thing again.

"Croyland," he said, considering. Why did that ring a bell? No one had mentioned Croyland so far in this case. Carradine had talked merely of a monkish chronicle somewhere.

He had been too often, in his professional life, faced with a fact that apparently destroyed his whole case to be dismayed now.

He reacted as he would have reacted in a professional investigation. He took out the upsetting small fact and looked at it. Calmly. Dispassionately. With none of poor Carradine's wild dismay.

"Croyland," he said again. Croyland was somewhere in Cambridgeshire. Or was it Norfolk? Somewhere on the borders there, in the flat country.

The Midget came in with his supper, and propped the flat bowl-like plate where he could eat from it with a modicum of comfort, but he was not aware of her.

"Can you reach your pudding easily from there?" she asked. And as he did not answer: "Mr. Grant, can you reach your pudding if I leave it on the edge there?"

"*Ely!*" he shouted at her.

"What?"

"Ely," he said; softly, to the ceiling.

"Mr. Grant, aren't you feeling well?"

He became conscious of The Midget's well-powdered and concerned little face as it intruded between him and the familiar cracks.

"I'm fine, fine. Better than I've ever been in my life. Wait just a moment, there's a good girl, and send a telegram down for me. Give me my writing-pad. I can't reach it with that mess of rice pudding in the way."

She gave him the pad and pencil, and on the reply-paid form he wrote:

Can you find me a similar rumor in France at about the same date?

Grant

After that he ate his supper with a good appetite, and settled down to a good night's sleep. He was floating in that delicious half-way stage on the way to unconsciousness when he became aware that someone was leaning over to inspect him. He opened his eyes to see who it might be, and looked straight into the anxious yearning brown irises of The Amazon, looking larger and more cowlike than ever in the soft lamplight. She was holding in her hand a yellow envelope.

"I didn't quite know what to do," she said. "I didn't want to disturb you and yet I didn't know whether it mightn't be important. A telegram, you know. You never can tell. And if you didn't have it tonight it would mean a whole twelve hours' delay. Nurse Ingham has gone off duty, so there was no one to ask till Nurse Briggs comes on at ten. I hope I haven't wakened you up. But you weren't really asleep, were you?"

Grant assured her that she had done the right thing and she let out a sigh that nearly blew the portrait of Richard over. She stood by while he read the telegram, with an air of being ready to support him in any evil news that it might contain. To The Amazon all telegrams conveyed evil tidings.

The telegram was from Carradine.

It said: "You mean you want repeat want that there should be another repeat another accusation questionmark—Brent."

Grant took the reply-paid form and wrote: "Yes. Preferably in France."

Then he said to The Amazon: "You can turn out the light, I think. I'm going to sleep until seven tomorrow morning."

He fell asleep wondering how long it would be before he saw Carradine again, and what the odds were against that much desired instance of a second rumor.

But it was not so long after all until Carradine turned up again, and he turned up looking anything but suicidal. Indeed he seemed in some queer way to have broadened out. His coat seemed less of an appendage and more of a garment. He beamed at Grant.

"Mr. Grant, you're a wonder. Do they have more like you at Scotland Yard? Or do you rate special?"

Grant looked at him almost unbelieving. "Don't tell me you've turned up a French instance!"

"Didn't you want me too?"

"Yes. But I hardly dared hope for it. The odds against seemed tremendous. What form did the rumor take in France? A chronicle? A letter?"

"No. Something much more surprising. Something much more dismaying, actually. It seems that the Chancellor of France, in a speech to the States-General at Tours, spoke of the rumor. Indeed he was quite eloquent about it. In a way, his eloquence was the one scrap of comfort I could find in the situation."

"Why?"

"Well, it sounded more to my mind like a Senator being hasty about someone who had brought in a measure his own people back home wouldn't like. More like politics than State, if you know what I mean."

"You should be at the Yard, Brent. What did the Chancellor say?"

"Well, it's in French and my French isn't very good so perhaps you'd better read it for yourself."

He handed over a sheet of his childish writing and Grant read:

Regardez, je vous prie, les événements qui après la mort du roi Edouard sont arrivés dans ce pays. Contemplez ses enfants, déjà grands et braves, massacrés impunément, et la couronne transportée à l'assassin par la faveur des peuples.

" 'Ce pays,' " said Grant. "Then he was in full flood against England. He even suggests that it was the will of the English people that the boys were 'massacred.' We are being held up as a barbarous race."

"Yes. That's what I meant. It's a Congressman scoring a point. Actually, the French Regency sent an embassy to Richard that same year—about six months later—so they had probably found that the rumor wasn't true. Richard signed a safe-conduct for their visit. He wouldn't have done that if they had been still slanging him as a murdering untouchable."

"No. Can you give me the dates of the two libels?"

"Sure. I have them here. The monk at Croyland wrote about events in the late summer of 1483. He says that there was a rumor that the boys had been put to death but no one knew how. The nasty slap in the meeting of the States-General was in January 1484."

"Perfect," said Grant.

"*Why* did you want there to have been another instance of rumor?"

"As a cross-check. Do you know where Croyland is?"

"Yes. In the Fen country."

"In the Fen country. Near Ely. And it was in the Fen country that Morton was hiding out after his escape from Buckingham's charge."

"Morton! Yes, of course."

"If Morton was the carrier, then there had to be another outbreak on the Continent, when he moved on there. Morton escaped from England in the autumn of 1483, and the rumor appears promptly in January 1484. Croyland is a very isolated place, incidentally; it would be an ideal place for a fugitive bishop to hide out till he could arrange transport abroad."

"Morton!" said Carradine again, rolling the name over on his tongue. "Wherever there's hanky-panky in this business you stub your toe against Morton."

"So you've noticed that too."

"He was the heart of that conspiracy to murder Richard before he could be crowned, he was in the back of the rebellion against Richard once he *was* crowned, and his trail to

the Continent is sticky as a snail's with—with subversion."

"We-ll, the snail part is mere deduction. It wouldn't stand up in court. But there's no peradventure about his activities once he was across the Channel. He settled down to a whole-time job of subversion. He and a buddy of his called Christopher Urswick worked like beavers in Henry's interest; 'sending preuie letters and cloked messengers' to England to stir up hostility to Richard."

"Yes? I don't know as much as you about what stands up in court and what won't but it seems to me that snail's trail is a very allowable deduction—if you'll allow me. I don't suppose Morton waited till he was overseas before beginning his undermining."

"No. No, of course he didn't. It was life and death to Morton that Richard should go. Unless Richard went, John Morton's career was over. He was finished. It wasn't even that there would be no preferment for him now. There would be nothing. He would be stripped of his numerous livings and be reduced to his plain priest's frock. He, John Morton. Who had been within touching distance of an archbishopric. But if he could help Henry Tudor to a throne then he might still become not only Archbishop of Canterbury but a Cardinal besides. Oh, yes; it was desperately, overwhelmingly important to Morton that Richard should not have the governing of England."

"Well," said Brent, "he was the right man for a job of subversion. I don't suppose he knew what a scruple was. A little rumor like infanticide must have been child's play to him."

"There's always the odd chance that he believed it, of course," Grant said, his habit of weighing evidence overcoming even his dislike of Morton.

"Believed that the boys were murdered?"

"Yes. It may have been someone else's invention. After all, the country must have been swarming with Lancastrian tales, part mere ill-will, part propaganda. He may have been merely passing on the latest sample."

"Huh! I wouldn't put it past him to be paving the way for their future murder," Brent said tartly.

Grant laughed. "I wouldn't, at that," he said. "What else did you get from your monk at Croyland?"

"A little comfort, too. I found after I had written that panic wire to you that he wasn't at all to be taken as gospel. He just put down what gossip came his way from the outer world. He says, for instance, that Richard had a second coronation, at York; and that of course just isn't true. If he can be wrong about a big, known, fact like a coronation, then he's not to be trusted as a reporter. But he *did* know about Titulus Regius, by the way. He recorded the whole tenor of it, including Lady Eleanor."

"That's interesting. Even a monk at Croyland had heard who Edward was supposed to have been married to."

"Yes. The sainted More must have dreamed up Elizabeth Lucy a good deal later."

"To say nothing of the unspeakable story that Richard based his claim on his mother's shame."

"What?"

"He says that Richard caused a sermon to be preached claiming that Edward and George were his mother's sons by some other father, and that he, Richard, was the only legitimate son and therefore the only true heir."

"The sainted More might have thought up a more convincing one," young Carradine said dryly.

"Yes. Especially when Richard was living in his mother's house at the time of the libel!"

"So he was. I'd forgotten that. I don't have a proper police brain. That's very neat, what you say about Morton being the carrier of the rumor. But suppose the rumor turns up somewhere else, even yet."

"It's possible, of course. But I'm willing to lay you fifties to any amount that it won't. I don't for one moment believe that there was any general rumor that the boys were missing."

"Why not?"

"For a reason that I hold to be unanswerable. If there had been any general uneasiness, any obviously subversive rumors or action, Richard would have taken immediate steps to checkmate them. When the rumor went round, later, that he was proposing to marry his niece Elizabeth—the boys' eldest sister—he was on to it like a hawk. He not only sent letters to the various towns denying the rumor in no uncertain terms, he was so furious (and evidently thought it of such importance that he should not be traduced) that he summoned the 'heid yins' of London to the biggest hall he could find (so that he could get them all in at one time) and told them face to face what he thought about the affair."

"Yes. Of course you're right. Richard would have made a public denial of the rumor if the rumor was general. After all, it was a much more horrifying one than the one that he was going to marry his niece."

"Yes; actually you could get a dispensation to marry your niece in those days. Perhaps you still can, for all I know. That's not my department at the Yard. What is certain is that if Richard went to such length to contradict the marriage rumor then he most certainly would have gone to much greater lengths to put a stop to the murder one, if it had existed. The conclusion is inevitable: there *was* no general rumor of disappearance or foul play where the boys were concerned."

"Just a thin little trickle between the Fens and France."

"Just a thin little trickle between the Fens and France. Nothing in the picture suggests any worry about the boys. I mean: in a police investigation you look for any abnormalities in behavior among the suspects in a crime. Why did X, who always goes to the movies on a Thursday night, decide on that night of all nights not to go? Why did Y take a return half as usual and very unusually not use it? That sort of thing. But in the short time between Richard's succession and his death everyone behaves quite normally. The boys' mother comes out of sanctuary and makes her peace with Richard. The girls resume their court life. The boys are presumably still doing the lessons that their father's death had interrupted. Their young cousins have a place on the Council and are of sufficient importance for the town of York to be addressing letters to them. It's all quite a normal, peaceful scene, with everyone going about their ordinary business, and no suggestion anywhere that a spectacular and unnecessary murder has just taken place in the family."

"It looks as if I might write that book after all, Mr. Grant."

"Most certainly you will write it. You have not only Richard to rescue from calumny; you have to clear Elizabeth Woodville of the imputation of condoning her sons' murder for seven hundred merks a year and perks."

"I can't write the book and leave it in the air like that, of course. I'll *have* to have at least a theory as to what became of the boys."

"You will."

Carradine's mild gaze came away from the small woolly clouds over the Thames and considered Grant with a question in it.

"Why that tone?" he asked. "Why are you looking like a cat with cream?"

"Well, I've been proceeding along police lines. During those empty days while I was waiting for you to turn up again."

"Police lines?"

"Yes. Who benefits, and all that. We've discovered that it wouldn't be a pin's-worth of advantage to Richard that the boys should die. So we go on looking round to see whom, in that case, it *would* benefit. And this is where Titulus Regius comes in."

"What has Titulus Regius got to do with the murder?"

"Henry VII married the boys' eldest sister. Elizabeth."

"Yes."

"By way of reconciling the Yorkists to his occupation of the throne."

"Yes."

"By repealing Titulus Regius, he made her legitimate."

"Sure."

"But by making the children legitimate he automatically made the two boys heir to the throne before her. In fact, by repealing Titulus Regius he made the elder of the two King of England."

Carradine made a little clicking sound with his tongue. His eyes behind their horn-rims were glowing with pleasure.

"So," said Grant, "I propose that we proceed with investigation along those lines."

"Sure. What do you want?"

"I want to know a lot more about that confession of Tyrrel's. But first, and most of all, I'd like to know how the people concerned acted. What happened to them; not what anyone reported of anyone. Just as we did in the case of Richard's succession after Edward's unexpected death."

"Fine. What do you want to know?"

"I want to know what became of all the York heirs that Richard left so alive and well and prosperous. Every single one of them. Can you do that for me?"

"Sure. That's elementary."

"And I could bear to know more about Tyrrel. About the man himself, I mean. Who he was, and what he had done."

"I'll do that." Carradine got up with such an on-with-the-charge air that for one moment Grant thought that he was actually going to button his coat. "Mr. Grant, I'm so grateful to you for all this—this——"

"This fun and games?"

"When you're on your feet again, I'll—I'll—I'll take you round the Tower of London."

"Make it Greenwich-and-back by boat. Our island Race have a passion for the nautical."

"How long do they reckon it will be before you're out of bed, do you know?"

"I'll probably be up before you come back with the news about the heirs and Tyrrel."

Chapter XIV

Grant was not, as it happened, out of bed when Carradine came again, but he was sitting up.

"You can't imagine," he said to Brent, "how fascinating the opposite wall looks, after the ceiling. And how small and queer the world looks right way up."

He was touched by Carradine's obvious pleasure in this progress and it was some time before they got down to business. It was Grant who had to say: "Well, how did the York heirs make out under Henry VII?"

"Oh, yes," said the boy, pulling out his usual wad of notes and drawing up a chair by hooking his right toe in the crossbar. He sat down on the chair. "Where shall I begin?"

"Well, about Elizabeth we know. He married her, and she was Queen of England until she died and he made a bid for the mad Juana of Spain."

"Yes. She was married to Henry in the spring of 1486—in January, rather; five months after Bosworth—and she died in the spring of 1503."

"Seventeen years. Poor Elizabeth. With Henry it must have seemed like seventy. He was what is euphemistically referred to as 'unuxorious.' Let us go on down the family. Edward's children, I mean. Fate of the two boys unknown. What happened to Cecily?"

"She was married to his old uncle Lord Welles, and sent away to live in Lincolnshire. Anne and Katherine, who were children, were married when they were old enough to good Lancastrians. Bridget, the youngest, became a nun at Dartford."

"Orthodox enough, so far. Who comes next? George's boy."

"Yes. Young Warwick. Shut up for life in the Tower, and executed for allegedly planning to escape."

"So. And George's daughter? Margaret."

"She became the Countess of Salisbury. Her execution by Henry VIII on a trumped-up charge is apparently the classic sample of judicial murder."

"Elizabeth's son? The alternative heir?"

"John de la Pole. He went to live with his aunt in Burgundy until——"

"To live with Margaret, Richard's sister."

"Yes. He died in the Simnel rising. But he had a younger brother that you didn't put in that list. He was executed by Henry VIII. He had surrendered to Henry VII under a safe-conduct, so Henry, I suppose, thought that it might break his luck to ignore that. In any case he had about used up his quota. Henry VIII took no chances. He didn't stop at De la Pole. There were four more that you missed out of that list. Exeter, Surrey, Buckingham, and Montague. He got rid of the lot."

"And Richard's son? John? The bastard one."

"Henry VII granted him a pension of £20 a year, but he was the first of the lot to go."

"On what charge?"

"On having been suspected of receiving an invitation to go to Ireland."

"You're joking."

"I'm not. Ireland was the focus of loyalist rebellion. The York family were very popular in Ireland, and to get an invitation from that direction was as good as a death warrant in Henry's eyes. Though I can't think why even Henry would have bothered about young John. 'An active, well-disposed boy,' he was, by the way, according to the 'Foedera.'"

"His claim was better than Henry's," Grant said, very tart. "He was the illegitimate only son of a King. Henry was the great-grandson of an illegitimate son of a younger son of a King."

There was silence for some time.

Then Carradine, out of the silence, said: "Yes."

"Yes to what?"

"To what you are thinking."

"It does look like it, doesn't it? They're the only two who are missing from the list."

There was another silence.

"They were all judicial murders," Grant said presently. "Murders under the form of law. But you can't bring a capital charge against a pair of children."

"No," agreed Carradine, and went on watching the sparrows. "No, it would have to be done some other way. After all, they were the important ones."

"The vital ones."

"How do we start?"

"As we did with Richard's succession. Find out where everyone was in the first months of Henry's reign and what they were doing. Say the first year of his reign. There will be a break in the pattern somewhere, just as there

was a break in the preparations for the boy's coronation."

"Right."

"Did you find out anything about Tyrrel? Who he was?"

"Yes. He wasn't at all what I had imagined. I'd imagined him as a sort of hanger-on; hadn't you?"

"Yes, I think I did. Wasn't he?"

"No. He was a person of importance. He was Sir James Tyrrel of Gipping. He had been on various—committees, I suppose you'd call them, for Edward IV. And he was created a Knight Banneret, whatever that is, at the siege of Berwick. And he did well for himself under Richard, though I can't find that he was at the battle of Bosworth. A lot of people came too late for the battle—did you know?—so I don't suppose that means anything particular. Anyhow, he wasn't that lackey-on-the-make person that I'd always pictured."

"That's interesting. How did he make out under Henry VII?"

"Well, that's the *really* interesting thing. For such a very good and successful servant of the York family, he seems to have fairly blossomed under Henry. Henry appointed him Constable of Guisnes. Then he was sent as ambassador to Rome. He was one of the Commissioners for negotiating the Treaty of Etaples. And Henry gave him a grant for life of the revenues of some lands in Wales, but made him exchange them for revenues of the county of Guisnes of equal value—I can't think why."

"I can," said Grant.

"You can?"

"Has it struck you that all his honors and his commissions are outside England? Even the reward of land revenues."

"Yes, so they are. What does that convey to you?"

"Nothing at the moment. Perhaps he just found Guisnes better for his bronchial catarrh. It is possible to read too much into historical transactions. Like Shakespeare's plays, they are capable of almost endless interpretations. How long did this honeymoon with Henry VII last?"

"Oh, quite a long time. Everything was just grand until 1502."

"What happened in 1502?"

"Henry heard that he had been ready to help one of the York crowd in the Tower to escape to Germany. He sent the whole garrison of Calais to besiege the castle at Guisnes. That wasn't quick enough for him, so he sent his Lord Privy Seal—know what that is?"

Grant nodded.

"Sent his Lord Privy Seal—what names you English have dreamed up for your Elks officials —to offer him safe conduct if he would come aboard a ship at Calais and confer with the Chancellor of the Exchequer."

"Don't tell me."

"I don't need to, do I? He finished up in a dungeon in the Tower. And was beheaded 'in great haste and without trial' on May 6, 1502."

"And what about his confession?"

"There wasn't one."

"What!"

"Don't look at me like that. I'm not responsible."

"But I thought he confessed to the murder of the boys."

"Yes, according to various accounts. But they are accounts of a confession, not—not a transcript, if you see what I mean."

"You mean, Henry didn't publish a confession?"

"No. His paid historian, Polydore Virgil, gave an account of how the murder was done. After Tyrrel was dead."

"But if Tyrrel confessed that he murdered the boys at Richard's instigation, why wasn't he charged with the crime and publicly tried for it?"

"I can't imagine."

"Let me get this straight. Nothing was heard of Tyrrel's confession until Tyrrel was dead."

"No."

"Tyrrel confesses that way back in 1483, nearly twenty years ago, he pelted up to London from Warwick, got the keys of the Tower from the Constable—I forget his name——"

"Brackenbury. Sir Robert Brackenbury."

"Yes. Got the keys of the Tower from Sir Robert Brackenbury for one night, murdered the boys, handed back the keys, and reported back to Richard. He confesses this, and so puts an end to what must have been a much canvassed mystery, and yet nothing public is done with him."

"Not a thing."

"I'd hate to go into court with a story like that."

"I wouldn't even consider it, myself. It's as phoney a tale as ever I heard."

"Didn't they even bring Brackenbury in to affirm or deny the story of the keys being handed over?"

"Brackenbury was killed at Bosworth."

"So he was conveniently dead too, was he?"

He lay and thought about it. "You know, if Brackenbury died at Bosworth, then we have one more small piece of evidence on our side."

"How? What?"

"If that had really happened; I mean: if the keys were handed over for a night on Richard's order, then a lot of junior officials at the Tower must have been aware of it. It is quite inconceivable that one or other of them wouldn't be ready to tell the tale to Henry when he took over the Tower. Especially if the boys were missing. Brackenbury was dead. Richard was dead. The next in command at the Tower would be expected to produce the boys. When they weren't producible, he *must* have said: 'The Constable handed over the keys, one night, and since then the boys have not been seen.' There would have been the most ruthless hue and cry after the man who had been given the keys. He would have been Exhibit A in the case against Richard, and to produce him would have been a feather in Henry's cap."

"Not only that, but Tyrrel was too well known to the people at the Tower to have passed unrecognized. In the small London of that day he must have been quite a well-known figure."

"Yes. If that story were true Tyrrel would have been tried and executed for the boys' murder, openly, in 1485. He had no one to protect him." He reached for his cigarettes. "So what we're left with is that Henry executed Tyrrel in 1502, and then announced by way of his tame historians that Tyrrel had confessed that twenty years before he had murdered the Princes."

"Yes."

"And he didn't offer, anywhere, at any time, any reason for not trying Tyrrel for this atrocious thing he had confessed."

"No. Not as far as I can make out. He was sideways as a crab, you know. He never went straight at anything, even murder. It had to be covered up to look like something else. He waited years to find some sort of legal excuse that would camouflage a murder. He had a mind like a corkscrew. Do you know what his first official action as Henry VII was?"

"No."

"To execute some of the men fighting for Richard at Bosworth *on a charge of treason.* And do you know how he managed to make it legally treason? By dating his reign from the day before Bosworth. A mind that was capable of a piece of sharp-practice of that calibre was capable of anything." He took the cigarette that Grant was offering him. "But he didn't get away with it," he added, with sober joy. "Oh, no, he didn't get away with it. The English, bless them, drew the line at that. They told him where he got off."

"How?"

"They presented him, in that nice polite English way, with an Act of Parliament that said that no one serving the Sovereign Lord of the land for the time being should be convicted of treason or suffer either forfeiture or imprisonment, and they made him consent to it. That's terribly English, that ruthless politeness. No yelling in the street or throwing stones because they didn't like his little bit of cheating. Just a nice polite reasonable Act for him to swallow and like it. I bet he did a slow burn about that one. Well, I must be on my way. It's sure nice to see you sitting up and taking notice. We'll be having that trip to Greenwich in no time at all, I see. What's at Greenwich?"

"Some very fine architecture and a fine stretch of muddy river."

"That all?"

"And some good pubs."

"We're going to Greenwich."

When he had gone Grant slid down in bed and smoked one cigarette after another while he considered the tale of those heirs of York who had prospered under Richard III, and gone to their graves under Henry VII.

Some of them may have "asked for it." Carradine's report had, after all, been a précis; innocent of qualification, insusceptible to half-tones. But it was surely a thundering great coincidence that *all* the lives who stood between the Tudors and the throne had been cut short so conveniently.

He looked, with no great enthusiasm, at the book that young Carradine had brought him. It was called *The Life and Reign of Richard III*, by someone James Gairdner. Carradine had assured him that he would find Dr. Gairdner well worth his while. Dr. Gairdner was, according to Brent, "a scream."

The book did not appear to Grant to be markedly hilarious, but anything about Richard was better than something about anyone else, so he began to glance through it, and presently he became aware just what Brent had meant by saying that the good doctor was a "scream." Dr. Gairdner obstinately believed Richard to be a murderer, but since he was a writer honest, learned, and according to his lights impartial, it was not in him to suppress facts. The spectacle of Dr. Gairdner trying to make his facts fit his theory was the most en-

tertaining thing in gymnastics that Grant had witnessed for some time.

Dr. Gairdner acknowledged with no apparent sense of incongruity Richard's great wisdom, his generosity, his courage, his ability, his charm, his popularity, and the trust that he inspired even in his beaten enemies; and in the same breath reported his vile slander of his mother and his slaughter of two helpless children. Tradition says, said the worthy Doctor; and solemnly reported the horrible tradition and subscribed to it. There was nothing mean or paltry in his character, according to the Doctor—but he was a murderer of innocent children. Even his enemies had confidence in his justice—but he murdered his own nephews. His integrity was remarkable—but he killed for gain.

As a contortionist Dr. Gairdner was the original boneless wonder. More than ever Grant wondered with what part of their brains historians reasoned. It was certainly by no process of reasoning known to ordinary mortals that they arrived at their conclusions. Nowhere in life, had he met any human being remotely resembling either Dr. Gairdner's Richard or Oliphant's Elizabeth Woodville.

Perhaps there was something in Laura's theory that human nature found it difficult to give up preconceived beliefs. That there was some vague inward opposition to, and resentment of, a reversal of accepted fact. Certainly Dr. Gairdner dragged like a frightened child on the hand that was pulling him towards the inevitable.

That charming men of great integrity had committed murder in their day Grant knew only too well. But not that kind of murder and not for that kind of reason. The kind of man whom Dr. Gairdner had drawn in his *Life and History of Richard III* would commit murder only when his own personal life had been *bouleversé* by some earthquake. He would murder his wife for unfaithfulness suddenly discovered, perhaps. Or kill the partner whose secret speculation had ruined their firm and the future of his children. Whatever murder he committed would be the result of acute emotion, it would never be planned; and it would never be a base murder.

One could not say: Because Richard possessed this quality and that, therefore he was incapable of murder. But one could say: Because Richard possessed these qualities, therefore he is incapable of this murder.

It would have been a silly murder, that murder of the boy Princes; and Richard was a remarkably able man. It was base beyond description; and he was a man of great integrity. It was callous; and he was noted for his warmheartedness.

One could go through the catalogue of his acknowledged virtues, and find that each of them, individually, made his part in the murder unlikely in the extreme. Taken together they amounted to a wall of impossibility that towered into fantasy.

Chapter XV

"There was one person you forgot to ask for," Carradine said, breezing in, very gay, some days later. "In your list of kind inquiries."

"Hullo. Who was that?"

"Stillington."

"Of course! The worthy Bishop of Bath. If Henry hated Titulus Regius, as a witness of Richard's integrity and his own wife's illegitimacy, he must still more have disliked the presence of its instigator. What happened to old Stillington? Judicial murder?"

"Apparently the old boy wouldn't play."

"Wouldn't play what?"

"Henry's pet game. Out goes he. Either he was a wily old bird, or he was too innocent to see the snare at all. It's my belief—if a mere Research Worker is entitled to a belief—that he was so innocent that no agent provocateur could provoke him to anything. Not anything that could be made a capital charge, anyhow."

"Are you telling me that he defeated Henry?"

"No. Oh, no. No one ever defeated Henry. Henry put him on a charge and conveniently forgot to release him. And never home came he. Who was that? Mary on the sands of Dee?"

"You're very bright this morning, not to say exhilarated." ·

"Don't say it in that suspicious tone. They're not open yet. This effervescence that you observe in me is intellectual carbonization. Spiritual rejoicing. An entirely cerebral scintillation."

"Well? Sit down and cough up. What is so good? I take it that something is?"

"Good is hardly the proper word. It's beautiful, perfectly-holy beautiful."

"I think you *have* been drinking."

"I couldn't drink this morning if I tried. I'm

bung full, full up to the gullet's edge, with satisfaction."

"I take it you found that break in the pattern we were looking for."

"Yes, I found it, but it was later than we had thought. Later in time, I mean. Further on. In the first months everyone did what you would expect them to do. Henry took over—not a word about the boys—and cleaned up, got married to the boys' sister. Got his own attainder reversed by a parliament of his own attainted followers—no mention of the boys—and got an act of attainder through against Richard and his loyal subjects whose service was so neatly made treason by that one day's ante-dating. That brought a fine heap of forfeited estates into the kitty in one go. The Croyland monk was terribly scandalized, by the way, at Henry's sharp practice in the matter of treason. 'O God,' he says, 'what security are our kings to have henceforth in the day of battle if their loyal followers may in defeat be deprived of life, fortune, and inheritance?'"

"He reckoned without his countrymen."

"Yes. He might have known that the English would get round to that matter sooner or later. Perhaps he was an alien. Anyhow, everything went on just as you would expect things to go with Henry in charge. He succeeded in August of 1485, and married Elizabeth in the following January. Elizabeth had her first child at Winchester, and her mother was there with her and was present at the baptism. That was in September 1486. Then she came back to London—the Queen-Dowager, I mean—in the autumn. And in February—hold on to everything—in February she was shut up in a convent for the rest of her life."

"*Elizabeth Woodville?*" Grant said, in the greatest astonishment. This was the very last thing he had expected.

"Yes. Elizabeth Woodville. The boys' mother."

"How do you know that she didn't go voluntarily?" Grant asked, when he had thought of it for a little. "It was not an uncommon thing for great ladies who were tired of court life to retire into an Order. It was not a severe existence, you know. Indeed, I have an idea it was fairly comfortable for rich women."

"Henry stripped her of everything she owned, and ordered her into the nunnery at Bermondsey. And that, by the way, *did* create a sensation. There was 'much wondering,' it appears."

"I'm not surprised. What an extraordinary thing. Did he give a reason?"

"Yes."

"What did he say he was ruining her for?"

"For being nice to Richard."

"Are you serious?"

"Sure."

"Is that the official wording?"

"No. That's the version of Henry's pet historian."

"Virgil?"

"Yes. The actual order of council that shut her up, said it was 'for various considerations.'"

"Are you quoting?" asked Grant, incredulous.

"I'm quoting. That's what it said: 'For various considerations.'"

After a moment Grant said: "He had no talent for excuses, had he? In his place I would have thought up six better ones."

"Either he couldn't be bothered or he thought other people very credulous. Mark you, her niceness to Richard didn't worry him until eighteen months after he succeeded Richard. Up till then everything had apparently been smooth as milk. He had even given her presents, manors and what not, when he succeeded Richard."

"What was his real reason? Have you any suggestion?"

"Well, I've another little item that may give you ideas. It certainly gave me one hell of a big idea."

"Go on."

"In June of that year——"

"Which year?"

"The first year of Elizabeth's marriage. 1486. The year when she was married in January and had Prince Arthur at Winchester in September, with her mother dancing attendance."

"All right. Yes."

"In June of that year, Sir James Tyrrel received a general pardon. On the 16th June."

"But that means very little, you know. It was quite a usual thing. At the end of a period of service. Or on setting out on a new one. It merely meant that you were quit of anything that anyone might think of raking up against you afterwards."

"Yes, I know. I know that. The first pardon isn't the surprising one."

"The *first* pardon? Was there a second one?"

"Yes. That's the pay-off. There was a second general pardon to Sir James exactly a month later. To be exact on the 16th July, 1486."

"Yes," Grant said, thinking it over. "That really is extraordinary."

"It's highly unusual, anyway. I asked an old boy who works next to me at the B.M.—he does historical research and he's been a wonderful help to me I don't mind telling you—and he said he had never come across another instance. I showed him the two entries—in the *Memorials of Henry VII*—and he mooned over them like a lover."

Grant said, considering: "On the 16th June, Tyrrel is given a general pardon. On the 16th July he is given a second general pardon. In November or thereabouts the boys' mother comes back to town. And in February she is immured for life."

"Suggestive?"

"Very."

"You think he did it? Tyrrel."

"It could be. It's very suggestive, isn't it, that when we find the break in the normal pattern that we've been looking for, Tyrrel is there, on the spot, with a most unconscionable break in his own pattern. When did the rumor that the boys were missing first become general? I mean, something to be talked openly about."

"Quite early in Henry's reign, it would seem."

"Yes; it fits. It would certainly explain the thing that has puzzled us from the beginning in this affair."

"What do you mean?"

"It would explain why there was no fuss when the boys disappeared. It's always been a puzzling thing, even to people who thought that Richard did it. Indeed, when you come to think of it it would be impossible for Richard to get away with it. There was a large, and very active, and very powerful opposition party in Richard's day, and he left them all free and scattered up and down the country to carry on as they liked. He had all the Woodville-Lancaster crowd to deal with if the boys had gone missing. But where interference or undue curiosity was concerned Henry was sitting pretty. Henry had got *his* opposition party safely in jail. The only possible danger was his mother-in-law, and at the very moment when she becomes capable of being a prying nuisance she too is put under hatches and battened down."

"Yes. Wouldn't you think that there was *something* she could have done? When she found that she was being prevented from getting news of the boys."

"She may never have known that they were missing. He may just have said: 'It is my wish that you should not see them. I think you are a bad influence on them: you who came out of sanctuary and let your daughters go to that man's parties!' "

"Yes, that's so, of course. He didn't have to wait until she actually became suspicious. The whole thing might have been one move. 'You're a bad woman, and a bad mother; I am sending you into a convent to save your soul and your children from the contamination of your presence.' "

"Yes. And where the rest of England were concerned, he was as safe as any murderer ever could be. After his happy thought about the 'treason' accusation, no one was going to stick his neck out by inquiring particularly about the boys' health. Everyone must have been walking on eggs as it was. No one knowing what Henry might think of next to make into a retrospective offense that would send their lives into limbo and their estates into Henry's kitty. No, it was no time to be over-curious about anything that didn't directly concern oneself. Not that it would be easy, in any case, to satisfy one's curiosity."

"With the boys living at the Tower, you mean."

"With the boys living in a Tower officialled by Henry's men. There was none of Richard's get-together live-and-let-live attitude about Henry. No York-Lancaster alliance for Henry. The people at the Tower would be Henry's men."

"Yes. Of course they would. Did you know that Henry was the first English King to have a bodyguard? I wonder what he told his wife about her brothers."

"Yes. That would be interesting to know. He may even have told her the truth."

"*Henry!* Never! It would cost Henry a spiritual struggle, Mr. Grant, to acknowledge that two and two were four. I tell you, he was a crab; he never went straight at anything."

"If he were a sadist he could tell her with impunity, you know. There was practically nothing she could do about it. Even if she wanted to. She mightn't have wanted to all that much. She had just produced an heir to the throne of England and was getting ready to produce another. She might not have the spare interest for a crusade; especially a crusade that would knock the ground from under her own feet."

"He wasn't a sadist, Henry," young Carradine said sadly. Sad at having to grant Henry even a negative virtue. "In a way he was just the opposite. He didn't enjoy murder at all. He had to pretty it up before he could bear the thought of it. Dress it up in legal ribbons. If you think that Henry got a kick out of boasting to Elizabeth in bed about what he had done with her brothers, I think you're wrong."

"Yes, probably," Grant said. And lay thinking about Henry. "I've just thought of the right adjective for Henry," he said presently. "Shabby. He was a shabby creature."

"Yes. Even his hair was thin and scanty."

"I didn't mean it physically."

"I know you didn't."

"Everything that he did was shabby. Come to think of it, 'Morton's Fork' is the shabbiest piece of revenue-raising in history. But it wasn't only his greed for money. Everything about him is shabby, isn't it?"

"Yes. Dr. Gairdner wouldn't have any trouble in making *his* actions fit his character. How did you get on with the Doctor?"

"A fascinating study. But for the grace of God I think the worthy Doctor might have made a living as a criminal."

"Because he cheated?"

"Because he didn't cheat. He was as honest as the day. He just couldn't reason from B to C."

"All right, I'll buy."

"Everyone can reason from A to B—even a child. And most adults can reason from B to C. But a lot can't. Most criminals can't. You may not believe it—I know it's an awful come-down from the popular conception of the criminal as a dashing and cute character—but the criminal mind is an essentially silly one. You can't imagine how silly sometimes. You'd have to experience it to believe their lack of reasoning powers. They arrive at B, but they're quite incapable of making the jump to C. They'll lay two completely incompatible things side by side and contemplate them with the most unquestioning content. You can't make them see that they can't have both, any more than you can make a man of no taste see that bits of plywood nailed on to a gable to simulate Tudor beams are impossible. Have you started your own book?"

"Well—I've made a sort of tentative beginning. I know the way I *want* to write it. I mean the form. I hope you won't mind."

"Why should I mind?"

"I want to write it the way it happened. You know; about my coming to see you, and our starting the Richard thing quite casually and not knowing what we were getting into, and how we stuck to things that actually happened and not what someone reported afterwards about it, and how we looked for the break in the normal pattern that would indicate where the mischief was, like bubbles coming up from a diver way below, and that sort of thing."

"I think it's a grand idea."

"You do?"

"I do indeed."

"Well, that's fine, then. I'll get on with it. I'm going to do some research on Henry, just as garnish. I'd like to be able to put their actual records side by side, you see. So that people can compare them for themselves. Did you know that Henry invented the Star Chamber?"

"Was it Henry? I'd forgotten that. Morton's Fork and the Star Chamber. The classic sample of sharp practice, and the classic sample of tyranny. You're not going to have any difficulty in differentiating the rival portraits, are you? Morton's Fork and the Star Chamber make a nice contrast to the granting of the right to bail, and the prevention of the intimidation of juries."

"Was that Richard's Parliament? Golly, what a lot of reading I have to do. Atlanta's not speaking to me. She hates your marrow. She says I'm about as much use to a girl as last year's *Vogue*. But honestly, Mr. Grant, this is the first time in my life that anything exciting has happened to me. Important, I mean. Not exciting meaning exciting. Atlanta's exciting. She's all the excitement I ever want. But neither of us is important, the way I mean important—if you can understand what I mean."

"Yes, I understand. You've found something worth doing."

"That's it. I've found something worth doing. And it's me that's doing it; that's what's wonderful about it. Me. Mrs. Carradine's little boy. I come over here with Atlanta, with no idea about anything but using that research gag as an alibi. I walked into the B.M. to get me some dope to keep Pop quiet, and I walk out with a mission. Doesn't that shake you!" He eyed Grant in a considering way. "You're quite sure, Mr. Grant, that you don't want to write this book yourself? After all, it's quite a thing to do."

"I shall *never* write a book," Grant said firmly. "Not even *My Twenty Years at the Yard*."

"What! Not even your autobiography?"

"Not even my autobiography. It is my considered opinion that far too many books are written as it is."

"But this is one that must be written," Carradine said, looking slightly hurt.

"Of course it is. This one must be written. Tell me: there's something I forgot to ask you. How soon after that double pardon did Tyrrel get that appointment in France? How soon after his supposed service to Henry in July 1486 did he become Constable of the Castle of Guisnes?"

Carradine stopped looking hurt and looked as malicious as it was possible for his kind woolly-lamb face to look.

"I was wondering when you were going to ask that," he said. "I was going to throw it at you on my way out if you forgot to ask. The answer is: almost right away."

"So. Another appropriate little pebble in the mosaic. I wonder whether the constableship just happened to be vacant, or whether it was a French appointment because Henry wanted him out of England."

"I bet it was the other way about, and it was Tyrrel who wanted to get out of England. If I were being ruled by Henry VII, I'd sure prefer to be ruled by remote control. Especially if I had done a secret job for Henry that might make it convenient for Henry if I didn't live to too venerable an age."

"Yes, perhaps you're right. He didn't only go abroad, he stayed abroad—as we have already observed. Interesting."

"He wasn't the only one who stayed abroad. John Dighton did too. I couldn't find out who all the people who were supposed to be involved in the murder actually were. All the Tudor accounts are different, I suppose you know. Indeed most of them are so different that they contradict each other flat. Henry's pet historian, Polydore Virgil, says the deed was done when Richard was at York. According to the sainted More it was during an earlier trip altogether, when Richard was at Warwick. And the personnel changes with each account. So that it's difficult to sort them out. I don't know who Will Slater was—Black Will to you, and another piece of onomatopoesis—or Miles Forest. But there *was* a John Dighton. Grafton says he lived for long at Calais 'no less disdained than pointed at' and died there in great misery. How they relished a good moral, didn't they? The Victorians had nothing on them."

"If Dighton was destitute it doesn't look as if he had done any job for Henry. What was he by trade?"

"Well, if it's the same John Dighton, he was a priest, and he was anything but destitute. He was living very comfortably on the proceeds of a sinecure. Henry gave a John Dighton the living of Fulbeck, near Grantham—that's in Lincolnshire—on the 2nd of May, 1487."

"Well, well," Grant said, drawling. "1487. And he, too, lived abroad and in comfort."

"Uh-huh. Lovely, isn't it?"

"It's beautiful. And does anyone explain how the much-pointed-at Dighton wasn't haled home by the scruff of his neck to hang for regicide?"

"Oh, no. Nothing like that. Tudor historians didn't any of them think from B to C."

Grant laughed. "I see you're being educated."

"Sure. I'm not only learning history. I'm sitting at the feet of Scotland Yard on the subject of the human mind. Well, that will be about all for now. If you feel strong enough I'll read you the first two chapters of the book next time I come." He paused and said: "Would you mind, Mr. Grant, if I dedicated it to you?"

"I think you had better dedicate it to Carradine the Third," Grant said lightly.

But Carradine apparently did not feel it to be a light matter.

"I don't use soft soap as a dedication," he said, with a hint of stiffness.

"Oh, not soft soap," Grant said in haste. "A matter of policy merely."

"I'd never have started on this thing if it hadn't been for you, Mr. Grant," Carradine said, standing in the middle of the floor all formal and emotional and American and surrounded by the sweeping folds of his topcoat, "and I should like to make due acknowledgment of my indebtedness."

"I should be delighted, of course," murmured Grant, and the royal figure in the middle of the floor relaxed to boyhood again and the awkward moment was over. Carradine went away joyous and light-footed as he had come, looking thirty pounds heavier and twelve inches more round the chest than he had done three weeks ago.

And Grant took out the new knowledge that had been given him, hung it on the opposite wall, and stared at it.

CHAPTER XVI

She had been shut away from the world; that indestructibly virtuous beauty with the gilt hair.

Why gilt, he wondered for the first time. Silver-gilt probably; she had been radiantly fair. A pity that the word blonde had degenerated to the point where it had almost a secondary meaning.

She had been walled up to end her days where she could be no trouble to anyone. An eddy of trouble had moved with her all through her life. Her marriage to Edward had rocked England. She had been the passive means of Warwick's ruin. Her kindnesses to her family had built a whole new party in England and had prevented Richard's peaceful succession. Bosworth was implicit in that scanty little ceremony in the wilds of Northamptonshire when she became Edward's wife. But no one seemed to have borne her malice. Even the sinned-against Richard had forgiven her her relations' enormities. No one—until Henry came.

She had disappeared into obscurity. Elizabeth Woodville. The Queen Dowager who was mother of the Queen of England. The mother of the Princes in the Tower; who had lived free and prosperous under Richard III.

That was an ugly break in the pattern, wasn't it?

He took his mind away from personal histories and began to think police-fashion. It was time he tidied up his case. Put it shipshape for presenting. It would help the boy with his book, and better still it would clear his own mind. It would be down in black and white where he could see it.

He reached for his writing-pad and pen, and made a neat entry:

CASE: Disappearance of two boys (Edward, Prince of Wales; Richard, Duke of York) from the Tower of London, 1485 or thereabouts.

He wondered whether it would be better to do the two suspects in parallel columns or successively. Perhaps it was better to finish with Richard first. So he made another neat headline; and began on his summing-up:

RICHARD III

Previous Record:
   Good. Has excellent record in public service, and good reputation in private life. Salient characteristic as indicated by his actions: good sense.

In the matter of the presumed crime:
   (a) He did not stand to benefit; there were nine other heirs to the house of York, including three males.
   (b) There is no contemporary accusation.
   (c) The boys' mother continued on friendly terms with him until his death, and her daughters attended Palace festivities.

(*d*) He showed no fear of the other heirs of York, providing generously for their upkeep and granting all of them their royal state.

(*e*) His own right to the crown was unassailable, approved by Act of Parliament and public acclamation; the boys were out of the succession and of no danger to him.

(*f*) If he had been nervous about disaffection then the person to have got rid of was not the two boys, but the person who really was next in succession to him: young Warwick. Whom he publicly created his heir when his own son died.

HENRY VII

Previous Record:

An adventurer, living at foreign courts. Son of an ambitious mother. Nothing known against his private life. No public office or employment. Salient characteristic as indicated by his actions: subtlety.

In the matter of the presumed crime:

(*a*) It was of great importance to him that the boys should not continue to live. By repealing the Act acknowledging the children's illegimacy, he made the elder boy King of England, and the youngest boy the next heir.

(*b*) In the Act which he brought before Parliament for the attainting of Richard he accused Richard of the conventional tyranny and cruelty but made no mention of the two young Princes. The conclusion is inevitable that at that time the two boys were alive and their whereabouts known.

(*c*) The boys' mother was deprived of her living and consigned to a nunnery eighteen months after his succession.

(*d*) He took immediate steps to secure the persons of all the other heirs to the crown, and kept them in close arrest until he could with the minimum of scandal get rid of them.

(*e*) He had no right whatever to the throne. Since the death of Richard, young Warwick was *de jure* King of England.

It occurred to Grant for the first time, as he wrote it out, that it had been within Richard's power to legitimatize his bastard son John, and foist him on the nation. There was no lack of precedent for such a course. After all, the whole Beaufort clan (including Henry's mother) were the descendants not only of an illegitimate union but of a double

adultery. There was nothing to hinder Richard from legitimatizing that "active and well-disposed" boy who lived in recognized state in his household. It was surely the measure of Richard that no such course had apparently crossed his mind. He had appointed as his heir his brother's boy. Even in the destitution of his own grief, good sense was his ruling characteristic. Good sense and family feeling. No base-born son, however active and well-disposed, was going to sit in the Plantagenets' seat while his brother's son was there to occupy it.

It was remarkable how that atmosphere of family feeling permeated the whole story. All the way from Cecily's journeyings about in her husband's company to her son's free acknowledgment of his brother George's boy as his heir.

And it occurred to him too for the first time in full force just how that family atmosphere strengthened the case for Richard's innocence. The boys whom he was supposed to have put down as he would put down twin foals were Edward's sons; children he must have known personally and well. To Henry, on the other hand, they were mere symbols. Obstacles on a path. He may never even have set eyes on them. All questions of character apart, the choice between the two men as suspects might almost be decided on that alone.

It was wonderfully clearing to the head to see it neat and tidy as (*a*), (*b*), and (*c*). He had not noticed before how doubly suspect was Henry's behavior over Titulus Regius. If, as Henry had insisted, Richard's claim was absurd, then surely the obvious thing to do was to have the thing reread in public and demonstrate its falsity. But he did no such thing. He went to endless pains to obliterate even the memory of it. The conclusion was inevitable that Richard's title to the crown as shown in Titulus Regius was unassailable.

CHAPTER XVII

On the afternoon when Carradine reappeared in the room at the hospital Grant had walked to the window and back again, and was so cock-a-hoop about it that The Midget was moved to remind him that it was a thing that a child of eighteen months could do. But nothing could subdue Grant today.

"Thought you'd have me here for months, didn't you?" he crowed.

"We are very glad to see you better so quickly," she said primly; and added: "We are, of course, very glad, too, to have your bed."

And she clicked away down the corridor, all blond curls and starch.

Grant lay on his bed and looked at his little prison room with something approaching benevolence. Neither a man who has stood at the Pole nor a man who has stood on Everest has anything on a man who has stood at a window after weeks of being merely twelve stones of destitution. Or so Grant felt.

Tomorrow he was going home. Going home to be cosseted by Mrs. Tinker. He would have to spend half of each day in bed and he would be able to walk only with the aid of sticks, but he would be his own man again. At the bidding of no one. In tutelage to no half-pint piece of efficiency, yearned over by no lump of out-sized benevolence.

It was a glorious prospect.

He had already unloaded his hallelujahs all over Sergeant Williams, who had looked in on the completion of his chore in Essex, and he was now yearning for Marta to drop in so that he could peacock in front of her in his new-found manhood.

"How did you get on with the history books?" Williams had asked.

"Couldn't be better. I've proved them all wrong."

Williams had grinned. "I expect there's a law against that," he said. "MI 5 won't like it. Treason or *lèse-majesté* or something like that it might turn out to be. You never know nowadays. I'd be careful if I was you."

"I'll never again believe anything I read in a history book, as long as I live, so help me."

"You'll have to make exceptions," Williams pointed out with Williams' dogged reasonableness. "Queen Victoria was true, and I suppose Julius Caesar did invade Britain. And there's 1066."

"I'm beginning to have the gravest doubts about 1066. I see you've tied up the Essex job. What is Chummy like?"

"A thorough little bastard. Been treated soft all his life since he started stealing change from his Ma at the age of nine. A good belting at the age of twelve might have saved his life. Now he'll hang before the almond blossom's out. It's going to be an early spring. I've been working every evening in the garden this last few days, now that the days are drawing out. You'll be glad to sniff fresh air again."

And he had gone away, rosy and sane and balanced, as befitted a man who was belted for his good in his youth.

So Grant was longing for some other visitor from the outside world that he was so soon to be a part of again, and he was delighted when the familiar tentative tap came on his door.

"Come in, Brent!" he called, joyfully.

And Brent came in.

But it was not the Brent who had last gone out.

Gone was the jubilation. Gone was his newly acquired breadth.

He was no longer Carradine the pioneer, the blazer of trails.

He was just a thin boy in a very long, very large overcoat. He looked young, and shocked, and bereaved.

Grant watched him in dismay as he crossed the room with his listless uncoordinated walk. There was no bundle of paper sticking out of his mail-sack of a pocket today.

Oh, well, thought Grant philosophically; it had been fun while it lasted. There was bound to be a snag somewhere. One couldn't do serious research in that lighthearted amateur way and hope to prove anything by it. One wouldn't expect an amateur to walk into the Yard and solve a case that had defeated the pro's; so why should he have thought himself smarter than the historians. He had wanted to prove to himself that he was right in his face-reading of the portrait; he had wanted to blot out the shame of having put a criminal on the bench instead of in the dock. But he would have to accept his mistake, and like it. Perhaps he had asked for it. Perhaps, in his heart of hearts, he had been growing a little pleased with himself about his eye for faces.

"Hullo, Mr. Grant."

"Hullo, Brent."

Actually it was worse for the boy. He was at the age when he expected miracles to happen. He was still at the age when he was surprised that a balloon should burst.

"You look saddish," he said cheerfully to the boy. "Something come unstuck?"

"Everything."

Carradine sat down on the chair and stared at the window.

"Don't these damned sparrows get you down?" he asked, fretfully.

"What is it? Have you discovered that there was a general rumor about the boys before Richard's death, after all?"

"Oh, much worse than that."

"Oh. Something in print? A letter?"

"No, it isn't that sort of thing at all. It's something much worse. Something quite— quite fundamental. I don't know how to tell you." He glowered at the quarrelling sparrows. "These damned birds. I'll never write that book now, Mr. Grant."

"Why not, Brent?"

"Because it isn't news to anyone. Everyone has known all about those things all along."

"Known? About what?"

"About Richard not having killed the boys at all, and all that."

"They've *known?* Since when!"

"Oh, hundreds and hundreds of years."

"Pull yourself together, chum. It's only four hundred years altogether since the thing happened."

"I know. But it doesn't make any difference. People have known about Richard's not doing it for hundreds and hundreds——"

"Will you stop that keening and talk sense. When did this—this rehabilitation first begin?"

"Begin? Oh, at the first available moment."

"When was that?"

"As soon as the Tudors were gone and it was safe to talk."

"In Stuart times, you mean?"

"Yes, I suppose—yes. A man Buck wrote a vindication in the seventeenth century. And Horace Walpole in the eighteenth. And someone called Markham in the nineteenth."

"And who in the twentieth?"

"No one that I know of."

"Then what's wrong with your doing it?"

"But it won't be the same, don't you see? It won't be a great discovery!" He said it in capitals. A Great Discovery.

Grant smiled at him. "Oh, come! You can't expect to pick Great Discoveries off bushes. If you can't be a pioneer what's wrong with leading a crusade?"

"A crusade?"

"Certainly."

"Against what?"

"Tonypandy."

The boy's face lost its blankness. It looked suddenly amused, like someone who has just seen a joke.

"It's the damnedest silliest name, isn't it!" he remarked.

"If people have been pointing out for three hundred and fifty years that Richard didn't murder his nephews and a school book can still say, in words of one syllable and without qualification, that he did, then it seems to me that Tonypandy has a long lead on you. It's time you got busy."

"But what can *I* do when people like Walpole and those have failed?"

"There's that old saying about constant water and its effect on stone."

"Mr. Grant, right now I feel an awfully feeble little trickle."

"You look it, I must say. I've never seen such self-pity. That's no mood to start bucking the British public in. You'll be giving enough weight away as it is."

"Because I've not written a book before, you mean?"

"No, that doesn't matter at all. Most people's first books are their best anyway; it's the one they wanted most to write. No, I meant that all the people who've never read a history book since they left school will feel themselves qualified to pontificate about what you've written. They'll accuse you of whitewashing Richard: 'whitewashing' has a derogatory sound that 'rehabilitation' hasn't, so they'll call it whitewashing. A few will look up the *Britannica*, and feel themselves competent to go a little further in the matter. These will slay you instead of flaying you. And the serious historians won't even bother to notice you."

"By God, I'll make them notice me!" Carradine said.

"Come! That sounds a little more like the spirit that won the Empire."

"We haven't got an Empire," Carradine reminded him.

"Oh, yes, you have," Grant said equably. "The only difference between ours and yours is that you acquired yours, economically, in the one latitude, while we got ours in bits all over the world. Had you written any of the book before the awful knowledge of its unoriginality hit you?"

"Yes, I'd done two chapters."

"What have you done with them? You haven't thrown them away, have you?"

"No. I nearly did. I nearly threw them in the fire."

"What stopped you?"

"It was an electric fire." Carradine stretched out his long legs in a relaxing movement and began to laugh. "Brother, I feel better already. I can't wait to land the British public one in the kisser with a few home truths. Carradine the First is just raging in my blood."

"A very virulent fever, it sounds."

"He was the most ruthless old blackguard that ever felled timber. He started as a logger and ended up with a Renaissance castle, two yachts, and a private car. Railroad car, you know. It had green silk curtains with bobbles on them and inlay woodwork that had to be seen to be believed. It has been popularly supposed, not least by Carradine the Third, that the Carradine blood was growing thin. But right now I'm all Carradine the First. I know just how the old boy felt when he wanted to buy a particular forest and someone said that he couldn't have it. Brother, I'm going to town."

"That's nice," Grant said, mildly. "I was looking forward to that dedication." He took his writing-pad from the table and held it out. "I've been doing a policeman's summing-up. Perhaps it may help you when you come to your peroration."

Carradine took it and looked at it with respect.

"Tear it off and take it with you. I've finished with it."

"I suppose in a week or two you'll be too busy with real investigations to care about a —an academic one," Carradine said, a little wistfully.

"I'll never enjoy one more than I've enjoyed this," Grant said, with truth. He glanced sideways at the portrait which was still propped against the books. "I was more dashed than you would believe when you came in all despondent, and I thought it had come to pieces." He looked back at the portrait and said: "Marta thinks he is a little like Lorenzo the Magnificent. Her friend James thinks it is the face of a saint. My surgeon thinks it is the face of a cripple. Sergeant Williams thinks he looks like a great judge. But I think, perhaps, Matron comes nearest the heart of the matter."

"What does she say?"

"She says it is a face full of the most dreadful suffering."

"Yes. Yes, I suppose it is. And would you wonder, after all?"

"No. No, there was little he was spared. Those last two years of his life must have happened with the suddenness and weight of an avalanche. Everything had been going along so nicely. England on an even keel at last. The civil war fading out of mind, a good firm government to keep things peaceful and a good brisk trade to keep things prosperous. It must have seemed a good outlook, looking out from Middleham across Wensleydale. And in two short years—his wife, his sons, and his peace."

"I know one thing he was spared."

"What?"

"The knowledge that his name was to be a hissing and a byword down the centuries."

"Yes. That would have been the final heartbreak. Do you know what I personally find *the* convincing thing in the case for Richard's innocence of any design for usurpation?"

"No. What?"

"The fact that he had to send for those troops from the North when Stillington broke his news. If he had had any foreknowledge of what Stillington was going to say, or even any plans to concoct a story with Stillington's help, he would have brought those troops with him. If not to London then to the Home Counties where they would be handy. That he had to send urgently first to York and then to his Nevill cousins for men is proof that Stillington's confession took him entirely unawares."

"Yes. He came up with his train of gentlemen, expecting to take over the Regency. He met the news of the Woodville trouble when he came to Northampton, but that didn't rattle him. He mopped up the Woodville two thousand and went on to London as if nothing had happened. There was still nothing but an orthodox coronation in front of him as far as he knew. It wasn't until Stillington confessed to the Council that he sends for troops of his own. And he has to send all the way to the North of England at a critical moment. Yes, you're right, of course. He was taken aback." He propped the leg of his spectacles with a forefinger in the old tentative gesture, and proffered a companion piece. "Know what I find the convincing thing in the case for Henry's guilt?"

"What?"

"The mystery."

"Mystery?"

"The mysteriousness. The hush-hush. The hole-and-corner stuff."

"Because it is in character, you mean?"

"No, no; nothing as subtle as that. Don't you see: Richard had no need of any mystery; but Henry's whole case depended on the boys' end being mysterious. No one has ever been able to think up a reason for such a hole-and-corner method as Richard was supposed to have used. It was a quite mad way to do it. He couldn't hope to get away with it. Sooner or later he was going to have to account for the boys not being there. As far as he knew he had a long reign in front of him. No one has ever been able to think why he should have chosen so difficult and dangerous a way when he had so many simpler methods at hand. He had only to have the boys suffocated, and let them lie in state while the whole of London walked by and wept over two young things dead before their time of fever. That is the way he *would* have done it, too. Goodness, *the whole point* of Richard's killing the boys was to prevent any rising in their favor, and to get any benefit from the murder the fact of their deaths would *have* to be made public, and as soon as possible. It would defeat the whole plan if people didn't *know* that they were dead. But Henry, now. Henry *had* to find a way to push them out of sight. Henry *had* to be mysterious. Henry *had* to hide the facts of when and how they died. *Henry's whole case* depended on no one's knowing what exactly happened to the boys."

"It did indeed, Brent; it did indeed," Grant said, smiling at counsel's eager young face. "You ought to be at the Yard, Mr. Carradine!"

Brent laughed.

"I'll stick to Tonypandy," he said. "I bet there's a lot more of it that we don't know about. I bet history books are just riddled with it."

"You'd better take Sir Cuthbert Oliphant with you, by the way." Grant took the fat respectable-looking volume from his locker. "Historians should be compelled to take a course in psychology before they are allowed to write."

"Huh. That wouldn't do anything for them. A man who is interested in what makes people tick doesn't write history. He writes novels, or becomes an alienist, or a magistrate——"

"Or a confidence man."

"Or a confidence man. Or a fortune-teller. A man who understands about people hasn't any yen to write history. History is toy soldiers."

"Oh, come. Aren't you being a little severe? It's a very learned and erudite——"

"Oh, I didn't mean it that way. I mean: it's moving little figures about on a flat surface. It's half-way to mathematics, when you come to think about it."

"Then if it's mathematics they've no right to drag in backstairs gossip," Grant said, suddenly vicious. The memory of the sainted More continued to upset him. He thumbed through the fat respectable Sir Cuthbert in a farewell review. As he came to the final pages the progress of the paper from under his thumb slackened, and presently stopped.

"Odd," he said, "how willing they are to grant a man the quality of courage in battle. They have only tradition to go on, and yet not one of them questions it. Not one of them, in fact, fails to stress it."

"It was an enemy's tribute," Carradine reminded him. "The tradition began with a ballad written by the other side."

"Yes. By a man of the Stanleys. 'Then a knight to King Richard can say.' It's here somewhere." He turned over a leaf or two, until he found what he was looking for. "It was 'good Sir William Harrington,' it seems. The knight in question.

"There may no man their strokes abide, the
    Stanleys dints they be so strong [the
    treacherous bastards!]
Ye may come back at another tide, methinks
    ye tarry here too long,
Your horse at your hand is ready, another
    day you may worship win
And come to reign with royalty, and wear
    your crown and be our king.
'Nay, give me my battle-axe in my hand, set
    the crown of England on my head so
    high.
For by Him that made both sea and land,
    King of England this day I will die.
One foot I will never flee whilst the breath
    is my breast within.'
As he said so did it be—if he lost his life
    he died a King."

" 'Set the crown of England on my head,' " said Carradine, musing. "That was the crown that was found in a hawthorn bush afterwards."

"Yes. Set aside for plunder probably."

"I used to picture it one of those high plush things that King George got crowned in, but it seems it was just a gold circlet."

"Yes. It could be worn outside the battle helmet."

"Gosh," said Carradine with sudden feeling, "I sure would have hated to wear that crown if I had been Henry! I sure would have hated it!" He was silent for a little, and then he said: "Do you know what the town of York wrote —wrote in their records, you know—about the battle of Bosworth?"

"No."

"They wrote: 'This day was our good King Richard piteously slain and murdered; to the great heaviness of this city.' "

The chatter of the sparrows was loud in the quiet.

"Hardly the obituary of a hated usurper," Grant said at last, very dry.

"No," said Carradine. "No. 'To the great heaviness of this city,' " he repeated slowly, rolling the phrase over in his mind. "They cared so much about it that even with a new régime in the offing and the future not to be guessed at they put down in black and white in the town record their opinion that it was murder and their sorrow at it."

"Perhaps they had just heard about the

indignities perpetrated on the King's dead body and were feeling a little sick."

"Yes. Yes. You don't like to think of a man you've known and admired flung stripped and dangling across a pony like a dead animal."

"One wouldn't like to think of even an enemy so. But sensibility is not a quality that one would look for among the Henry-Morton crowd."

"Huh. Morton!" said Brent, spitting out the word as if it were a bad taste. "No one was 'heavy' when Morton died, believe me. Know what the Chronicler wrote of him? The London one, I mean. He wrote: 'In our time was no man like to be compared with him in all things; albeit that he lived not without the great disdain and hatred of the Commons of this land.' "

Grant turned to look at the portrait which had kept him company through so many days and nights.

"You know," he said, "for all his success and his Cardinal's hat I think Morton was the loser in that fight with Richard III. In spite of his defeat and his long traducing, Richard came off the better of these two. He was loved in his day."

"That's no bad epitaph," the boy said soberly.

"No. Not at all a bad epitaph," Grant said, shutting Oliphant for the last time. "Not many men would ask for a better." He handed over the book to its owner. "Few men have earned so much," he said.

When Carradine had gone Grant began to sort out the things on his table, preparatory to his homegoing on the morrow. The unread fashionable novels could go to the hospital library to gladden other hearts than his. But he would keep the book with the mountain pictures. And he must remember to give The Amazon back her two history books. He took them out so that he could give them to her when she brought in his supper. And he read again, for the first time since he began his search for the truth about Richard, the schoolbook tale of his villainy. There it was, in unequivocable black and white, the infamous story. Without a perhaps or a peradventure. Without a qualification or a question.

As he was about to shut the senior of the two educators his eye fell on the beginning of Henry VII's reign, and he read: "It was the settled and considered policy of the Tudors to rid themselves of all rivals to the throne, more especially those heirs of York who remained alive on the succession of Henry VII. In this

they were successful, although it was left to Henry VIII to get rid of the last of them."

He stared at this bald announcement. This placid acceptance of wholesale murder. This simple acknowledgment of a process of family elimination.

Richard III had been credited with the elimination of two nephews, and his name was a synonym for evil. But Henry VII, whose "settled and considered policy" was to eliminate a whole family was regarded as a shrewd and far-seeing monarch. Not very lovable perhaps, but constructive and painstaking, and very successful withal.

Grant gave up. History was something that he would never understand.

The values of historians differed so radically from any values with which he was acquainted that he could never hope to meet them on any common ground. He would go back to the Yard, where murderers were murderers and what went for Cox went equally for Box.

He put the two books tidily together and when The Amazon came in with his mince and stewed prunes he handed them over with a neat little speech of gratitude. He really was very grateful to The Amazon. If she had not kept her school books he might never have started on the road that led to his knowledge of Richard Plantagenet.

She looked confused by his kindness, and he wondered if he had been such a bear in his illness that she expected nothing but carping from him. It was a humiliating thought.

"We'll miss you, you know," she said, and her big eyes looked as if they might brim with tears. "We've grown used to having you here. We've even got used to *that*." And she moved an elbow in the direction of the portrait.

A thought stirred in him.

"Will you do something for me?" he asked.

"Of course. Anything I can do."

"Will you take that photograph to the window and look at it in a good light as long as it takes to count a pulse?"

"Yes, of course, if you want me to. But why?"

"Never mind why. You just do it to please me. I'll time you."

She took up the portrait and moved into the light of the window.

He watched the second-hand of his watch.

He gave her forty-five seconds and then said: "Well?" And as there was no immediate answer he said again: "Well?"

"Funny," she said. "When you look at it for a little it's really quite a nice face, isn't it?"

Topics for Writing and Research

1. Through a general analysis of pertinent sources, discuss the moral implications involved in the controversy over Richard III.
2. Write a full exposition of the three points of view on Richard as expressed in sources in this book.
3. In a well-known essay, "Getting at the Truth," Marchette Chute points out that in biographical writing truth is often distorted by two kinds of "desire": (*a*) the writer's desire to use his subject's life to illustrate a thesis of his own, or (*b*) the desire that occurs when a writer gets emotionally involved with his subject and shapes it according to what he thinks it ought to be. Write a paper in which you attempt to detect these types of "desire" on the part of More, Markham, Tey, and other writers about Richard.
4. Select certain episodes from the life of Richard as described by More and analyze their credibility, bringing to bear as much evidence from other sources as possible.
5. Write an essay assessing the influence of Sir Thomas More on the reputation of Richard.
6. Write a comparison of More and Polydore Vergil in their treatments of Richard's career.
7. Compare Polydore Vergil and the author of the Croyland Chronicle in their treatments of Richard's career.
8. Analyze the basis of the "revisionist" position.
9. Analyze the nature of the moralistic import which fifteenth and sixteenth century writers saw in Richard's career.
10. Evaluate the frequently presented view that the actions of Elizabeth Woodville were simply those of a "silly woman."
11, 12, 13, 14.
    Compare and contrast the characters of one or more of the following as they are presented in Shakespeare and in the historic sources: (11) Elizabeth Woodville,
(12) Duke of Buckingham, (13) Lord Hastings, (14) Anne Neville.
15. Analyze the primary sources for real evidence of Richard's unpopularity.
16. Compile a detailed account of the Battle of Bosworth Field.
17. Discuss the murder of the princes, carefully separating fact from fiction.
18. Analyze Richard's career in terms of its effect on Lord Hastings, Jane Shore, the Duke of Buckingham, and Elizabeth Woodville.
19. Examine evidence for the existence of rivalry between the Woodvilles and the older nobility.
20. Discuss the validity of the idea that Richard was primarily motivated in his actions by the influence of those around him.
21. Discuss Shakespeare's use of his sources.
22. Discuss Tey's use of her sources.
23. Write an essay comparing Shakespeare and Tey in their use of sources.
24, 25, 26, 27.
    Analyze the particular role of one or more of the following in the events of 1483: (24) Elizabeth Woodville, (25) Duke of Buckingham, (26) Lord Hastings, (27) Marquess of Dorset.
28. Compare Shakespeare's picture of Richard on the night before Bosworth with that which emerges from the historic sources.
29. Compare and contrast More, Walpole, and Markham on the murder of the little princes.
30. Evaluate the death of Queen Anne as a part of the Tudor propaganda.
31. To what extent, in his appraisal of Richard, does Myers escape from the moral necessity of "proving a villain"?
32. Compare More and Shakespeare in their presentations of Richard's efforts to win approval of the city of London.
33. How does Shakespeare's Henry Tudor compare with that of Markham?
34. Analyze Bacon's attitude toward Richard

in terms of the specific evidence he mentions.

35. Discuss the basis of Bacon's praise of Richard.

36. Discuss Shakespeare's manipulation of chronology.

37. Describe the additions which Shakespeare made to his historical sources.

38. Examine Myers' criticism of Markham's thesis.

39. Discuss the various presentations of Jane Shore and analyze her role in the events of 1483.

40, 41, 42, 43.
Using the primary sources only, write character sketches of one or more of the following: (40) Elizabeth Woodville, (41) Duke of Buckingham, (42) Anne Neville, (43) Lord Hastings.

44. Discuss the credibility of the charge that Richard planned to seize the crown even before his brother's death.

45. Examine the role played by Lord Stanley during the period 1483–1485.

46, 47, 48.
The following three subjects will require the use of library materials as well as sources in this book: (46) Compare the actions of Richard III with those recommended by Machiavelli in *The Prince*. (47) Using the Battle of Bosworth Field as a particular example, write a paper on the art of warfare in the late Middle Ages. (48) What were the rules and customs of "sanctuary" in the late fifteenth century?

49. Assuming Richard's position, write an account of the day of Hastings' death.

50, 51, 52, 53, 54, 55, 56.
Write the story of Richard's seizure of power from the personal point of view of: (50) Elizabeth Woodville, (51) Duke of Buckingham, (52) Lord Hastings, (53) Henry Tudor, (54) Jane Shore, (55) Edward V, (56) A merchant of London.

57. If you had been Richard, would you have fought the Battle of Bosworth? Explain your decision.

58. Write an essay clarifying the confusion in the sources concerning Elizabeth Lucy and Eleanor Butler.

59. Make a careful comparison of More and Holinshed and evaluate Holinshed as a source.

60. Compare the moral attitudes of More and Dickens toward Richard.

61. Show how Shakespeare develops in *Richard III* the character suggested by Gloucester's speech from *3-Henry VI*.

62. Answer Horace Walpole's question: "Does a lie become venerable from its age?"

63. Write a character sketch of Richard based on observation of his portrait.

64. The following historical references taken from Tey's *Daughter of Time* may serve as subjects for brief papers prepared from library resources: Canute's courtiers and the sea, Raleigh's cloak, Nelson's farewell to Hardy, ship money, Rye House Plot, benevolences, Peasants' Revolt of 1381, Alfred and the cakes, Cromwell's wart, tonnage and poundage, Laud's liturgy, Triennial Acts, maintenance and livery, the Scot's sale of Charles I.

65. In *Daughter of Time*, Miss Tey suggests a number of historical mysteries or misinterpretations which parallel that of Richard III in one way or another. The student may add to his enjoyment and understanding of the novel—and of historical mysteries—by undertaking papers on the following topics: The Casket Letters, Perkin Warbeck, Louis XVII, Russian troops in England, Tonypandy, The Man in the Iron Mask, Lucrezia Borgia, the death of Amy Robsart, the Boston Massacre, the Wigtown Martyrs.

Bibliography

General History

The best treatment of the general history of the period will be found in E. F. Jacob, *The Fifteenth Century 1399–1485* (Oxford, 1961), which is Vol. VI in *The Oxford History of England*, ed. Sir George Clark. Other useful surveys include Charles Oman, *The History of England from the Accession of Richard II to the Death of Richard III (1377–1485)* (London, 1918); K. M. Vickers, *England in the Later Middle Ages* (7th ed., London, 1950); V. H. H. Green, *The Later Plantagenets* (London, 1955); A. R. Myers, *England in the Late Middle Ages* (London, 1952); C. H. Williams, "England: The Yorkist Kings, 1461–1485," *The Cambridge Medieval History* (Cambridge, 1936), Vol. VIII, Ch. 12; and Sir J. H. Ramsay, *Lancaster and York 1399–1485* (Oxford, 1892).

Charles L. Kingsford's *Prejudice and Promise in XVth Century England* (Oxford, 1925) is an outstanding interpretation of the period. Paul Murray Kendall, *The Yorkist Age: Daily Life During the Wars of the Roses* (New York, 1962), and V. B. Redstone, "The Social Condition of England during the Wars of the Roses," *Transactions of the Royal Historical Society*, n.s. XVI (1902), provide background material for Robert B. Mowat's *The Wars of the Roses* (London, 1914) and Albert Makinson, "The Wars of the Roses: Who Fought and Why?" *History Today*, IX (1959).

Biography

The best point of departure for biography is James Gairdner's *History of the Life and Reign of Richard the Third* (2nd ed., London, 1879), which presents the standard condemnation of the king. The restoration of Richard's fame was undertaken by A. O. Legge, *The Unpopular King* (London, 1885), and most notably by Clements R. Markham, *Richard III* (London, 1906), who was followed by Philip Lindsay, *King Richard III* (London, 1933). Paul M. Kendall's *Richard the Third* (London, 1955) is now the standard biography, but see Mortimer Levine, "Richard III–Usurper or Lawful King?" *Speculum*, XXXIV (1959). The most recent and convenient study of the critical campaign is Albert Makinson, "The Road to Bosworth Field," *History Today*, XIII (1963).

The fate of Edward V and his brother is pursued by James Gairdner's reply to Markham, "Did Henry VII Murder the Princes?" *English Historical Review*, VI (1891); Lawrence E. Tanner and William Wright, "Recent Investigations Regarding the Fate of the Princes in the Tower," *Archaeologia*, LXXXIV (1935); D. E. Rhodes, "The Princes in the Tower and Their Doctor," *English Historical Review*, LXXVII (1962); and Hugh Ross Williamson, "The Princes in the Tower," *Historical Whodunits* (New York, 1956). Vivien B. Lamb offers an interesting hypothesis in *The Betrayal of Richard III* (London, 1959).

Richard's predecessors have been described by Mabel E. Christie, *Henry VI* (Boston, 1922); Cora L. Schofield, *The Life and Reign of Edward the Fourth* (London, 1923); and J. R. Lander, "Edward IV: The Modern Legend: And a Revision," *History*, n.s. XLI (1956). C. W. C. Oman's *Warwick the Kingmaker* (London, 1891) and P. M. Kendall's *Warwick the Kingmaker* (London, 1957) are of use, as is Kendall's "Warwick the Kingmaker," *History Today*, VII (1957). Concerning lesser figures, there is M. A. Hookham, *The Life and Times of Margaret of Anjou* (London, 1872); David MacGibbon, *Elizabeth Woodville* (London, 1938); and Dorothy M. Stuart, "The King's Brother-in-Law, Antony Wydeville, Second Earl Rivers," *History Today*, IX (1959). John W. Spargo wrote an interesting essay on "Clarence in the Malmsey-Butt," *Modern Language Notes*, LI (1936).

THE SOURCES

Advanced students should, of course, consult such guides as the bibliographies of E. F. Jacobs' *The Fifteenth Century*, P. M. Kendall's *Richard the Third*, Charles Gross's *The Sources and Literature of English History* (2nd ed., New York, 1951), and C. L. Kingsford's *English Historical Literature of the Fifteenth Century* (Oxford, 1913). Dominic Mancini's *The Usurpation of Richard III*, ed. C. A. J. Armstrong (Oxford, 1936), is an important recent addition. A number of rare literary materials are gathered in Geoffrey Bullough's *Narrative and Dramatic Sources of Shakespeare* (New York, 1960), Vol. III. More extensive versions of Thomas More's *History of King Richard III* may be found in J. Rawson Lumby's bowdlerized edition (Cambridge, 1883), and in *The English Works of Sir Thomas More*, Vol. I, ed. W. E. Campbell (London, 1931). The latter volume includes R. W. Chambers' important essay on "The Authorship of the 'History of Richard III,'" a revised edition of an article in *Modern Language Review*, **XXIII** (1928). The latest edition is that by Richard S. Sylvester, *The History of King Richard III* (*Complete Works of St. Thomas More*, Vol. II, New Haven, 1963). Shakespeare's use of Holinshed, is further illustrated by W. G. Boswell-Stone, *Shakespeare's Holinshed, The Chronicle and the Historical Plays Compared* (London, 1896), and *Holinshed's Chronicle as Used in Shakespeare's Plays*, ed. A. and J. Nicoll (London, 1927). Lily Bess Campbell has edited *The Mirror for Magistrates* (New York, 1938).

The student who wishes to consider Shakespeare's *Richard III* against its literary and political backgrounds should see Lily Bess Campbell, *Shakespeare's "Histories," Mirrors of Elizabethan Policy* (San Marino, Cal., 1947); L. C. Knights, *William Shakespeare: The Histories* ("Writers and Their Work," 151, London, 1962); Irving Ribner, *The English History Play in the Age of Shakespeare* (Princeton, 1957); and E. M. W. Tillyard, *Shakespeare's History Plays* (New York, 1947).

NOVELS AND PLAYS

Among the historical novels set in this period are Margaret Campbell Barnes, *The Tudor Rose* (New York, 1953); Patrick Carleton, *Under the Hog* (New York, 1938); Francis Leary, *Fire and Morning* (New York, 1957) and *The Golden Longing* (New York, 1959); Edward Bulwer Lytton, *The Last of the Barons* (London, 1843); Carola Oman, *Crouchback* (New York, 1929); Thomas G. F. Paget, *The Rose of London* (London, 1934), *The Rose of Raby* (London, 1937), and *The Rose of Rouen* (London, 1940); Marguerite Vance, *Song for a Lute* (New York, 1958).

Before Shakespeare pre-empted the field, two dramatists grappled with the subject. A curious and determined reader might look at Thomas Legge's *Richardus Tertius* (microfilm ed., Ann Arbor, 1958) and the anonymous *True Tragedy of Richard III*. More recently, Elizabeth Mackintosh dramatized her subject in "Dickon," *Plays by Gordon Daviot* (London, 1953–1954). Film versions include *The Tower of London* (Universal Pictures, 1939); *Richard III* (London Films, 1955), starring Sir Laurence Olivier; and *An Age of Kings* (B.B.C., 1961). Vincent Price's *The Tower of London* (Admiral Pictures, 1962) is the ultimate in historical horrors.